Sweet Grapes for Cold Climates

Easy Picking for Kids

Nutritious Nuts

Best Fruits for Small Spaces

Unusual Fruits to Try

The Fruit Gardener's Bible

The Fruit Gardener's Bible

A Complete Guide to Growing Fruits and Nuts in the Home Garden

Lewis Hill and Leonard Perry

The mission of Storey Publishing is to serve our customers by publishing practical information that encourages personal independence in harmony with the environment.

Edited by Elizabeth P. Stell and Carleen Madigan
Art direction and book design by Dan O. Williams and Carolyn Eckert
Text production by Liseann Karandisecky and Jennifer Jepson Smith

Front cover photography: from top left: *gooseberries* © Joshua McCullough; *strawberries* © bravo1954/iStockphoto.com; *grapes* © Mark Bolton/GAP Photos Ltd.; *blueberries* © Ewa Brozek/iStockphoto.com; *cherry trio* © Red Helga/iStockphoto.com; *pear* © craftvision/iStockphoto.com; *blackberries* © Jonathan Buckley; *currants* © Valentyn Volkov/iStockphoto.com; apricots © house_red/iStockphoto.com; *cherries* © John Glover/GAP Photos Ltd.; *almonds* © Alexandr Tovstenko/iStockphoto.com; *plums* © Jonathan Buckley; *raspberries* © Floortje/iStockphoto.com; peaches © Kutay Tanir/iStockphoto.com; *loganberries* © Zara Napier/GAP Photos Ltd.; *walnuts* © Kevin Dyer/iStockphoto.com; *apples* © Jerry Pavia
Back cover and spine photography: *pruning* © Friedrich Strauss/GAP Photos Ltd.; *blueberries* © Tim Gainey/GAP Photos Ltd.; *pear* © Nickos/iStockphoto.com; *raspberries* © Ewa Brozek/iStockphoto.com
Interior photography credits appear on pages 310 and 311
Illustrations by Beverly Duncan

Indexed by Christine R. Lindemer, Boston Road Communications

Portions of this text were originally published under the title *Fruits & Berries for the Home Garden*, 1992.
Editorial revision by Leonard Perry

Storey Publishing
210 MASS MoCA Way
North Adams, MA 01247
www.storey.com

Printed in the United States by R.R. Donnelley
10 9 8 7 6 5 4 3 2 1

Library of Congress Cataloging-in-Publication Data

Hill, Lewis, 1924–
The fruit gardener's bible / Lewis Hill and Leonard Perry.
p. cm.
Includes index.
Previous eds. published as: Fruits and berries for the home garden.
ISBN 978-1-60342-567-4 (pbk. : alk. paper)
ISBN 978-1-60342-984-9 (hardcover : alk. paper)
1. Fruit-culture. I. Perry, Leonard P. II. Title. III. Title: Fruits and berries for the home garden.
SB355.H655 2012
634—dc23

2011024870

Contents

Acknowledgments

UNTIL ONE IS INVOLVED with writing, or in this case extensively revising, a book of this magnitude, one cannot imagine the number of people who help to make it a reality, to grow mere words into a beautiful and useful gardening reference. I am most thankful to Carleen Madigan for inviting me to undertake this project, and then for providing extra time to make some needed changes. In addition, I'm grateful to the reviewers, the artist, the photographers, and the many other production personnel I've not had the pleasure to meet. Thanks especially to Liz Stell for her patience as we worked on all the details to reorganize the material and create a book even more reader-friendly.

To make this book applicable beyond where I garden, in New England, I'm indebted to the many nurseries, specialist growers, and cooperative extension professionals coast to coast and north to south who shared useful information on cultivars and practices for their particular regions. I hope this book has succeeded in tapping into, and accumulating in one place, this wealth of knowledge.

Even with so much new information added to this book, Lewis's voice still rings throughout it. I'm grateful for the chance to have known Lewis and Nancy Hill so well, and to have enjoyed good visits and learned much from them over the years. Finally, thanks to my family for giving me up for so many weeks behind the computer.

— *Leonard Perry*

It took me about twenty years to learn how to grow good fruit. I hope this book will help you accomplish it in less time — a whole lot less. — *Lewis Hill*

Preface to the New Edition

EVERY TIME THERE IS A RECESSION, there is a renewed interest in food gardening. What may start out as an activity to save some money on the food bill often turns into much more. The reasons for growing your own fruits and berries that Lewis mentioned in his original first edition of this book — *Fruits and Berries for the Home Gardener* — are still applicable. The safety of what we eat, knowing what chemicals have been applied (if any), and the increased flavor and nutrition of fresh fruits from the garden are still good reasons why people turn to growing their own fruit. What wasn't such an issue in the previous editions of this book is a concern about global warming and our "carbon footprint" — how much fuel is spent transporting those fruits from all over the country and from around the globe.

Since then, our lives seem to have become even busier, more hectic, often chaotic. Growing your own fruit can provide a welcome refuge, a sense of order and control, an opportunity for a family activity, and the exercise many of us lack because of desk jobs and time spent in vehicles.

Because many people have less time to garden, they often need to quickly locate the information they need. The layout of this book has been revised with this in mind. More information has been added for beginners, to encourage more people to enjoy the benefits of growing their own food.

This edition also addresses some of the changes in gardening practices. There have been advances in sustainable practices, notably biological pest and disease controls. Deer have become a major problem in many parts of the country. Incorporating fruits and nuts into ornamental landscapes, for both their aesthetics and food functions (for people and wildlife), is gaining in interest. There are many new varieties, and some gardeners are becoming interested in new fruit crops. Each of these topics is thoroughly covered in this new edition.

Until his passing, Lewis was a dear friend for almost three decades. I knew and worked with him, along with his wife Nancy, professionally through the University of Vermont Extension. I am excited to have this opportunity to update his wonderful and useful reference. Lewis was a true Vermonter who had a practical, engaging, and humorous style of writing, as if you were talking with him in person. He wrote based on a lifetime of experience in horticulture. I have attempted to maintain his style, and hope my own many years of similar experiences, both in the South and in the North, continue to provide what you, the gardener, will find really useful.

For those of you who already grow fruits and nuts, I hope you find much new, and easily accessible, information in this revised edition. For those of you who are just beginning, or thinking about doing so, I hope you'll quickly learn what you need for success. This book will help you deal with the challenges that nature throws at us, turning them into successes, opportunities for learning, or perhaps new practices and crops. Even if you begin growing fruits and nuts for a purely functional reason — to save money or to ensure food safety — I hope you'll soon discover the other benefits and pleasures of fruit growing and harvest, just as Lewis did and I still do.

— *Leonard Perry*

PART ONE

Getting Started *with* Fruits *and* Nuts

With a little planning and proper site selection, you can have a yard that produces fruits and nuts instead of just flowers.

ONE OF THE BEST THINGS ABOUT WALKING the mile to our country school when I was six was cutting through our old and rather decrepit orchard and picking pockets full of apples to eat on the way. The early 'Yellow Transparents' and 'Tetoskys' were ready on the first day of school, and even a child could eat a lot of them without feeling stuffed. Later came the "heavier" apples — the zippy-flavored 'Duchesses', the 'Astrachans' with their waxy red skins, golden 'Peach' apples with rosy blooms, and the 'Wealthys', which ripened a week or so later. The 'Bethels', 'Pound Sweets', and 'Tolmans' ripened even later, and we stored those in the cellar for winter eating.

Lots of other apples grew in the orchard, too. We didn't even know their names, so we called them by their flavor or appearance: the pear, the pumpkin, the banana, the sugar. All the kids in the neighborhood knew where the best apples in each orchard grew, and when they were at their best. Like the raccoons that stole them at night, we could go unerringly to the choicest trees.

One reason for the success of those early orchards was the kind of care the old-timers gave their fruits and berries. A century ago, the orchard was as important to people as their grain, animals, woodlot, or vegetable garden. They never neglected the annual fertilizing, pruning, and insect control, even though the latter might consist only of flinging wood ashes through the trees now and then, or perhaps an occasional spray of soapsuds and water. They fenced out the farm animals except in late fall, when pigs or cattle were let in for a short time to eat any unused fruit in which insects and disease could spend the winter.

As I grew older, I remembered how much better I had liked the homegrown fruits and was already sentimental about the stately old orchard and the heaps of apples that fell on the ground there each fall. So I decided to plant some apple trees. I couldn't find any of the old favorites, so I had to order new kinds from tantalizing catalogs sent by faraway nurseries. Their assortment in the 1940s was small, consisting mostly of the same varieties as those that were displayed in our local stores each fall: 'Red Delicious' and 'Yellow Delicious', 'Rome Beauty', 'Jonathan', 'Winesap', and 'Grimes Golden'. I learned a lot the hard way, including the knowledge that when I bought fruit trees it was wise to study the catalogs carefully, because a tree suitable for Oregon might not be happy in New England.

Growing apples was my stepping-stone to trying other fruits, and a few years later we were harvesting plums, pears, grapes, cherries, and a large assortment of berries, just as our ancestors had done. We no longer needed to depend on the small selection in the supermarket, because the dozens of different kinds of fruits growing in our backyard gave us an exciting variety of good eating. Unlike Grandpa and Grandma, we had the advantage of a home freezer, which let us enjoy our produce all year. It seemed good not to have to wash a raft of sprays and waxes off our fruit and berries before we ate them, or to worry about whether our apple pie contained more preservatives than vitamins.

In fact, just about everything connected with fruit growing was a pleasure, especially the harvest. When I picked the first red strawberry of the season, or the first juicy ripe raspberry, or the first crisp tangy apple, any battles with insects or weeds were quickly forgotten. Instead, my boyhood memories of the majestic old orchard returned, and I was filled with hopeful anticipation of all the fabulous harvests ahead.

Often, fruiting plants can be incorporated into ornamental settings. This normally shrubby gooseberry bush has been trained to a single trunk and surrounded with nasturtiums.

CHAPTER 1

Fruits and Nuts in the Home Garden

Our orchard and our berry patch aren't large, but each year we put hundreds of packages of fruit into the freezer, in addition to all the fruits we store in our root cellar or preserve in other ways. All summer and fall we eat pies and shortcakes, drink lots of juice, and give away quantities of fruit. I won't even mention the amount we eat right off the trees and bushes while we're picking. Naturally, it would cost a tidy sum to buy all this food in the local market, and it wouldn't taste nearly as fresh as homegrown. In small towns like ours, we can't always get these fruits, and when we can they're usually shipped in from places or countries we'll never visit. I find that growing our own fruit means we tend to eat more, which is good for our health. Increasing prices, concerns about food safety, our need to eat more fruits and vegetables daily for our health, and thinking about all the fuel burned to ship fruit thousands of miles — these reasons make us appreciate our orchard and berry patch even more.

Fruiting plants are not a big initial investment in light of all the future dividends you reap from them. A fruit tree can cost as little as a bushel of fruit, and for the cost of a quart of strawberries you might buy enough plants for 4 quarts. Why buy fruit drinks, fruit pies, and fruit ice cream when you can make your own? By raising their own fruits and berries, families can save a lot on their food bills. Just two mature semidwarf apple trees, for instance, can yield 6 bushels each, which translates to about 480 pounds.

If you have only a small lot, you can still grow fruit. Many dwarf trees grow to full size within an 8-foot circle. Strawberries thrive in crocks, hanging baskets, pyramids, and barrels. A short row of raspberries will produce quarts of fruit every year. Some fruits can even be grown in large patio containers.

If you don't have much time, start small. Once planted, blueberries provide the most return for the least effort. The truth is, if you choose the right kinds of fruits and give them a suitable place to live and a little attention, fruit trees and especially berries require no more — and often less — care than many other plants.

Including Fruits in Your Yard

One nice way to enjoy fruit, especially on a small lot, is to landscape with fruit trees and bushes instead of ornamental trees and shrubs. If you're planting around your home for the first time or replacing existing landscaping, why not use blueberries, currants, and gooseberries as functional substitutes for some of the ornamental foundation plants and hedges around your house? Many fruiting plants have attractive shapes, leaves, and fall color, and of course provide food for wildlife. Fruit trees can replace flowering trees and shrubs, and nut trees are good substitutes for shade trees. Although our plantings bear little resemblance to those in formal botanic gardens, we find pleasure and satisfaction in growing plants that are beautiful in all seasons and also produce a product that can be put into a tasty pie or poured into a pitcher.

Incorporating perennial edible plants into a landscape is an important aspect of what is known as permaculture. This system of planning the landscape is gradually gaining recognition among gardeners who want to be ecological and sustainable in their plantings and practices. In permaculture, landscapes are seen as both aesthetic and functional, providing food for both humans and wildlife.

You don't have to wait long. Dwarf fruit trees begin to bear within two or three years, some berries produce big crops within three years, and you can pick everbearing strawberries even the first year. If you sell your property, an orchard and a berry patch may even add to its value.

Here are eight ways to fit fruits into your landscape. Some fruits fit more than one of these functions:

Screens and hedges. Hedges are planted to define a space, or to provide an "outdoor wall." They can be formal (clipped to a strict shape) or informal (utilizing the natural shape of plants). Hedges, such as a dense planting of blueberries or a less dense but thorny row of brambles, also provide a physical barrier. Brambles, blueberries, and currants make good hedges. Just make sure that if you use a spreading fruit, you can contain the hedge easily through pruning, cultivation, or mowing.

Screens are more often planted as a visual or noise barrier, and they're commonly used to provide privacy. If planted as a wind barrier, a screen is called a windbreak. As a visual barrier, a screen can be denser, as in a wide bed of shrubs closely spaced, or more open and merely suggesting a visual barrier. Tall-growing elderberries can serve as a screen and provide good fall eating and an invitation to birds. They're a good choice for soils that are too moist for other fruits, and they will even grow on the north side of a building. Other screening plants are chokeberries, espaliered fruit trees, and grapes on trellises.

Shade trees. Most fruit trees are just as lovely as flowering ornamental trees. Not only do they bloom, but their crop also gives the effect of a second flowering. We have a 'Dolgo' crab apple in the front yard that thrills us with its profusion of white blossoms each spring and is covered with gorgeous, bright red apples every fall — plenty for us, our friends, the

Why settle for an ordinary fence? An espaliered apple or pear will serve some of the same purposes while producing fruit and adding aesthetic value.

freezer, and even a flock of migrating Canadian robins that include us on their route south each fall.

Make sure when choosing a shade tree to consider its mature height and spread. Think about where it will go. Will it provide the shade you want for your home or patio in summer or will it cast unwanted shade on your vegetable garden? Will it be in the way of future utility repairs or overhead utility lines as it grows?

Nut trees such as black walnut, butternut, pecan, and hickory are prime choices for large shade trees — those over 60 feet high. For medium-size trees, between 30 and 60 feet high, consider standard apples, red mulberry, American persimmon, Chinese chestnut, and walnut. Most other fruit trees are in the small size category — under 30 feet high at maturity — and include crab apples, pears, peaches and nectarines, plums, cherries, and semidwarf apples.

Foundation plantings. When including fruits in a foundation planting, keep them away from the building. If they're too close, moisture will be trapped behind them, which can rot siding and weaken bricks. A roof overhang may prevent rainwater from reaching plant roots. Mature height is another important consideration; you don't want plants that will grow to block windows and doors.

Although most trees are too large to plant near a foundation, dwarf apples are good for flanking an entrance and at the corner of a building. Large shrubs such as serviceberries and Nanking cherry work well on home corners. When siting larger trees such as pears and plums, place them out from a corner at least half the width of their mature canopy. Gooseberries and currants work well along the foundation. With their red fall leaves, blueberries (especially the half-high varieties) are a good substitute for burning bush (*Euonymus alata*). Clove currant, which sports yellow flowers, is a good substitute for forsythia. Put the sun-loving blueberries on the east and south sides; the currants and gooseberries will grow best on the west and north.

Beds and borders. Island beds within lawns and borders (the beds along the edge of a wall or property

Grapevines trained to cover a pergola benefit from the sturdy support of the timbers, while offering shade to a sitting area below.

line) are usually planted to shrubs and perennials or a combination. For these areas, consider some of the foundation plants such as saskatoons, red or clove currants, blueberries, and gooseberries. Be careful of raspberries and elderberries; these spread and will take over an entire bed. Save these shrubs for a berry patch.

Place larger shrubs toward the back of a border, or in the center of an island bed. Mass lingonberries, cranberries, or lowbush blueberries in the front. Strawberries, particularly the alpines, which clump rather than spread, are also good for the front. Intersperse small trees or plant them toward the back of a border. Just make sure you leave space between other plantings, or a path, to access your fruits for picking.

Arbors, pergolas, and trellises. These terms are often used interchangeably, although an arbor is simpler and less extensive than a pergola. An arbor is usually constructed of wood. Pergolas are common over seating areas such as patios. Arbors, pergolas, and trellises are excellent supports for vining fruits, such as grapes, kiwifruit, and in warmer climates, muscadine grapes. For a decent fruit crop, you'll need to prune the vines annually. Be aware that pruning is more difficult on an arbor or a pergola; unlike on a trellis, most of the growth on these structures is overhead.

Espaliers. Remember the caution not to plant trees too close to a building? You can disregard that advice if you grow an espalier. This form not only grows well in close quarters, but it also provides a decorative way to grow fruits. Though labor-intensive, when well cared for an espalier produces an abundance of fruit. Create a small-scale orchard with several kinds of fruits growing in close quarters, or train one up a wall to create a landscape feature. For more on this specialized technique, see page 253.

Ground covers. Some low-growing fruits are perfect for steep terrain or to replace a lawn area. They need a mostly sunny site to be vigorous and bear fruit. Also, make sure the site is fairly weed-free before you plant. Most are deciduous (lingonberries, however, are evergreen). Most are trailing. The alpine strawberry is an exception, and it looks wonderful as a massed planting. (Ordinary strawberries don't grow densely and therefore don't compete well with weeds.) Trailing brambles that are usually trained on a trellis can be allowed to ramble along the ground to create a mounded effect; keep in mind that they will bear less fruit this way than they would if grown on a trellis.

Containers. Smaller fruits can work well in containers. Plant half-high blueberries or dwarf fruit trees in large pots or raised planters. You can even grow grapes in a pot if you train the vine onto some form of trellis or attractive structure such as an obelisk. Container grapes will make smaller plants than those field-planted and trained on a trellis, but containers may enable you to grow grapes in places that otherwise would not be possible.

Since containers are aboveground, they dry out quickly and don't benefit from the moderating effects of deep soil. Plants in containers are also less hardy. In cold-winter areas, move container plants in into an unheated space such as a garage — but not one subject to freezing temperatures — for the winter.

Another important part of container plantings is the soil. The physical properties of a growing medium in a container are different from those in a ground bed; regular garden soil is not a good choice for containers. Instead, mix garden soil with at least half organic matter such as peat moss or compost, or purchase an already prepared potting mix.

Learning to Grow Good Fruit

EVERYONE WANTS PLANTS that produce well, but a surprising number of people seem to forget that plants are living and growing organisms that need care. Especially in recent times, with so much attention paid in the press to "decorating" outdoors — as if plants were living room furniture to be purchased, placed, then forgotten — this little fact is often overlooked. Many times along country roads you've probably seen abandoned farms where there are dozens of sturdy old apple trees growing miles from civilization. They obviously get no care whatsoever, yet they appear to be growing well and producing fruit. Still, it's very likely that sometime, long ago, someone helped those trees get off to a good start. You'll want to do the same for your fledgling fruit trees. It's easy. All you have to do is think from a tree's point of view.

Before you make a purchase, think about where in your yard the plant will grow best. Then, when your new tree or shrub arrives, treat it like the living infant it is. No responsible person would buy a puppy and dump it in the backyard to fend for itself; yet gardeners often buy a helpless little tree, plant it far too quickly and carelessly, and promptly lose interest in it or figure their work is done. Unlike the pup, a tree can't go hunting for food and water, or even howl to remind you it's being neglected. Plant it carefully, check up on it frequently, and — most important — make sure that its roots never lack moisture.

Strawberries Fit into Any Landscape

Strawberry plants make a charming edging for a flower bed and are useful in other ornamental ways. I've seen them in hanging baskets, grow bags, window boxes, jars and pots, barrels with large holes drilled in them, and pyramids. They can even be used in plantings on a wall, known as a green or living wall. The everbearing cultivars are most commonly used for edible landscaping, because unlike June bearers they begin to produce fruit the first year. Alpine strawberries don't need a large container; they grow well in smaller pots, including the classic strawberry pot.

Plant everbearing strawberries in barrels, window boxes, hanging baskets, or flower borders to make use of limited space.

What a Fruit Plant Needs to Thrive

Your tree or shrub has the same basic requirements as any other living thing:

A place to live. The earth around the tree or shrub will be its permanent home, so be sure the soil is to its liking. Can the soil accommodate the huge root system of a mature tree and, with a little help from you, properly nourish it? Is the soil well drained, not too dry, but also not too wet? Fruit trees deteriorate quickly if water ever covers their roots for more than a few days at a time. Even if you've chosen the right variety for your climate, trees can be fussy about where they're planted.

This gnarled old grapevine is more likely to survive neglect than a newly planted young vine would.

Water and nutrients. A fruit plant or tree needs water and nourishment, and both should be readily available, especially in early summer when a plant makes most of its growth. The roots take in nitrogen, phosphorus, potassium, and other minerals from the soil, but because soils are seldom well supplied with all these nutrients, you'll probably need to provide additional amounts. Enriching the soil will help the roots; then the tree or bush will grow better and produce more fruit. See chapter 15 to learn how to both improve the soil and add proper nutrients.

Sunlight. Most plants need light, and most fruits need a great deal of it throughout much or all of the day — at least 8 hours a day is usually recommended. Sunlight is necessary for photosynthesis, which is the process by which plants convert energy from the sun into the carbohydrates necessary for plant growth. If a building or large trees block out sunlight, your trees and bushes won't thrive.

Room to grow. No tree or bush should be crowded. Be sure not to plant too close to other trees, a road, a path, a building, or — if the tree will get tall — under overhead wires. Also make sure there are no young shade trees nearby that will grow to block the needed light. Bear in mind that it's not just the tops of trees that present a problem; the roots of large trees will steal valuable nutrients and moisture from your plants. A tree produces as much growth underground as there is above, and in areas where the soil is not deep, the roots of a large shade tree often reach out 60 feet or more in every direction.

The right climate. Each spring, post offices and delivery trucks in the northern states are filled with peach, fig, and apricot trees that have no more chance of survival than a walrus caravan crossing the Sahara. You can try various schemes to protect your trees from frost, but the best way to outwit the weather is to choose cultivars that are suited to your climate. Gardeners in a warm climate can't grow just any fruit, either. In order to produce fruit, most temperate-zone trees need a period of cool temperatures so they can get a good rest. This required chilling period is often long, as much as a few hundred hours each year. (See Choosing Hardy Fruits, page 27.)

Fruiting plants need regular watering, especially right after being planted.

Protection. Animals, insects, machinery (especially lawn mowers and weed trimmers), children, and weather all take their toll on trees and shrubs each year, especially newly planted ones. Although a grown tree can stand a little neglect, you must give a young tree or fruit plant careful protection. Keep an eye on your young acquisition and be ready to spring to its rescue whenever danger threatens. You may need to protect the trunk of a young tree from winter mouse feeding. In many areas, you will need some form of repellent or fencing to save your plants from deer browsing.

Sex and the Single Tree

Despite the childhood lectures about the birds and the bees, pollination is still a mystery to many people. They don't realize they need two of most fruit trees to get fruit, or they're unsure about whether they'll get the best pollination with two trees of the same cultivar or two different kinds. Others think pollination could change the variety of fruit, or that planting several kinds of berries near each other could eventually result in a grand mix-up. People have asked me whether a plum can pollinate a cherry, if apples will mate with stone fruits or pears, and if all the thousands of apple cultivars are compatible. One new gardener thought the year-old plants in his raspberry patch might be male and the young new plants female.

Like all other plants, a fruit plant's biological duty is to reproduce itself. It does this by blooming and bearing fruit that contains seeds. As in the animal world, both genders are involved. The male and female parts of blossoms must join together for offspring — fruit and seed — to occur.

No mate? No fruit. Almost all fruit trees and some bush fruits do better with a mate. Having at least two trees planted near each other (even in a neighboring yard), is the most reliable way to get consistently heavy crops. The catch is that the trees have to be two different cultivars of the same fruit; two alike won't cross-pollinate. Having two identical apples is no different from having only one tree. You need to plant two separate kinds — perhaps a 'Honeycrisp' and a 'Freedom'. Likewise, if you want to grow plums, plant two different plum cultivars. Only then can you be sure of true cross-pollination.

Cross-pollination is important for fruit quality as well. Lopsided apples and small or lopsided raspberries and strawberries are the result of poor pollination. Although a few fruit trees are "self-fertile"

It's important to plant fruit trees in groups for cross-pollination. This stand of apple trees also provides a shady area for outdoor dining.

or "self-fruitful," which means that a single tree can bear fruit by itself, most are "self-infertile" or "self-unfruitful." They need cross-pollination, which requires a partner nearby. Even though in some cases two trees or bushes are not needed for pollination, it bears repeating that they produce far better if several are planted together. Trees listed as self-fertile often produce better yields with cross-pollination from another cultivar. You'll find pollination requirements for each type of fruit in the box at the beginning of each fruit chapter.

In order to cross-pollinate, the trees must be in the same family group. Apples can't pollinate pears; pears can't pollinate plums. You therefore need at least two of each type of fruit tree you plant. If you want to grow pears, plant two pear trees. If you want to grow plums, you need two plum trees. Because crab apples and apples are related, they can be used to pollinate each other, so you can plant one apple and one crab apple.

Make sure the cultivars you select bloom at the same time. For example, there are early-, mid-, and late-season apples; to get fruit, you need two trees that bloom in the same season. For more information on the pollination requirements of specific fruits, nuts, and berries, see the appropriate chapters.

The Process of Pollination

This is how pollination happens. The pollen (male cells) from the flower on one plant must be moved to the female portion of the same flower (if it is a self-pollinating cultivar) or to a flower on another plant for cultivars that require cross-pollination (cross-fertilization). How does all this pollen get around? Though forest trees (pines, maples, oaks) are pollinated by the wind, fruit trees and bushes are pollinated by insects — primarily bees. The bee is an innocent party to these goings-on; she accidentally fertilizes flowers as she goes about her business of gathering nectar to take to the hive. On a good day, one busy bee may visit 5,000 blooms!

The flowers of most fruit plants are perfect, which means that each contains both male and female organs. The male portion is the cluster of little upright projections in the center, the stamens (see illustration, right). These are covered with pollen — the brown, red, yellow, or orange powder you get all over your nose when you sniff a flower up close. The female part of the blossom, the pistil, is the long, slender green tube that is slightly taller than the stamens and in the midst of them. For most fruit trees and many berries to bear fruit, pollen from the stamens of Plant A must be moved to the pistil of Plant B. The pollen then germinates — just as a seed does — growing a pollen tube down to unite with (fertilize) the female cell in the ovary. This is the beginning of a fruit, which is the enlarged and ripened ovary.

Fruits with a single seed or pit need only one grain of pollen. Apples, which have ten seeds, need ten grains. An apple has five compartments (carpels) in the center, each with two seeds in most varieties. If the pistil of an apple receives only one or two pollen grains, the developing fruit will fall off soon after it forms. If it takes in only five or six grains, an apple may still develop, but it will be lopsided. Similarly, if your raspberries or strawberries are small and lopsided, they probably weren't pollinated sufficiently. On blueberries, poor pollination means fewer berries.

THE PARTS OF A FLOWER

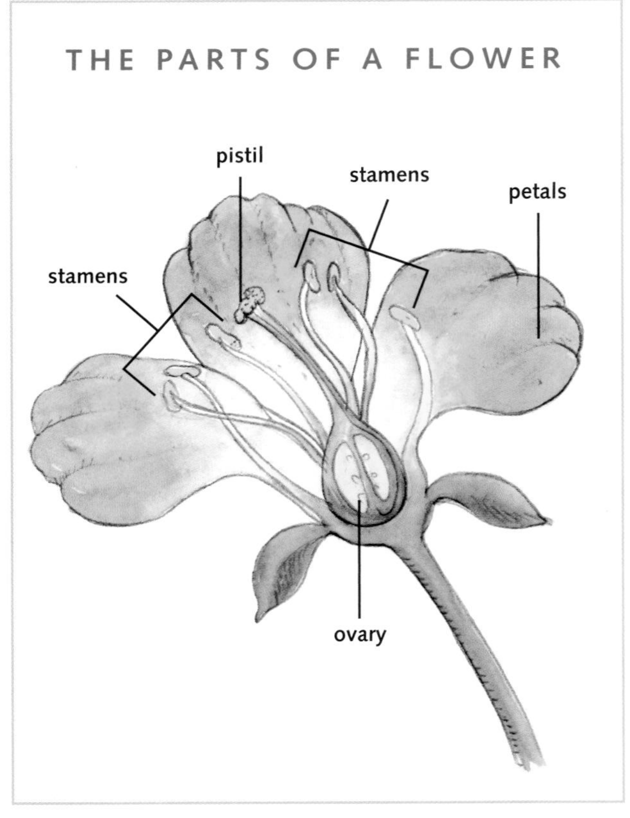

Don't worry about whether the quality of your fruit will be affected by the pollen of your tree's partner, or that pollen from a sour wild tree might produce sour apples. The mating tree's pollen influences only the genes in the seed and therefore only a plant grown from that seed. The fruit is merely the host for the seeds; it will stay the same whether bees bring pollen from a sour crab apple or a high-quality grafted tree. Any trees grown from the seeds, however, will vary widely, each producing fruit quite different from its parents and from each other.

No More Johnny Appleseed

It's fun to think of growing an apple tree from the seed of something you eat, but, alas, you won't get good fruit that way — and you certainly won't get the same apple you started with. Unlike shade and forest trees, fruit tree cultivars will not, if propagated from seed, be like their parents. Even seeds from the best apples, plums, peaches, and pears are likely to grow into trees that produce poor fruit. The fruit from Johnny Appleseed's famous trees weren't good for much except hard cider.

Your new little 'Liberty' apple tree is most likely two trees joined together by a surgical operation called a graft. The part that will grow and produce fruit was started from a short piece of branch called a scion (pronounced SYE-on), which was taken from a large 'Liberty' apple tree (or whatever cultivar you bought). The scion determines the shape of the tree, and what the size, color, and quality of the fruit will be. If this scion is just a bud, as is often the case, the process is called budding. The rootstock, or rooted portion of your tree (also called understock), came from a different plant. Although once it would have been grown from a seed, now, more likely, it was cloned from a cutting. The rootstock greatly influences the size of the tree, its vigor, its hardiness, and its ability to grow in various types of soil; it may also provide some disease resistance. Grafting is common with fruit trees, even with some woody ornamental plants.

You can easily locate the graft on a young fruit tree. It will be a good-sized bump or slight bend in the stem, either at ground level or a few inches above it. As the tree grows, the bump gradually disappears, but the different kinds of bark are often noticeable years later.

What you need to know about grafted trees is that everything growing below the graft will produce poor-quality fruit if allowed to grow shoots (suckers). That means you should cut off any sprouts from that part of the tree immediately. If mice or rabbits should chew the bark and kill the tree above the graft, any growth coming from below the graft will be the rootstock and not the cultivar you bought and want. Unless you regraft one of these sprouts with a scion from a good variety, it's better to dig up the roots and replace with a new tree.

Your new grafted fruit tree is the result of centuries of improvement over the fruits that the early Greeks cultivated, even those your great grandparents grew. Newer selections have better yields and shorter and more compact habits. Many have good resistance to diseases. Your new little 'Liberty' apple tree is now ready to enrich your life with its beauty and bounty, asking only for a little care and attention in return.

On grafted fruit and nut trees, be sure to prune off suckers that grow from the rootstock; they'll produce poor-quality fruit.

Helping the Bees

It's always a delight to walk through the orchard when it's in bloom and hear a loud buzzing coming from each tree. More bees means better pollination, which means more and larger fruit, so anything that aids bees also improves fruit production. This is just as important for blueberries and strawberries as it is for tree fruits. Gardeners who live where late-spring frosts are a problem especially appreciate a strong colony of bees in the neighborhood. If the flowers are pollinated soon after they bloom, they can resist a light frost better than blooms just opening.

Helping the bees begins at planting. As a rule, the busy little bees should not be forced to fly more than 500 feet to bring about the mating of two blossoms, although they can, and do, travel much farther if need be. Closer spacing is better, since bees don't fly as far if it's windy or if the weather is cold or wet. Ideally, you should plant semidwarf apples within at least 50 feet of each other; dwarf apples, within 20 feet. The recommended spacing given for specific fruits will result in the best pollination.

A hedgerow, or dense planting of native species, growing near your fruits provides habitat for wild bees. It may provide a windbreak too, an advantage because bees are less active on windy days and in windy sites. Bumblebees are especially good pollinators for blueberries, raspberries, and currants. Bumblebees work better than honeybees when it's cold, cloudy, and windy.

If you grow lots of fruit, consider keeping bees, especially if you aren't getting good pollination. (See Resources, page 307.) A hive of bees is good fruit insurance, because wild bees may be in short supply in early spring. Along with better fruit set, you'll also get honey! If you keep bees, don't place the hives right under the trees; if you need to spray, you'll endanger the bees. Never spray during bloom; in addition to killing bees, many pesticides will damage the pollen growth in the flowers.

You can still get fruit when only one kind of fruit tree is blooming and there appears to be no suitable partner blossoming anywhere in the neighborhood. Here's how we do it: When only one of our pear trees is in bloom, we drive across town to an abandoned farm where a big, ancient pear tree always blossoms at the same time as ours. We cut off a few branches, bring them home, and put them in a bucket of water under our tree. The bees take over from there.

Keeping bees (opposite) is an excellent way to ensure that your fruiting plants are properly pollinated. Most commercial orchard owners hire beekeepers to truck in hives of bees (left) while the trees are in bloom. The bees fly from flower to flower, covered in pollen (right), as far as a mile from the hive.

Picking fruit is an activity the whole family can enjoy. If you have children, consider including them in the discussion when you're deciding which fruits to plant.

CHAPTER 2

What to Grow and Where

The word *orchard* may stir up visions of acres of well-spaced trees, or at least a dozen big old gnarled specimens around Grandpa's house in the country, but a modern orchard can consist of three or four dwarf fruit trees, a few grapevines, and a small berry patch — all on a half-acre lot. Intensive gardening has always been necessary in tiny, backyard city lots, and it's now common in suburban and even rural areas. The size of the lot isn't the only reason people plant on a miniature scale. You may prefer to limit the size of your plantings because you have only a small family or because you lack the time to garden.

Whatever the space of your gardening area, you'll find that although neighbors or the local zoning board might raise a ruckus if you were to keep a few pigs or even chickens, no one is likely to find an ordinance prohibiting a few trees. In fact, planting a tree almost anywhere is encouraged.

Before you buy plants, consider what you want to grow. Figure out which fruits you like to eat. What do you buy most often at the store or farmer's market? Think about whether you have the time and energy to put up some of the harvest. When you have your answers, it's time to identify which varieties will grow best in your climate. All these factors will help you determine which, and roughly how many, trees and berries to plant. Resist the temptation to crowd in too many if your space is limited. Even if you have a large lot, don't let enthusiasm get the best of you. In the quiet of winter, too many of us succumb to colored catalog pictures and tantalizing descriptions of fruits and berries. Soon we've made out quite an order, and only when the trees arrive in the spring or we come home from the nursery do we realize that we overestimated not only the space available, but also our time, energy, and needs.

It's impossible to suggest the precise number of plants that would be right for every family, as each has different needs and tastes. It makes a difference, too, whether you want to consume all the fruit fresh or preserve enough to enjoy through winter.

Before you choose the exact location of your berry patch or orchard, investigate anything that goes on there that might affect your plantings, now or in the future. Will your neighbor's row of little trees, or even your own plantings, grow to powerful heights and shade your fruit plants? Do heavy rains or melting snows form pools of water that could drown them? Will road salt drain onto them? Is the spot a neighborhood trail for motorcycles, snowmobiles, or hikers? Will you or someone else eventually have to dig to repair a cable, a waterpipe, or a sewer line? Will an orchard block off an area where you may need service vehicles to drive through someday?

If you have only a small lot, you don't have much choice about where to put things. Within the boundaries you do have, though, try to find a place where your fruit plants will have full sun, good deep soil, and plenty of room to grow.

It's good insurance to plant fruit near your home, where you can keep a watchful eye on any troubles before they get serious. Fruit trees planted close to a busy sidewalk may be tempting to passersby, and you'll likely have competition for your bounty from all the neighborhood kids. To reduce temptation, plant berries and fruit trees in a slightly less convenient place.

Planting on a slope assures good soil drainage and reduces damage from a late frost. East- or north-facing slopes are best for reducing frost risk.

Choosing Hardy Fruits

When buying fruit plants, select varieties that are acclimated and can stand the weather expected for your region. If you have extra room, though, it's always fun to experiment with a few that are intended for a different zone. For most of your planting, you'll want to stack the odds in your favor with those proven for your region. There can be a great difference in hardiness among cultivars, so pay attention to the hardiness level indicated for each. Just because a particular fruit type is listed for a certain hardiness range doesn't mean all cultivars will live in all the zones listed. (See the USDA Plant Hardiness Zone Map on page 306.)

To be successful in your yard, a fruit tree or berry bush must meet several requirements. In colder climates, it must be able to make its growth during the first half of the growing season, then stop and harden up before the first frost. Don't assume that a plant's hardiness is determined only by the cold temperature it can tolerate. Actually, a short growing season may limit your choice of fruits more than the lowest temperatures will. Certain peaches, plums, and nuts are often advertised as being hardy to –20°F. What is left unsaid is that the trees need a long growing season to properly harden the wood so that it can withstand those low temperatures. Some tree fruits — as well as many grapes, nuts, blackberries, and blueberries — that were developed in warm zones are still growing when the first fall frosts hit parts of Zones 3, 4, and 5. Because their new wood is still green and soft, the moisture-filled cells freeze and then rupture.

Plants native to a region have become adjusted to local conditions, and the shortening days trigger mechanisms to stop growing and harden their wood before frost. Plants imported from a milder region are often unable to do this; they not only continue to grow late into the fall, but also may start to grow during the first warm week in early spring. Your plant should be able to ripen its fruit before the first killing frost of autumn. Many late-ripening apples, such as 'Granny Smith', can't do this and therefore are unsuitable for cold-climate gardens. Plants from one zone can acclimate to another zone if they're able to survive long enough. Those vastly unsuited for another climate, however, have little chance of adaptation. Nectarines may never adjust to North Dakota, and the 'McIntosh' apple will probably never grow well in Louisiana.

During the winter, the entire tree or vine — fruit buds, branches, trunk, and roots — should be able to withstand the most likely coldest temperatures. It should also stay dormant all winter, and not begin to grow during a midwinter thaw. Plants that bloom too early in the spring won't produce fruit if the flowers are killed by a late frost. If you garden in a cold climate, look for selections listed as blooming late.

In addition to the other factors that determine hardiness, different parts of a tree may have different tolerances to cold. Often the roots and tops of some plants are perfectly hardy but their blossom buds are tender. Peach, plum, and pear trees tend to bloom early, which makes them a special target of Jack Frost, but even later-blooming fruits, such as apples and grapes, can be hit in areas that

TIPS FOR PLANNING YOUR FRUIT PLANTINGS

- Determine how much space you have; make sure your space won't conflict with other activities.
- Decide what fruits you like and would like to grow.
- Make sure your site has the right soil, sun, and climate for these fruits.
- Read up on your fruits, to make sure you have the time to give them the care they need.
- Make a plan to scale — figure how many of each fruit for the yield you want, and where they will go — then use the plan to fit your ideas to your actual space.

Gardeners in cold climates need to select plants that will be cold hardy, and growers in warm climates must be careful to select varieties of plants (like these almonds) that will produce fruit with a relatively short winter dormancy. These are often referred to as "low-chill" varieties.

are prone to late-spring frosts — or in an unusual year. If you have a fruit tree that always leafs out and grows but never seems to bear fruit, this may be the cause.

Although knowing your hardiness zone helps a great deal when choosing plants, every gardener soon finds out that within each zone there are many microclimates, small areas that are a zone or two warmer or colder than the surrounding area. Uneven elevations, air drainage patterns, fog, frost pockets, prevailing air currents, proximity to bodies of water or buildings, and many other conditions cause these variations. So a fruit tree that may be damaged in a low spot on your property where frost settles may be fine higher up or on a slope.

Gardeners in mild-winter areas such as the Deep South and southern California must be careful to choose the right plants for their climate too. Plants grown in temperate zones need a certain period of chilling during their dormant period, and can't grow in the tropics. The length of winter chill needed varies from a long period for gooseberries to a far shorter one for pecans. There may be quite a range of chilling needs among cultivars, especially for apples (see page 142, Low-Chill Apples).

Although the requirements for a specific fruit tree might seem to limit your chances for growing it successfully, each region has a number of cultivars of a fruit that will thrive there, and you have only to discover which do best in your area. Ask your local garden center if its plants were grown locally or are adapted to local conditions. Nurseries and mail-order firms that focus on a specific fruit or region provide a much wider selection than what you can usually find locally. See the chapters describing each fruit for help in making your choices.

How Much Room Do You Need?

PLAN THE SPACING of your fruit crops so that no plant will touch any other when all are fully grown. Be sure, too, that they won't eventually rub against a building or overhang a street, sidewalk, or property line. Allow enough room between the bushes and trees so that sunlight will reach the entire leaf surface of every plant.

Keep in mind that some fruit trees are susceptible to disease and insects, and will need spraying from time to time. Don't plant these near a pool, birdbath, dog run, clothesline, water supply, or the vegetable garden or berry patch. Consider all the possibilities, even though most will never come to pass, so you can avoid trouble in the future. After all, a large tree is difficult to move and a disappointment to lose.

Unless you incorporate fruiting plants into your home landscape, you'll find that planting in rows simplifies cultivation and harvest. For example, plant strawberries in hills or rows (see pages 51-52). If space is limited, choose smaller cultivars and trees with more-upright shapes, or consider growing your fruit plants in containers. If you plant fruit trees, for the first few years you can use the space between them for growing strawberries or vegetables until the trees begin to bear and shade the ground underneath.

Starting Small: The Efficient Fruit Garden

Having a tiny yard isn't the only reason people plant smaller gardens. Limiting the size of your plantings makes sense when you have a small family or have limited time to spend gardening. It makes even more sense if you're a beginner. In fact, it's better to wait to make any large plantings of fruits until you've tried growing just a few for several years in your area. This advice comes from experience — I've learned it's better to make mistakes on a small scale!

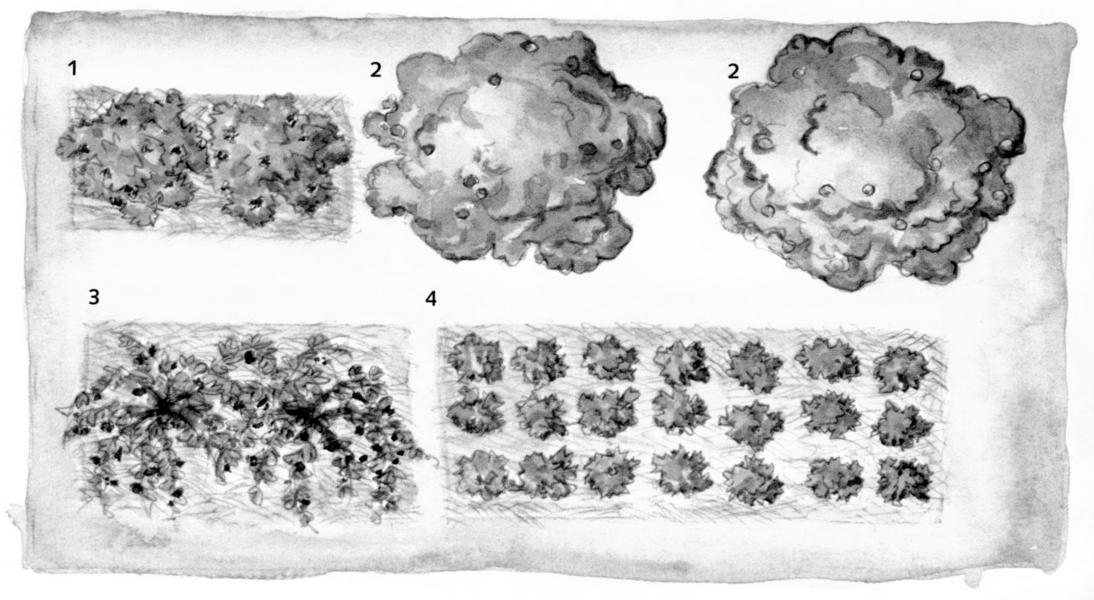

KEY TO PLANTS

1. blueberries
2. apple
3. blackberries
4. strawberries

If you're planting fruit for the first time, remember: it's better to start with just a few plants! You can always add more, if you find the maintenance schedule to be manageable and the amount of fruit to be insufficient.

Whether you're a beginner or a busy gardener, berries are an ideal choice:

- They require little space
- They need less care than fruit trees
- The initial cost is small
- They bear quickly
- They supply abundant yields, and for many years

Strawberries, currants, gooseberries, and elderberries are all easy to grow, attract few pests, and require no specialized pruning. Gooseberries and red and white currants are well behaved; they'll stay 4 to 5 feet high and wide for many years. They take up little space, and you need only one bush to get some fruit. Elderberries take minimal effort, but they take up more room, and they aren't always the first fruits people want to eat. Blueberries need minimal pruning. Fall raspberries are simple to prune; summer-bearing raspberries take only a little more time and skill.

Maybe it's time that limits you. If you're busy, consider planting two dwarf fruit trees, a couple of raspberry bushes, and a few blueberries. (You need more than one for cross-pollination; see page 19) You'll get a lot of fruit for a small amount of labor. If time is short and/or you want to minimize effort, it's important to choose disease-resistant cultivars.

Thinking Big: The Home Fruit Garden

If you plant your vegetable garden with the seedlings too close together or in the wrong spot, or if you choose the wrong varieties, you'll lose only one season. But if you make similar mistakes with fruit trees, it may be a few years before you find out there's a problem and longer before you can get new trees into full production. That's why planning is so important for fruit growing. Plant fruits on paper first, then put the trees in the ground.

KEY TO PLANTS

1. pear
2. cherry
3. peach
4. nectarine
5. plum
6. grapes
7. late apple
8. blueberries
9. blackberries
10. early apple
11. strawberries
12. elderberries
13. red raspberries
14. yellow raspberries

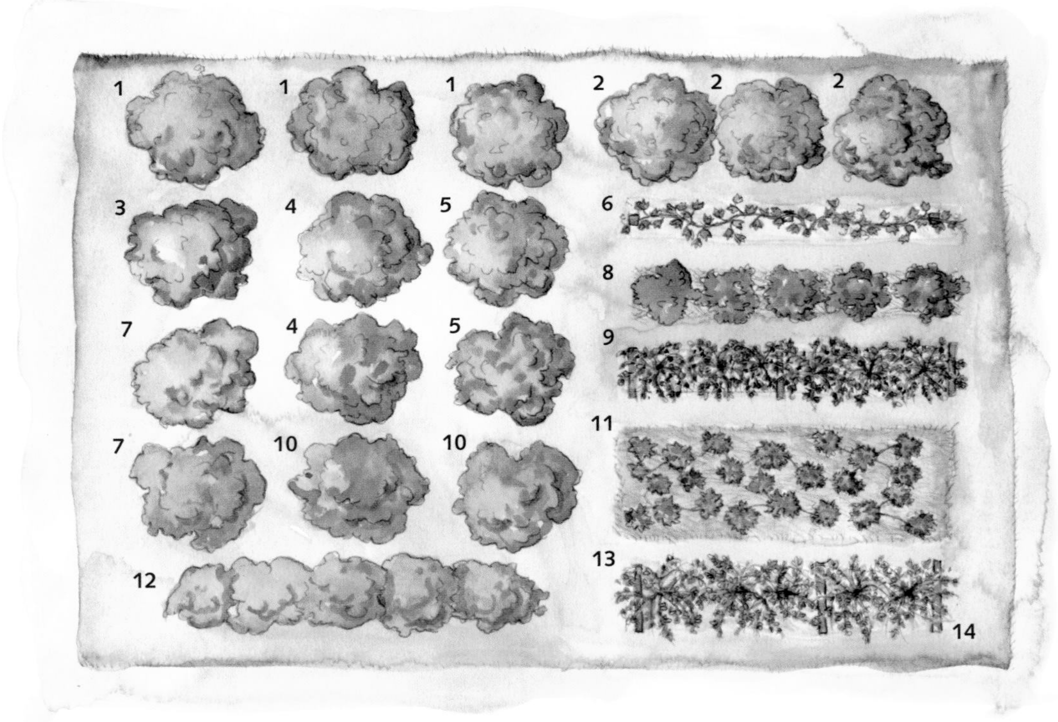

With a well-laid plan and a good sense of the amount of maintenance and harvest to expect, there's no reason not to set aside space for a large fruit garden.

Ripening Times

Generally, cherries are the first of the stone fruits to ripen (first the sweet, then the sour), followed by apricots and plums, then peaches. Following are general guidelines. Ripening times vary with climate and culture: later in the range for colder areas; earlier in the range for warmer regions. Ripening times for different cultivars vary within the range for each fruit.

CHERRIES: late May–late July
APRICOTS: late May–early July
PLUMS: late June–mid-September
PEACHES: late May–mid-September
NECTARINES: late June–early September
PEARS: late July–late October
APPLES: early July–late November

A plan will help you put everything in the most favorable location, especially if you spread your planting over several years. Keep your plan up-to-date, because labels invariably get lost, and whenever a tree begins to bear you'll want to know what it is. Also, if a tree does poorly or dies, you'll want to replace it with a better variety.

Try using a piece of graph paper to draw your plan. If you set each square to equal 1 foot, and a tree at maturity is described as being 10 feet across, draw a circle 10 squares in diameter. An easy way to try out different ideas is to cut out shapes for each mature tree, bed size, or row length you need. Rearrange them on the graph paper until you get what you want. Make sure to leave plenty of space for rows. Think about where the sun will come from, so you don't end up placing tall trees on the south side of a berry patch, which would cause too much shade.

A plan will help you put everything in the most favorable location

Selecting Plants

THE CURRENT ASSORTMENT of fruit trees and berry plants offered by nurseries and garden centers is much larger and better suited to the home gardener's needs than the choices of a half century ago. Even so, many chain stores and seasonal garden shops have little knowledge of local conditions, and their suppliers are as likely to ship the same assortment of fruit trees and plants to northern Maine as they do to southern Kentucky.

Try to buy your plants at a nearby nursery or a full-service garden center with trained professionals and plants as their main focus. Where this isn't possible, or the selection is limited, look for well-established nurseries or mail-order houses that are in your region or can recommend plants for your climate (see Resources, page 307).

When shopping for fruit trees, you may wonder what size and age to select. Bare-root trees come in all sizes, from a few inches tall to more than 10 feet. They may be from 1 to 4 years old, and are priced accordingly. Bare-root trees that are 1 or 2 years old, lightly branched, and 4 to 6 feet tall tend to be the best choice for planting. They become established sooner, grow faster, and usually bear earlier than a large tree, which needs time to get its big root system reestablished. On the other hand, small trees can be difficult to protect from lawn mowers and other hazards. You may also need to devote more care to train them, because some will try hard to grow into poor shapes for fruit-bearing.

If you buy a tree with its roots intact and wrapped in burlap or plastic (this is called "balled-and-burlapped"), almost any size is practical as long as you can lift, transport, and handle it. When you plant it, there is no setback, because every root is intact, and the plant will get off to a fast start. Just be sure it's in fresh, healthy condition and not dried out.

When you buy a tree that's balled-and-burlapped or in a pot, it helps to buy from a local nursery or garden center. Many potted plants sold through mass markets are really bare-root plants that were only recently potted up for sale. If, when you take it out of the pot, all the soil falls off, leaving a few major roots, you just bought a bare-root plant — so treat it as one.

Space Requirements and Average Yields

The following are only approximate. Some varieties will be larger or smaller and yield more or less. Yields for the same variety will vary in different regions and different growing conditions; trees also may grow differently in varying soils and climates.

Fruit Tree	SPACING (FEET)		AVERAGE YIELD (PER MATURE PLANT)
Apples (standard size)	25–35		8–18 bushels
Apples (semidwarf)	15–20		4–10 bushels
Apples (dwarf)	7–10		1–6 bushels
Apricots (standard)	18		3–5 bushels
Apricots (dwarf)	8		1–2 bushels
Cherries (sweet)	20–25		60–80 quarts
Cherries (sour)	15–20		60–80 quarts
Peaches, nectarines (standard)	18–20		4–6 bushels
Peaches, nectarines (dwarf)	7–8		1–2 bushels
Pears (standard)	15–20		2–8 bushels
Pears (dwarf)	8–10		1–2 bushels
Plums (standard)	18–20		2–6 bushels
Plums (dwarf)	18–20		1–2 bushels
Small Fruits	**FEET APART IN ROW**	**FEET BETWEEN ROWS**	**AVERAGE YIELD (PER MATURE PLANT)**
Blackberries	3	6–7	1–4 quarts
Blueberries	5–6	6–9	3–8 quarts
Currants	5	6–8	1–8 quarts
Elderberries	5	8–10	3–7 quarts
Gooseberries	5	6–8	2–6 quarts
Raspberries	2–3	6	1–4 quarts
Strawberries	1½	3	½–2 quarts
Grapes, muscadine	16	8–9	30–60 pounds
Grapes, table	8	8–9	5–15 pounds
Nut Tree	**SPACING (FEET)**	**MATURE HEIGHT (FEET)**	**YIELD (IN POUNDS, PER MATURE TREE)**
Almonds	15–20	20–30	10–20
Black walnuts	35–50	50–75	60–75
Butternuts	35–50	50–75	60–75
Chestnuts, Chinese	30–40	40–60	60–75
Filberts	15	15–18	20–25
Hazelnuts	15	15–18	20–25
Hickories	35–50	70–100	60–75
Nut pines	20–25	30–40+	10–30
Pecans	30–50	70–100	60–75
Walnuts	40–50	40–60	60–75

"Balled-and-burlapped" is a common way for fruit trees to be sold. All wrappings must be removed prior to planting.

Choosing Cultivars

If you're growing trees for the first time, choose cultivars that are easy to grow. Although it may be tempting to plant French wine grapes, sweet cherries, Japanese plums, and English walnuts, it makes more sense to start with kinds that need less painstaking care. Start with some disease-resistant apples, for example, or try strawberries, blueberries, or pears. Don't plant named selections just because they're familiar, as they may not be adapted to your region or may require more spraying or pruning than you care to do. 'Delicious' apples, for instance, are common in the grocery store, but they require much spraying. Bypass another favorite, the late-ripening 'Granny Smith', unless you live where there's an extra-long growing season. Of course, if you've been gardening for years, go ahead and try plums, peaches, grapes, and anything else that will grow well where you live.

After you've decided which fruits to grow, pick out the cultivars that are best suited to your geographical region. Many of the best apple, peach, and plum cultivars ripen their fruits over a long season, a good choice for home gardeners who don't want all their harvest at one time. The chapters on the various fruits and berries will help, and you may also want to consult your favorite garden store, the local Cooperative Extension Service, state university professionals, or staff at public gardens in your region. They know not only which trees are best for your climate, but also what insects and diseases you're likely to encounter.

Master Gardener networks, which exist in many parts of the United States and Canada, are there to answer questions. If you seek out information on one of the many online sites, keep in mind that these gardeners are usually writing from personal experience. If their conditions and climate are different from yours, their answers may lead you in the wrong direction.

Regional Recommendations

The following fruits are good choices for beginners in these general geographic regions. Check with local or specialty nurseries or your local Cooperative Extension Service, as not all selections of a particular fruit may grow well even within a region. Strawberries, grapes, apples, pears, and plums will thrive in all regions if you choose an appropriate type or cultivar.

Northeast: black currants, blueberries (highbush, lowbush, half-high), cherries (in warmer areas), raspberries

Midwest: black currants, black walnuts, blueberries (highbush, lowbush, half-high), butternuts, cherries, peaches (in warmer areas), raspberries

South: black raspberries (in cooler areas), black walnuts, blueberries (rabbiteye), butternuts, English walnuts, peaches, pecans, red currants (in cooler areas)

Western mountains: black currants, black walnuts, butternuts, cherries

Northwest (including northern California): blueberries (highbush), black walnuts, butternuts, cherries, currants, English walnuts, peaches, raspberries

Southwest (including southern California): English walnuts, peaches, pecans, red currants, almonds

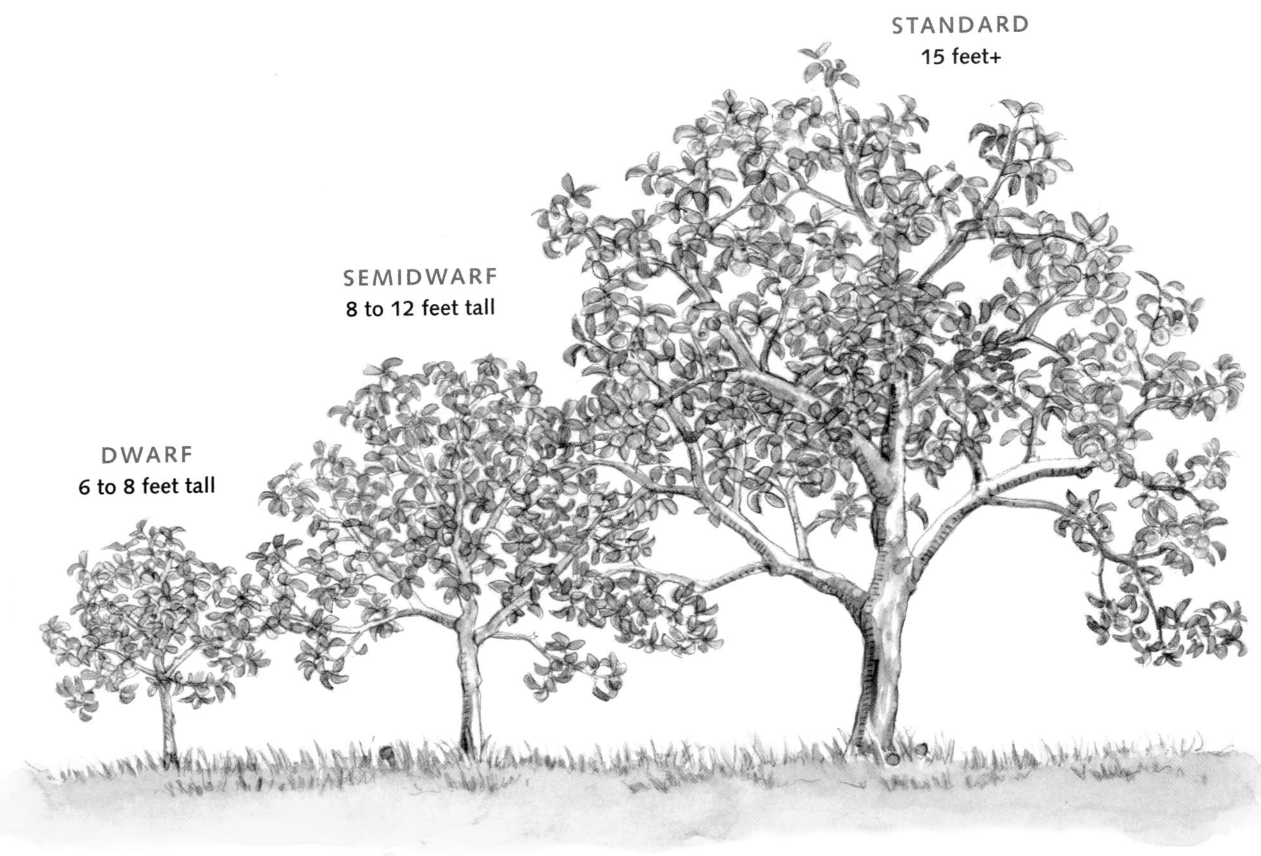

Six to twelve or more dwarf trees will grow in the space it takes to grow one standard (full-size) fruit tree.

Standard, Dwarf, or Semidwarf?

When shopping for fruit trees, you have a choice of trees grafted on dwarf, semidwarf, or standard rootstocks. The size of the mature tree is determined by its rootstock, in addition of course to pruning practices. (See page 21.) This means that even within each category, sizes of trees will vary.

A standard tree — that is, one growing on its own roots or grafted onto a rootstock that results in a tree of normal or "standard" size — may reach 30 feet tall for apples, 10 to 15 feet for peaches, and in between for other tree fruits. Standard trees are hardier than dwarf versions and thus better for the coldest climates. Because they're taller and larger overall, they're also more of a challenge to maintain and harvest. They usually don't bear fruit early in their early life, either, unlike dwarf varieties, but they live longer. Many provide nice shade as landscape trees, however.

Many dwarf cultivars of apples, cherries, pears, plums, and peaches are now available. Dwarfs generally grow 6 to 8 feet tall (slightly taller for apples) and spread about the same amount. Almost all dwarfs have the nice habit of growing quite rapidly when they're young and then slowing down, which means not only that pruning is easier on these trees but also that less of it is required. Dwarfs usually bear at an earlier age than standards, but their fruit is the same size. Of course, a dwarf tree produces considerably less fruit than a full-size tree does, but because so many more trees can grow in the same space, the total yield per acre compares favorably.

Unfortunately, some dwarfs are not as hardy as standard trees. Check the hardiness before ordering, especially if you live in a cold climate. Some dwarf trees are rather brittle and tend to break in high winds. Also, because they're shallow rooted, the wind may tip them over unless they're firmly staked. Deep, heavy snow can cause problems when it settles in spring, possibly tearing off the buried lower branches and devastating much of the rest of the tree. In some areas, dwarfs appear to be more susceptible to disease and insect damage than trees grown on native rootstocks. Despite these drawbacks, dwarf fruit trees may be the perfect choice if you have the right conditions for growing them and realize their needs and drawbacks.

Fortunately, semidwarf trees don't have the same drawbacks, yet they offer most of the same advantages. Semidwarf cultivars reach 8 to 15 feet in height and are about as wide.

Useful Terms

Here are some terms you'll come across when shopping for fruit trees and plants:

CULTIVAR. This is short for "cultivated variety." This is the correct designation for almost all named selections of fruits, although you'll see the term "variety" used interchangeably in various references and catalogs. They both refer to the same plants, so don't let this confuse you. A variety, by definition, is a plant that comes about from natural selection and occurs in the wild. A cultivar is a horticultural variety that came about through some process of breeding or selection; it doesn't occur naturally in the wild.

PATENTED PLANT. Sometimes in catalogs you'll find a fruit tree listed with a U.S. patent number, such as PP 16,859 for the Brunswick strawberry. Most new gardeners are surprised to find that trees can be patented, but over the years thousands of plants have been developed that were unusual enough to be registered and given a number. A patent does not mean that a plant is superior to any other named cultivar, merely that it's unique and that only the person or firm holding the patent, or those licensed by the holder, can propagate it commercially.

CHILLING HOURS. You'll run across this term often with tree fruits. It means the number of hours below 45°F a particular plant needs during winter in order to flower and fruit. It's not really an issue for cold-climate gardeners, but it's important for those in mild climates such as Florida and southern California. Chilling hours are cumulative during the season. If the temperatures go above 60°F the effect is reversed, so for each hour above 60°F subtract an hour. For example, if day one has 10 hours below 45°F, that's 10 chilling hours. Suppose day two has 15; the total is now 25. If day three has 5 hours above 60°F, you subtract this from the total, which leaves 20 cumulative chilling hours.

Most cherries and apples need at least 600 chilling hours, which is why they're grown in cooler climates. But each cultivar has a particular chilling requirement, and low-chill apples are available for warmer climates.

5-IN-1 TREE. Color nursery catalogs sometimes display a photo of a gorgeous "orchard-in-one-tree," which means that several cultivars have been grafted on a single tree. A beginning orchardist should avoid these 3-in-1 or 5-in-1, multiple-grafted fruit trees. The different cultivars seldom grow at the same rate and are difficult to prune. And if you're not careful as you prune, you could cut off an entire cultivar. On the other hand, if you want something really unusual, or if you have only a small space, and if you're willing to give it the special care it needs, the multiple-graft tree could be ideal for your backyard.

COLUMNAR TREE. Many nurseries sell small "beanpole" trees. These are a form of espalier (see page 253), small trees trained to a single trunk with no side branches. A pair of columnar trees takes up very little room, which makes it possible to grow fruit trees in a very small space.

Proper pruning of fruiting plants will help maximize harvest and minimize problems with pests and disease.

CHAPTER 3

Seasonal Care of Fruits and Nuts

Getting the feel of an orchard is best accomplished by actually being there to observe what takes place from week to week. When you get in tune and begin to feel the extraordinary cycle of a fruit tree, what you might have considered a difficult chore and performed nervously will become a delightful experience, and your trees will thrive. "The footsteps of the owner are a garden's best fertilizer," according to an old proverb. The same applies to one's orchard, vines, and berry bushes.

"To everything there is a season." This is especially true for fruit growers. Although the harvests of autumn may be what tree-fruit growing is all about, I enjoy the rest of the year in the orchard, too. Watching the trees gradually come to life in springtime is exciting. First comes the swelling of the buds as the sap begins to move, and not long after, the leaves appear. Still a bit later come the flower buds, and finally the flowers.

Winter Care

THE FRUIT GARDENING SEASON starts in winter. Even if the garden is asleep under snow, you need to get busy if you want to order plants by mail. Catalogs start arriving before the new year, and many nurseries sell online.

Late winter is the time to shape new trees and to remove winter damage from established trees and shrubs. In cold climates, most gardeners prune on warm days in early spring while it's still cold but the temperature is above freezing. This is before any growth begins or buds begin to swell. In warmer climates, you can safely prune all winter, as long as the trees or bushes are dormant. You'll find more information about pruning in chapter 17.

Spring Care

A STROLL THROUGH an orchard in bloom is one of the most delightful of experiences. The rich, sweet fragrance of the blossoms is a perfume no chemist could possibly capture. The trees delight the eyes, whether you're looking at small new trees bravely blooming for the first time or a gnarled, ancient specimen now well into its second century. Birds also seem to enjoy the beauty, and their songs and chirps blend cheerfully with the humming of thousands of bees. No matter how much there is to do on a spring day, a fruit grower should never become too busy to pause for a few minutes and enjoy springtime.

This is the time we hope for a week of warm, sunny weather, so no frost will harm the tender blooms and the bees will have a chance to gather the nectar and spread the pollen. Rainy, cold days or frosty nights when trees are flowering means a poor crop, and sometimes none. Soon the petals will fall and new fruits will begin to form.

It's a busy time. The birds have already started their nests, and insect eggs laid last fall will soon begin to hatch. Every creature is at work and so, too, must be the orchardist. It is the time to check the orchard frequently to see that insects, diseases, animals, and any other dangers are not threatening it. Insects tend to increase rapidly when the weather is warm, and diseases abound in cool, humid conditions. Some springs, unfortunately, provide an abundance of both! Scavenging animals swiftly pass the word to their friends to join them to dine on your succulent young twigs and forming fruits. If you spray, make sure to not spray during bloom so you don't kill off the pollinators your flowers need to set fruit.

Trees need a good supply of nutrients and moisture, because they should be growing their fastest at this time. Where the growing season is short, trees have to grow rapidly during the long days of spring and early summer to make the same growth they would during a longer period farther south.

Make sure that plenty of fertilizer and moisture is available, and that your trees get the first chance at

To protect pollinators, avoid spraying for pests or diseases while fruit trees are in bloom.

that nourishment. No new little tree is going to be able to compete with healthy, green-blooded weeds. The only way to deal with weeds and tall grass is to be firm and demand that they leave. Dig them out, keep them mowed, spray them with an herbicide, or smother them with a heavy mulch.

Early spring is the time to encourage birds and beneficial insects in your fruit grove. Birdhouses, hedges, windbreaks, and a few evergreens offer all sorts of protective nesting places for these helpful creatures, and they will reward you by feeding their new broods on the thousands of hungry larvae busily hatching everywhere, and eagerly waiting to feast on your leaves and young fruits. Although natural predators are your best ally in the battle against bugs, some other controls are usually necessary as well (see chapter 18). Remember that the more blemishes you can tolerate, the less intervention you'll need.

Checklist of Activities for Fruits and Nuts

WINTER

- ☐ Order new plants
- ☐ Perform dormant pruning of trees, shrubs, and vines (after the coldest weather, but before buds open)
- ☐ Tighten wire supports for grapes and brambles, if necessary

SPRING

- ☐ Remove frost protection from strawberries as soon as the top few inches of ground have thawed
- ☐ Plant new trees and bushes, also strawberries
- ☐ On raspberries and other brambles, cut out weak canes, thin remaining canes, and cut to ground level all canes that bore fruit the previous year (if not done in fall)
- ☐ Protect new shoots from browsing by deer
- ☐ Remove plastic winter tree guards from young trees
- ☐ Spray with dormant oil before tree fruits bloom and leaf out
- ☐ Check at least weekly for pests and diseases; use appropriate remedies
- ☐ Spread compost and fertilize
- ☐ Weed
- ☐ Renew mulch

SUMMER

- ☐ Prune off suckers and water sprouts
- ☐ Hand-thin fruits, as needed
- ☐ Water new plantings thoroughly each week; water established plants when dry
- ☐ Keep weeds removed, grass mowed
- ☐ Check for pests and diseases and use appropriate remedies
- ☐ End sprays a month before harvest, or according to directions on spray labels
- ☐ Install bird netting or scare devices just before fruits start to color
- ☐ Harvest berries at the right time for each cultivar

FALL

- ☐ Harvest at the right time for each cultivar and for your intended use
- ☐ On raspberries and other brambles, cut to ground level all canes that bore fruit; also cut out weak canes, thin remaining canes
- ☐ Clean up fruit drops and fallen leaves
- ☐ Keep grass mowed to discourage small mammals
- ☐ Replace winter tree guards for sun protection on young trees
- ☐ Add winter protection against browsing deer
- ☐ Install row covers or straw over strawberries as frost protection when ground starts to freeze

Summer Care

CONTINUE YOUR PEST PATROL through the summer. Early summer brings pruning needs too. Remove all the suckers, the shoots that spring from the roots. These suckers are parts of the rootstock, and because they sap the energy of the tree, they should be removed as soon as they sprout. Also remove branches arising from the lower part of the trunk and from just below pruning cuts. These water sprouts add too much foliage and take away energy the tree needs for fruiting.

Early summer is the time to thin developing fruits (see page 257). By removing at least half of the developing fruits, you'll end up with fewer but larger apples, peaches, or pears — the same size harvest but in much more usable form.

Through the summer, keep weeding. Take care not to cultivate too near plants, and don't go too deeply around shallow-rooted ones such as blueberries. During dry spells and in dry climates, keep plants watered, especially new ones. Ample water is crucial while fruits are forming. See individual fruit chapters for additional summer tasks, such as renovating strawberry beds after June harvest, tipping back branches of tall brambles, and spreading young branches of upright fruit trees to make them more horizontal.

Toward the end of summer, fruits increase in size rapidly. Insects and diseases may still be a problem, especially in years that are unusually wet or dry, so keep a watchful eye out for them. Check plants at least weekly for new pests and diseases, and deal promptly with those that can become serious problems.

Check trees that are bearing to be sure the crop is not overloading the branches. In a good year, a large tree may produce almost a ton of fruit, and even lighter loads put a strain on weak branches. Place wide boards or planks of the proper length upright under sagging branches to prop them up until the fruit is harvested.

Resist any temptation to use a fast-acting fertilizer to increase the size of the fruit. Feeding a plant in late summer will stimulate the tree to grow when it should be getting ready for its long winter nap.

Thinning out individual fruits is an important task for early summer. The remaining fruits will grow larger and will be less prone to disease.

Harvest Time

PICKING AND USING your fruit at its peak is what home fruit growing is all about. Not only does homegrown fruit taste better and need less sweetening, but also it contains more vitamins. Commercial growers that aren't local must harvest fruits before they're ripe, while they're still firm enough to ship. Large-scale commercial growers have no choice but to pick all the fruit at once; it's inefficient in a big operation to select only the fruits that are really ready for picking.

How can you tell when a fruit is ripe? Until you've had some experience, it isn't always easy. Squeezing and poking are natural impulses, but they leave bruises and aren't always reliable. Most varieties of tree fruits fall soon after ripening, so as soon as the fruit will separate from the branch with an easy twist it's ready. Most fruits change color as they ripen. Plums, blueberries, and grapes become covered with a powdery white "bloom." Cherries, apples, peaches, and pears each develop a characteristic color and blush, so you should be aware of what that color is for each variety. Some of the best-flavored apples are yellow, green, or russet brown, not red. If you're in doubt about the ripeness of an apple or pear, pick a sample fruit and cut open. If the seeds are dark brown, the fruit is ripe and ready to pick.

Only pears, a few varieties of peaches, and late apples that finish ripening in storage should be picked before they're tree ripened. If you leave pears on the tree until they're soft enough to eat, they'll quickly rot. Instead, pick them just before they're ripe and store them in a cool place. They'll be perfect for eating within a few days or weeks, depending on the variety.

The taste test is the most reliable when it comes to judging berries, but there are other clues. Strawberries become red all over and begin to soften. They and raspberries stay at their prime for only a short time and then deteriorate rapidly, so try to pick them every day during their season. A raspberry slips off its core freely when it's ripe. Blackberries, currants, and gooseberries are ready for picking when they have developed their full color. Sample some to see if they pass the taste test. Blueberries take 7 to 10 days after they turn fully blue to be truly ripe. With many varieties of blueberries, the stems change from green to a reddish color when ripe. Grapes are a good example of when you can't rely just on color, as they change color and appear ripe before they're sweet. Don't pick grapes until they're completely ripe — when flavor is sweet and clusters separate easily from vines — as they will not continue to ripen after picking.

Color of fruit isn't always the best way to determine when to pick, as varieties have different colors. You'll learn this quickly with experience.

TIPS FOR PROPER PICKING

- Harvest at the proper stage of ripeness (see box, opposite; pick slightly unripe for canning and baking, or for storing some late apple cultivars)
- Pick when fruits are dry
- Leave stems on the fruit
- Chill fruits as soon as possible after picking
- Wait to wash fruits until just prior to use or processing
- For fruits like strawberries and raspberries that don't store well, pick often, and pick only what you can eat soon or process for long-term storage
- Pick raspberries and other brambles into small, shallow containers as they crush easily
- Handle gently — avoid bruising, denting with fingernails, especially with peaches, which are softer than most other fruits

Use caution on ladders, with heavy loads of fruit, and when picking in hot weather.

Fruit growers warn their pickers to treat all fruits as if they were eggs. Pick each one by hand; never club or shake it from the tree or bush. For tree fruits, bend each fruit upward and twist it gently; if it's ripe, the stem will separate easily from the tree and stay on the fruit. Never pull out the stem, as that will leave a hole where rot will quickly develop. Be careful, too, not to damage next year's crop by breaking branches or fruit spurs as you pick. You'll find more on harvest and storage in each fruit chapter.

Storing Fresh Fruit

Bruised fruit starts to rot quickly, and rot will spread rapidly to all the fruit it touches. The old proverb that one rotten apple can spoil a whole barrel is all too true. Use all windfalls and any damaged fruit immediately.

Many tree fruits keep well for months in controlled storage. Some fruits will keep well for a short time in a cool, unheated room. Some of our friends use a small air conditioner in their basement, which has a concrete floor. A spare refrigerator in good running condition makes a good storage unit, too.

Home growers can keep apples and pears in a simple root cellar. Although home root cellars can't duplicate the scientifically controlled conditions that large growers maintain, they make it possible to eat good fruit through much of the winter. We have a small one partitioned off in a corner of our basement. It is insulated, and it has an outside window for ventilation when necessary and a dirt floor to increase humidity. 'Cortland' apples will keep there until April, if we don't eat them all first. We can't always maintain the ideal climate of 34°F and 85 percent humidity, but our fruits stay remarkably firm. Cellars of homes with forced air or whole-house heat stay too warm for long-term fruit storage; even 50° to 55°F is too warm.

You need to store apples separately from other fruits and vegetables, or as far away as possible. Try also to keep fruits apart from vegetables. Apples give off ethylene gas, which can cause other fruits to ripen more quickly, potatoes to sprout, and carrots to turn bitter. Potatoes can give apples a musty flavor. Strong odors from cabbages and turnips and onions can be absorbed by apples and pears.

Is It Ripe?

Unlike most fruits, pears should be picked before they're fully ripe and kept in a cool, dark place. Wrapping pears in vented plastic bags will keep them from shriveling.

In general, fruits are ripe when they develop good color and flavor. Ripe fruit should pull easily from the plant with an upward twisting motion. Some cultivars ripen their fruit over a long period, so look for the ripe ones and leave the rest to finish ripening.

Apples: seeds are dark brown; taste ripe

Cherries: good color and flavor; use soon after picking

Peaches: pick when almost ripe and color is good but before fruits are soft; should separate easily from twigs; won't ripen after picking but will soften, so pick when you can press and make a little dent; softer than most other fruits, so handle gently

Pears: pick before fully ripe, when still firm and seeds are dark brown

Other tree fruits: good color and flavor

Blueberries: good color for a week with white powdery bloom; softened; sweet flavor; stems often turn color; rings around stems show berries are ready to detach

Raspberries: colored well; softened; good flavor; slip easily off core; use soon after picking

Strawberries: red all over; softened; good flavor; use soon after picking

Other berries: good color; softened

Grapes: brown seeds; sweet flavor; clusters separate easily from vines

What to Do with All Your Fruit

MY FAVORITE WAY to eat most fruit is fresh off the tree, with no middleman — direct from tree to me. But I also love applesauce, strawberry shortcake with whipped cream, raspberry ice cream, blueberry pie, apple pandowdy, peach sherbet, a cherry tart. Once your kitchen shelf is laden with beautiful fruits, you'll find any number of wonderful things to do with them. Much of our surplus fruit goes into preserves for the pantry.

There are many good books on processing and storing fruits, and lots of recipes are available on the Internet. Hardware, farm, and garden stores can supply many of the items you'll need for harvesting and preserving. See Resources, page 307 for other sources for harvesting supplies, home cider mills, and orchard equipment.

Freezing

We freeze most berry and tree fruits raw in plastic bags or sealed containers, and they come out of the freezer tasting almost like fresh. We freeze the berries on a rimmed baking sheet before placing

Freeze small berries and slices of larger fruits by spreading them out in a single layer on a tray and placing the tray in the freezer. When fruits are frozen, transfer them to a zip-lock bag and return them to the freezer.

A Simple Way to Freeze Fruit

These instructions are for peaches, but they apply to other tree fruits as well. For best fruit quality use plastic bags or containers designed especially for freezing. Or freeze fruit in the right shape to pop into a piecrust: Mix fruit slices with sugar and spices for your favorite peach pie recipe before bagging, then lay the plastic freezer bag in a pie plate until the contents are frozen.

Sugar helps maintain texture, but you can omit it if you'll be cooking the fruit later, as for jam. In addition to sweetening and improving texture of the thawed fruit, sugar helps prevent freezer burn, drying out, and browning — benefits an artificial sweetener won't provide. If you don't want to use sugar, try apple, peach, or white grape juice; these all work well.

If using a vacuum sealer you can skip the juice or sugar syrup, just treat fruits with a fruit preservative to prevent browning. Freeze individual berries or slices first before bagging and vacuum sealing.

1. Peel two pounds of peaches, cut in half, remove the pits, and slice. (You can freeze halves without slicing, but slices take up less space.) You should have 4 cups of sliced peaches.
2. To prevent browning, prepare a fruit preservative — either ascorbic acid as the label directs (usually by dissolving a small amount in a little water), or half a squeezed lemon.
3. For every 4 cups of sliced peaches, also add 2/3 cup sugar; mix in gently.
4. Fill freezer bags or containers. Lay the bags flat and squeeze the air out, then seal to freeze.

Glazed, dehydrated apple chips are an excellent way to preserve the harvest from a bountiful apple tree.

them in plastic bags, so they will separate easily. We then partially thaw them to enjoy strawberries blended into milkshakes, blueberries baked into muffins, and raspberries in pies and cobblers. All make tasty and nutritious toppings for cereal. Just-thawed, spiced, whole crab apples on their stems have become our traditional garnish for Thanksgiving turkey. Berries make excellent jams, jellies, conserves, marmalades, and "butters" that brighten up the breakfast table during the dark days of winter. They're also welcome homemade gifts.

Canning and Drying

If you don't have a lot of freezer space, fruits are easy to can using the water-bath method. Apples, peaches, pears, cherries, and plums work well as canned fruits; I think pears taste better canned than frozen.

Drying is an excellent, old-fashioned way to preserve fruits. Electric or solar-powered food dryers work best, though an ordinary or microwave oven will do the job. Apricots, apples, and peaches cut into thin slices dry well; blueberries, elderberries, and black currants should be dried whole. When stored in glass jars, dried fruits will keep for months on the pantry shelf.

Juicing

If you have more apples than you know what to do with, cider is the answer. Apple cider-making with our old Sears & Roebuck press is a fall ceremony we wouldn't want to miss. A modern electric juicer is an easy option for smaller quantities. Most years we freeze large quantities and put aside a gallon or two to turn into vinegar.

Several years ago we began to question why we were drinking so much tropical fruit juice when our own New England fruits were so good and healthful. We've since remedied that situation by freezing lots of apple juice and cider, as well as berry juices such as strawberry and black currant. Elderberry, crab apple, and raspberry juices are some of our favorites. We either use a juice steam extractor or cook the fruit briefly and strain it through a jelly bag or wire strainer before canning or freezing. In winter we enjoy the thawed juices straight or sweetened with orange juice or cider. For a sparkling punch, we combine the juices with ginger ale or club soda. If we're too busy during the harvest season, we freeze the raw fruit and make juice later.

Making fruits attractive and accessible is a key way for both you and your children to incorporate more of these healthful foods into your diet. Growing and preserving your own is a great way to increase the appeal of fruit. Fresh berries, fruit pieces, and dried fruit slices make great snacks. Keep some handy at work, and pack some in children's lunch boxes and when you travel. Try some with pudding or yogurt as a dip, or with toppings. Spread peanut butter on apple slices. Make a fruit smoothie. When you make juice, freeze some into juice bars. When baking cakes, replace some of the oil with applesauce. In a salad, mix fruits that quickly turn brown, such as apples and pears, with either lemon juice or acidic fruit such as orange and pineapple.

PART TWO

The Small Fruits: Berries, Bushes, and Brambles

Small fruits are often the best plants to start with, if you've never grown fruit before. They take up less space, often cost less to purchase, and produce relatively soon after planting.

WE COULDN'T BUY ALL THE DIFFERENT BERRIES we harvest each year, even if we wanted to. Where would we find yellow and purple raspberries, black currants, elderberries, jostaberries, and red gooseberries? Strawberries imported from far away can't match the flavor of a pint just picked. The small fruits cost us very little money and take far less work than our vegetable garden. We feel that their undeniably superior flavors, and the convenience of having them in our own backyard, more than offset the effort it takes to grow them.

If you must make a choice between growing tree fruits and small fruits, the latter offer several advantages. They take up little space and the initial cost is small. They bear soon after planting, and most go on producing abundantly for decades. Many books say that a raspberry patch can produce berries for ten years, but we're still picking bushels of fruit each year from a patch set thirty years ago, and there's no sign of its retirement. Some of our currant, gooseberry, and elderberry plants are even older. It's the care you give them that makes the difference in both productivity and longevity.

It's important to buy plants that are suited to your climate. Berries developed especially for one region often don't grow well in another, even if climatic differences seem slight. Luckily, experimenters in every section of the temperate United States and Canada have been introducing cultivars for many years. Whether you live on the North Carolina seacoast or on a prairie in Manitoba, there are now plants suitable for you to grow. Experimenting is fun, but to count on a crop, plant the cultivars you're sure will produce in your corner of the world.

Plants are available at most nurseries and garden centers. It's not a good idea to accept gift plants from a generous neighbor, even though strawberries, blackberries, and raspberries create new plants at a fast rate. The trouble is that gift plants might bring along a variety of diseases and insects that will give you a peck of trouble ever after. Nurseries take great care to grow disease-free plants. Make life easier for yourself by starting with a bug-free, disease-free berry patch.

The best location is where you can mow around the bed to keep the plants' spread under control. Raspberries, blackberries, and elderberries sucker badly, so don't plant them near a vegetable garden, strawberry patch, or flower bed. Plant them a good distance from shade trees, whose roots will rob your berries of water and nutrients. Also keep them away from fruit trees, which may need spraying during the summer — just when your berries are ripening. When you plant small fruits, be careful not to crowd them; set plants at the recommended spacing for good air circulation and the most abundant yields. Uncrowded plants make pruning and picking easier, too.

The number of plants you grow depends on how many people will be eating them and their preferences, whether you intend to preserve the fruit, and how much room is available for growing. If you have time and space, many berries are a good cash crop, so plant extra for a bit of extra income. Yields will vary with different cultivars, also with different growing conditions. The chart on page 32 gives you a general idea of what to expect.

Few pleasures compare to the taste of a perfectly ripe strawberry, picked on a sunny morning in late spring.

CHAPTER 4

Strawberries

During a Sunday service in our little church when I was a child, a visiting minister remarked that he was thoroughly sick of hearing about Heaven's pearly gates and golden streets. He visualized Heaven, he said, as a land where, among other pleasant happenings, juicy, red strawberries ripened eternally. Probably lots of other people would agree; it's hard to find anyone who doesn't like strawberries.

Like many other gardeners, we have often risen in the dead of a late-spring night, looked at the thermometer with half-opened eyes, and suddenly come wide awake in shock. Soon we're grabbing blankets, quilts, tablecloths, boxes, and anything else we can find to cover up the tender blossoms that have foolishly opened just before the temperature plunged.

Are strawberries worth fighting the frost, the bugs, the diseases, the weeds, and the quackgrass? Every strawberry lover will answer a booming "Yes!" The reward comes on a bright summer morning when you gaze at the reddening row in hungry anticipation and then pick the first big, luscious ripe berry of the season.

June-Bearing or Day-Neutral?

THE STRAWBERRY WE CULTIVATE today (*Fragaria × ananassa*) is one of the few fruits that originated in the United States. These large, beautiful berries were developed throughout the last couple of centuries in North America and Europe from the same small-fruited wild strawberries that the early explorers found growing in the New World.

Because of the popularity of strawberries, a great many cultivars have been developed. There are kinds that grow well all over the continental United States, as well as in parts of Alaska, Canada, and even the warmest sections of Florida. Because there is such a wide range of cultivars, be careful to choose the ones that are best adapted to your region.

Most cultivars bear in June and so are called June bearers. These fruit from flower buds that were formed the previous fall as days got shorter. Those referred to as everbearing consist of a couple of different types of plants. The older everbearing cultivars really fruit only twice, once in June and then a lesser crop late in the season. Fruits of the everbearing types tend to be smaller than the June bearers, but overall yields are about the same over the season as they bear more often. Most retailers no longer sell these older everbearing cultivars.

The newer everbearing cultivars are called day-neutral, as they bloom and fruit regardless of the length of the day. Many of the day-neutrals have two or three cycles of fruiting each season. They fruit earlier in the season than June bearers (as long as the blossoms don't freeze), and with protection they can fruit into October and even November. They may pause in the heat of hot summers and in hot climates. Fruits are smaller than those of June bearers and everbearers. If you want strawberries over a long season, these are the varieties to seek out. If you want to finish picking strawberries before you switch to picking bush fruits, though, opt for June-bearing cultivars.

If you want to harvest strawberries over a long season, choose a day-neutral variety.

Strawberry Fast Facts

USDA Hardiness Zones: 3–9, varies with cultivar

Height: 6–10 inches

Spacing: 15 inches in rows 3 feet apart for matted rows; for hills 12 inches in rows 12 inches apart with paths between every third row

Pollination: self-fertile

Pruning: The first year, pick off all blooms on June bearers; only the first cluster on day-neutral cultivars

Special requirements: Replant rows after they fruit (the second year), or replant hills after 4–6 years; replant in a new location

Years to bearing: 2

Yield per plant: ½–2 quarts per plant; varies with cultivar, age of planting

Two Ways to Grow

BEFORE YOU PREPARE BEDS or purchase plants, you need to decide how you're going to grow your berries. This is really a decision about how you're going to manage the abundant runners that each strawberry plant produces. Runners are tiny plants on very long stems that will root where they touch the ground and then grow into new strawberry plants. Although we usually associate the name of this fruit from the straw used for mulch, another explanation comes from the verb "to strew," referring to the plant's habit of strewing runners about.

The matted-row system is commonly used for June bearers. If you keep the beds well weeded, renovate each year, and plants are healthy and vigorous, matted rows will produce well for 3 to 5 years for June-bearing cultivars. Or plants may be treated as biennials; this means each spring you set out new plants that will be harvested the summer of the following year and then plowed under. Everbearers and day-neutral cultivars should be replaced every third year in matted rows since bed renovation isn't recommended for these.

The hill system takes more plants initially and requires more attention than the matted row. It saves the work of renovation, though (or the cost of annual replanting, if June bearers are treated as biennials). It is ideal for home gardeners with little growing space. Anyone who likes to raise plants organically with a deep mulch should try this method. The hill system is more commonly used for day-neutral (everbearing) cultivars.

Though strawberries are perennial, they don't last forever. Even with proper care of hills or renovating rows yearly, you may get 4 to 5 years of good crops from hill culture, or 3 to 5 years of good crops from matted-row culture, before it's time to start new a bed elsewhere. If you start a new bed a year before the old one has run its course, you'll continue to get fruit while the new bed gets established. It may be tempting to save money by digging extra strawberry plants from your old patch for replanting, but to avoid problems with viruses and other diseases buy new ones.

Matted-Row System

The matted-row system is the usual method, but it takes up a lot of space. Set the plants in a row, 15 to 18 inches apart. If you plant more than one row, keep the rows at least 3 feet apart — even wider if you plan to use a power tiller for cultivation. As the plants send out runners, steer these offshoots so they fill in the empty spaces to make a row "matted" with strawberry plants (see illustration). Keep the row no wider than 18 inches; 12 inches is better.

Shortly after harvest, renovate rows of June bearers if the plants are still healthy and vigorous, up to 5 years old. If they're older than that, replant in a new location. Grow a cover crop such as winter rye, oats, wheat, or clover in the old rows for 2 or 3 years before replanting strawberries there. When you turn it under, the cover crop adds organic matter to the soil. Crop rotation helps prevent diseases such as verticillium and red stele from becoming established.

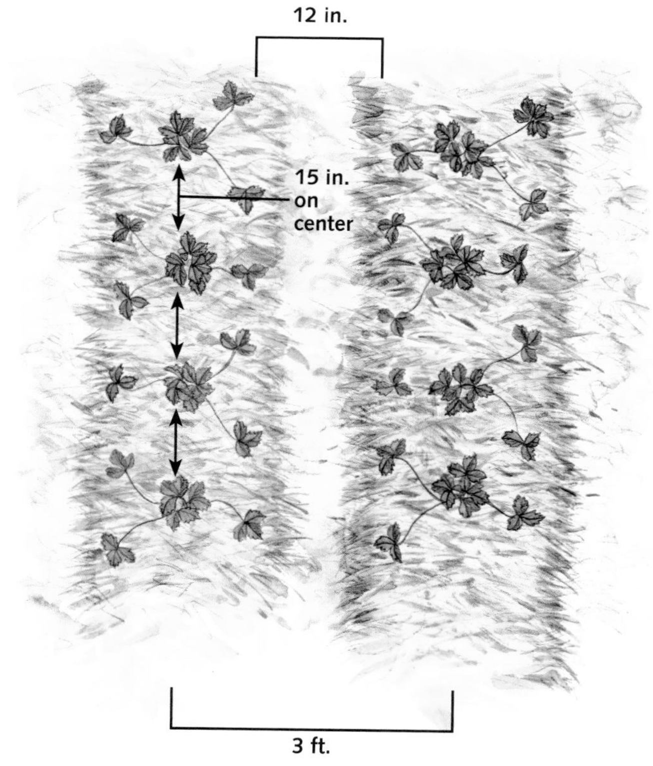

In the matted-row system, runners are allowed to take root and fill in the empty space around the mother plant.

Hill System

The "hill" in this system refers to the mounded appearance of the large plants, and not to planting strawberries on a mound of soil. In this system, plants are set 12 to 15 inches apart in a bed consisting of three rows, which are also spaced 12 to 15 inches apart (see illustration). The bed can extend for as long as you like, but leave openings every 20 feet so you can cross over between the rows. If you set more than one bed, leave 2 or 3 feet of walking space between the beds.

Mulching is essential to control weeds. It's difficult to cultivate plants grown in this system, because as they mature they will grow very close to each other. Some growers set the plants in slits cut in heavy black plastic, which they then cover with hay, wood shavings, or another material to protect the plastic from deteriorating in the sun. Mulching also keeps soils cooler, which is especially important for many day-neutral cultivars, as they're sensitive to warm soils.

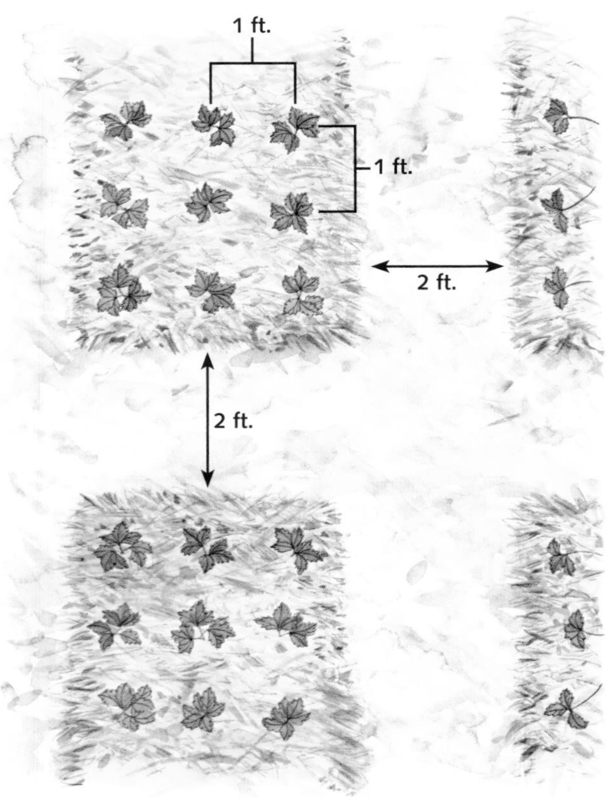

In the hill system, all runners are cut off, so the plant puts all of its energy into producing fruit. Because of this, the plants that are grown in the hill system often produce larger fruits than plants grown in the matted-row system.

In the hill system you must cut off all runners before the plantlets root (unlike the matted-row system in which you let runners to grow to fill the row.) In other words, treat the strawberry plants like the perennials they are. As none of the plant's energy goes into producing runners and making new plants, both the plant and its berries can get quite large. The part of the plant that produces the leaves and flowers is called the crown. In the hill system, plants will produce more crowns from the original; these are referred to as branch crowns. These are referred to as branch crowns. In just 2 years, a plant can produce many crowns, and too many branch crowns over time will eventually reduce berry size. If getting the largest berries is your goal, you may need to replant hill systems more often, every 2 or 3 years.

Preparing the Soil

CHOOSE YOUR SITE WITH CARE. The ideal spot gets at least 8 hours of sun a day and is on a slight rise for better drainage and reduced risk from a late frost. Avoid the bottom of a slope; cold air will settle there on quiet nights. Low spots are also frost pockets — areas that freeze before the rest of the yard — and a good site may save you from running out with blankets as the temperature drops. Low spots also are prone to drainage problems. If the soil is heavy or drains poorly, plant in raised beds to minimize disease problems.

Your strawberry plants will be growing in the same spot for at least two years, so it's important to prepare the soil thoroughly. It should be slightly acid (pH between 5.5 and 6.5 is ideal) and rich in humus (compost, well-rotted manure, or peat) so it will hold moisture even during the driest spells. Above all, it must be well drained to minimize disease problems.

Soils that grow good vegetables also grow good strawberries. For the best crops, plant them on land that has been cultivated with other crops for at least a year to get rid of the grass, weeds, and grubs. White grubs live in grass-covered soils, and because one of their favorite foods is strawberry roots, they're one of the strawberry's worst enemies. Well-prepared soil helps eliminate them.

Don't plant in a spot where you've grown potatoes, tomatoes, eggplant, melons, raspberries, blackberries, or other strawberries in the last 2 or 3 years. Verticillium wilt often lurks in such soils and can infect a new crop of strawberry plants months later. Never plant strawberries in soil infested with nematodes. (See Birds, Insects, and Diseases on page 57.)

Prepare the planting area well. For the best crops in a new bed, control weeds for at least a year before planting strawberries. Or start plants in pots and wait to set them into the ground until you've cleared out the first flush of weeds. Your strawberry plants won't have much of a chance if you set them into ground with a large reservoir of weed seeds. Incorporate lots of humus to improve the soil's moisture-holding ability. (See page 216.) Also enrich the soil with a balanced, all-purpose, low-analysis fertilizer worked into the top 6 inches. Follow the amounts recommended on the label, as application rates for different fertilizers vary greatly.

Planting and Care

SPRING IS USUALLY REGARDED as the best time to plant strawberries. Exceptions are southern California and similarly mild climates: there fall is best for many cultivars. In the South, planting hills in the fall may help you to grow strawberries where diseases are a problem; harvest the following spring before diseases take hold, then dig up and start new plants elsewhere. Ask the nursery where you buy your plants, or your local Cooperative Extension Service, their recommendation for planting in your area. Whichever growing system you choose, be sure to set your strawberry plants at the correct depth.

Water after planting and throughout the growing season. Water before the plants get too thirsty; for the best berries, make sure plants get at least an inch of water a week from you if not from rain. You'll need to provide even more in sandy soils. Strawberry roots are shallow, so don't let the soil dry out. After growth starts, the most crucial times to keep June bearers watered are late summer (when plants are forming next year's buds), before and during harvest, and after renovation.

A mulch helps soil retain water. Soaker hoses placed along rows, underneath mulch, are an efficient and easy means to water. They keep water off the leaves, and dry leaves are less susceptible to diseases.

Not Too Deep, Not Too Shallow

Plant strawberries at the proper depth, which means the crown should be at ground level. If the crown is buried in soil, the plant will smother; if it extends too high above the soil, it will dry out. In either case, your plants will die. If you cultivate or hoe the bed, never let soil pile up around the crowns, as you would with corn and beans.

12 TIPS FOR GROWING STRAWBERRIES

1. Choose a site with well-drained soil and abundant sun. Don't plant in low areas, which might be frost pockets.
2. Determine which planting system you will use (matted-row or hill) so you know how many plants to buy.
3. Select cultivars appropriate for your area and needs. Buy only what you will have time to keep weeded.
4. Prepare weed-free soil; enrich with a balanced fertilizer.
5. Plant in early spring in most areas, fall in mild areas such as California and the South if soil diseases are a problem. Set plants at the right depth, with the crown at the soil surface.
6. Remove the first blossoms to encourage a good crop. Do this the entire first year on June bearers; on day-neutrals pick off only the first blooms (first cluster of flowers).
7. In matted-row beds, sweep runners into rows; in hills, remove all runners.
8. Keep beds watered (at least an inch of water a week if not supplied by rain) and weeded.
9. In late fall, cover with straw or a similar organic material.
10. In early spring, uncover plants and use the straw for mulch.
11. Fertilize everbearers when leaves appear and again after fruiting; wait to feed June bearers until after renovation.
12. Renovate June bearers after fruiting; replace the plants that aren't vigorous.

The first year, if leaves begin to lose their dark green color several weeks after planting, this may indicate low nitrogen. Watering with fish emulsion is an easy way to give new plants a nitrogen boost. (Follow label directions.) The best plant growth will occur if you fertilize once a month until mid-September.

In the years after planting, don't fertilize June bearers early in the season, as this will lead to excessive runners, disease, and soft fruit that doesn't keep well. Fertilize these cultivars after bed renovation. Day-neutral cultivars need fertilizer when growth starts in the spring, again after the first flush of fruit, and once more after the second flush of fruit.

Remove First Flowers

The first year, don't let any fruit develop on your June-bearing strawberry plants. Picking off the blossoms is time consuming but essential. Growing and ripening even a single berry will weaken a new young plant so much that the following year's production will be drastically reduced. Pick off all the blooms as soon as they form; it will take several pickings.

Everbearing and day-neutral strawberries are an exception to this rule. Pick off their first flower cluster the first year, but from then on allow them to flower and bear naturally. After midsummer, plants should be well enough established to support the late-summer crop.

During the first spring after planting June-bearing strawberries, pick off any flowers that develop, to ensure a good crop the following year.

Renovating Strawberry Rows

1. After harvesting June bearers, use hedge clippers to remove leaves that are more than above 2 inches above the crown. (A mower set high enough to miss the crowns may work.) Make sure not to injure the crowns.
2. With a hoe, cultivate between rows to remove plants that have encroached, or use a tiller to turn them under. Narrow the rows to 10 to 12 inches wide. The goal is to leave five or six plants per square foot of row, with plants about 6 inches apart.
3. Detach and replant rooted runners (daughter plants) to fill in the bare spots, and to replace any 3- to 4-year-old mother plants.
4. Apply an all-purpose fertilizer, following directions on the label; avoid getting it on the leaves. Water it in soon after application.
5. Keep plants well watered for at least 6 weeks after renovating a bed. This will encourage large, healthy plants by the time buds start forming in September.

Rooted runners can be clipped off and planted up to fill in bare spots or to replace old plants whose production has declined.

Control Weeds

Weed control is essential for strawberries. Grass and weeds shade leaves and compete with shallow-rooted berry plants for nutrients and moisture. Weed or cultivate frequently the first year. Use a thick mulch between rows in subsequent years; you can use the same straw you covered plants with for overwintering.

Make sure you buy straw rather than hay, which is full of weedy seeds. If you use a grain straw such as wheat, soak it in water first to germinate any seeds. In subsequent years as the strawberries grow together, their matted growth habit will help keep down many weeds, but you'll still need to pull out some as they sneak through.

Provide Winter and Frost Protection

Even though strawberry plants vary considerably in hardiness, in almost every spot north of the Mason-Dixon line — and in some of the South — you must protect them over the winter in order to get good yields. The fruit buds, rather than the plants themselves, are most vulnerable to freeze damage, which can occur even before the buds begin to show in spring. Cultivars such as 'Cavendish' listed for colder regions are generally hardy in Zones 3 to 7; those such as 'Chandler', for warmer climates, are for Zones 5 to 8. Cultivars listed for warm and cold climates such as 'AC Wendy' should produce well in Zones 3 to 8.

Straw was once cheap, fairly weed-free, and plentiful, so gardeners buried their plants beneath thick layers of it before winter. When they uncovered them in the spring, the leftover straw provided a perfect mulch that conserved moisture and kept the ripening berries free from dirt. Straw (not hay!) is still an excellent winter cover, if it's available locally. You can often find it at farm supply or feed stores, and even in some complete garden stores. One straw bale will cover about 100 square feet of bed or rows.

Shredded leaves, salt hay, and pine needles are all good winter covers too. Or use a heavier weight of row cover — a thick felt fabric through which rain can pass and plants can breathe. Because we have plenty of evergreen boughs, we use them as coverings.

Cover strawberry plants in the fall about the time hard frosts start to freeze the ground (late November to mid-December in most areas). Covering strawberries earlier, before plants are fully dormant, leads to reduced yields.

Uncover in spring when the ground has thawed a few inches deep and no temperatures below 20°F are forecast in the foreseeable future. (The time will vary from year to year; start checking in early March.) Strawberry yields are increased by access to light and increasing day length in very late winter and early spring. Yields are reduced more by leaving the mulch on too long and having plants start to grow under it than by taking the mulch off too early. If there are tender white shoots showing, the mulch has been taken off way too late and yields will be drastically reduced because the plants will have used up much of their stored reserves to produce this growth.

Strawberry blossoms are sensitive to spring frosts, which turn the centers black and ruin a fruit crop. Some years you'll probably need to cover plants when late-spring frosts occur at blooming time. Use row covers, old blankets, sheets, or simply the straw you removed from plants from winter and placed in the paths. With row covers, make sure to get the heaviest weight possible, which may provide 5 degrees of temperature protection (twice the protection of lightweight row covers). Two layers will provide slightly more protection. If you're sure a frost is coming, cover the plants in late afternoon while the soil is still warm. Some gardeners turn lawn sprinklers on their beds, similar to methods commercial growers use for frost protection.

Whatever method you use, listen to weather forecasts at blooming time and watch the thermometer closely, especially on clear nights. The temperature can be a balmy 60°F at dusk and plunge to well below 30°F by 2 a.m. Keep in mind that the temperature near the ground may be a few degrees colder than at your thermometer mounted by a window. No one wants to work all year and then lose the crop in one night. For extra insurance invest in a frost alarm, available now on many wireless home-temperature monitors.

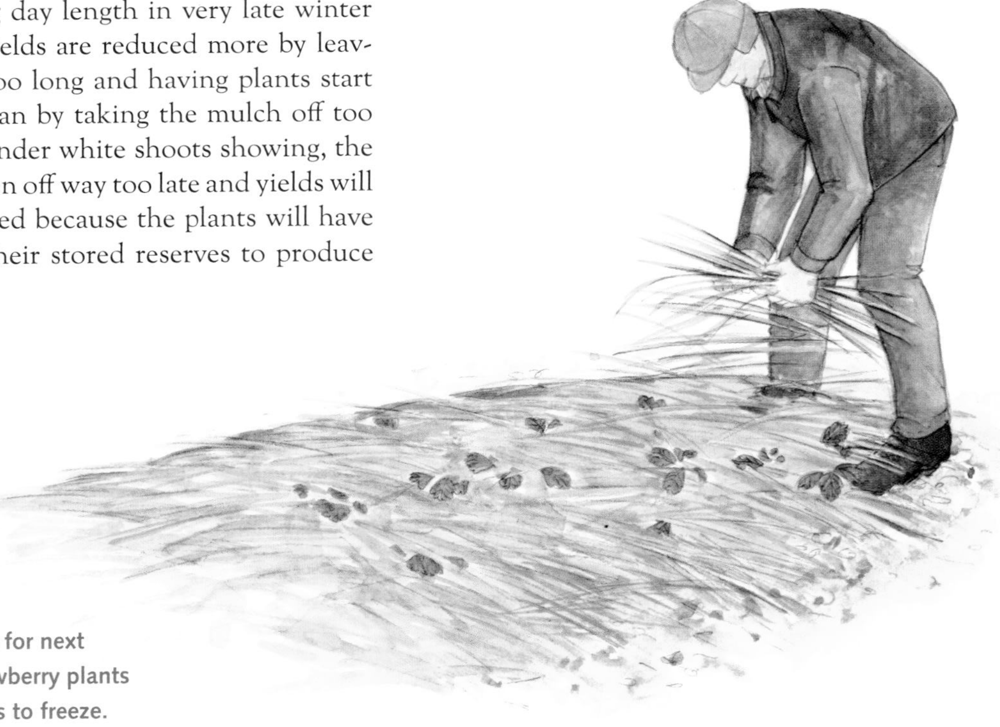

To protect flower buds for next year's crop, cover strawberry plants when the ground starts to freeze.

Strawberries off the Ground

One of the classic methods of growing strawberries is in a strawberry pot, a taller-than-wide clay or plastic container with planting holes in the sides. When you set one or a few plants in the top, their runners root into the side pockets of soil. A variation is the pyramid, a short stack of ever-smaller raised beds. A newer option is a tall, thin bag filled with soil that you hang. You can incorporate strawberries into hanging baskets, or in a "green wall," which is a structure similar to a tray with mesh to hold the soil you plant and then set upright. For hanging, day-neutral or everbearing cultivars are best; remove any runners as they form.

Such containers allow you to grow strawberries on the patio or in a small yard if you don't have room (or time) for a strawberry bed. Fill containers with a soilless medium, and add a slow-release fertilizer. You can also add a water-absorbing gel to help retain water. In cold climates, containers need to be protected from freezing, as in an unheated garage, over winter.

Birds, Insects, and Diseases

If you find the birds are up earlier than you are and beating you to the ripe berries, place bird netting over rows. Many garden stores and online catalogs sell this. Drape it over wire hoops or some sort of frame to keep birds from reaching through to get at the berries. Anchor it with tent stakes, or 6- to 8-inch wooden stakes in the ground angled outward. There are other bird repellents such as noisemakers and eye balloons, with varying effectiveness.

Diseases. If you buy virus-free plants and don't plant them where you recently raised susceptible crops (tomatoes, eggplants, potatoes, melons, raspberries, blackberries, or other strawberries), you'll have some insurance against verticillium wilt, red stele, and other diseases carried in the soil. A good way to minimize leaf diseases is to use soaker hoses or drip irrigation near plants underneath mulch to keep water from getting on the leaves. Keeping strawberry flowers from getting wet during bloom, and then keeping the strawberries picked, will help keep gray mold disease (botrytis) from growing on fruit. In addition to the common gray mold (page 270) and verticillium wilt (page 272), other diseases to watch for on strawberries are leaf scorch, leaf spot, and red stele.

Leaf scorch begins as reddish purple pinpoints on leaves, or blotchy areas. These may cause leaves to turn brown and curl at the edges — a scorched appearance. Flowers may be damaged, resulting in no fruit, or fruit may have dead stems. Remove and destroy (burn or bag) any dead plant parts. To minimize the need for fungicides, choose resistant cultivars, allow plenty of air circulation, and don't over-fertilize, in addition to destroying afflicted plant parts.

Leaf spot is a widespread disease that causes reddish to purple spots of varying shapes and sizes on leaves and fruit. If severe, leaves may fall off. Controls are the same as for leaf scorch (see above).

Red stele is a root rot found particularly on cool, wet soils. It is most active in early spring and late fall and causes roots to rot from the tips and turn reddish on the insides. As this disease is most commonly introduced on new plants, make sure you buy disease-free stock, and plant on good soils. If soils are poorly drained, incorporate plenty of organic matter prior to planting to form raised beds, and make sure you don't overwater.

Insects. As for insects, you're likely to encounter at least a few, among them Japanese beetles, aphids, thrips, mites, sap beetles, leafhoppers, and leaf rollers. (See chapter 18 for controlling these pests.) Fortunately, very few of these pests are likely to become a problem in a backyard garden; they're more likely to target large plantings grown on the same land for years.

Some strawberry growers plant a marigold between every plant to help repel soil nematodes. Although it's unclear whether this really works, marigolds attract beneficial insects such as lacewings, lady beetles, and parasitic wasps. (For more information on preventing nematodes, turn to page 274.)

In addition to the general pests mentioned above, others are also fond of strawberry plants. Tolerate small populations, and remember that even organic sprays are toxic to bees and other pollinators. Make sure any product you use is listed as safe for strawberries, and follow label directions carefully.

White grubs are root-eating pests that can devastate a new planting in short order. They develop into those big May beetles that hang on the windows and buzz around lights during early summer nights. Because they live mostly in sod, the best prevention is to plant your berries on ground that was cultivated the previous year.

Tarnished plant bugs are brown insects about 1/4 inch long, with black and yellow markings (see page 281). Watch for these pesky pests as plants begin to bloom, as that's when they search out one of their favorite foods — strawberry blossoms. Feeding by tarnished plant bugs causes fruit to be misshapen; sometimes hard green "buttons" develop instead of fruit. Though you can tolerate a few of these insects, for severe infestations consider spraying

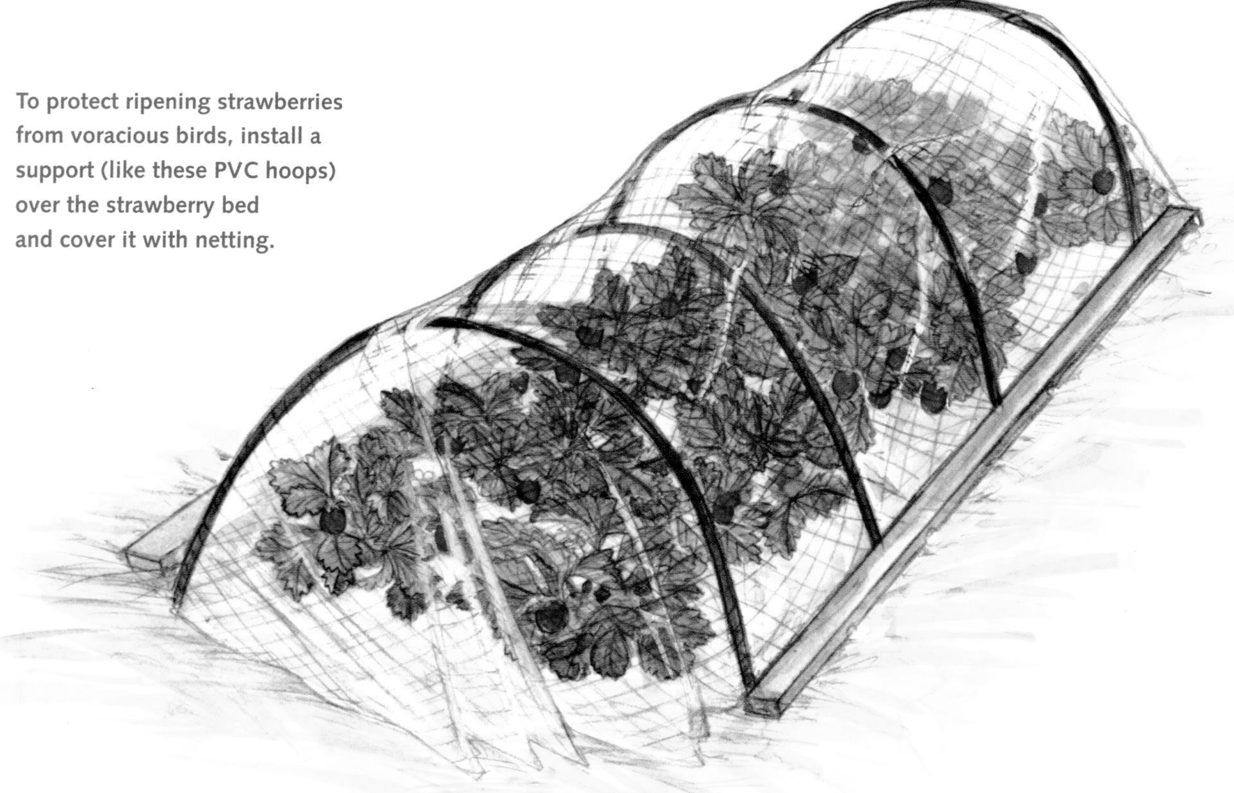

To protect ripening strawberries from voracious birds, install a support (like these PVC hoops) over the strawberry bed and cover it with netting.

To avoid diseases like strawberry leaf spot, purchase resistant cultivars and grow plants where other susceptible crops have not been planted recently.

Damage like this is a sure sign that slugs are present. To trap them, try placing a deep saucer of beer in the bed; slugs will be drawn to the yeast in the beer and will drown.

just as bud clusters start to develop. (Don't spray after the blooms open or you'll kill pollinating bees.) Tarnished plant bugs tend to be more of a problem on later-blooming varieties. If you don't want to spray, plant only early-blooming varieties, keep the bed free of weeds, and be prepared to do more frost protection.

Weevils are one of the most serious problems, especially strawberry bud weevils. They lay their eggs in a bud cluster, partly severing it from the plant. Insecticides can control them, but you must be careful to use one that you can wash off later and stop spraying once blooms open to protect pollinators. Pyrethrum and rotenone, both organic insecticides, wash off the fruit easily.

Spittlebugs are appropriately named, surrounding themselves with a foamy white "spittle." These insects are common on strawberries early in the season and feed on young plants. Although they weaken plants, they seldom cause serious damage unless they're present in abundance. They're more a concern to gardeners than to the plants, and both you and the plants should be able to tolerate them.

Slugs and snails are slimy pests easily recognized by most people. They especially like to eat ripe or nearly ripe strawberries. They're not a problem in all years in all places, but watch for them in damp seasons and climates. Not much is worse than picking a ripe strawberry, only to find a slug on it, particularly as you're about to eat the fruit! Keeping fruit off the ground on straw makes it less accessible to slugs and snails. You can also place rolls of newspaper or boards in the garden for slugs to crawl in or under by day, thus concentrating them for easy removal. One of the most popular controls is a saucer of beer. Copper strips are sold as slug guards, as slugs and snails won't crawl across copper. You can use diatomaceous earth as a barrier, but you need to replace it after a heavy rain. Coffee grounds are also a deterrent. A weak ammonia spray kills slugs on contact, as will a sprinkle of table salt.

Place rolls of newspaper or boards in the garden for slugs to crawl in or under by day, thus concentrating them for easy removal.

Harvesting Strawberries

FOR THE BEST FLAVOR and highest vitamin content, pick strawberries on the day they ripen, which usually means daily picking during the peak of the season if it's warm. This is June in many areas, but can be as early as April in warmer climates. Check plants at least every couple of days during the harvest season. Overripe fruit spoils quickly and can lead to disease and insect problems, so pick all ripe and overripe fruit often. In the early morning, while the air is still cool and just after the dew has evaporated, is the best time to pick. Put the berries in a cool place immediately after picking them so they'll stay fresh a bit longer. The crisper drawer of a refrigerator works best, but even there it's hard to keep strawberries more than a few days. Don't wash them until just before using; wet berries spoil very quickly.

Yields vary with cultivar, season, and age of the planting. Figure on 1 to 2 pounds of strawberries per plant, perhaps a quart. (A quart of mounded strawberries usually weighs about 1½ pounds.) A 50-foot row yields at least 20 quarts.

Raw berries, either whole or mashed with sugar, freeze very well. Remove the stems (caps) and wash in a strainer under running water. You may prefer to slice large berries, or freeze them crushed. Freezing with sugar, even just a little sprinkled on berries, helps retain texture and prevent bitterness upon thawing. For a quart of berries, mix with up to ¾ cup of sugar; if you use an artificial sweetener, follow recommendations for the equivalent amount. To freeze in syrup, dissolve 4 cups of sugar in 4 cups of lukewarm water. Chill this syrup, then pour over berries before freezing. When using frozen whole berries, serve before fully thawed so they won't be merely a mush.

If you don't have a lot of freezer space, there are other means of preserving. Drying and making fruit leathers are two options. A great many of our berries are turned into jam.

A sprinkling of sugar will help draw out the juices in strawberries.

Strawberries All Season

Popular June-bearing strawberries

EARLY: 'Earliglow', 'Surecrop'
MIDSEASON: 'Allstar', 'Honeoye'
LATE-SEASON: 'Lateglow', 'Sparkle'

Popular day-neutral (everbearing) strawberries

'Albion', 'Quinault', 'Tribute', 'Tristar'

Strawberry Cultivars

NEW AND IMPROVED strawberry cultivars are introduced every year (as many as some vegetables). So many cultivars make it hard to choose. Contact your local Cooperative Extension Service or regional websites (see Resources, page 307) for the latest and best varieties for where you live. You can usually rely on local full-service garden centers to sell some cultivars appropriate for your area. It is most important to buy those that are right for your climate and resistant to local diseases.

If you want a few berries at a time over a long season, grow day-neutral cultivars. If you prefer to harvest more strawberries at one time, perhaps preserving or freezing what you don't eat, focus on the June bearers. For preserves and jams, look for cultivars with firmer fruit. Most June-bearing cultivars are suited to both eating fresh and freezing; most everbearing are best for eating fresh.

By planting early, midseason, and late cultivars of June bearers with some everbearers you can enjoy fresh strawberries for much of the summer. Don't have that much room? Plant one bundle (usually 10 or 25 plants) of a June-bearing cultivar and one of a day-neutral. Remember to pick off just the first flower clusters that appear on your day-neutral plants, as you want them to produce a bigger late crop after the June bearers have finished. (On the June-bearing plants, you need to pick off all the flowers for the first year.)

Alpine Strawberries

If you want strawberries but don't want to spend so much time renovating beds or removing runners, consider growing alpines. Also known by their French name *fraises de bois,* they are a different species (*Fragaria vesca*) from the common strawberry. The berries are small, like wild strawberries, with wonderful flavor, and plants may last for several years without needing renovating or replanting. Alpine strawberries grow in most parts of Zones 3 to 10. They're attractive massed as a groundcover, for edging flowerbeds, in edible landscapes, and even in hanging baskets.

Unlike the more familiar strawberry, these stay in clumps and don't spread with runners. They grow best with at least 6 hours of sun. The white, fragrant flowers bloom throughout the season, producing berries right along. Because they're soft when ripe and rather perishable, they don't store well, so eat them soon after picking.

Ordinary strawberry cultivars don't come true from seed and so must be started from cuttings or divisions. Alpine strawberries, however, have been grown from seed for many years; seeds and plants are readily available online and from catalogs. (If you start them from seeds, be warned that they germinate slowly — often taking 3 to 6 weeks — so be patient.)

'Alexandria', 'Mignonette', and 'Sweetheart' are good cultivars. 'Yellow Alpine' and 'Yellow Wonder' produce white-to-yellow fruits; these are less attractive to birds, so you may get more of the berries for yourself!

Alpine strawberries are much smaller than most cultivated varieties, but many people think their flavor is also more concentrated.

Blackberries taste best when they're picked dead ripe,
but won't store for more than a day or two.

CHAPTER 5

Raspberries and Blackberries

If we had room for only one kind of fruit, we would choose the red raspberry. Nearly everybody we know loves them, and they're one of the easiest fruits to grow. The plants usually produce a big crop by the third year after planting, and big annual crops after that are almost guaranteed. We expect each foot of row to produce at least a pint of berries during the season, and they seldom fail to live up to our expectations. A 10-foot row, with five initial plants, provides several people enough berries to eat fresh, and enough left over to freeze or turn into jam.

Raspberries have lots of other good qualities to recommend them as a home fruit. They blossom late, so spring frosts never ruin the crop. The diseases that trouble them are easy to control if you buy virus-free plants and opt for resistant cultivars. They need little care. And maybe best of all, they're easy to pick without much bending. In my opinion, the raspberry is a near-perfect fruit.

The other brambles are just as easy to grow. Blackberries can be distinguished from black raspberries because they retain their central core when you pick them. Black and red raspberries leave the core behind, resulting in a hollow center, or a fruit shaped like a thimble. The main trick to growing any of the brambles is faithfully removing the canes once they've finished bearing. Neglected brambles quickly become an impenetrable thicket of dead branches.

Getting to Know the Brambles

RASPBERRIES, BLACKBERRIES, and other brambles are all members of the large rose family. The ancient Greeks and Romans mentioned raspberries, which were first cultivated in North America in the mid-1700s. Black raspberries and blackberries are both native to North America. Though they have been cultivated here only since the mid-1800s, Europeans imported wild blackberries and began cultivating them in the 1600s. The purple raspberry — a hybrid of the red and the black — came about shortly after black raspberries entered cultivation.

Red raspberries (*Rubus idaeus*) are by far the most familiar. The reds come in both one-crop (summer-bearing) and two-crop (fall-bearing) varieties. The one-crop type bears fruit that matures in midsummer on canes that have grown the previous season. After bearing, the canes die. Two-crop raspberries are often called everbearers, which they really aren't. Instead, they bear once during the summer on canes grown the previous year and produce an additional crop in the fall on canes grown the current year.

Many red raspberry cultivars are hardy far into Canada. Others have been developed for Zones 5 through 8. Most fall-bearing red raspberries are winter-hardy, but in Zones 3 and 4 many fail to ripen their second crop before the early frosts.

Yellow raspberries, which are closely related to the reds and blacks, vary in color from yellow to pale pink. These are so fragile that they're seldom seen in stores. They're ideal for home gardens, however, and many fruit lovers regard the ripe golden or yellow raspberry as the finest tasting fruit in the world. A handful tossed together with a few red and black raspberries makes an elegant dessert. Most are fall bearing, with hardiness similar to the reds. The downside is that they're more susceptible to viruses. Be careful to buy only certified virus-free plants; you want to avoid unknowingly introducing viruses to your other raspberries.

Black raspberries (*Rubus occidentalis*), or "black caps," as wild ones are called in some areas, have an unusual flavor that many people like very much, a slightly musky aroma and taste. Unlike red raspberries, they produce few suckers. Instead, they start new plants when their long canes bend over and the tips touch the soil and root. Their fruits tend to have more seeds than the reds, and the plants are less hardy.

Red raspberries (left) are familiar to most fruit lovers. The less-common golden raspberry 'Fall Gold' (right) offers a welcome autumn harvest after the main raspberry season is over.

Bramble Fast Facts

USDA Hardiness Zones: Depends on cultivar; raspberries Zones 3–8; blackberries Zones 5–9

Height: 4–6 feet (pruned)

Spacing: Upright cultivars 2 feet apart within rows, trailing cultivars 4–6 feet apart within rows; space rows at least 6 feet apart (10 feet apart for blackberries)

Pollination: Raspberries are self-fruitful; some blackberries need cross-pollination

Pruning: Remove spent canes in the second and subsequent years (after fruiting), weak canes, and any canes closer than 6 inches apart

Special requirement: Annual pruning

Years to bearing: 2

Yield per plant: 1–4 quarts

Purple raspberries are closely related to the blacks, and have a similar flavor. Of all the raspberries, the purples are usually most tolerant of drought. They're among the most vigorous, and the most resistant generally to pests and diseases, but they're usually less hardy than the reds. Some cultivars such as Sodus have a less-suckering growth habit. Other purple raspberries, such as 'Brandywine' and 'Royalty', behave more like the reds and send up suckers in the same way.

Blackberries come in two types, upright and trailing, and both are available as thornless cultivars and with thorns. There are a few different species. The original wild types were the thorny upright blackberries, which have the best flavor, but their

Black raspberries (left), also known as "black caps," have an unusual, slightly musky taste. Purple raspberries (right) are related to them, and are generally thought to be the most drought tolerant of all the raspberries.

Lesser-Known Brambles

Raspberries and blackberries have some less common relatives. All are basically cultivars of blackberry, and the differences in color and flavor are not great, without getting into highly subjective taste descriptions. As mentioned above, dewberry is the name applied to a group of several trailing (often sweeter) blackberry species that generally grow as evergreen shrubs in Zones 5 to 9. The southern species is often found growing along roadsides and railway tracks. 'Austin' and 'Lucretia' are widely available improved selections.

Several hybrids of red and black raspberries are grown mainly in the Pacific Northwest and California, as they aren't very hardy. They have trailing habits, and their berries cling to the central core (receptacle), similar to the habit of blackberries. The youngberry is trailing, with purplish black fruit that ripens earlier than blackberries. The loganberry, hybridized in the early 1880s, is a parent of several modern hybrids. Crossing the loganberry with a raspberry led to the tayberry (named after the Tay River in Scotland), with red fruits that are larger and sweeter than those of the loganberry. Tummelberries produce deep red, conical fruits that retain their core when picked. Similar to the tayberry is the thorny wyeberry, which looks and tastes like a red raspberry with some boysenberry flavor, with higher yields than many raspberries. Dark boysenberries, popular in syrups and jams, came from a three-way cross among the loganberry, a raspberry, and a blackberry.

The tayberry is a cross between the loganberry and the raspberry, and is named after the Tay River in Scotland.

Marionberry is actually just the 'Marion' cultivar of the thorny blackberry, a hybrid of two other blackberries. Similarly, olallieberry is the cultivar 'Olallie'. Three uncommon but related species are the wineberry (*R. phoenicolasius*), the thimbleberry (*R. parviflorus*), and the salmonberry (*R. spectabilis*).

vicious thorns make harvesting a challenge, so they aren't grown much.

The trailing types are sometimes called dewberries, but these are considered to be a separate group of trailing species of blackberries. The trailing types grow canes from a central crown; the upright ones form canes from both a crown and roots, similar to how raspberries grow.

Most blackberry cultivars have hardy roots. Their canes are not as hardy as those of raspberries, however, and in cold climates are apt to die to the ground over the winter. Most upright ones are hardy in Zones 6 to 8, some growing to Zone 9, and some are hardy just to Zone 5 ('Darrow' may grow into Zone 4). Less hardy are the thornless upright cultivars. The least cold hardy are the thornless trailing blackberries, developed in the 1960s by the U.S. Department of Agriculture. The berries are tart but the plants are vigorous where they can be grown. Most are suitable only in Zone 7 and warmer climates, although some will grow into Zone 5. For this reason they are grown mainly in southern states and the Pacific Northwest. Least common are the thorny trailing types, both with less cold hardiness and a need for more chilling than many southern gardens can provide. For this reason, you'll see these mainly in the Pacific Northwest, where they may be called western trailing blackberries.

Plant and Site Selection

START WITH certified disease-free plants, as brambles are susceptible to several viruses that impair yield and are difficult to eradicate. Avoid the temptation to accept new plants from friends (you get their problems along with their plants), or to dig wild raspberries. Wild raspberries may taste good, but named cultivars have been bred for traits such as larger fruit, easier picking, no thorns, and higher yields.

Caring for Bare-Root Plants

Mail-order plants are usually shipped bare-root, and there's a good possibility they'll be dry when they arrive. Unwrap them as soon as possible and soak their roots for several hours in a tub of water, out of the sun, before planting. If you can't plant right away, "heel them in," out of direct sun, by covering the roots with moist sawdust, moist burlap, or wet newspapers. Or lay the roots in a shallow trench, tops angled out, cover the roots with soil, and water well.

Don't let the sensitive roots dry out while planting. Keep blackberry roots in the dark (under cover), or better yet plant on a cloudy day. The roots are sensitive to light and don't grow well if they were exposed to the sun.

Heel in bare-root canes that can't be planted right away.

Separate black and purple raspberries from red and yellow raspberries by at least 100 feet, because they often have a virus that can spread to the red and yellow cultivars, even when the host plants appear healthy. Upright blackberries need isolation from any other plantings, because their long roots send up suckers many feet from the parent plants.

Because red raspberries and blackberries sucker so prolifically, locate the planting where you can control the "volunteers" that spring from the vigorous roots. Mowing is the easiest way, so plant in narrow rows with grass on either side (and between rows).

If you purchase your plants from a local nursery or garden center, they'll be either bare-root or growing in pots. The potted ones, although more expensive, will get off to a faster start because of their established root system. These are worth the extra money, unless you're planting a large number of them. To plant other than in spring, these will be your only choice. Make sure if setting out mature plants in summer that they don't dry out.

Planting and Care

PREPARE THE GROUND THOROUGHLY, as described in chapter 15. Incorporate organic matter and a balanced, complete fertilizer, following application rates on the label. Brambles prefer a slightly acidic soil (pH 5.5 to 6.5).

Follow the spacing recommendations in the Fast Facts box on page 65 but note that trailing cultivars need more room. Set each plant to the same depth as it grew originally in the ground or pot. A common mistake is to plant too deeply — make sure the green or white buds near the base can see the light of day. Soak the soil heavily with water to which you have added a weak (no more than quarter strength) solution of liquid fertilizer.

Continue to water the newly set plants thoroughly every 2 or 3 days for 3 weeks (unless it rains heavily). Water is cheap insurance for a good fruit crop. Soaker hoses placed along rows, underneath mulch, are an efficient and easy means to get water to the roots. Because this method bypasses leaves, stems, and berries, it helps to prevent diseases. If

When planting brambles, upright cultivars should be spaced 2 feet apart in rows. Don't plant them too deeply; make sure the green or white buds near the base are above the soil line.

you don't use soaker hoses, direct watering to the base of plants. About a month after planting, feed with a balanced fertilizer, following label directions.

When you purchase well-rooted potted plants, no pruning is necessary at planting time. If when you remove the plant from its container the soil falls off, it's obvious that it was only recently potted; treat as you would a bare-root plant. With bare-root plants, set them in, then cut back the canes to 4 to 6 inches above the ground (unless they were pruned back by the nursery). If you don't cut them back, the tops will start to grow and there will not be enough corresponding root growth to support them. The result is weak plants that are likely to give up entirely or take years to recover. Plants that have been cut back will not produce any berries the first year, but the idea is to develop a lot of canes that will produce heavily in the future.

In subsequent years, once plants are established, they grow best with annual feeding and a steady supply of water. Sprinkle fertilizer at recommended rates along rows in the spring, keeping away from the base of plants. If your soil is especially fertile, you may only need to add nitrogen. Fish emulsion is an easy way to supply nitrogen to established plants; follow label directions. Reapply at half-strength in midsummer for fall-bearers.

Ample amounts of water improve the quality of the berries. Aim for 1 to 2 inches of water per week for best yields. More may be needed on sandy soils or when fruits are forming.

Mulch for Weed Control

Grass and weeds are some of the worst enemies of brambles, especially during the first year while they're getting established. They compete with the plants for nutrients, limit their growth, reduce production, and give the berry patch a messy, unkempt appearance. Rototilling or hoeing can easily damage bramble roots, so heavy mulching is a better way to control grass and nourish your plants at the same time. The exception is on heavy or clay soils, where continued heavy mulching in subsequent years provides good conditions for root-rot diseases. If you have heavy or clay soils, plant in raised beds that are 6 to 8 inches higher than the surrounding ground and build up the beds with lots of organic matter such as compost.

A thick layer of shredded bark, shredded leaves, wood shavings, or straw is an excellent mulch for brambles. Sawdust packs too tightly unless composted first, and it steals nitrogen from the soil, but you can compensate with a second application of fertilizer. Several inches of mulch (4 to 6 inches of straw) will provide enough shade to suffocate sprouting weed and grass seeds, yet the new berry canes will push through it easily.

Some gardeners lay black plastic, cardboard, newspapers, or weed-control fabric between the rows and cover it with wood chips. This prevents the growth of sucker plants and weeds.

Provide Support

For better yields and easier picking, provide some means of support to keep raspberries and upright-growing blackberries from falling over. Some berry growers tie the canes to stakes or posts placed every 3 feet along the row. Others put up a fence consisting of strands of smooth wire on each side of the row. Two-crop cultivars won't need staking if you grow for only one fall crop: Mow or cut canes to the ground each fall or spring to produce short new canes and a single late crop of berries.

Shorter varieties will do fine without support. The sturdy 'Boyne' raspberry is less likely to need staking than taller-growing cultivars such as 'Royalty' and 'Latham'.

Trailing types of blackberries must be tied to a wire fence or some other support during the fruiting season. String a single wire between two posts. Use fabric strips, thick cord, or wide plastic ties to tie canes to the wire. (Don't use string, as it will cut into the canes.)

Black raspberry cultivars that grow from a central crown (rather than from suckering canes) are often grown tied to a central stake.

Taller cultivars are easier to pick and care for when supported by a trellis.

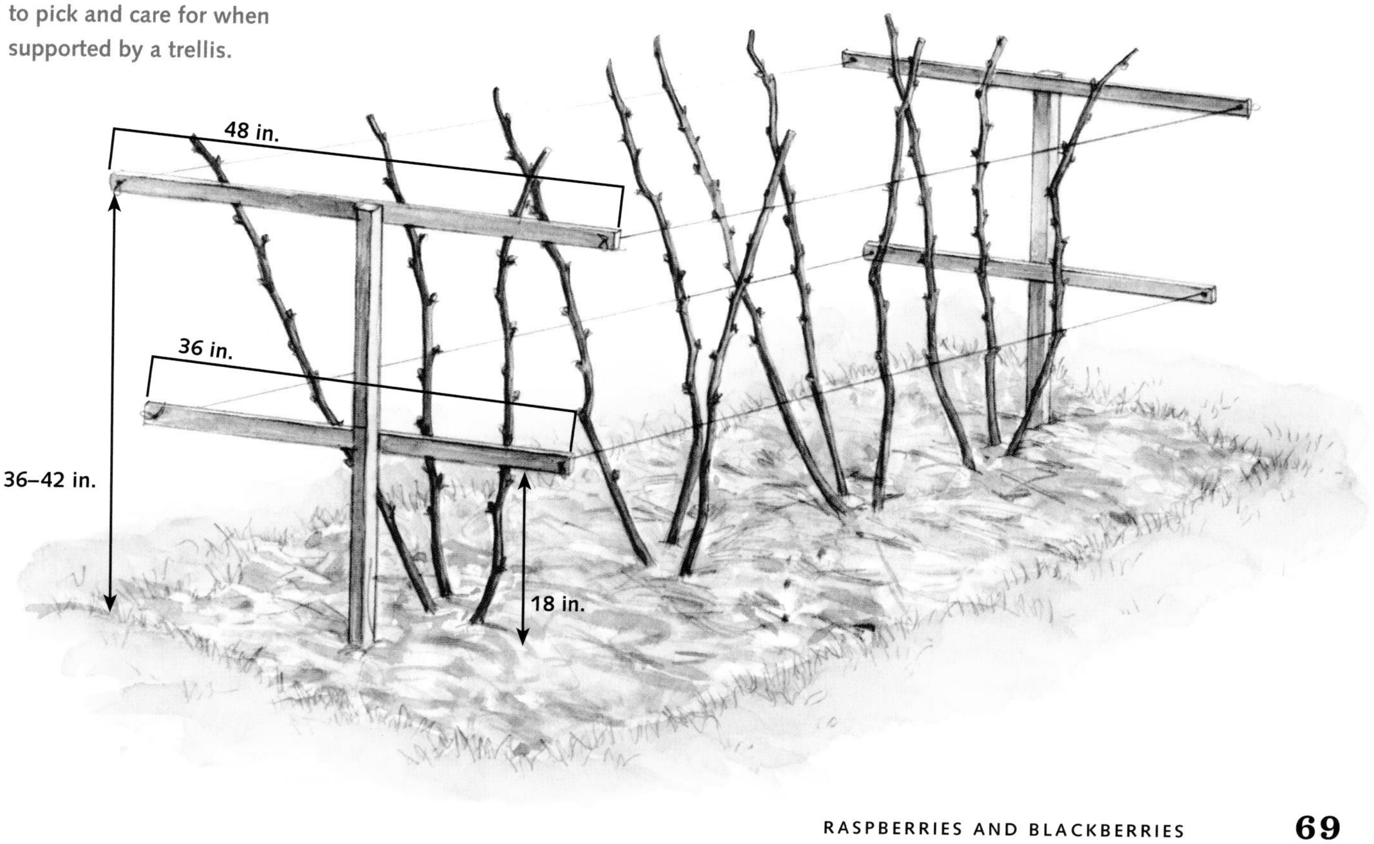

48 in.

36 in.

36–42 in.

18 in.

Essential Pruning

If you neglect to cut out the old canes in your bramble patch each year, the planting will deteriorate rapidly. Both raspberries and blackberries have roots that are perennial, but their canes are biennial. In other words, the roots live for many years, but each cane sprouts and grows to its full height in one year (then called a primocane), bears fruit the following year (then called a floricane), then dies immediately. The fall-bearing, or two-crop, raspberry cultivars bear most their fruit in fall on primocanes. Neglected raspberries and blackberries become a jungle of dead canes after a few years, and both fruit size and quantity will suffer.

To keep your patch productive, cut each dead cane to ground level in the fall after it has finished bearing. You'll recognize the dead ones by their pallid color and brittle appearance. Hand-held clippers are ideal for this job, and you'll probably want to wear thick gloves to handle the thorny canes. Rose gloves work well as they're thicker so thorns can't penetrate, and they have long gauntlets to protect your lower arms when reaching among the thorny canes. Because insects and diseases winter over in the old canes, don't put them in the compost pile. Instead, remove them to the local landfill or burn them as soon as possible.

With purple and black raspberries and upright blackberries, you'll also need to prune back or "tip" new first-year canes in summer. This will promote shorter and stronger canes and more lateral branches, which will produce fruit the second year. When canes reach 3 to 4 feet high, remove the top 3 to 6 inches. If you're supporting them on a trellis or a stake, you can wait until they reach about 5 feet to tip back. In early spring (when you're pruning to remove dead, broken, or excess branches), also tip back the side branches to about 6 inches long on purple and black raspberries, 12 inches for upright blackberries.

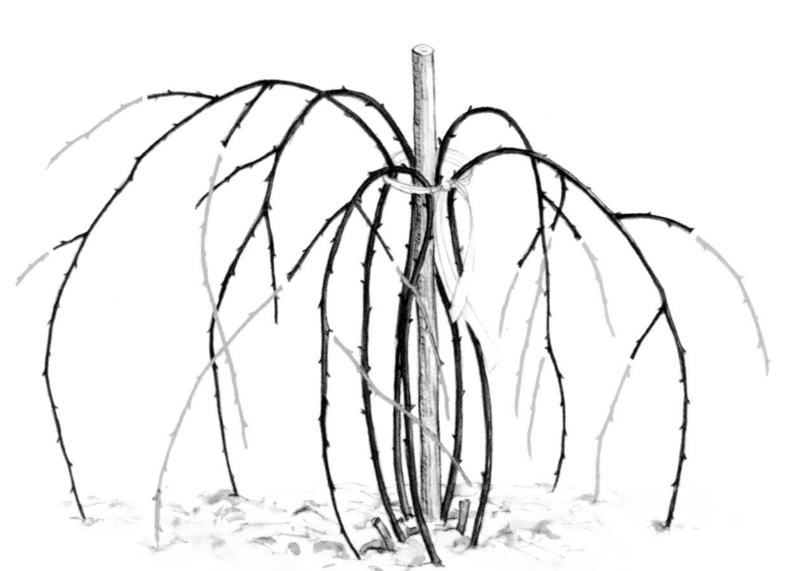

Purple and black raspberries — as well as upright blackberries — produce long side shoots. Prune them back to about 6 inches (slightly longer for blackberries) in early spring.

Cut dead canes to the ground after the plant has finished fruiting.

TIPS FOR GROWING RED RASPBERRIES AND OTHER BRAMBLES

- Choose a site with well-drained soil and abundant sun. Don't plant red and yellow raspberries within 100 feet of wild berries or black and purple raspberries.
- Buy cultivars that grow well in your region.
- Prepare weed-free soil and plant in early spring. Space raspberry and blackberry plants 2 feet apart within rows (trailing cultivars 4 to 6 feet apart within rows); space rows at least 6 feet apart (10 feet apart for blackberries). For bare-root plants only, cut back to 4 to 6 inches above the ground.
- Water well after planting; for the first year, provide at least an inch of water weekly if not supplied by rain.
- Install stakes for individual plants, or stakes with parallel wires for rows, to support berry-laden branches.
- Mulch with a thick layer of wood shavings or shredded bark to control weeds; supplement annually. (Mulch heavily only the first year where root-rot diseases are a problem.)
- Keep rows to 2 feet wide by mowing or cutting off sprouts that pop up outside the rows.
- Each spring, feed with a balanced fertilizer; follow rates on label.
- Keep an eye out for any wilted tips and diseased leaves or branches; prune out immediately and destroy.
- In the fall in second and subsequent years, cut spent fruiting canes down to the ground. In spring, remove weak (small-diameter) canes, winter-damaged wood, and vigorous canes closer than 6 inches apart.
- If you want to grow one fall crop from two-crop cultivars, cut all canes to the ground each spring. (Don't do this for one-crop cultivars.)
- For the best berry crops, keep plants well-watered during the growing season — especially during the 3 to 4 weeks prior to harvest when fruits are forming.

Trailing blackberries are pruned in a slightly different way. Unlike the upright ones, which produce canes from both the crown and the roots, the trailing types produce canes only from the crown. The first year, just leave primocanes on the ground, trailing along the row. This way they can be protected over winter with straw. Don't tip these back. Then the second season, in spring pull the canes (now floricanes) up onto a trellis. Remove the lower 2 to 3 feet of lateral shoots, then tip back the remaining laterals to stubs 2 to 4 inches long. These are what will produce the fruit. Prune off the floricanes after fruiting in fall, or the following spring prior to training up the previous season's canes.

As your berry patch ages, more pruning will be necessary because the suckering plants produce too many new canes each year. Cut off all the weak new canes and thin out any remaining canes that are closer together than 6 inches (12 inches for blackberries). Otherwise, the berries will be small and there will be fewer of them. Do this either when you remove the spent canes in fall, or in early spring before growth resumes. With proper pruning your plants will be less prone to disease, and may last 10 years or more.

Keep the rows of red and yellow raspberries and upright blackberries no more than 2 feet in width, and those of black and purple raspberries and trailing blackberries no more than 1½ feet wide. This makes harvesting and pruning easier and also allows better air circulation, which reduces the chances of diseases.

Trailing blackberries need more intensive pruning than other brambles. The first year (left), leave trailing canes in rows on the ground. The second year (right), remove all side shoots on the lowest 2 to 3 feet of each cane; prune remaining (upper) side shoots back to only 2 to 4 inches.

How to Prune Brambles

Brambles need pruning every year. Neglected raspberries and blackberries become a jungle of dead canes after a few years, and both fruit size and quantity will suffer.

- For bare-root plants, cut back to 4–6 inches after planting.
- For everbearing (two-crop) cultivars, cut back all canes in spring if you want only one fall crop and don't want to stake.
- In summer, cut 6 inches from tips of canes on purple and black raspberries and on upright blackberries, when they reach 3–4 feet; the following spring, cut back side branches to 6 inches.
- Cut back spent fruiting canes of one-crop cultivars in fall.
- In the third and subsequent years, remove weak and diseased canes, and thin remaining canes to 6 inches apart (12 inches for blackberries). Mow or trim shoots that pop up outside a roughly 2-foot-wide bed.

Diseases

Starting with disease-free plants is important to maintain healthy brambles. Choosing a site with good air circulation and thinning canes to 6 inches apart will prevent many diseases.

Before assuming something is a disease, check the physiological problems on page 266. If for some reason your raspberries crumble when picked, this could be from poor pollination of flowers (as from cool, rainy weather or insufficient bee activity — even though plants are self-fruitful they need some help from bees), cool summers, or a virus. If you have this problem over 2 or 3 years, it is probably a virus. On brambles, marbled green or greenish yellow mottled leaves on new canes is another symptom of a virus disease.

Brambles are susceptible to some of the same diseases as other fruits, particularly gray mold, root (crown) gall, and viruses (see chapter 18). Verticillium wilt (page 272) is one of the most troublesome diseases in some areas; it is usually more serious with black and purple than red raspberries and blackberries. In addition, be on the lookout for the following:

Anthracnose is a blight that shows up on the cane bark as gray blotches with purple edges, and as scabs on the fruit. Black raspberries are most susceptible. If you encounter this disease, be rigorous about thinning plants and sterilize pruning tools between cuts (see Disinfecting Pruning Tools, page 273). A fungicide should control severe cases; follow label directions. Look for resistant cultivars of red raspberries such as 'Chilcotin' and 'Heritage'.

Cane blight is a fungus and causes darkened areas at the base of canes, eventually girdling and killing them. Prune out infected canes during dry weather, then destroy them.

Double blossom rosette causes compressed and abnormal blooms which then don't bear fruit. Watch for this disease if you garden in southern areas where this disease mainly occurs. If you see any signs, cut out and destroy all flowering canes. The cultivar 'Humble' is resistant.

Rusts are fungal diseases that often appear as rusty colored or tan spots. Several rusts, mainly orange rust, affect most brambles except for red and purple raspberries. In spring, leaves may pale, deformed, and stunted. In summer, look for bright orange spores on the undersides of leaves and on the canes. Cut off and destroy any infested leaves or branches, or remove the entire plant, as rusts are not easy to treat (especially the one that attacks black raspberries). Many wild blackberries have the disease, so remove any wild brambles within 500 feet. (Some recommend 1,000 feet.)

Spur blight can be a problem during a rainy spring. When the berry patch sends out beautiful leaves that then suddenly turn yellow and the canes die, the cause is likely spur blight. Look for small dark spots on the lower parts of canes around the leaf nodes of red raspberries, and leaves with brown V-shaped areas with yellow borders. Because the disease affects only the old canes, new ones will replace them over the summer, but your crop for that year will be lost. If this is a recurring problem, spray with a copper- or sulfur-based fungicide in the spring just as the leaves appear, and later according to label recommendations. A few cultivars may have some resistance, such as 'Brandywine' (purple) and 'Latham' (red, one-crop).

Insects

Although many types of insects bother brambles, surprisingly few ever become serious in a home planting. Keeping beds free of weeds helps. If insect populations do build up, remove the mulch and burn it; this may control the problem.

The cane borer is one of the most common pests, and rare is the bramble grower who doesn't encounter it sooner or later. If the top of a new canes suddenly wilts and falls over, this critter may be at work. Inspection will reveal two circles near the top of the cane. If you open the cane at this point, you may find a larva sitting there as though it had every intention of making this plant its summer home. If you leave it there undisturbed, it will bore down the cane, kill it, and continue on to infect other canes, with increasing damage to your patch in future years. Happily, it is easy to control the borer without sprays. As soon as a wilted end appears, simply cut it off below the bottom ring and burn it.

On the other hand, if canes wilt after they have fruit maturing on them, this is likely a sign of previous damage by the raspberry crown borer. Remove and destroy infected plants.

Japanese beetles, aphids, leafhoppers, and spider mites can be pesky. One particular aphid, the raspberry aphid, can transmit the raspberry mosaic virus among plants. Sawflies, sap beetles, strawberry bud weevils (see page 59), and tarnished plant bugs may attack brambles in certain areas of the country. Luckily, they seldom show much interest in small berry patches. See chapter 18 for more on managing these pests.

Cane borer

Harvesting Bramble Fruits

RASPBERRIES HAVE a long ripening season, beginning a few weeks before blackberries, so you'll enjoy fresh picking every day for several weeks. To extend the season even more, plant early, mid-season, and fall-bearing raspberry cultivars, as well as the various colors. Black raspberries are the first to ripen, followed by the red and yellow, then the purple, and then blackberries. The black and purple often ripen over a 2-week period; the red and yellow over 4 to 6 weeks. In most areas, raspberry harvest is in July and August. In warmer climates, blackberry harvest often starts as early as in May in southern states. In the northwestern states, picking may start in July, and not until fall in the Midwest. From a 50-foot row of mature plants, expect 30 quarts of raspberries and 50 or so quarts of blackberries (depending on cultivar, culture, and climate). A single mature bramble plant generally yields 1–2 quarts, but some blackberries may yield up to 20 quarts.

Pick in the morning, while the berries are still cool but after any dew has evaporated. Use only small, shallow containers for picking raspberries, because too many piled atop each other will crush those on the bottom. We use a pail we hang on our belts so we have both hands free. Avoid handling the berries any more than necessary, and move freshly picked berries out of the sun and into the refrigerator as soon as possible.

When blackberries first turn black, they may still be rather tart. Leave them on the bush for a few more days until they almost fall off when you touch them, at which time you'll find them much sweeter.

Raspberry pavlova

Bramble Cultivars

To help you select cultivars, consider taste, plant hardiness, time of ripening, whether you can deal with thorns, and final use of the berries (fresh, frozen, or jams, for example). The flavor of some raspberry cultivars may vary with soil type and season, perhaps milder on sandy soils or in wet seasons. The following are only a few of the many cultivars you'll encounter. Unless noted, all these have thorns. Consult the text for each fruit type to determine suitability in your region.

Cultivar	Zones	Berry Size	Fruiting Season	Comments
SUMMER (ONE-CROP) RASPBERRIES				
'Boyne'	3–8	medium	early	Deep red berries, vigorous, erect, good yield, some disease resistance
'Canby'	4–8	medium	mid	Light red berries, sweet, vigorous, thornless
'Latham'	3–8	large	mid	Bright red berries, few thorns, good disease resistance
'Taylor'	4–8	large	early	Light red berries, vigorous, long harvest, heavy yield
FALL (TWO-CROP OR EVERBEARING) RASPBERRIES				
'Anne'	4–8	large	fall	Soft yellow berries, very sweet, disease resistant
'Fall Gold'	4–8	large	fall	Soft gold berries
'Heritage'	4–9	large	fall	Firm bright red berries, late ripening, good disease resistance
'Jaclyn'	4–8	medium	fall	Dark red and firm berries, vigorous, erect, pest- and disease-resistant
BLACK (SUMMER) RASPBERRIES				
'Bristol'	4–8	large	early	Fairly resistant to mosaic, berries in easy-to-pick clusters
'Jewel'	4–8	large	early	Vigorous, good yield, resistant to anthracnose
PURPLE (SUMMER) RASPBERRIES				
'Brandywine'	4–9	large	mid	Tart, good yield, few suckers, good for jams and cooking
'Royalty'	4–8	large	mid to late	Pick red (immature) or purple (mature), large sweet fruit, good resistance to insects
UPRIGHT BLACKBERRIES				
'Arapaho'	6–10	medium	early	Very small seeds, thornless
'Darrow'	4–8	large	early to mid	Large thorns, rust resistant
'Illini'	5–10	medium	late	One of hardiest, long harvest season
'Kiowa'	5–9	large	early	Long harvest season
TRAILING BLACKBERRIES				
'Chester'	5–7	large	late	Vigorous, semi-upright, some cane blight resistance, good in hot weather, thornless
'Triple Crown'	5–9	large	mid	High yield, semi-upright, long harvest period, thornless

A blueberry plant that's given a sunny spot with acid soil and lots of organic matter will produce delicious berries every summer for decades.

CHAPTER 6

Blueberries

Maybe the expression should be changed to "as American as blueberry pie," because blueberries (*Vaccinium* species) are a North American fruit and apples are an import. This popular fruit grows on an ornamental bush, a favorite of those creating edible landscapes. In early summer bushes are covered with white or pink-tinged flowers, followed by the attractive berries in various shades of blue. In fall the foliage often turns brilliant dark red to red-orange.

Gardeners just about everywhere can grow blueberries (except in the tropical tip of Florida). Given well-drained, acidic soil rich in organic matter and some pruning, blueberry plants should produce well for several decades. You may get a few berries the first year if you start with 2- or 3-year-old plants, but these slow growers take 4 to 8 years to reach full production. A little pruning each year will reward you with bigger berries and bigger yields. Bushes will bear if you skip pruning, but the berries will be smaller, yields will shrink over time, and diseases will reduce production and fruit quality.

Different Types for Different Regions

SEVERAL SPECIES OF wild blueberries grow in various sections of the United States and Canada and have been harvested and processed commercially. Since the 1950s, hundreds of large-fruited cultivars have been developed. Five types of blueberries are the most commonly grown in North American gardens.

Hardiest are the lowbush blueberries (*Vaccinium angustifolium*), which grow only a foot or so tall. Wild lowbush blueberries are grown commercially in some northern states, particularly Maine. They're grown more in cold climates not only because they tolerate lower temperatures, but also because their short stature holds up better under snow than highbush cultivars. Also, it doesn't take much snow to cover them, and snow provides insulation. Gardeners who grow lowbush blueberries in their backyard can expect about a pint of berries for each foot of row. Though the yields are lower than for highbush blueberries, they're particularly attractive for landscaping.

A few lowbush cultivars have been developed for their berries, and a few selected for their ornamental qualities as a spreading ground cover, but often they're just found as a species. 'Brunswick' and 'Ruby Carpet' have especially good red fall foliage. The popular variety 'Top Hat' has good fall color and a globe-shaped habit, and produces large berries. All these are hardy in Zones 3 to 7.

The northern highbush (*Vaccinium corymbosum*) is the most popular in many areas, for both home gardeners and commercial growers. Bushes grow from 6 to 15 feet tall and produce large berries. Yields vary widely among cultivars, but gardeners can expect from 5 to 15 pounds per bush, or 4 to 8 quarts. Although less hardy than the lowbush, some cultivars do well in Zone 3 when planted in a spot sheltered from the wind. They usually thrive where the growing season is at least 160 days. Many cultivars require a chilling period of at least 600 hours below 45°F, making them unsuitable for hot and mild climates. (See page 87 for more about chilling hours.)

Crossing highbush and lowbush blueberries has produced midsized cultivars, which are often called half-high hybrids. Growing 3 to 4 feet tall, they're better protected by snow than are taller bushes, so they should survive better in colder climates than many highbush cultivars. Yields on the half-high hybrids are slightly lower than on the highbush.

The rabbiteye blueberry (*Vaccinium ashei*) can't survive low winter temperatures, but produces good crops in the southern United States. Though sometimes listed as southern highbush, this term really refers to the next group. Rabbiteye cultivars have a low chilling period (100 to 200 hours below 45°F), but this is enough to make them unsuitable for tropical

Lowbush blueberries (left) grow close to the ground and produce small, flavorful berries that are usually harvested with a special rake. Highbush blueberries (right) can grow to be 15 feet tall and produce much larger berries that are picked individually by hand.

Blueberry Fast Facts

USDA Hardiness Zones: Rabbiteye, Zones 6–10; lowbush, Zones 3–7; northern highbush, Zones 4–7; southern highbush, Zones 6–10 (ranges may vary with cultivar)

Height: Under 1 foot (lowbush) up to 15 feet (highbush and rabbiteye; can be pruned to 6 feet for easier picking)

Spacing: Highbush and rabbiteye, 5–6 feet apart in rows 7–9 feet apart; half-high hybrids, 4–5 feet apart in rows 6–8 feet apart; lowbush 1 foot apart in rows 3 or more feet apart

Pollination: Some are self-fertile, but plant at least two cultivars for best yields

Pruning: When plants are 5 feet tall, remove old wood, thin crowded branches, cut back tops that are too high

Special requirements: Well-drained and acidic soils (pH 4.5 to 5.5), high organic matter; don't let plants dry out

Years to bearing: 4–8 for full production (some berries in second year)

Yield per plant: 2–15 pounds (varies with type), or 3–8 quarts

climates. Generally those listed for warmer zones, or as very early, have the lowest chilling requirement. Rabbiteyes tolerate drier soils than the highbush cultivars, but in hot climates most need some type of irrigation. Yields of 20 pounds of fruit per bush are not unusual, with a range of 8 to 25 pounds.

Southern highbush cultivars are the best blueberries for the warm West, Deep South, some south-central states, Texas, and Florida. Many have a very low chill requirement, but this can vary from 100 hours to more than 600. Despite their low chill needs, they don't grow well in the Southwest, which for the most part has alkaline soil (water for irrigation is often too alkaline as well). They're a relatively new group, created from crosses of northern highbush cultivars with southern species. Often you'll find them listed with the rabbiteyes, but there are significant differences. They're typically smaller and slower growing, and their leaves are thick and crinkled compared with those of the rabbiteyes. Many flower quite early, often in midwinter, and thus are susceptible to freezes. They are also more susceptible than the rabbiteyes to soil diseases and less tolerant of dry soils. Yields are similar to those of the other highbush cultivars, ranging from 8 to 15 pounds per plant, occasionally even 20 pounds.

Native huckleberries (*Gaylussacia* spp.) are similar in fruit and culture to their close relative the blueberry. Hardy throughout a wide range of Zones 3 to 8, their berries tend to be darker, on plants only 1½ to 3 feet tall and wide, and plants sport gorgeous red leaves in fall. A number of species grow in the Pacific Northwest, such as the red huckleberry (*Vaccinium parvifolium*), the evergreen huckleberry (*V. ovatum*), and the thinleaf huckleberry (*V. membranaceum*). The latter, the state fruit of Idaho, bears large, flavorful fruits and is best suited to higher elevations. Huckleberries are often found growing in some shade. They'll be more open in habit under this condition, and fruiting will be less than if grown in full sun.

Meeting Soil Requirements

BLUEBERRIES ARE extremely particular about soil acidity, like their relatives the azaleas, mountain laurel, and heathers. You must meet their soil requirements in order to get good crops. They do best with a soil pH of 4.5 to 5.5, which is too "sour" for most other garden plants. If you plan to grow blueberries, first test the pH of your soil. Soil pH higher than this may cause yellowing of leaves. Either buy an inexpensive testing kit, or send a sample to a soil laboratory (see Sources and Resources). A professional soil test from your local Cooperative Extension Service will factor in the several variables that affect soil pH, and will provide specific recommendations for how to change it.

If your soil tests from 5.5 to 6.0, you can probably grow blueberries if you mix in lots of sphagnum peat moss, which is very acidic, to the soil before planting. You may also incorporate cottonseed meal, composted pine needles or oak leaves, or compost made from pine, oak, or hemlock bark to help acidify the soil. After planting, mulch with pine needles, oak leaves, or shavings from oak, pine, or hemlock to help maintain acidity. Ammonium sulfate, a form of nitrogen fertilizer, acidifies the soil, as do other ammonium fertilizers. Be aware, though, that another fertilizer formerly prescribed for lowering acidity, aluminum sulfate, is now known to be toxic to soil organisms and noticeably changes the flavor of the blueberries. Organic methods for lowering soil pH are safer — and their acidifying effects last much longer.

If your soil test indicates a pH higher than 6.2, you'll have to work hard to grow blueberries. It's likely that the subsoil contains lime, which will dissolve into the topsoil with each rain. The tasks of lowering the acidity and maintaining it may not be not worth the trouble and expense. One day a gardening friend who lives in a limestone region showed us her beautiful, giant-sized bushes, heavily laden with blueberries. "Do you like them?" she asked. "I estimate that the berries on those bushes have cost about a dollar each." Don't despair of enjoying fresh-picked blueberries, though; see Growing Blueberries in Containers, page 82.

If you must lower your soil's pH more than half a point, do this over at least 2 years to avoid disrupting soil organisms and nutrient balance. Use powdered sulfur or the less dusty but more expensive sulfur pellets. Either should be spread on soil at least 2 years in advance of planting. The amount of sulfur required depends on soil type, as heavier soils buffer changes in acidity or alkalinity.

To lower the pH half a point, for sandy soils use 1/2 pound of sulfur for each 100 square feet; for loamy soils, 1 pound; and for clay soils, 2 pounds. Test soil pH the following year and if it's 6.0 or less, you may

To help acidify the soil, add cottonseed meal when planting blueberry bushes. Top-dress with cottonseed meal every year thereafter, to maintain the level of acidity.

Blueberries at a Glance

Use this table as a general guide. Some cultivars may grow in other regions, and both heights and yields vary with climate, culture, and cultivar.

Type or Grouping	HEIGHT (FEET)	YIELD PER BUSH	ZONES	BEST REGIONS
Lowbush	1–2	pint/row foot	3–7	Coldest areas (Northeast, Upper Midwest), higher elevations
Northern highbush	6–15	5–15 lbs.	4–7	North, Midwest, Northwest
Half-high hybrids	3–5	2–8 lbs.	3–7	Cold regions, higher elevations, Northwest
Rabbiteye	6–10	8–25 lbs.	6–9	South, south-central U.S.
Southern highbush	6–10	5–15 lbs.	6–10	Deep South, Florida, southern California

TIPS FOR GROWING BLUEBERRIES

1. Choose a site with well-drained soil and full sun. Rabbiteye and lowbush will tolerate some afternoon shade in hotter portions of their range.
2. Test soil pH; amend as needed to bring it below 6.0 (4.5–5.5 is ideal). This may take a year or two to accomplish before you can plant.
3. Incorporate plenty of organic matter (peat moss, compost) before planting.
4. Choose cultivars adapted for your area; buy at least two to ensure good pollination and large berries.
5. Follow spacing recommendations for each type and cultivar (5–7 feet apart for larger cultivars).
6. Apply a thick mulch, ideally pine needles (for acidity). Weed by hand to avoid disturbing shallow roots.
7. Water often so surface roots don't dry out.
8. Protect from birds before berries begin to turn blue.
9. Prune annually in late winter for the biggest berries and best yields.
10. Feed with a balanced fertilizer (such as 5-3-4) just before buds start to open. In warm climates, you may fertilize again just after harvest.

plant now. If it's still not acidic enough, incorporate more sulfur and wait another year.

Two other aspects of soil are important but often overlooked. Good soil drainage is essential, especially near the surface. Blueberries have many shallow surface roots, which in poorly drained soils are starved for oxygen. And abundant organic matter is necessary for good drainage and to make a loose, crumbly soil for these surface roots. Before planting, spread copious amounts of peat moss or compost on top of the soil and then work it in. The mulches mentioned above will help maintain abundant organic matter.

Planting and Care

CHOOSE A SITE that gets sun most of the day. (Only a few varieties tolerate shade. One of these is 'Well's Delight', a creeping lowbush good in Zones 6 to 8.) Don't plant in a low area, or plant in raised beds or on mounds to provide better drainage. After you've made sure that the soil is acidic enough, spread a couple of inches of compost, sphagnum peat moss, or other organic matter over the entire planting area. Mix everything in thoroughly with a spade, garden fork, or tiller.

Identify which type of blueberry is best for your climate. Plant at least two cultivars to ensure cross-pollination. It's best to plant three, for improved pollination and so that if one doesn't make it, two will still be left. Choose cultivars from the same group (such as rabbiteye or highbush) that bloom about the same time. Blueberry blossoms are not especially fragrant and therefore not as attractive to bees as are most other flowers, so mix up your plantings and keep the different cultivars close to each other (within 20 feet). If you set 20 'Jersey' plants in one block and 20 'Earliblue' in another some distance away, the same bee may not find both kinds.

You can plant potted blueberry bushes almost any time that the ground isn't frozen, but plant bare-root varieties only in the spring in the North and in spring or fall in the South. Set highbush and rabbiteye blueberries 5 to 6 feet apart in rows, spacing the rows 7 to 9 feet apart. Set half-high hybrids 4 to 5 feet apart in rows 6 to 8 feet apart. Set lowbush plants 1 foot apart in rows at least 3 feet apart. Unlike other types, lowbush blueberries spread by underground rhizomes, and will quickly make a low, thick hedge or fill in a whole bed as a ground cover.

Growing Blueberries in Containers

Where soils are too alkaline for blueberries, grow them in large containers such as a half whisky barrel filled with a peat-based, soilless mix. Containers are also perfect for those with little space or time to garden, or with poorly drained or clay soils. Because many cultivars get quite large, choose half-high or lowbush types, such as 'Top Hat' lowbush in colder climates and Sunshine Blue (a popular low-chill cultivar) in the South, California, and the Pacific Northwest.

Plants growing in containers are much less hardy; roots will be exposed to air temperatures and will die when the thermometer goes much below freezing. Except in mild climates, use smaller containers that can be moved to a protected site during winter, such as an unheated shed or garage. (A rolling platform with casters works well.) Look for a lightweight plastic container 18 to 24 inches wide and at least 12 to 16 inches deep. When potting, leave a couple of inches on the top for an organic mulch to help keep roots moist.

Keep plants in a cool spot; the ideal is just above freezing. Too warm, and plants will begin to grow. Remember blueberry bushes' shallow roots are susceptible to drought, so water well before moving, and water periodically (when the soil is very dry) during winter.

If containers aren't overly large and you have the garden space, consider burying them in the ground. Dig some holes and plant the containers, bushes and all. Leave them there over the winter or year-round. To remove them each spring, use the pot-in-pot method. Bury an empty pot the same size as or a bit larger than the one a bush is in, then sink the planted pot into the one in the ground. This way you don't have to dig a new hole each year. Even though they're in the ground, plants in a pot will still dry out more often, so check often and keep them watered.

Water the small bushes immediately after planting, and continue to water every other day. Once plants are established, a month to 6 weeks after planting, lightly fertilize with a product formulated especially for acid-loving plants, following label directions. One option is to sprinkle 1 tablespoon (½ ounce) of ammonium sulfate (not aluminum sulfate) around each bush, staying 6 inches away from stems. Rabbiteyes are quite sensitive to fertilizer, so for them, use a very light hand or even wait to fertilize until the second growing season.

Add a thick mulch to protect sensitive roots, conserve moisture, and reduce weed growth. Even with a mulch, shallow-rooted blueberry bushes are apt to dry out during a prolonged dry spell, so you may have to water often during their first growing season. Hoeing and cultivating can damage the shallow roots, so pull out by hand any weeds that penetrate the mulch.

Annual Upkeep

In subsequent years, fertilize plants twice in spring: first when leaves start to emerge and again once plants stop blooming. In warm climates where the growing season is long (Zones 8 and 9), blueberries benefit from a third feeding in summer. So plants can harden properly for winter, don't fertilize after July in Zones 6 and colder or after August in warmer climates.

Use fertilizer formulated for acid-loving plants (such as for hollies and azaleas), or a balanced blend such as 5-3-4; follow application rates on the label. Or use a cup of cottonseed meal or soybean meal per bush (use greater amounts as the plants grow). Scatter around each plant, then add more mulch. Or pull back the mulch and spread an inch of compost over the entire growing area. If you use a synthetic fertilizer, check the ingredient list for nitrates (one form of nitrogen) and chloride compounds. These chemicals may injure blueberry plants, so select a different fertilizer. Blueberries are sensitive to too much fertilizer of any kind, so don't overfertilize.

Pruning

For the first five or so years, blueberries need little pruning. Each spring, remove broken branches and any that are crossing and rubbing on others. Remove weak and wayward branches to encourage a sturdy upright shape as plants mature. This is about all that lowbush blueberries ever need, except to thin out some of the thickest growth periodically.

Highbush and rabbiteye blueberries need annual pruning once they reach 5 or 6 feet in height in order to produce large crops of big berries. In Zones 3 and 4, where highbush blueberries grow more slowly, you may be able to wait until plants are 12 years old.

A mild day in late winter or early spring is a good time to get out there with your clippers. Different cultivars grow in different ways, so try to prune according to the needs of each. Cut back the tops of any plants that are growing too tall. Each year, cut a couple of the oldest branches (those at least 5 years old or more than 1 inch thick) completely to the ground. Thin out branches that are crowding each other by cutting back to a main branch. Where the twiggy end branches appear too thick, thin them. This will open up the bush and let in sunshine, so the berries will ripen better, and you can harvest them more easily.

Blueberries have many shallow surface roots, which in poorly drained soil are starved for oxygen.

Annual pruning, once plants reach 4 to 5 feet tall, will give you bigger blueberries and better yields.

Birds, Insects, and Diseases

One of the nicest features of blueberries is the small number of insects and diseases that bother them. Large commercial plantings can be vulnerable, but home gardeners may never encounter any serious diseases or harmful insects. You can avoid most problems by choosing a site with well-drained soil and good air circulation, and buy purchasing certified disease-free plants. See chapter 18 for more on managing pest problems.

Insects. The plum curculio may show up on early cultivars, leaving the same crescent-shaped scars as on other fruits (see page 279). The blueberry maggot and the cranberry and cherry fruitworms are the most common troublesome insects. If you see a small hole in a berry, open it and check the fruit first before you bite into it. The small white maggots eat and live in the berries. The presence of either fruitworm is signaled by the webbing they create (more common with the cranberry), and berries turning blue prematurely. If you find any of these, clean up all the old fruit each year before winter to discourage these pests. For an unusually serious infestation, remove and burn all mulch before winter. If the pests return and you don't have the patience to sort through and remove the bad berries, check with your local garden store or Cooperative Extension Service for the latest and safest remedies.

Diseases. Three diseases to watch for on blueberries are mummy berry, stem canker, and botrytis tip blight. Mummy berry causes fruits to turn pink, shrivel, and fall off prior to ripening. (Shriveled berries on the ground are termed "mummies.") To prevent mummy berry, keep the berries picked and destroy those that fall, so the disease can't overwinter on the ground. Where this disease is a recurring problem, pay special attention when its prime

Yellowing leaves (below) may indicate a pH problem or a nitrogen deficiency. By comparison, healthy leaves (above) will be a deep, glossy green.

If you have a problem with birds eating too many of your blueberries, you might consider building a cage around them and covering it with bird netting.

conditions occur, when leaves stay wet for 6 to 12 hours and temperatures are above 60°F. In these conditions you may need to apply an appropriate fungicide after buds form. Avoid spraying once plants start to bloom.

Stem canker may cause cracks in the canes and then death, particularly on northern highbush cultivars. Many of the top rabbiteyes and some newer cultivars are resistant, so look for these if you're starting a patch.

Botrytis tip blight kills new growth. When this disease occurs, prune to improve air circulation.

Many newer cultivars have resistance to some of the major diseases, so look for these selections. Check with your garden store to see what specific fungicides are available for treatment if your plants become infected.

Virus diseases such as stunt really have no controls, and invariably result in the gradual deterioration of the plant. Remove and destroy infected plants so they don't infect others. Control aphids and leafhoppers (see pages 376 and 378), as these insects can spread viruses from infected plants to healthy ones.

Other problems. If areas between the leaf veins turn yellow, check the soil's pH; this is usually a nutrition problem, not a disease. If the soil has a pH above 5.5, soil alkalinity may be causing iron deficiency. Apply an iron chelate product, following label directions; spray leaves for a short-term boost. To prevent a recurrence, amend soils (see Meeting Soil Requirements, 79) and use an acidifying mulch such as pine needles.

Stunted growth, yellow or reddish leaves, or red dots on leaves may indicate that nitrogen is lacking. If you see this, apply liquid fish emulsion fertilizer at recommended rates.

Animal pests. Though animals seldom bother blueberries, birds are unusually fond of them. You may be able to scare away some birds by installing balloons with "eyes" or Mylar ribbons sold for this purpose. Put these in place before any berries ripen. If you don't grow enough blueberries to share with avian visitors, cover the bushes with bird netting. Tight is the key, as birds will try to find their way inside and then get trapped. To make picking easier, drape netting over a frame made of wood or PVC pipe, creating a cage inside which you can stand. Modern bird netting is a black plastic material, visually unobtrusive in the landscape. You could also wrap plants with row cover, a white, lightweight material sold to create shade or for frost protection.

Harvesting Blueberries

IN COOLER CLIMATES, blueberry season usually starts in July and runs through August. In milder climates such as much of the Midwest and the Northwest, the season runs from July into September. In the warmest areas, it runs from May or June (April in Florida for southern highbush cultivars) through July. Most cultivars ripen over a 3- to 4-week period; with some, the picking period is up to 6 weeks; with others, there's a concentrated 2-week ripening period. Southern highbush cultivars generally ripen over a long time (4 to 6 weeks) except for 'Star', which ripens over 3 weeks.

Unlike strawberries and raspberries, blueberries ripen over a long season and hold well on the bush, so there's no need to pick them daily. Picked berries will keep for several days if you keep them cool and dry.

For the best flavor, don't pick blueberries until they have developed a rich bloom and come off easily in your hand. Taste a few to determine exactly when each variety is at its peak. The fruits of different cultivars turn various shades of blue when completely ripe, so color is not a good measure of ripeness. Unripe berries still have a bit of pink where the stem joins, though you may not be able to see this when you're picking.

Cooks never run out of ways to use fresh blueberries. They're a treat on morning cereal and in muffins, and in pies, puddings, and other desserts. They make wonderful jams and conserves. They're easy to freeze for winter feasts — just wash, drain, and pour into plastic freezer bags. Figure on about a quart of berries to make a pint canned (this will vary with size of berries). Drying in a slow oven (140°F) or food dehydrator is another good way to preserve blueberries.

Blueberry Cultivars

For the longest harvest from the fewest bushes, choose pairs of cultivars with various ripening times (for example, two different early cultivars, two midseason, and two different late ones). These are just a few of the more popular cultivars; check with a local nursery or your Cooperative Extension Service for others suited to your area. For the warmest climates, such as Florida and southern California, select cultivars that require the fewest chilling hours.

Cultivar	SEASON	FRUIT DESCRIPTION	COMMENTS
NORTHERN HIGHBUSH			
'Bluecrop'	mid	medium-large	Adaptable to many areas
'Darrow'	late	large	Some disease resistance, good for Pacific Northwest
'Duke'	early	large	Resists mummy berry
'Elliott'	very late	medium	Low chill requirement, some disease resistance, good for Pacific Northwest
'Jersey'	mid–late	medium	Resists mummy berry
'Nelson'	late	large	Some disease resistance
'Pink Lemonade'	mid–late	medium	Pink berries when ripe, good in mild climates, low chill requirement
HALF-HIGH HYBRIDS			
'Northland'	early–mid	medium	3–4 ft. tall, large spread increases yields, hardy
'North Sky'	mid	small	1–1½ ft. tall, great flavor and sweetness, good for freezing, very hardy, good at front of ornamental border
'Patriot'	early	very large	4 ft. tall, good flavor, hardy, leaves orange-red in fall
RABBITEYES			
'Brightwell'	early–mid	medium	Vigorous, upright, Zones 7–9
'Legacy'	mid–late	medium-large	Stores well, Zones 5–8, bright orange fall color
'Tifblue'	late	large	Standard cultivar, Zones 7–9
'Woodard'	early	large	Zones 7–9
SOUTHERN HIGHBUSH			
'Misty'	early–mid	medium	Low chill need (300 hours), Zones 5–10
'Sharpblue'	very early	medium	Classic cultivar, needs 200 chill hours, Zones 7–10
'Sunshine Blue'	mid	medium	Low chill need (150 hours), tolerates higher pH, Zones 5–10
'Star'	early	large	Short ripening period, needs 400 chill hours, may get botrytis in wet spring weather, Zones 6–9

Why not try growing something a little more unusual?
This tasty white currant is cold-hardy and easy to grow.

CHAPTER 7

Ribes, Elderberries, and Other Bush Fruits

For many years, we had a large gooseberry bush in our front yard that "belonged" to the boys in my 4-H club, who frequently visited us. It was mutually agreed that they could eat freely from it if they ignored those in the back garden. The bush produced so lavishly year after year that it always supplied more than their needs, even though it was not unusual to find several boys sitting around it eating with both hands.

Like the brambles, the bush fruits come in many colors, making them ornamental as well as edible. There are red, white, and black currants; green, amber, pink, and red gooseberries; and wine-dark jostas and elderberries. They begin to bear at an early age, yield big crops each year, and add exciting variety to any home grower's fruit collection. In Europe, currants and gooseberries have long been considered gourmet foods. Many of our best cultivars have been developed there and in Canada. Even if you don't have room for a full patch, you can incorporate these bush fruits into home landscapes as ornamentals.

Among the hardiest of fruits, these berries are a boon for gardeners in cold regions. They grow best in the Northeast, Midwest, and Pacific Northwest, and in cooler parts of northern California. Gardeners in warm climates should console themselves with other fruits.

Getting to Know the Bush Fruits

GOOSEBERRIES AND red and white currants are well behaved; they will stay 4 to 5 feet tall and wide for many years. They take up relatively little space, and you need only one bush to get some fruit. Black currants and jostaberries are likely to spread, but usually not enough to be troublesome. Although currants and gooseberries are often found growing and bearing on abandoned farms where they're choked with grass and receive no care, they produce much better when they get a little attention.

The elderberry is extremely hardy, tolerates warmer climates than currants and gooseberries, grows in almost any soil that is somewhat moist, and requires almost no care. It has attractive flowers, berries, and yellow to red-orange leaves in fall. So what's wrong with it? Not much, though it's perhaps a bit too easy to grow, so it spreads rapidly, both by seed and by root suckers. Fortunately, we have plenty of room, and by keeping the grass mowed all around the bushes, we keep them under control.

Pick gooseberries ripe for jams and jellies. Unripe, bake them into a tart pie.

The Ribes: Currants, Gooseberries, and Jostaberries

Currants and gooseberries belong to the genus *Ribes*. The genus name is often used as a common name for this group of diverse fruits. Red currants (*Ribes rubrum*) are just that, although also they come in white and pink. Fruits are small, about the size of a small blueberry, and ripen in mid- to late summer, as do other currants. Depending on cultivar, berries can be sweet or sour; the pink are the sweetest. Use the sour cultivars in cooking, jams, and juices; the sweeter cultivars are delicious fresh. Black currants (*R. nigrum*) have a musky flavor and fragrance and are used more for cooking rather than eating fresh. Black currant juice is popular in Europe, partly because the berries provide up to five times the amount of vitamin C found in oranges.

Currants are a good source of vitamin C, and they make tasty juices and jellies.

The jostaberry is a cross between the European black currant and a North American dessert-type gooseberry.

Clove currant, also called Buffalo currant (*R. aureum* var. *villosum*, sometimes seen as *R. odoratum*), makes a nice ornamental shrub. In spring, clusters of yellow, trumpet-shaped flowers exude a spicy fragrance of clove and vanilla. These shrubs are native to the middle section of North America. Larger than their currant cousins at 5 to 6 feet tall and wide, they produce black fruits over a long period, from mid- to late summer.

TIPS FOR GROWING BUSH FRUITS

- Verify that it's legal to grow currants, gooseberries, and jostaberries in your area. Select disease-resistant cultivars.
- Choose a sunny site with well-drained soil for all except elderberries, which prefer moist soil. (In warmer areas, plants tolerate more shade.)
- Set currants and gooseberries 3–5 feet apart in well-weeded soil; jostaberries and elderberries, 6–8 feet apart.
- Apply a thick mulch for weed control; keep weeded, but don't disturb shallow roots once established.
- Water deeply the first month, or until established.
- Feed plants with compost each year, and replenish mulch.
- After 4 or 5 years, prune in spring to thin out old branches.

Currant, Gooseberry, Jostaberry, and Elderberry Fast Facts

USDA Hardiness Zones: All except elderberries Zones 3–7, but best in Zones 5 and colder; not for the South or Southwest; elderberries Zones 3–9

Height: Currants and gooseberries, 4–5 feet; jostaberries, 5–6 feet; elderberries 6–12 feet

Spacing: Currants and gooseberries, 3–5 feet apart; jostaberries and elderberries, 6–8 feet apart

Pollination: Red and white currants and gooseberries are self-fertile; many black currants and jostaberries need another cultivar for cross-pollination; elderberries produce better with cross-pollination

Pruning: After 4 or 5 years, prune in early spring to thin out old branches

Special requirements: Make sure currants are legal to grow in your area; select varieties that are resistant to blister rust

Years to bearing: 2; full production in 3 or 4 years

Yield per plant: Currants, 3–10 pounds; gooseberries, 5–10 pounds; jostaberries and elderberries, 8–12 pounds

Contraband Currants

Just as blueberry growing is restricted by its fussiness about acid soil and peach growing by its insistence on a mild climate and light soil, the gooseberry and its cousins have a major obstacle to being widely grown. Members of the *Ribes* clan are denied admittance to some areas because they can't always get along with their neighbors. They are, unfortunately, one of the Typhoid Marys of the plant world. The plants can be an alternate host to blister rust, a disease that infects and kills native white pine (*Pinus strobus*).

Blister rust seldom noticeably affects the *Ribes* plants themselves, but its spores travel to nearby white pines. First a few limbs on the pine die; ultimately, the whole tree succumbs. Curiously, the disease does not spread from one pine tree to another: it needs an intervening host plant. The main culprits are the European black currant (now naturalized in many parts of North America) and the native wild gooseberry, which is equally widespread. Many of the newer cultivars of red and black currants, jostaberry, and gooseberry are resistant to blister rust and thus cause no problem.

Canada has no laws prohibiting the planting of *Ribes,* but laws in some states still ban the sale of these plants. Other states require that all *Ribes* be planted at least 900 feet from any white pine (and other five-needled pines, such as the Swiss pine), and even farther from a nursery raising white pine seedlings. Your Cooperative Extension Service can tell you whether any restrictions apply in your area.

There are two species, the American gooseberry (*Ribes hirtellum*) and the European (*R. uva-crispa*). Cultivars of the European species are more common because they bear larger berries (to 2 inches across) with better flavor. American cultivars tend to be more resistant to powdery mildew and also more productive. Some cultivars are hybrids.

The josta or jostaberry (pronounced YOS-ta-berry), *Ribes × culverwellii,* sometimes listed as *R. nidigrolaria,* was developed in Germany in 1922 yet not introduced to North America until 1977. It's a complex hybrid involving a cross between the European black currant and a North American dessert-type gooseberry, delivering the best traits of both and usually just found as the species. Bushes are thornless, quite hardy, and resistant to both blister rust and mildew. They're such vigorous growers that they need heavier pruning and more space than gooseberries or currants; space plants 8 feet apart.

Before they're fully ripe, jostaberries often taste more like gooseberries; they taste more like black currants when ripe. Even though the flavor doesn't appeal to everyone, their advocates declare that jostaberry preserves are superior to those made of other *Ribes.* Like currants, the berries are rich in vitamin C, and their size is between a currant and gooseberry.

Clove currant produces spicy-scented flowers followed by small, edible fruits.

Low-maintenance, ornamental, and high in antioxidants, elderberries are a good choice for edible landscaping.

Elderberry blooms are not only ornamental but also edible. Fry them in batter for a special treat.

Elderberries

Undemanding elderberries require just about the least amount of work of any of the cultivated fruits and will make it on their own with very little attention. The main species, *Sambucus nigra,* is a complex of several subspecies such as *S. nigra* subsp. *canadensis* (sometimes listed just as *S. canadensis*). In addition to being extremely hardy, elderberries let us make use of land that, even if it's not swampy, is too wet for other fruits. In fact, these bushes don't do well on very well drained or dry soils. Our two rows of 6- to 7-foot-tall bushes are each about 20 feet long and 3 feet wide, and produce gallons of highly flavored fruit from late summer into early fall.

The flowers, which look like large white umbrellas, are quite showy in early summer. The flavor of elderberries is somewhat like that of blackberries but richer and somewhat tart. The fruit is fun to pick because the bushes are thornless and there's no bending over. Fruits of hybrids are much larger than the wild berries, usually about the size of chokecherries. Elderberries are high in antioxidants that help strengthen the immune system. It's likely that the ladies of bygone days who had their glass of elderberry wine each afternoon "for medicinal reasons" knew exactly what they were doing. The berries make a nice juice and are delicious in pies and jams. Strain out the many seeds through several layers of cheesecloth or a fruit strainer.

Our biggest problem with elderberries is that birds love them as much as we do. Every year they try to grab all the fruit, usually by picking it a day or two before it's ready. To make matters worse, the heavy birds occasionally break off whole clusters by perching on them. Because the tall bushes are impossible to cover, we usually resort to beating the birds at their own game: we too pick a day or two before they're really ripe, then we let them finish to perfection in a warm room. Fortunately, in our cool climate some of the new hybrids ripen so late that many berry-eating birds have already gotten sick of wild elderberries and headed south before the crop from the cultivars turns color.

Planting and Care

WHEN YOU'RE JUST STARTING out with bush fruits, it's best to buy disease-free plants from a nursery. If you decide to beg a plant or two from a neighbor who has exactly what you want, sever a small offshoot from a large bush in early spring with a quick thrust of a sharp spade. Be sure the fledgling plant has good roots, leave the soil around it intact, plant it in your own garden as soon as possible, and water well. You can enlarge your own plantings with such offshoots as well.

Set out potted plants any time the ground isn't frozen. Because every root is intact, these get off to the fastest start. Plant bare-root stock in early spring (before growth starts) for best results.

The culture of all the bush fruits is much the same. Although they'll grow and produce in light shade (members of the *Ribes* clan were at one time planted in orchards among the fruit trees), they have fewer diseases when grown in plenty of sun with good air circulation. Gooseberries tolerate more heat than currants, and elderberries tolerate more heat than either. Give most bush fruits well-drained loamy soil with a pH of 5.5 to 7.0. An exception is the elderberry, which prefers a moist (but not continually wet) location. All thrive in soil rich in organic matter. Plants benefit from annual generous additions of compost topped with mulch.

Red and white currants and gooseberries are self-fertile, so one bush usually produces abundantly with no partner. Many black currants and jostaberries, on the other hand, will need a partner nearby to produce fruit. Make sure both partners bloom at the same time, and don't expect a red or white currant to pollinate a black. You'll get larger harvests from your elderberries if you plant two different hybrids.

You don't need soil that is as carefully prepared as that required for strawberries or brambles. Start with soil as weed-free as possible. Simply dig a large hole, mix an equal amount of well-rotted manure or compost with the soil you remove, and fill the hole with water. Set in the plants at the same depth they grew originally in the pot, or if bare-root, the same depth before they were dug, and refill with the amended soil. Prune tops of bare-root plants back to 6 to 10 inches, leaving at least two buds.

Mulching bush fruits provides many benefits. It keeps grass and weeds from choking them, helps maintain abundant organic matter in soil, and protects shallow surface roots. Apply a thick layer of organic mulch around each bush at planting time and add to it each year. Pull any weeds that sneak through by hand so as not to damage the surface roots on established plants.

Water heavily two or three times a week for the first few weeks. Feed with a liquid fish emulsion, or with a complete balanced fertilizer at half the recommended rate, a month after planting.

Each spring, in subsequent years, put a shovelful or two of compost or composted manure under the mulch. If plants look healthy, vigorous, and dark green, there is no need for fertilizer. If plants look a bit anemic (light yellow leaves), feed them with fish emulsion or a complete, balanced fertilizer (follow application rates on the label). Avoid fertilizers containing chlorides (such as potassium chloride, also called muriate of potash), as currants and gooseberries are sensitive to this element. Don't overfertilize with nitrogen, and don't fertilize once fruits begin to form.

Pruning

Young *Ribes* plants require little or no pruning. Even after they begin to bear heavily, the only pruning they need is the removal of broken branches and some of the older wood. Black currants produce best on wood that is 1 or 2 years old; on red and white currants, 2- and 3-year-old shoots produce the most fruit. Cut the older, less productive branches to the ground. You can usually tell the age of shoots by their color: 1-year-old stems are tan, 2-year-olds are gray, and canes 3 or more years old are dark gray to blackish.

Gooseberries bear on 2- to 4-year-old stems, so wait a year longer to prune these. Prune large-fruited gooseberry cultivars more heavily than the smaller-fruiting ones so the berries will grow to their ultimate size. Be sure to use heavy gloves when you tackle the thorny gooseberries. The vigorous jostaberries need even heavier pruning. If mildew has been a problem, thin out more of the branches so sun and air can better dry out the interior of the plant.

Gooseberries and currants don't need much pruning. Each year, cut a few of the oldest branches back to the ground.

Ideally, elderberries should have six to eight mature upright stems. On established plants, in early spring, before growth starts, prune away older branches and some side shoots. We cut out all winter-killed branches and are never alarmed if there are a lot of them, as the fruit is produced on the new sucker growth each year, as well as on 2-year-old stems that have several side branches.

If any of these fruit bushes has become overgrown, prune out all old and weak shoots right to ground level. Or you can sacrifice a year's harvest and cut back the whole plant to the ground.

Insects and Diseases

Our elderberry plants have never been bothered by insects or disease, but you may encounter either. If you spot a lot of aphids, dislodge them with a stream of water from the hose, though they'll probably disperse on their own before long. The elder shoot borer makes itself known by bits of sawdust at the base of canes where they enter. Prune out and destroy infested and dead canes.

The gooseberry sawfly caterpillar may attack any of the *Ribes* in early summer, and is the most serious pest, particularly of gooseberries. The caterpillars chew leaves in spring and again in late summer, although spring damage is usually more severe. If there aren't too many, check them by handpicking or by using rotenone spray (don't use near a waterway; rotenone is toxic to fish).

Tomato ringspot virus and several leaf diseases may be found on elderberries, but these seldom cause enough damage to warrant controls. If a plant becomes stressed, fungal cankers may ring the stems and kill it. Again, prune out infected and dead canes and destroy them.

A common disease to watch for with *Ribes* is powdery mildew, which appears as a white powdery growth that covers twigs, leaves, and fruit, in severe cases making them inedible. Anthracnose, a less common disease on *Ribes,* shows up as leaf discolorations, in contrast to leaf spots from other diseases. For more on controlling these diseases and other pests and diseases, see chapter 18.

Gooseberry sawfly caterpillar

Harvesting Bush Fruits

WE DON'T PICK CURRANTS and gooseberries when they first turn color, because both improve in flavor when they stay on the bush awhile until fully ripe. Watch them closely, though, because birds like them, too. Unlike most other berries (including elderberries), which last for only a few days, these store well in the refrigerator up to 2 weeks.

With all currants, fruits are produced on flexible stems called strigs. Look for cultivars with fruits produced in large clusters; they make for easiest picking.

The red, white, and pink currants ripen fairly uniformly, so wait until about 3 weeks after they begin to color to harvest. Pick a whole strig (stem), being careful not to damage the fruit spurs. Or use the tines of a fork to strip currants from the stem. Black currants don't ripen uniformly along a single strig, so pick berries individually as they're ready. Avoid picking wet currants, or spread them on a towel to dry before storing, as the fruits mold easily. Expect to harvest 3 to 10 pounds of currants per bush.

Thorny cultivars of gooseberries can be a bit tricky to pick. Try wearing a leather glove on one hand to hold up the branches while you pick with the other hand. Long-sleeved "rose gloves" are great for this purpose; most garden-supply stores and catalogs sell them.

Gooseberries resemble small kiwifruits in texture and flavor. Different cultivars vary widely in size, color, and sweetness. When fully ripe, the berries are soft, and many are delicious right off the bush. Some people prefer to pick when slightly underripe for tart sauce and pies. Gooseberries will continue to ripen off the bush if you pick them before they're fully flavored. Expect 5 to 10 pounds per mature bush.

The red currant is a bit tart, and thus is best when cooked, although as a boy I liked to eat them fresh off the bush. Red currants are high in pectin (until they become overripe), which makes them ideal for jelly making. Use a mixture of ripe and half-ripe red currants for jelly recipes with no added pectin; ripe ones are good for jam. Use slightly overripe ones in juice and wine. The same is true for black currants; the dead-ripe ones are best for juice.

Red currant jelly has long been a gourmet treat accompanying meat dishes as well as desserts. Black currant jelly and jam are just as tasty. I'll never forget

One effective way to strip currants from their strigs is to use the tines of a fork.

our first jar of Confiture de Cassis, which we picked up on a trip to Montreal — a delight that made me want to start growing them right away. Some people make black currants into juice and wine or dry them. (Note: The small, dark dried fruits sold as "currants" or zante currants are actually raisins, the dried form of a small, sweet black grape.)

Gooseberries also are delicious in jam, jelly, and something really special — gooseberry fool (a traditional English dessert of gooseberries cooked with sugar and then mixed with whipped cream). Traditionally, the cook "tops and tails" the berries before using them, but for most recipes this painstaking job is unnecessary.

Because elderberries are ready to harvest in early fall, when we're up to our necks processing the apples, cider, plums, and vegetables, we pick them and freeze them immediately without processing. Later in the season or in winter, when time isn't quite so precious, we cook them into syrups that we freeze for delicious drinks or make them into jellies, pies, and juice. The vitamin C–loaded juice (highest content of any fruit except currants) mixed with orange juice, cider, or ginger ale is our winter health tonic to ward off colds and flu. Make sure to pick only ripe berries, as unripe ones are mildly toxic (do not eat leaves, stems, and especially roots, as they are toxic).

Bush Fruit Cultivars

There is little difference in hardiness among the following cultivars. All except elderberries grow in Zones 3 to 7 but are best in Zones 5 and colder. (These fruits are not good choices for the South or Southwest.) Elderberry cultivars grow in Zones 3 to 9.

Cultivar	Fruit	Comments
RED, WHITE CURRANTS		
'Gloire des Sablons'	pinkish white, medium	Good disease resistance
'Jonkeer Van Tets'	red, medium	Vigorous, popular, may get some powdery mildew
'Rovada'	red, large	Ripens late, easy to pick, good yield
BLACK CURRANTS		
'Crandall'	very large, sweet, and tart	Fragrant yellow flowers in spring, good in jams and juices, tolerates heat
'Crusader'	large and sweet	Not self-fertile, good rust resistance
'Titania'	large	Good disease resistance, matures in only three seasons
GOOSEBERRIES		
'Pixwell'	pink-red, medium	Easy to pick, vigorous
'Poorman'	red, sweet, small	Vigorous, few spines
ELDERBERRIES		
'Nova'	large, very dark	Fruits heavily, early
'Samdal'	large	Bears on shoots from ground second year, prune after fruiting
'Samyl' (Sandvil)	large	Good yield, later to flower
'York'	large	Flowers with 'Nova', fruit ripens after 'Nova'

Unusual Bush Fruits

Check these out if you're looking to expand your fruit collection, or to get some fruits not otherwise available locally. Many make nice additions to ornamental landscapes or a wildlife garden.

Chokeberries (*Aronia* spp.), include the black chokeberry (*A. melanocarpa*) and the red chokeberry (*A. arbutifolia*). Purple-fruited chokeberry (*A.* × *prunifolia*) is a cross between the two. All are attractive additions to the landscape, sporting attractive white flowers in late spring and red fall foliage. Native to eastern North America, they grow in Zones 4 (possibly 3) to 9. Research shows these fruits to be among the top natural sources of antioxidants and other healthful compounds.

Generally reaching 5 to 6 feet tall, these suckering shrubs can grow to 10 feet. Chokeberries are adaptable to most conditions, from wet to dry soils and part to full sun. They need little care other than pruning out some of the older branches.

Fruits form in late summer to fall and last on the plants until winter. They're easy to pick but so astringent that they're said to cause choking (hence the name). Sugar tones down the tartness, and because of their high level of pectin, they make good jam by themselves or added to low-pectin fruits. The cultivar 'Nero' has especially good yields of larger fruits high in vitamin C and with better flavor. 'Viking' is similar, but more vigorous with bright red fall leaves.

Lingonberry (*Vaccinium vitis-idaea*) is a low-growing ornamental plant closely related to the cranberry, except that it's easier to grow and has slightly smaller berries with a better, less tart flavor. The berries will keep for weeks in the refrigerator. Plants are hardy in Zones 3 to 7 and attractive year-round with small, glossy evergreen leaves. They grow a foot tall and slowly spread to two feet wide; massed, they make a good ground cover. Small white or pink bell-shaped flowers yield berries in late summer to fall. In mild climates with a longer season, there may be a second, smaller harvest. You'll need two or more plants to get fruit; with a couple of different cultivars or clones, expect a pound of fruit per mature plant.

Though less tart, lingonberries can replace cranberries in sauces. They're good in beverages, mixed with other fruits, on ice cream and pancakes, with yogurt, and even in wine and liqueurs. They're rich in vitamin C and, similar to blueberries, have many healthful properties.

Lingonberries produce best in sun but will tolerate light shade. They don't like hot summers. With shallow roots, they need sufficient water but well-drained, acidic soils, and to be kept weeded. Grow as you would blueberries (see page 81). Among the few cultivars are 'Balsgard' with flavorful, large fruit; 'Koralle', bearing medium-size berries in midseason on upright, compact plants; the taller 'Red Pearl' (to 16 inches), which spreads more rapidly than most, with many large fruits; upright and compact 'Sanna' with medium-size dark

Chokeberries are both ornamental and delicious; they're high in vitamin C and taste somewhat like pomegranate.

A close cranberry relative, lingonberry produces colorful, tart fruits on low-growing plants.

red berries; 'Splendor', which begins bearing at an early age and has somewhat frost-tolerant buds; and 'Sussi', boasting abundant and larger berries on plants only 4 to 8 inches high.

Pineapple guava (*Acca sellowiana,* formerly *Feijoa sellowiana*) is a subtropical evergreen shrub that can grow to 15 feet high and wide. It grows in Zones 8 to 10. In early summer, plants bear attractive, 1-inch white flowers with red stamens. The petals, which are edible, impart their sweet flavor when you add them to a salad. Rounded to egg-shaped fruits are 1 to 3 inches long and have a distinctive scent. Waxy blue-green skin covers a greenish white, juicy pulp that tastes like a minty pineapple and is used fresh or in drinks. This low-maintenance shrub is often grown as an ornamental. Plant at least two bushes to ensure cross-pollination and good yields.

The saskatoon (*Amelanchier alnifolia*) is one of the few fruits that not only survive the sub-zero temperatures of the prairie provinces and Northern states, but also produce tremendous crops. With beautiful early-spring blooms and attractive fall color, saskatoon makes a pretty ornamental. Several related species are known as serviceberries, Juneberries, shad, and shadblow. Because birds love the ripening fruits, some growers plant a hedgerow of wild saskatoons nearby, hoping birds will get their fill on these and leave the cultivated fruits alone.

Although commonly called a berry, its fruit is actually a small pome, like an apple or a pear. Most wild bushes produce ¼-inch to ⅜-inch fruits; those on improved cultivars are much larger and sweeter. They resemble blueberries in appearance and flavor and can be used the same way. The bushes grow from 8 to 12 feet tall, and cultivars can produce 6 quarts of fruit per bush. It takes 3 to 4 years for plants to start producing fruit and 7 or 8 for big yields. Saskatoons are only partly self-fertile, so for more-abundant harvests, plant more than one kind or even some wild plants or related serviceberries.

The bushes are quite hardy (Zones 2 to 7), but a late-spring frost may damage the crop. To avoid frost damage, choose a spot where air drainage is good. Grow as you would elderberries, only plant in well-drained soil amended with plenty of organic matter. Also, don't prune off too much young growth. Unlike elderberries, saskatoons produce fruit on wood that grew during the previous season.

Cultivars include the large-fruited 'Honeywood', which blooms late and thus may avoid spring freezes, and 'Martin', with good-size fruits and uniform ripening. 'Northline' is hardy to Zone 2 and bears large and flavorful fruits at a young age on plants only to 6 feet tall. 'Regent' produces good fruit on compact plants 4 to 6 feet tall and wide. 'Smoky' is perhaps the most common commercial cultivar, with large, mildly sweet fruits. 'Thiessen' is very hardy (to Zone 2) and bears large, flavorful fruits on plants to 15 feet tall. It's early-blooming and so may be injured by spring freezes.

In warm climates, pineapple guava is often grown as a landscape plant. It also produces fruits with a juicy pulp that tastes like minty pineapple.

Saskatoon is a true all-season plant: it produces beautiful white blooms in early spring, tasty fruit in summer, and attractive orange and yellow foliage in fall.

Discovering the flavor and variety of the many kinds of grapes is one good reason to grow them yourself.

CHAPTER 8

Grapes for Every Region

According to Aesop's ancient fable, a fox once found a beautiful bunch of grapes growing on a vine just out of his reach. He leaped at it a couple of times and then backed up and took several running jumps, all to no avail. He just couldn't reach the grapes. Finally, he trotted off, muttering, "They're probably too sour to eat anyway." Aesop not only gave us the expression "sour grapes," but he may have helped name the wild North American fox grape as well.

When the early settlers came to America, they brought with them European vines (*Vitis vinifera*). Most of their plantings failed because the Old World grapes could not adapt to the climate, diseases, or insects of eastern North America. Native grapes, however, were thriving, including those the Vikings found when they named the country Vinland. Among them were the fox grape (*Vitis labrusca*), which may get its "foxy" name for its pungent aroma rather than from Aesop's tale. Muscadine grapes (*V. rotundifolia*) grew from Maryland to Florida and west as far as Kansas.

Getting to Know Grapes

'CONCORD' IS A TABLE GRAPE developed in Concord, Massachusetts, in the mid-1800s. Ephraim Bull, a gold beater by trade, abandoned his occupation to experiment with grapes. He is said to have grown more than 22,000 seedlings before he developed the vine that ushered in the American grape industry. A century and a half later, the 'Concord' and its hybrids are still the leading grapes grown in the northeastern United States and southern Canada. These vigorous, hardy vines adapt easily to many different soils and produce an abundance of good-quality fruit for eating, juice, and wine.

The French-American hybrids grown in many areas are another interesting story in breeding. In the nineteenth century, American grape plants were exported to France in an attempt to breed resistance to powdery mildew. Also exported, unknowingly, was the root-feeding grape phylloxera. The American grapes, which had developed with this insect, were resistant. The result in France, however, was the fairly rapid destruction — over just a few years — of the French grape and wine industry. This led to breeding American and French grapes for flavorful hybrids with resistance to both grape phylloxera and powdery mildew. Crosses made with various native grapes and other hybrids have provided us with hundreds of red, white, and blue cultivars, many suitable for home culture.

Grapes are delicious eaten fresh from the vine or made into health-promoting juice, jelly, or wine. The seedless kinds are also good in pies. Grape leaves, picked in early summer, are often used in Mediterranean cooking, as in stuffed grape leaves. You can make wreaths from the dormant vines you prune off. One of the advantages of growing your own grapes is that you avoid the chemical sprays that commercial growers are likely to apply.

The secret to growing good grapes is pruning. Because grapes grow so vigorously, a lot of wood must be cut away each year — often as much as 90 percent — once plants reach maturity. Unpruned grapevines become so overgrown and dense that the sun can't reach into the areas where the fruits should form, and the lack of air circulation gives diseases a green light. Also, the greater the distance from the main stem that the grapes are produced, the smaller the crop is likely to be. Because vines tend to produce more fruit than the plants can support, thinning out some fruit clusters is required. A bonus is that this thinning improves yields, too.

Most grapes are self-fruitful, so you can plant just one. There are exceptions, and a nursery will usually indicate when a pollinator is necessary for a particular cultivar. Some muscadines, for example, are female and will need a self-fertile cultivar nearby.

Grape Fast Facts

USDA Hardiness Zones: European, 6–9; French-American, 5–9; native, 4–9; muscadine, 8–10

Height: Depends on the support structure

Spacing: 8 feet; muscadines, 16 feet

Pollination: Most grapes are self-fruitful, so cross-pollination seldom necessary

Pruning: French-American and native types, cane pruning; European and muscadine types, spur pruning; remove 70 percent or more of top growth each year

Special requirements: Rigorous annual pruning; thinning fruit clusters

Years to bearing: 3–4 (remove any flowers the first 2 years, so plants will develop strong roots)

Yield per vine: 5–15 pounds; muscadines, 30–60 pounds

'Concord' grapes are the variety you'll find in most kinds of grape juice. They're very cold hardy and commonly grown in the Northeast.

'Niagara' is a white table grape that is also processed into juice and wine, particularly in areas where other white grapes aren't hardy.

'Golden Muscat' is a golden table grape with a citrusy flavor. It's best grown in hot, dry climates.

'Merlot' is a very common red wine grape that is most often grown on the West Coast.

Choices for Cold and Hot Climates

CLIMATE IS A limiting factor in growing grapes. The minimum temperature for most European cultivars is about –10°F; it's –15°F for the hardier French-American hybrids and most American cultivars. The hardiest American cultivars should survive temperatures below –15°F. This effectively rules out Zones 3 and 4 and parts of Zone 5 as prime grape-growing country.

The length of the growing season is also a factor. Grapes are one of the last fruit plants to start growth in the spring, and they blossom much later than any of the tree fruits. Most grapes require at least 150 continuous frost-free days:

- 'Concord' grapes and northern natives, along with their cultivars, need the shortest season, 150 days or fewer.
- Early-maturing European cultivars will produce in areas with at least 160 frost-free days.
- European and French-American hybrids need a growing season of 170 to 180 days.
- Late-ripening European cultivars need 200 days
- Muscadines need 200 frost-free days.

Muscadines are warm-climate grapes that produce large, flavorful fruit with a thick skin.

If you garden in Zones 6 to 8, you'll have little trouble growing most grapes offered by nurseries. In the Deep South and other regions in Zones 8 to 10, consider growing muscadines, which tolerate heat. Muscadines won't survive below 0°F, so they're not an option for much of the country. In short-season areas, such as the Dakotas, Minnesota, northern New England, and Canada, look for those cultivars that require fewer than 120 warm days to ripen their fruit.

Some of the hardy Minnesota cultivars withstand temperatures colder than –15°F. In Zones 3 and 4, you may be able to grow these hardier cultivars by planting them in heat pockets. A heat pocket is a site where a building, a wall, or a hill forms a cove, or a corner faces southeast. This location protects against the cooling north wind and traps the warm sunshine in spring and fall. South-facing slopes warm up faster than north-facing ones, and light, sandy soils warm up faster than clay.

In northern Vermont, where the climate is often compared with that of the Arctic, we know of a steep southerly slope that drops sharply to a small lake. It's protected by woods and hills and gets all the morning and mid-afternoon sun. Here, year after year, the late-ripening 'Concord' has found a perfect home. It's protected from the wind, tilts toward the sun, and is warmed by the gentle air currents arising from the lake on cool fall nights.

Climate isn't the only factor in determining which type(s) of grape to grow. Look for disease-resistant cultivars, especially if you live in a humid area prone to grape diseases. Some cultivars are listed as resistant to skin cracking. "Cracking" or "splitting" refers to soft fruit skins splitting, which enables disease organisms to enter and fruit to spoil; this happens more often after a heavy rain. Also take note of what part of the season a particular grape ripens in. Those ripening late are less prone to being eaten by birds. Consider growth habit and vigor, too.

Some grapes are multipurpose; others are more specialized. Choose your cultivars according to whether you want them for table use, juice and jelly, or wine making. Some good for fresh eating also make good juice, and juice is what you need for making jelly and wine. Muscadine cultivars are sweeter than the species, and although good fresh, they're best in jams and for a sweet dessert wine. A few cultivars often used for wine are quite tasty eaten fresh, but don't assume this as a general rule. Be bold and experiment with different applications, but choose cultivars suited to your intended use.

Why not start out with one or two of the old reliable 'Concords' if your season is long enough, one of the newer Minnesota cultivars if you live where it's cold, or one of the muscadines if you live in the South? Add others one by one, as your skill improves. Who knows, you may one day become known as the Bacchus of your block.

Grapes Need Support

GRAPES ARE VINES, and they need something to climb on. A support system of one or two wires installed between posts makes it easy to prune and train vines. Because they get heavy when laden with fruit, make sure the posts are sturdy and well anchored.

Figure out how much space you need before you order plants or install posts. Posts should be 7 to 9 feet long, as you need a finished height of at least 5 feet, and you must sink them 2 to 3 feet into the ground. If you have more than one row, keep the rows at least 8 feet apart. You'll need to install a post midway between each plant and one on each end of the row. Space vines about 8 feet apart; space vigorous American cultivars slightly more, the less robust European cultivars slightly less. Because muscadines are more vigorous, figure on posts 16 to 20 feet apart and only one plant between posts.

String strands of smooth 9- to 11-gauge wire between the posts. To keep the wires from sagging under the weight of fruit-laden vines, install bracing wires attached to each end post, or extend the wires and bury them around an anchor (called a deadman) in the ground. For the anchor, use a tree anchor that landscapers use, a screw anchor, or an object such as a cinderblock buried 2 to 3 feet to which the wire is attached. Finally, install a turnbuckle or other means of tightening on the wire between the end post and where it enters the ground, as well as one on the other side of the end post to tighten the wires the vines are growing on. Install the first trellis wire 2 to 3 feet above the ground and the second 2 to 3 feet higher.

TIPS FOR GROWING GRAPES

- Choose a site with well-drained soil and good air drainage. In colder climates, look for a warm pocket; avoid a low area that is subject to early frosts.
- Select one or more disease-resistant cultivars adapted for your area.
- Install supports. Plant vines 8 feet apart (16 feet for muscadines), in rows 8 to 9 feet apart. Mulch to control weeds.
- Plant in spring. If vines were not pruned before purchase, cut back to two or four plump buds after planting.
- Water frequently the first year. In subsequent years, water only if there's a drought, and fertilize lightly in early spring.
- Weed as needed, being careful not to disturb roots.
- Prune as described on page 110.
- Watch for pests and diseases. Use bird netting, if necessary, as grapes ripen.
- Harvest when grapes are sweet and fully ripe, not when they change color, which is usually too early.

Five Training Options

1. The easiest way for beginners to manage a backyard vineyard is on a two-wire fence using a method called the four-cane **Kniffien system**. After a couple of years of training, you end up with a main trunk supporting four shoots, or "canes," two on each wire trained to grow in opposite directions away from the trunk. This system is particularly suited for American cultivars, whose shoots tend to grow downward, and those of moderate to low vigor.
2. The **single high-wire system** is generally used for muscadines, if they're not grown on a trellis. With this system, all but two canes are removed. These remaining canes are trained to grow along a single wire located 4 to 6 feet off the ground, one cane in each direction from the trunk. If these canes are allowed to hang, they form a curtain effect, hence the alternate name, curtain system. When trained in an arching manner from the top of the trunk, forming an umbrella shape, this is called the umbrella system. The single-wire system, often called high-wire cordon, is best suited for vigorous cultivars, as the upper canes would shade any lower ones if they were trained in the two-tier Kniffen method.

   A cross of these first two is the **umbrella Kniffen system** of training. It's similar to the high-wire cordon in that vines are trained only from a point onto two high wires. Instead of being trained along these upper wires, though, they're allowed to hang down to form an arching or umbrella (in two dimensions) shape. These shoots are then tied to the lower wires. This method is often used for vigorous American grapes.

3. For the European cultivars and most French-American hybrids, a single low-wire system (often called a **low-wire cordon**) is effective because shoots of these grapes tend to grow upward. Similar to the high-wire, train two canes along the wires but use only the lower wires, one cane in each direction. The upper wire will hold shoots that grow off the canes. You may need a couple of strings or wires in between to help support the shoots as they grow upward, or strings between the wires to which you tie the canes.

High-wire cordon

Vines aren't pruned quite as severely in this system. The second winter, leave 8 to 10 buds on each cane (as opposed to the four or five in step 3 of the four-cane Kniffen system; see page 110). The third and subsequent winters, cut back future fruiting canes to 15 to 20 buds, more for vigorous, mature plants.

Either single-wire system is worth considering if you live in a cold climate, as it makes it easier to provide winter protection. Remove each vine in late fall and lay it on the ground, then cover it with straw or soil for winter protection. (Soil is best if you have mice and voles, which may live in straw and eat bark from the vines.) Remove the covering as soon as the frost leaves the ground before buds swell, and reattach to wires.

4. A simple option for small gardens is **umbrella or head training** of grapevines. This system requires only one stake and takes up less space, but yields are lower. If you don't need many grapes, this could be the system for you. It's the best for growing grapes in a large container, too. Once the vines mature, the trunk is self-supporting and no stake is needed.

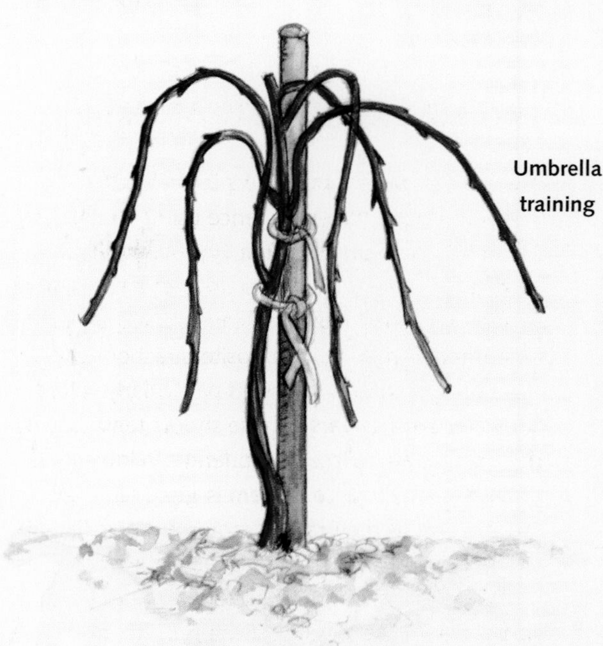

Umbrella training

5. Another option is growing grapes on a sturdy **trellis or pergola**. If you are thinking of growing grapes in a more ornamental manner, keep in mind that vines on latticework, arbors, and trellises are particularly difficult to prune. If your goal is shade rather than a huge crop of grapes, you don't have to prune as hard, but you still must prune the vines to keep them healthy and under control.

Low-wire cordon

Planting and Care

CHOOSE A SITE with good air circulation. In cooler climates, a southern-facing slope may give you a slightly longer growing season. If you don't have such a spot, try creating a heat trap. Fiberglass fences, plastic tents, and other artificial structures can be used to intensify and hold heat for sun-worshiping grapes. It also helps to mulch vines with clear plastic or crushed rock, both of which attract and hold heat better than do organic mulches. Avoid a low spot; it may be a frost pocket. Orient rows north to south if possible, so vines get maximum light.

The ideal soil for grapes is slightly sandy, so it will warm up fast and stay warm. Grapes tolerate many soils, though, as long as they're well drained, including ones that are quite rocky. The soil pH should be between 5.5 and 6.5. American grapes grow best in more acidic soils (pH 5.0 to 6.0), and European grapes grow best with a pH closer to neutral (6.0 to 7.0). Soils should not be excessively fertile, or vines will grow too fast and won't bear well. Grapevines have deep roots and can go searching for their nourishment better than can most other small fruits.

Prepare the site as described on page 221. Before you plant, make sure the site is free of perennial weeds. Work in some compost; abundant organic

Growing Grapes in Containers

Grapes are adaptable to growing in containers, great for a small garden, a balcony, or a patio. They tend to put on only as much top growth as root growth, so if the roots are confined, the tops will grow in proportion. A 5-gallon pail or pot, with good drainage holes, works well and is easier to move about than a larger pot. Large clay pots and wooden containers (not treated with toxic chemicals) are more attractive than plastic. Unlike many other plants, grapes do better in a sandy loam than in a soilless potting mix. If you don't have such a soil, mix (by volume) 7 parts potting soil, 3 parts peat moss, and 2 parts sand. Unless your pot is next to a trellis, anchor a stake or frame within the pot. When planting in a wooden tub, simply tie the stake to U-shaped nails on the sides. Otherwise, drill holes in the rim of a plastic container to affix support wires. Train to an umbrella form, as shown on page 107.

Choose cultivars with fruit clusters close to the trunk rather than toward the ends of canes. Try 'Canadice' or 'Interlaken' seedless cultivars, or the seeded 'Seyval' and 'Swenson Red'.

Water regularly, but reduce watering in late summer. Fertilize weekly the first year, and monthly in subsequent years, with a low-concentration product (or an ordinary fertilizer at half the recommended rate), but stop in midsummer to start plants on the process of hardening off for the winter. Don't overfertilize, or you may get all leaves and no fruit.

As with trellis grapes, train into a trunk with several shoots or canes. Allow four shoots to develop the second year, then prune these back in late winter to spurs, each with two or three buds. In subsequent years, remove all fruiting wood similarly, leaving a few buds to develop fruiting shoots the coming year.

In the second year, remove flower clusters, then allow only one per shoot to develop in the third year. Subsequently, when plants are more established, keep 10 to 15 clusters per vine in a 5-gallon pot (15 or so for larger pots, no more than 10 for less vigorous plants).

Where temperatures drop below freezing, move grapes growing in pots to a nonfreezing location (as an unheated garage or shed, for example) for winter protection. Keep soil just barely moist while plants are dormant.

Each spring before growth begins, slip the plant out of the pot to check the roots. If roots crowd the pot, prune off some and loosen the others. Gently knock off some of the old soil and repot in fresh soil.

matter is especially beneficial in heavy clay soils. You don't need to incorporate fertilizer before planting. Avoid feeding plants with anything other than compost for the first 2 years: Too much fertilizer increases the chance of winter injury. Once plants start bearing, overfertilizing may delay the coloring and ripening of the fruit.

In most of North America, spring planting is best because grapes need an abundance of heat and sunlight to get established before winter. This may be early February to mid-March in warm climates and April to mid-May in cooler areas.

Buy plants locally whenever possible, as some states have restrictions on shipping grapes and you'll get cultivars best suited to your area. Make sure they're certified disease- and pest-free. Look for the highest grade of 1-year-old vines. Two-year-old plants may have been grown from weak, leftover plants from the previous year.

Install supports before planting, as described on page 105. Set most vines about 8 feet apart, vigorous American cultivars slightly farther apart, and muscadines 16 to 20 feet apart. You can add a string between the lower and top wires of the trellis to help support the vines the first year. A stake, tied to the wires, works also. Make sure tendrils attach to the support and not to the vine itself; otherwise, they may end up strangling the young vine.

Grapes bought in containers have probably already been pruned, or are established, so they don't need pruning. When you buy vines bare-root, however, you may need to cut them back to 5 or 6 inches long and leave just two or three fat buds. This pruning will encourage the roots to start growing rapidly and help them to keep up with the top growth.

Water well to settle the soil around the roots. Water the vines frequently the first year. Use an organic mulch such as straw the first year to help retain soil moisture and decrease the need to weed. If you cultivate around plants to control weeds, keep it shallow (1 to 3 inches deep) to avoid injuring roots. Allow vines to grow freely without further pruning the first year.

In subsequent years, plants won't need watering unless you garden in an area with little rainfall. The vigorously growing muscadines will need some watering regardless of the climate. Avoid wetting leaves while the fruits are forming, as this promotes fruit rot diseases.

Grapes don't need much fertility. Spread compost around plants yearly. If your soils are reasonably fertile, you may not need to add fertilizer. Or apply a balanced organic fertilizer according to directions. (If the label doesn't give amounts for grapes, use half the amount recommended for other fruits and ornamentals.) Better to fertilize too little than too much, as excess fertility reduces yields (and in muscadines, it causes fruit drop).

In cool climates, cultivation is better than mulch for weed control after the first year. Grapes need warm soils to grow well and to fruit abundantly, and mulches keep soils cooler. In warm but dry climates, though, mulching may reduce the need for supplemental watering.

Grapes must establish a good root system to support the plants for the long haul (maybe 50 years!), so during the first couple of years, don't let them put energy into fruits. Remove any flowers the first two years, the first three years if plants aren't vigorous. This pruning will pay off in the long term.

If grape culture at first glance looks a bit involved, don't worry. Once you learn and master the basics, it will become second nature.

If your yard has a south-facing stone wall, consider growing grapes along it, to take advantage of the warm microclimate the wall creates.

THE KNIFFEN SYSTEM

Spring, year one

Summer, year two

Essential Pruning

Pruning is an important part of grape culture, and one that must not be neglected. Don't be afraid of doing it wrong. Plants will grow back if you don't get it quite right. And, in fact, there isn't any exact way to prune, as the method varies with the shoots and growth on each plant. With grapes, it's better to err on the side of pruning more than too little. Just keep in mind the following simple principles and basics, and the process won't be overwhelming. You'll see this as soon as you begin pruning.

- Grapes produce more top growth than roots can support.
- Grapes bear fruit on 1-year-old wood; the goal is to remove older wood and keep new growth coming.
- For the best fruit, remove 70 to 90 percent of the wood produced the previous year — more in warm climates, where plants are more vigorous.
- Grapes vary in vigor with the season, climate, and cultivar; prune back vigorous growth more than you would on weaker plants.

The time for pruning is late winter or very early in spring, when the plants are dormant and before the buds start to swell. This is January through March in many areas. Later is better for muscadines, which, if pruned in early spring, may ooze sap, or "bleed." If this happens, don't despair: it doesn't hurt the plants.

In addition to cutting back the vines, and difficult as this may seem, you'll need to prune away or thin out fruit clusters during the season. Grapes may produce more fruit than the plants can handle, decreasing vigor and even stunting young plants. This thinning is more important on cultivars that bear large fruit clusters.

Pruning Grape Vines: Four-Cane Kniffen System

The Kniffen system (cane pruning) is the easiest way to grow grapes. This method is good for most types, especially American cultivars such as 'Concord' and French-American hybrids.

In most climates, one trunk is the goal. In colder areas where trunks may suffer winter injury, keep two trunks, the second as a backup during the first year. At the beginning of the second year, if both are alive, remove the less vigorous trunk. If a trunk suffers an injury in a subsequent year, train a sucker shoot during the following season as a new trunk.

1. After planting, if vines are not already pruned, cut them back to 5 or 6 inches long, leaving two to four buds. Allow shoots to grow from these. Remove any flower buds that form. Loosely tie shoots to the horizontal support wires, or support them with thin stakes, to make sure they grow vertically.
2. In late winter the first year after planting, remove all but one main upright shoot (two in

Summer, year three

Winter, year three

cold climates), which will become the trunk. Remove all side shoots. During the second growing season, train two main side shoots (canes) from the trunk(s) in opposite directions along each wire. Pinch or prune off any other shoots and any flower buds that form. Secure vines loosely until the curling tendrils grasp the wires. Plastic-coated ties (as come with trash bags) work well; tight string can constrict stems as they grow.

3. The second winter, prune back each cane along the wire, leaving four or five buds. These will produce the fruit-bearing shoots in the third season.
4. During the third season, train shoots (from the four or five buds you left on the previous year's canes) along wires. Fruit will develop on this season's new growth. Once fruits begin forming (when grapes are no more than ⅛ inch in diameter), thin clusters to leave only one or two bunches of grapes per new shoot.
5. In the third winter, remove the previous year's fruiting canes, cutting back the horizontal stems along wires. Leave four of these canes (cordons) close to the trunk for each wire. Cut back two canes from each wire to two buds. These are the "renewal spurs" that will form the fruiting canes for the year after the coming one.
   Tie the remaining two canes to the wires, as before, with one in each direction, again leaving four or five buds per cane. These buds will develop into the shoots that will produce the fruit for this coming season. These four shortened canes are called arms. Do this training during mild weather, as cold canes break easily.
6. In subsequent years, repeat steps 4 and 5. Remove the old arm in late winter with the fruiting canes from the past season. Select canes for new arms growing from last year's renewal spur. At this point the plants are larger, so they can support more fruit. During winter cane pruning, you can now leave 10 to 15 buds on each fruiting cane (the higher number for vigorous plants), or a total of 40 to 60 per plant.

Mature vine

SPUR PRUNING FOR MUSCADINES

Before pruning

Muscadine types grow best with a system called spur pruning. This is effective for some wine grapes too, although many are cane-pruned. Follow the same steps as with cane pruning for the first 2 years (see 110). Then continue with these steps:

1. In late winter or early spring of the third year, don't touch the horizontal stems (cordons) along wires; cut back only the previous season's fruiting canes that arose from these, leaving two or three buds per pruned cane (spur). These buds will give rise to the shoots that will produce fruit the next year.
2. Prune out excess spurs so what's left are 6 inches apart along the cordon. The result should be four to six buds per foot of cordon.
3. Once fruits begin forming (when grapes are less than 1⁄8 inch in diameter), thin clusters to leave only one or two bunches of grapes per fruiting shoot.
4. For mature plants, in subsequent years, repeat these three steps. Leave no more than 50 buds per vine (20 to 30 for wine grapes).

After pruning

Diseases

Vines in an isolated home garden usually escape most of the diseases that large growers must cope with. Sooner or later, though, one of the problems described below will show up. Most can be controlled with good sanitation and rigorous pruning for good air circulation. Inspect your vines regularly, as all problems are easier to manage when they're caught early. If you spot just a few infected leaves, remove and destroy them. Problems vary depending on where you live; look for disease-resistant cultivars if you garden in an area prone to plant diseases. Steer clear of the European cultivars that get many of the American diseases if you live in a warm and humid climate and don't want to face such problems and their controls. 'Concord' is fairly disease resistant, as are 'Frontenac', 'Mars', and 'Seyval'. If you experience recurring problems despite good sanitation and decide to spray, check to make sure the product is safe for use on grapes and follow label directions carefully. Never spray grapes when they're in bloom as you risk killing pollinators. Some grapes are sensitive to sprays; don't use sprays containing copper or sulfur on 'Concord' grapes.

Fruit drop on muscadine grapes is usually not a disease problem; inadequate pollination, too much or too little water, and too much fertilizer all can lead to this. Similarly, what appears to be a disease — stunted and deformed growth — may be a reaction to herbicides if these are used nearby, or to a weed-and-feed lawn product such as is used on the grass between rows. Grapes are particularly sensitive to herbicides, so it's best not to use one in the vicinity of grapevines.

Grapes get some of the same diseases as other fruits, such as crown gall, powdery mildew, and viruses (see chapter 18). In addition, be on the watch for the following.

Black rot is a fungal disease, particularly common in eastern and midwestern states. It covers the leaves with brown spots and black pimples, and turns the fruit black, rotten, and shriveled. It can occur any time during the season under warm and wet conditions. Good sanitation by cleaning up old fruit and leaves will help greatly by preventing its spores from overwintering.

Dead arm is a fungus that, if left unchecked, gradually kills a plant. Canes and arms die back, hence its other name, dieback.

Phomopsis on a grapevine

Black rot

Phomopsis cane and leaf spot is similar but less damaging. It appears more often in the humid East and South. The most effective control is to cut off and burn the infected parts, making sure to sterilize pruning tools between cuts. (See Disinfecting Pruning Tools, page 273.)

Downy mildew is an especially serious disease in the humid East. It covers leaves, new shoots, and fruit with a gray down, and eventually rots the fruit. European cultivars are highly susceptible. Bordeaux mixture or powdered sulfur is sometimes used where mildew problems are severe, but a modern fungicide may work better.

Fruit rots are caused by gray mold (botrytis) and several other diseases that flourish when conditions are moderately warm and wet, especially on cultivars with dense fruit clusters. Early in the season, buds and young fruit turn brown. During the season, you may see large, reddish brown dead areas on leaf edges. Fruits turn color and rot. To alleviate the problem, remove infected leaves and prune to improve air circulation.

Insect and Animal Pests

In spite of Aesop, I've never heard of a fox actually eating grapes, but the succulent fruits are favored by raccoons, skunks, and opossums. The best control for these critters is a low electric fence, 6 inches from the ground. In regions where birds steal the fruits, purchase some bird netting. Or grow 'Concord' grapes, which birds usually don't bother. Other bird repellents (for example, aluminum pie plates blowing in the wind) are only marginally effective; placing paper bags over each cluster works only for people with the time and patience for such things.

Fortunately, few insect pests bother home plantings of grapes. Inspect your vines frequently and practice good sanitation to keep insect problems to a minimum. Keep the grapes picked, and remove all prunings to prevent the overwintering of insect larvae. (For general control strategies, such as traps, see chapter 18.)

Even more than diseases, the insects you're likely to encounter depend on your area. In addition to Japanese beetles and aphids, which are familiar pests of other fruits and even ornamentals, you may meet up with leafhoppers, leaf rollers, mites, and nematodes; see chapter 18 for controlling these pests. Here are some other common insect pests to watch for on grapes:

Grape flea beetle

The **cane girdler** is a shiny black weevil that lays its eggs in shoots, girdling them (cutting off the water and nutrient flow inside) around this point. The result you see is shoot tips wilting and dying back, then breaking off. This isn't serious unless fruits are being produced from these shoot tips.

The **grape flea** beetle is a small, steel-blue insect (often called a steely beetle) that emerges from leaf litter in spring to feed on buds and young shoots. Later, it will attack a vine and its leaves. Keep the ground beneath plants clean, areas between rows tilled, and adjacent woodlots and waste areas cleared. Knocking adult beetles into a jar of soapy water may be difficult, as they often jump when disturbed.

The **climbing cutworm** causes similar damage, but later in bud development, and produces more-ragged holes. The larvae are gray or brown, a bit over an inch long, but you aren't likely to see these as they hide in the ground during the day, climbing the stems to feed at night. Keep the ground nearby clear of plant debris, weeds, and sod if this insect shows up.

The **grape berry moth** is the primary source of wormy grapes, and perhaps the main pest in many areas. Tiny, pale, maggotlike larvae feed on flowers and tender young growth in spring, then enter young fruit in order to eat the pulp. Look for the webbing they often encase themselves in, or reddish spots on berries. You can control small infestations by picking off infected fruit. Other

Inspect your vines frequently and practice good sanitation to keep insect problems to a minimum.

Rose chafer

Grape berry moth larva

Skunk

Raccoon

controls are removing leaf litter under plants in fall and using an insecticide spray early in the season.

The **grape root borer** weakens, and may kill, a vine by tunneling and feeding in the larger roots and base of the plant. If a vine appears stressed and wilts easily, check the roots for the white larvae. Keep wild grapes away from desired plants, rake up fallen leaves and debris under plants, and use a plastic mulch should this pest appear.

Phylloxera are small sucking insects similar to aphids (technically lice) that feed on and damage roots. They attack European grapes and are a major pest on the West Coast and in heavy soils. Susceptible grapes are grafted onto resistant rootstocks, as this is the only control other than ensuring that plants are phylloxera-free at the outset. (These pests can live on resistant plants, even if they don't cause damage to them.)

Rose chafers eat blossoms, buds, and newly formed fruits early in the season. The straw-colored beetles, about half an inch long, also skeletonize leaves in June and July. Usually they're most troublesome on vines grown on sandy soil. If there are just a few, knock them off into a jar of soapy water. Check frequently, as more are apt to fly in.

Yellowjackets are familiar to gardeners and nongardeners alike. They're attracted in late summer and fall to the sweet sugars of overripe fruit. They can damage ripe fruits before you get them picked or injure the picker! Keeping fruit picked, and fallen grapes raked up, will help keep away these insects.

Harvesting Grapes

WITH PROPER TRAINING and pruning, a mature grapevine will produce 5 to 15 pounds of grapes (30 to 60 bunches) each year, depending on the cultivar. A mature muscadine yields 30 to 60 pounds of fruit a year. Although you can start getting fruit the third year, try not to let plants bear heavily until vines are at least 4 years old. You may see grapes, other than muscadines, grouped together under the term "bunch grapes." They form their fruit in bunches rather than the loose clusters of a few muscadine fruits that ripen at different times. As muscadines tend to drop when they're ripe, an easy way to harvest is to spread a tarp under the vines and shake them, which causes the ripe grapes to fall.

Muscadines ripen in late summer through early fall. Other grapes ripen as early as July and August in southeastern states. Harvest time in the Northwest is mid-September to mid-October; it's September in the Northeast.

Ripe grapes should be snipped from the vine in whole clusters, leaving the stem handle intact. It's best to harvest on a dry day, so that the grapes keep longer.

Don't rely on skin color to determine whether grapes are ready to pick. Grapes often change color before they're fully ripe. Ripe grapes have brown seeds and taste sweet (if they're table grapes), and the clusters separate easily from the vines. Birds starting to eat your fruit may be an indication of ripeness!

Wine grapes are ready when their sugar content is around 22 percent. This is easy to measure with an inexpensive hygrometer, available at home winemaking–supply stores. Hygrometers measure sugar content using what's called the Brix scale. At 22 percent Brix, grapes yield a wine with 10 to 12 percent alcohol.

Don't pick your grapes early; unlike many other fruits, they won't go on to ripen off the vine. If average temperatures drop below 50°F, fruits won't continue to ripen, nor will they if frost has killed the leaves. If you intend to use the fruit for jelly, though, you can harvest them while they're slightly "green."

Pick grapes on a dry day, as wet grapes don't keep well. Pick whole clusters, leaving the stem "handle" intact. Try not to bruise or rub off the whitish bloom; they'll last longer. Grapes keep in a refrigerator for several weeks if they're dry and the temperature is just above freezing.

Most grapes are usually eaten whole, but muscadines are generally eaten by squeezing and sucking out the pulp. Discard the skins. Such grapes are often called slipskins.

You can dry seedless grapes to make your own raisins. Wash and remove stems and damaged fruit. Dip whole grapes in boiling water for 30 seconds to crack the skins. If you've cut large ones in half, dip them in ascorbic acid for 10 minutes to kill any surface microbes. Drain well after either treatment, then dry using low heat (140°F) or in an electric dehydrator until they're leathery, with no moisture inside. In a warm and arid climate, you can dry them in the sunlight on screens. Just cover the screens with cheesecloth to keep off dust and birds.

Figure on 2 quarts of grapes to make four half-pint jars of jelly, a bushel of grapes to make 16 quarts of juice. To make wine, you'll need about eight bunches for each bottle. A vine that yields 40 bunches should produce enough to make five bottles of wine.

Table and Wine Grape Cultivars

The following are only a few of the many good grapes for eating or using fresh, often called table grapes, and those used primarily for wines. Table-grape cultivars have seeds unless noted otherwise. "FH" are French-American hybrids; "E" are European cultivars, which can be more difficult to grow and less hardy. For color, those listed as black are often more purplish or blue-black; those listed as white are often yellow-green. The season is based relative to that of the 'Concord', a midseason grape. Cultivars are noted as best for certain regions (C = coldest climates, such as northern New England and the Upper Midwest; W = warmest climates, such as the Lower Midwest, the Upper South, and the south-central and mid-Atlantic states; WC = West Coast; NW = Pacific Northwest).

Cultivar	USES	FRUIT	SEASON	REGION	COMMENTS
'Aurore'	wine	white	early	NW, C	FH; hardy, tends to split; good for sweet wine, blending
'Cabernet Sauvignon'	wine	red	late	W, WC, NW	E; the famous red wine of France; needs a long season; susceptible to disease
'Canadice'	table	red	early	C, W, NW	FH; hardy; very sweet; juice; seedless
'Catawba'	table	red	late	W, NW, C	Hardy; needs a long growing season
'Cayuga'	wine	white	mid	C, W	FH; hardy, late blooming; vigorous, high yields; light, dry wine
'Chambourcin'	wine	black	mid	W	FH; tart, red claret wine with peppery and spicy flavors
'Chardonnay'	wine	white	early	W, WC	E; top white wine grape; fruit may crack after rain; best on West Coast
'Concord'	table	blue	mid	C, NW, W	Hardy; juice (main juice cultivar), wine; also found as a seedless cultivar
'Delaware'	wine	red	early	C, W	Native; hardy; best on fertile soils; fruit may crack with rain; mild flavor
'Frontenac'	wine	blue	mid	C	Hardy; good disease resistance; large clusters of small fruit
'Gewürztraminer'	table, wine	white	early	WC, NW	E; good in cooler regions; good table use; sweet wine
'Golden Muscat'	table	golden	mid	C, W, NW	Fruit cracks after rain, so best in a hot, dry climate; citrus flavor; large fruit
'Himrod'	table	white	early	C, W, NW	Hardy; golden when ripe; honeylike flavor; cane-prune; seedless
'Maréchal Foch' ('Foch')	wine	black	very early	W, WC	FH; hardy; fruity, light wines or burgundy type
'Mars'	table	blue	early	W	Hardy; disease resistant; vigorous; good for the South; seedless
'Merlot'	wine	black	mid	WC	Imparts berry notes to wine; best for drier regions
'Neptune'	table	white	mid	W	Resists cracking; large clusters; mild and fruity; good for the South; seedless
'Niagara'	table	white	mid	C, W, NW	Hardy; wine, juice; most popular native white
'Pinot Gris'	wine	white	late	WC, NW	Thought a mutant clone of Pinot Noir, Italian clone is Pinot Grigio

Table and Wine Grape Cultivars *(continued)*

Cultivar	USES	FRUIT	SEASON	REGION	COMMENTS
'Reliance'	table	red	mid	W	FH; hardy; skins may crack in wet weather; juice; good for the South; seedless
'Riesling'	wine	white	late	W, WC, NW	E; dry to sweet wines, flowery aroma; best on West Coast; top white wine grape
'Sauvignon Blanc'	wine	white	mid	WC, NW	May get gray mold; good flavor; top white wine grape; prefers a dry climate
'Seyval'	wine	white	mid	C, W, WC	FH; high yields, disease resistant; prune heavily; good for the South
'Syrah' ('Shiraz')	wine	red	early	WC, NW	E; popular in France, Australia, and California
'Thompson' ('Thompson seedless')	table	white	late	WC	The standard found in stores; thin for larger fruit; good in Southwest
'Vanessa'	table	red	early	C, NW	FH; hardy; resists cracking, some pest resistance; juice, pies; seedless
'Venus'	table	blue-black	early	W	FH; red-orange fall leaves; juice; seedless; good for the South
'Vidal' (blanc)	wine	white	late	WC, W	FH; heavy yield, mildew resistant; needs a long season
'Vignoles' ('Ravat')	wine	white	mid	WC, W	FH; late to flower; sweet wine with high acidity
'Worden'	table	blue	early	C	Similar to 'Concord' but hardier (Zone 4); vigorous; few problems; good for short seasons
'Zinfandel'	wine	red	mid	WC	E; best in mild climates

Muscadine (Scuppernong) Cultivars

Most muscadine cultivars are self-fertile. Those marked (F) are female; these cultivars require a self-fertile cultivar with male flowers for cross-pollination. (These may be listed in catalogs as "male.") Those with pink or red to bronze skins are often called scuppernongs. Following are some of the more popular and better cultivars.

Cultivar	FRUIT COLOR	SEASON	COMMENTS
'Black Beauty'	black	mid	F; large fruit, edible skin, good black
'Carlos'	bronze	early	Good for wine or juice
'Darlene'	bronze	mid	F; large uniform fruit, one of the best bronzes
'Ison'	black	early	Good pollinator; large clusters, good yields
'Jumbo'	black	mid	F; large fruit; disease resistant; sweet
'Fry'	bronze	late	F; vigorous; large clusters; high yields
'Nesbit'	black	mid	One of the more cold tolerant
'Noble'	black	early	Some cold tolerance; good for red wine
'Supreme'	black	mid	F; very large fruit; resists disease; edible skin
'Tara'	bronze	mid	Sweet, similar to 'Fry'

Unusual Vine Fruits

Hardy kiwi. When most people think of kiwifruit, they're thinking about the brown fuzzy fruit the size of an egg sold in stores. This is the common or fuzzy kiwi (*Actinida deliciosa*), sometimes known as the Chinese gooseberry. It needs to be peeled, revealing a soft green pulp with small edible seeds. Less well known is the Chinese or golden kiwi (*A. chinensis*). Fruits of the Chinese kiwi are less fuzzy (more like the skin of a peach) and more rounded, with green or gold flesh. Both species are tender and can't be grown in areas colder than Zone 8.

But don't despair if you want to grow kiwis and live in a colder climate. The hardy kiwi (*A. arguta*) and the arctic or Russian kiwi (*A. kolomikta*) both grow in Zones 5 to 8, even colder for some selections. Plants need at least 150 frost-free days to bear fruit, and some chilling, although they're adaptable to low-chill areas. In cold-climate regions, spring frosts can nip the early flowers, and even the pollen may be damaged by cold, which will cause uneven fruiting.

Hardy kiwi is a vigorous, cold-hardy vine that produces a bounty of small fruits that are smaller than, but similar to, their tropical cousins.

The hardy kiwi is usually grown for its fruits. The less vigorous arctic is often grown as an ornamental, for its variegated leaves; these start out purplish, then turn green with some white and pink. Both these kiwis bear smaller fruits than do their more tropical kin, with a sweeter flavor. (Botanically, they're berries.) They produce fruits the size of large grapes, greenish with perhaps reddish tints, with smooth skin that doesn't need peeling. The fruits are sweeter than those of the common kiwi (sugar content of 15 to 30 percent, depending on the cultivar).

Kiwis are vigorous vines, often growing 20 feet in a season, so they need sturdy supports. You can grow them on a trellis system similar to the one used for grapes. The more usual method, however, is to grow them on T-shaped supports, 6 to 8 feet high, with wires strung between them. The look is of a very sturdy clothesline. Vines climb by twining rather than with tendrils, so they need some help in attaching to a trellis. They make effective visual screens too, or grow on a pergola to shade the patio.

The vines are ornamental, sporting large, heart-shaped leaves that tend to hide the slightly fragrant but rather inconspicuous greenish spring flowers. Male and female flowers grow on separate plants; thus, you'll need a male plant so the females will bear. Plant at least one male for every six to nine female vines, and of course in close proximity. Some cultivars may be self-fruitful, but, as with many other such fruits, even these produce higher yields with cross-pollination. Fruiting usually begins when plants are at least 5 years old. Then, kiwifruit ripen in early fall.

Kiwi vines are easy to grow. They produce best in full sun, although they'll tolerate some shade. Give them somewhat acidic (pH 5.0–6.5) and well-drained soil and plenty of water during the season. Plant about 10 feet apart in soil enriched with compost, or, in a warm climate, grow in large containers. Don't fertilize the first year. Wait until the second year, then fertilize lightly, and increase the amount a little each year after. Compost helps, as does straw mulch; just keep the mulch away from the stems to prevent rot.

Maypop is a hardier version of the tropical passionflower. It produces stunning, unusual flowers followed by delicious fruits that taste something like guava.

Because kiwi vines are quite vigorous, you'll need to prune heavily, almost as much as for grapes. Allow them to put on as much growth as possible the first season. Flowers form on the previous year's growth, so when you do start pruning, don't remove these shoots. Prune when dormant. Shoots more than 3 years old seldom produce flowers, so remove these. During the growing season, cut back as desired, or so just a few leaves are left beyond the last flower. In summer, cut off vigorous upright shoots (water sprouts) as well.

Problems are rare. Crown and root rots, gray mold, and powdery mildew are diseases that may attack the hardy kiwi. Well-drained soil and good air circulation will aid in disease prevention. Plants may be troubled by scales, nematodes, spider mites, leaf rollers, thrips, and Japanese beetles. Like catnip, kiwis seem to attract cats, which uproot and shred plants. A chicken-wire cylinder around stems will keep away the neighborhood felines.

Expect mature hardy kiwis to yield 50 to 100 pounds of fruit per (female) vine, depending on the season and cultivar. As with some apples, kiwis may bear heavier crops on alternate years, with little or no fruit in between. Pick fruits before they're fully ripe, while they're still tart, and they'll continue to ripen. To speed up the ripening process, put them in a plastic bag together with an apple or a banana (both give off ethylene gas, which promotes ripening of fruits). They'll keep several weeks in the refrigerator.

Maypop. For a vine with stunning flowers and delicious edible fruits, grow the hardiest of the passionflowers, the maypop (*Passiflora incarnata*). This temperate version of the tropical passionflower is native to the southern states, but also grows well in the Midwest, West, and Mid-Atlantic regions (Zones 6 to 9).

The attractive, climbing vine grows 8 to 12 feet long and produces glossy, deeply cut leaves that are 6 inches wide and long. It serves as a good ornamental plant for fences and trellises. Because of its sprawling habit, it's best planted in informal and natural gardens. Maypop is also fairly low maintenance; prune as needed to direct growth. In regions where the top growth dies in winter, cut the vine back to the ground in spring

In summer, unusual rounded, purplish white flowers give way to egg-shaped fruit that starts off greenish and turns light orange when ripe. True to its name, the fruit goes "pop" when broken. Eat the jellylike pulp around the seeds, as you would a pomegranate. The flavor resembles that of guava. The vines do need cross-pollination, so you must grow at least two in order to get fruit.

PART THREE

Tree Fruits *and* Nuts

Once you've grown a few small fruits, try your hand at tree fruits (like apricot, above) and nuts (like hazelnut, in flower at right). They require more of an investment of time and money, but will produce a large harvest, year after year.

THE FIRST IMAGE THAT COMES TO MIND WHEN many hear the word "trees" is a huge specimen in a lawn or park or forest. This applies to many nut trees, which may require a considerable area, but there are some — such as almonds, filberts, and hazelnuts — that are suited for small properties. Most fruit trees you now find for sale are of smaller stature, either as semidwarfs or dwarfs (see page 34), and even some newer upright columnar selections. Fruit trees, particularly apples and pears, lend themselves to growing vertically in two-dimensional espalier patterns (see page 253) where space is limited, or to create a more visually interesting garden or landscape.

To ensure success with tree fruits and nuts, you'll need to give them a bit more forethought before buying, and ground preparation before planting, than you might with the small fruits. One reason is that just a few fruit trees can produce many bushels of fruit, so you don't want to end up with lots more than you can eat or put away for winter. If you do end up with an excess, local food pantries are usually happy to help you put it to good use.

Fruit and nut trees will be in one place for many years, so good ground preparation and proper planting are essential. Small fruits are in the ground fewer years than tree fruits generally, or are easier to move if misplaced. Tree fruits and nuts usually grow much taller than the small fruits, and this needs to be allowed for when you're planning, both to avoid obstructing views and utilities, and to avoid casting shade where it's not wanted — on your sun-loving perennials, for example.

It's also important to pay attention to the right choices of tree fruits for your particular region and climate. Factors such as the length of the growing season, the amount of cold needed to flower and fruit, and timing of flowering are crucial to success with many tree fruit cultivars, with specific details following in the individual chapters.

Growing your own apples enables you to try a wide variety of shapes, colors, and tastes.

CHAPTER 9

Apples and Crab Apples

When the wicked old witch selected an apple to tempt the beautiful Snow White, she knew exactly what she was doing. So did the serpent when he made his proposal in the Garden of Eden. We grow many different kinds of fruits, and I love them all, but every time a nursery catalog arrives, I automatically turn to the apple section first, to be tempted by the best new selections.

Despite the expression "as American as apple pie," the apple (genus *Malus*) came to this country from elsewhere. As early as 8000 BCE, nomads moved apples throughout the Fertile Crescent of the Mideast. Homer, in his Odyssey (800 BCE), makes mention of apples. In China, around 5000 BCE, a diplomat was recorded as having given up his job in order to concentrate on grafting fruit trees, including apples.

Apples for Every Climate

ONE GOOD REASON for the apple's popularity among home fruit gardeners is its ability to adapt to different soils and climates. One cultivar or another will grow in all 50 states, and home gardeners everywhere have a good selection from which to choose. Many popular cultivars will grow in many regions. Gardeners where winters are mild, such as southern California and Florida, should seek out apples that require very little cold during winter (see page 142). Most apples need more than 600 hours below 45°F; some require more than 1,000. Low-chill cultivars need less than 500 hours.

Apples are among the hardiest of tree fruits, and many cultivars will grow where peaches, apricots, and pears haven't a chance of survival. There are apples that will thrive in the northern, windswept prairies of Saskatchewan and Alberta. During the big freeze in the winter of 1917, when temperatures stayed below –40°F for days, many tender apple varieties in the northern United States and Canada were knocked out, including the then-popular 'Jonathan'. This event paved the way for increased planting of the hardy Canadian 'McIntosh' and other members of its huge family.

'Cox's Orange Pippin'

'Jonagold'

'Egremont Russet'

'Granny Smith'

Apple Fast Facts

USDA Hardiness Zones: 3–9 (varies with cultivar)

Height: Standard, 20–30 feet; semidwarf, 12–15 feet; dwarf, 7–10 feet

Spacing: Standard, 25–35 feet; semidwarf, 15–20 feet; dwarf, 7–10 feet

Pollination: Need cross-pollination; plant at least two cultivars for good yield

Pruning: Central leader (modified central leader for mature trees); late winter

Special requirement: Thin fruits to improve quality of harvest

Years to bearing: Standard, 5–8; semidwarf, 3–5; dwarf, 2–4

Yield per tree (bushels): Standard, 8–18; semidwarf, 4–10; dwarf, 1–6

Pollination Matters

You must plant at least two cultivars near each other for cross-pollination by bees. Even the few cultivars listed as self-fertile (such as 'Liberty', 'Empire', and 'Golden Delicious') will produce more with cross-pollination. "Near" means within 75 feet for standards, 45 feet for semidwarf, and 20 feet for dwarf cultivars. In a large planting, it means every third tree in a mixed row or every fifth row of single-cultivar rows. If you have lots of ornamentals, even weeds such as dandelions, in flower at the same time, you may find the bees are lured away by these and won't pollinate your apple trees as well as they might. You need to make it easy for bees to find the different apple trees.

Just have one tree? Then place a few branches you get from a friend's apples or a crab apple in bloom into a bucket of water hung within the tree. Where space is too limited for two trees, seek out a tree with at least two cultivars grafted onto it; that will solve the problem.

Often, a crab apple flowering nearby at the same time will suffice. Be aware, though, that crab apples are susceptible to the same diseases as are apple trees. For that reason, if you don't need them for pollination it's a good idea to site your apple trees at least 100 yards away from ornamental crab apples unless you know they're disease resistant.

'Winesap', 'Mutsu', 'Jonagold', and some other apples are infertile, which is usually mentioned in their descriptions. This means they produce no pollen, or sterile pollen, to cross-pollinate another apple cultivar. You need another apple cultivar to pollinate a 'Baldwin', but it can't reciprocate, so if you have a 'Baldwin' or another infertile cultivar,

TIPS FOR CHOOSING APPLES

For the best crops for your conditions, consider the following.

- Tree size: dwarf, 7–10 feet tall; semidwarf, 12–15 feet; standard, more than 15 feet. Yields proportional to tree size
- Suitability to climate (cold or warm winters), problem soils
- Resistance to pests and diseases
- Flowering time: buy at least two cultivars, flowering near the same time, for cross-pollination
- Fruit qualities: color, flavor, and texture (crisp or soft), best uses
- Yield: desired ripening times, whether biennial or annual bearing

you'll actually need three trees: the 'Baldwin', a second cultivar to pollinate it, and a third cultivar to pollinate the second.

As there are so many apples varieties, there's quite a range of bloom times. Make sure cultivars blossom at the same time. As a rule, apples are divided into early, mid-, and late season. Apples usually bloom over about 10 days, so there's some overlap: an early apple generally will pollinate a midseason one and midseason cultivars can pollinate most early- and late-season ones.

If all this information about pollination sounds complicated, just look in catalogs for tables that show what cultivars will cross-pollinate each other. Flowering time may be listed as pollination group; if you don't see this information in cultivar descriptions, ask at your local nursery or Cooperative Extension Service whether the trees you want to buy will cross-pollinate.

Emerging bud

Apple blossom, ready to open

Developing fruit

Ripe fruit

Standard, Semidwarf, or Dwarf?

AS YOU STUDY various fruit catalogs, you may be surprised that sometimes the same apple cultivar is available as a full-size standard, a medium-size tree (semidwarf), and a small (dwarf) tree. This is due in large part to the rootstock — the trunk and roots onto which the apple cultivar is grafted. Tree size varies also with vigor of the cultivar grafted onto the rootstock, soil fertility, tree age, climate, and of course pruning practices. A "standard" tree to which dwarf and semidwarf are compared may be 40 feet high in one area, 30 feet in another, and 15 feet in the Far North because of these factors.

If you have space enough for large trees, don't mind working on a ladder, and want a huge, old-fashioned, spreading tree for kids to climb, by all means grow standard (full-sized) apples. If you don't want them too tall, do as we do: prune to keep them low. Although full-size trees require more pruning than their dwarf and semidwarf relatives do, and make it more difficult to manage pests, as a rule they suffer from fewer diseases, live longer, bear more fruit, and in the coldest climates are more hardy. Most people opt for dwarf or semidwarf apples, as they don't have the room for two full-sized trees and don't want to wait 5 to 8 years for fruit. Dwarf apples should bear 2 to 4 years after planting; semidwarfs usually begin in 3 to 5 years.

Understanding Rootstocks

There is really no other plant crop for which so much attention is paid to the roots! Almost any apple tree you buy is grafted onto a rootstock. The main reason for this is to control ultimate tree size (not fruit size). A particular rootstock may also be used to make a tree hardier or more tolerant of a particular soil type, to confer some pest or disease resistance, to control suckering, or to provide strong roots for better anchorage in windy areas.

You don't have to worry about the rootstock — what you do need to know is how tall the tree you're buying will get, so you'll know how much space it requires and how much pruning. Learning about the rootstock onto which your apple is grafted, however, gives you helpful information, such as whether you'll need to stake the young plant. Many of the dwarfing rootstocks have a poor root system that won't anchor a tree well, so trees may topple or lean if not staked. If a rootstock is said to sucker — producing vigorous shoots from the base — just plant it deeper. As you get more involved in apple growing, you can custom-order rootstock combinations from specialty nurseries or even create your own tree by grafting.

You may see the term "interstem," which refers to grafting the main cultivar onto a stem section, which in turn is grafted onto the rootstock, making two graft unions. The purpose is to impart traits of both, such as vigor and soil adaptability from a rootstock and hardiness from the interstem.

Before cloned rootstocks came into prominence in the middle of the 20th century, apple cultivars were generally grafted onto seedlings. This is still the norm in many lesser-developed parts of the world. Seedlings were brought to North America by the early settlers, and were used through the 1800s, even after dwarfing rootstocks had begun to be imported. Seeds were most often collected from juice and processing operations. Although they may

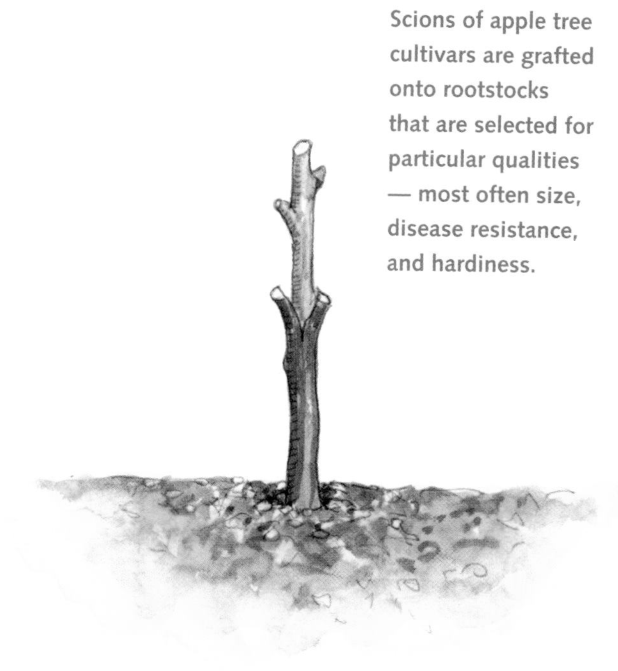

Scions of apple tree cultivars are grafted onto rootstocks that are selected for particular qualities — most often size, disease resistance, and hardiness.

result in a fairly uniform stand of trees, those trees won't bear as early or be as productive compared to apples grafted onto rootstocks. A few named seedlings are still used for grafting, such as Antanovka, used in Europe for cold hardiness and the recent Novole from New York, which shows some resistance to vole damage and certain diseases.

Popular Apple Rootstocks

Some common and popular rootstocks are Bud.9, M.7, M.9, M.26, and MM.111. The descriptions below are generalizations; heights in particular will vary.

Semidwarf

(between dwarf and standard in size, about 15 feet tall)

M.26: Slightly larger growing than M.9 but smaller than M.7; early bearing; hardy; needs staking; doesn't grow in wet/heavy soils; susceptible to fire blight and crown rot; may not be compatible with some cultivars; produces burr knots

M.7: Widely used semidwarf stock; anchors the tree well; resists crown rot and fire blight; leads to productive trees; hardy; tolerates heavy soils; is early bearing; tends to sucker

MM.111: Vigorous; one of largest of the semidwarfs and more upright; drought-resistant and tolerates wet soils, good anchoring; resists fire blight; produces burr knots

Dwarf

(ideal for home gardens, 50 percent smaller than standard, about 10 feet tall)

Budagovsky 9 (Bud.9 or B.9): Productive and very early to bear; needs support; hardy; susceptible to drought; suckers; resistant to powdery mildew, crown rot, and apple scab (but not to fire blight); popular with both growers and home gardeners

M.9: Productive and early to bear; needs support; grows well in well-drained soils but tolerates heavy soils; suckers; resistant to crown rot but susceptible to fire blight and aphids

Rootstocks are often included in catalog descriptions. They're identified by a name, often shortened to a single letter, that gives their origin. This may be followed by an identifying number. The common Malling (pronounced MAUL-ing) rootstocks, for example, are indicated by M (sometimes listed as EM), named for the East Malling Research Station in England. Crosses between these Malling cultivars and 'Northern Spy' were given the prefix MM after a joint effort between the John Innes Horticulture Institute at Merton and East Malling. EMLA signifies East Malling/Long Ashton rootstocks. Several have been released from the Geneva, New York, agricultural experiment station, which you may see listed either with the prefix G or more recently CG (an effort between the U.S. Department of Agriculture and Cornell University), such as G.11 and G.16.

If you want to try your hand at grafting, you'll need to learn more about rootstocks in order to ensure compatibility. For example, to grow a cultivar that isn't particular vigorous, you should select a vigorous rootstock. Otherwise, you'll get little growth or fruit. If you purchase trees at a nursery, you don't need to worry about rootstock compatibility.

Planting and Care

IF YOU'RE CAREFUL to follow the general directions for planting and growing fruit trees in chapter 16, you should be picking apples within a few years. As with most other fruit trees, apples like full sun and deep, well-drained soil. Don't plant in a low area; it may collect water and be prone to spring frosts, which would injure flower buds. If your soil is less than desirable, seek out rootstocks for your conditions; M.7 and M.9, for example, tolerate heavy soils.

Set a tree in its hole so the graft union sits 2 to 4 inches above the soil (the higher above the soil, the more dwarfing influence from the rootstock). If the tree has an interstem (a double graft), set the tree so that the lower graft (where interstem joins the rootstock) sits 2 to 4 inches above the soil. If you know your apple tree's rootstock is prone to sucker (such

TIPS FOR GROWING APPLES

- Select a site with well-drained soil and good air circulation.
- Choose cultivars appropriate for your site (see page 140)
- Keep up with pruning in the first few years, but make only the cuts necessary to develop a central leader and main (scaffold) branches.
- Once trees begin to bear, prune in late winter to maintain a pyramid or cone shape, or for a more topped modified leader, remove upper branches as needed.
- Watch for pests and diseases and take appropriate control measures; a dormant oil spray before bloom will prevent many problems.
- Practice good sanitation to minimize pest/disease problems: keep the ground clear of fallen leaves and fruit, and keep the grass mowed.

as Bud.9), plant the tree lower — with the graft union at soil level — to reduce this tendency.

Staking during the first 4 or 5 years will help trees get established better and more quickly. It's an essential procedure for apples grafted onto dwarfing rootstocks that don't provide adequate anchorage, such as M.9 and Bud.9.

Pruning Apples

Apples are the classic subject for the central and modified leader systems (see chapter 17). Pruning is slightly different for spur and non-spur apples. Spurs are short, stubby wrinkled stems on a branch. All apples trees have them; some types produce more, and more closely spaced, spurs. These are referred to as spur-type apples. Although spurs can live many years, they only develop flower buds the second year and fruit beginning in the third year.

Some apples are identified by the "spur" via their name ('Crimson Spur Red Delicious'). Spur types produce more fruit per same length of branch as a non-spur type does. Botanically speaking, they're strains, generally mutations of normally growing cultivars.

A spur-type tree is generally three-quarters the size of the non-spur version of the same cultivar, so it's a good choice for a small property. It also produces fewer limbs; these branches are often stronger and more vertical than on a non-spur type, so the tree takes up less space. A big plus is that with fewer branches, these trees require less pruning, which

Spur-type apples make fewer limbs and thus require less pruning than a regular tree does; head back some branches to encourage more spurs to form.

Non-spur apple trees produce their fruits on spurs too, just spaced apart along the branches; prune these normally.

PRUNING TIPS

Young Apple Trees

- Train to a central leader (see page 246).
- Remove upright branches that compete with the central leader.
- In the early years, identify the main scaffold branches; remove the others.
- If most branches grow upright, spread some to make horizontal scaffolds (see page 246).
- Remove diseased, damaged, dead, and rubbing branches.

Mature Apple Trees

- Switch to modified central leader pruning if you want to keep trees lower; not needed for dwarf trees (see page 246).
- Remove more from the upper portion than from the lower, to let in more light.
- Prune off limbs that form narrow angles to the trunk.
- If a tree is too tall, remove whole upright limbs from the top, flush with the bark of lower horizontal limbs. Note: Use this "bench cut" sparingly.
- Each year, thin fruits early in the season (see page 257).
- Thin out the longest branches; don't head them back.
- Prune spur types less than you would other apples; head back some branches to promote more spurs.
- Remove diseased, damaged, dead, and rubbing branches.

makes them popular with home gardeners as well as commercial growers.

Whenever a tree produces too many of these spurs, snip off some to reduce the amount of fruit thinning you'll need to do later. To increase the number of spurs on a branch, shorten (head back) the branch. After you have grown these trees for a few years, you'll be able to judge the right amount to leave, according to each tree's strength and fruit production.

A few apple cultivars (usually older ones, such as 'Golden Russet') are tip-bearers, meaning they produce fruit at the tips of shoots more than 4 inches long. For the tip-bearers, leave the shoots without pruning if last year's growth is under 9 inches long. If longer, prune back to four or five healthy buds. These will grow into shoots that will fruit the following year.

Some apples such as 'Northern Spy' are partial tip-bearers. That is, they produce fruit both at tips and on spurs. Prune these as you would a spur-type apple.

To help a young tree put its energy into forming good branches and growth, remove all fruit the first couple of years. The third year, remove all fruit from only the central leader. The fourth year, remove some of the fruits from the whole tree, a process called thinning.

Once a tree begins bearing, help nature thin developing apples to ensure good fruit size and quality. Thin after the June drop (see page 257) or when they're the size of a dime; leave one fruit per cluster and 5 to 6 inches between fruit. This is difficult for many growers to do, but it will make a dramatic improvement in the size and quality of the harvest. In addition, you'll be encouraging the tree to produce a good crop each year, rather than the biennial bearing most apples do if left to their own devices.

Pruning Mature Apple Trees

Remove limbs at narrow angles to the trunk.

Thin out the longest branches rather than heading back.

Remove broken or rubbing branches.

Insects and Diseases

Apple trees, like any other living thing, suffer their share of life's ills. As you read the list of potential problems, don't be overwhelmed. Practicing good sanitation and choosing disease-resistant cultivars will minimize problems. Keep a constant watch on your orchard, and use control measures quickly before a minor outbreak of insects or a disease threatens to become epidemic. If you grow ornamental crab apples, plant your apple trees at least 100 yards from them, if possible, as they're prone to some of the same diseases.

The main insects apple trees are most likely to encounter are apple maggots, codling moths, and — in the East — plum curculios. You may also see aphids, spider mites, sawflies, and San Jose scale. Descriptions and controls for all except apple maggots are discussed in chapter 18 (beginning on page 261).

Apple maggots, also known as railroad worms, are in my opinion among the meanest villains in the fruit world, and many a beautiful crop of apples has been wrecked by these persistent pests. They can reduce a good-looking apple to a pulpy brown mess. An insect closely resembling a smallish housefly pierces the skin of the growing fruit and lays its eggs in the fruit flesh. Then the larvae hatch, often in large numbers, and "railroad" through the fruit. Larvae live in apples that are left on the ground during the fall, then burrow underground for the winter, ready to emerge as flies the following summer. Sometimes you can see swarms of these flies buzzing under fruit trees in late summer in unsprayed orchards.

Cleaning up all the old fruit and using maggot traps provide the best control. The traps are red apple-shaped spheres, coated with a sticky substance, that attract and capture the egg-laying females. If you have only a few small trees, bag individual fruits after thinning to keep the insects from reaching them. Simply place a plastic sandwich bag over each fruit, secure with a twist tie or staples, and poke a hole to let water drain out. On larger trees, bag the apples you can reach and leave the upper ones for the insects. If the apple maggot becomes a serious problem, once-a-week spraying during the early and middle part of the summer (after petal fall) may be necessary. Kaolin clay products can be sprayed on weekly, beginning in midsummer, to

A Sample Organic Spray Schedule for Apples

Use a spray only if it's essential, and always follow label directions even if they differ from the guidelines below. (The exception is dormant oil, which is applied before pests and diseases appear.) This schedule is designed to control the main diseases (apple scab and powdery mildew, for trees that aren't resistant) and insect pests (apple maggots and codling moth). See chapter 18 for descriptions of the developmental stages along with additional control strategies.

Stage	Spray
Dormant	Dormant oil: overwintering eggs of aphids, mites; some diseases
Green tip	Sulfur (not within 3 weeks of oil) for disease prevention; insecticidal soap or neem oil if aphids or mites are a problem
Open cluster	Sulfur spray (not lime sulfur) for disease prevention; neem oil if aphids are persistent; Bt to control pest caterpillars (don't mix with sulfur spray; apply separately)
King/first bloom	Repeat sulfur and Bt, if needed (don't use other insecticides at this time, as you don't want to harm pollinating bees)
Petal fall	Repeat sulfur and Bt and again 7–10 days later, if needed, or begin weekly kaolin clay spraying
Fruit set	Sulfur spray or Bordeaux if there are signs of disease, every 10–14 days, as fruits develop; stop 30 days before expected harvest; pyrethrum (or similar) for pests, on the same schedule

help keep away these and other apple pests. If possible, control these pests on other hosts within a half mile, such as other fruit trees, crab apples, and ornamental hawthorns.

The four main diseases to watch for on your apple trees are apple scab, cedar apple rust, powdery mildew, and fire blight. Fortunately, there are cultivars resistant to some or all of these. Descriptions often mention a range of susceptibility; cultivars that aren't completely resistant may tolerate a disease, so generally you won't have to spray these trees. Unsprayed trees may be susceptible to black rot and some of the other fungal diseases described in chapter 18.

Apple scab, the most common apple disease, is a fungus that attacks both leaves and fruit. It causes olive-colored and velvety splotches on leaves, often making them warped and curly. Infected fruits are covered with dark, hard, unsightly blotches and cracks. Fruits that become diseased early in the

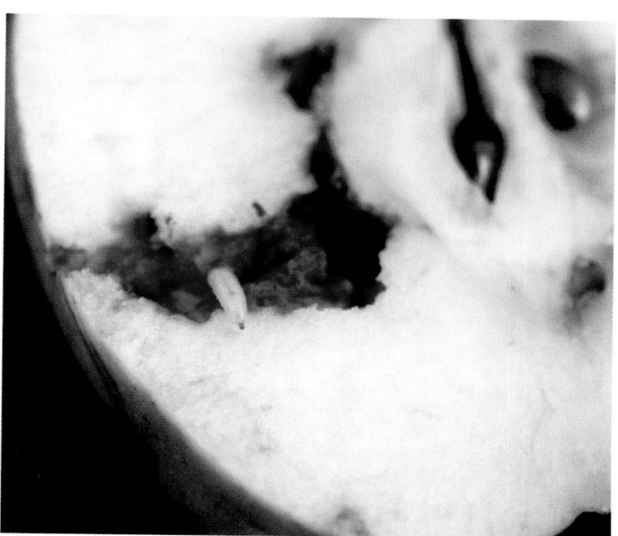

Apple maggot

Bitter pit

Apple scab

Cedar apple rust

season may fall before maturing, and those contaminated later are often unfit to eat. Scab usually doesn't present a problem if the year is dry, but in rainy summers you may need to spray from silver-tip stage (see page 282) until a few weeks before harvest to get healthy fruit. Dormant oil sprays help to prevent infestations of apple scab, but fungicides are likely to be the only way to control it throughout the season. Because scab overwinters in apples and in leaves on the ground, careful orchard sanitation helps prevent the disease.

Cedar apple rust is the worst of several rusts that infect apple trees. It attacks both leaves and fruit, causing very noticeable yellow-orange raised spots on the undersides of leaves, then on fruit. Leaves will drop if severely infected. To complete its life cycle, the disease must have a juniper or an eastern red cedar nearby, so eliminating that plant controls it completely. If this is impossible, you can control it with one of the fungicides recommended for that purpose. Silver tip through petal fall are the best stages for control with fungicides.

Bitter pit may look like a disease, but it's actually a physiological problem. It begins as small, water-soaked spots on fruits, eventually turning brown, depressed, and spongy below after a month or two in storage. This is caused by climate and cultural practices that lead to a calcium imbalance in fruit. Most susceptible are young trees just starting to bear, immature fruit, and fruit on upright, leafy branches rather than on horizontal wood nearer the main limbs. Cultural practices will help: don't over-thin fruit, maintain adequate soil moisture by mulching trees and watering when rainfall is scant, and refrain from over-pruning and overfertilizing (both cause excessive shoot growth).

Because scab overwinters in apples and in leaves on the ground, careful orchard sanitation helps prevent the disease.

Harvesting and Storing Apples

AS YOU MUST WAIT a few years for your trees to produce, keep good records of your plantings.

We've heard of gardeners who lost their whole crop of luscious yellow apples because they were patiently waiting for them to turn red. Other friends picked their 'Delicious' apples too early because they didn't realize that "winter" (late-ripening) apples must stay on the trees for a few weeks after they begin to show color in order to develop their flavor. A few light frosts don't hurt these hard-fleshed apples a bit.

This raises an important question. When is an apple ripe enough for picking? If it separates easily from the tree, it should be ready. If you're picking apples that are slightly unripe, grasp an apple in your palm, then lift sideways and upward, twisting a bit while doing so. Be careful not to break off any spurs that will produce next year's fruit. As apples ripen, they often change color outside and the flesh becomes less green and more white or yellow. If you're uncertain, cut open an apple. If the seeds are still white, it's not ripe, so wait until the seeds turn brown. The best indicator is when an apple tastes crisp and juicy and sweet.

You can use apples for cooking before they're fully ripe. Sometimes you just can't wait for that first pie or dish of applesauce — and raccoons, birds, and deer don't wait either. In fact, if you plan to store them, do pick apples before they're fully ripe.

Some cultivars ripen their fruits more or less all at once; others call for several pickings. Among those that have a short harvest season are 'Baldwin', 'Cortland', 'McIntosh', and 'Northern Spy'. Those that ripen over a longer season are especially good home varieties, as you won't have to use all the fruit at once. Among these are 'Gravenstein', 'Jonathan', 'Wealthy', and 'Winesap'.

In most areas, early apples ripen beginning in August; late apples, in October. In warmer climates, early cultivars may ripen as early as June or July and the late ones in November. Most apples ripen over a period of 10 days to weeks, but some — 'Cortland',

'Red Delicious', 'Northern Spy', and 'Granny Smith', for example — ripen over about 3 weeks.

Wash and refrigerate soon after picking, as apples will ripen much more quickly when they're left at room temperature. Ripe apples should last 4 to 6 weeks in the refrigerator. Early-ripening apples and those described as "soft" generally don't store as well as the later-ripening cultivars do. While the early 'Lodi' may store for up to 2 weeks, some later cultivars ('Cortland', 'McIntosh', 'Red Delicious' and 'Golden Delicious') keep for up to 4 months. A few apples —'Winesap', 'Rome', and 'Granny Smith' — can last up to 5 months. For long-term storage, keep apples in a spot with high humidity and temperatures below 40°F.

Choosing Apple Cultivars

A CENTURY AGO, if you wanted to buy apple trees, you'd have had a tremendous selection from which to choose — some 700 cultivars in all shapes and colors. There were a great many nurseries selling them, and each stocked all the local favorites. In the 1950s, when I first went scouting for trees, most catalogs listed only half a dozen commercial varieties, which needed a lot of spraying (at least in New England) and a long growing season. Now, because of increased demand and more breeding, the selection is even better, especially for smaller home gardens. One estimate has 2,500 apple cultivars in the United States alone, and 7,500 worldwide.

How Many Apples Can You Use?

A mature dwarf tree should yield 1 to 6 bushels of apples. A mature semidwarf will produce 4 to 10 bushels. Expect 8 to 18 bushels from a mature standard tree. A bushel averages 40 to 42 pounds; 1 pound is approximately two large, three medium, or four or five small apples. To help figure what you'll need to make a particular recipe, 1 pound of apples peeled and cut or sliced yields about 3 cups, so figure on 2 pounds of apples for a standard 9-inch pie. A bushel of apples should be enough for 20 pies or 12 to 18 quarts of applesauce or frozen slices.

Once sliced, apples rapidly turn brown (a few cultivars are exceptions). Eat slices within a couple of hours, or refrigerate to be used later. To delay the discoloring, soak slices in a mix of 1 part lemon juice to 3 parts water, or apple juice fortified with vitamin C. You could also use a commercial anti-browning product such as ascorbic acid.

For longer storage, freeze or dry slices. Soak as above to prevent browning prior to drying or freezing. Spread slices on a baking sheet, freeze, then pack into freezer bags or containers. Make sure your containers are designed for freezing; other plastics may allow moisture to enter. Whenever a recipe calls for fresh apples that will be cooked, you can substitute the frozen ones. We thaw them in a microwave oven just enough to be able to break them apart.

You can also soak slices in a sugar and water syrup (2–3 cups of sugar, depending on taste, to 4 cups of water), then freeze both syrup and slices. Don't add more sugar, as this will spoil their natural flavor and crisp texture.

With a microwave, you can quickly turn apple slices in syrup into applesauce: Thaw, adjust sugar to taste, add some cinnamon (optional), and cook on high power until the slices are soft. Some apple cultivars, such as 'Cortland' and 'Empire', make a chunkier sauce; 'McIntosh' and its relatives make a smoother sauce. To make a smooth sauce, process in a blender; for a chunky sauce, use a potato masher instead. Using at least some red apples, skin on, produces a pink sauce.

For drying, dehydrators work best, and the slices should be thin. Use your favorite cultivar, or try mixing several for different flavors. To use dried slices, simmer in boiling water for 5 minutes to reconstitute; use a cup of water for each cup of fruit. Or you can soak slices in fruit juices, even in fruit liquors.

Heirlooms

Specialty nurseries are once again propagating old-time apples, which are often referred to as heirlooms, heritage apples, and antique apples. There's no real definition of what constitutes an heirloom: the name can designate an older cultivar, or one grown 50 or 100 years ago, or one available now but not grown commercially. Many places showcase a region's heirlooms. The Tower Hill botanic garden in Massachusetts, for example, boasts heirlooms dating from before 1900. Whatever the definition, heirlooms are worth searching out for their unique flavors and qualities (see the appendix for sources).

Backyard Growing

Experiment stations are developing cultivars especially suited for home culture. These are bred for good flavor in addition to disease resistance, adaptability, and other desirable traits. Catalog descriptions are so glowing that you almost dread making a choice for fear of missing out on something better. A good place to start is your local nurseries, as they should know what grows and produces best where you garden. A cultivar may grow well in a number of regions but produce better-tasting fruit in certain climates. 'McIntosh', for example, develops best where there are warm fall days and cool nights, as in the upper Northeast; 'Jonathan', on the other hand, develops best where temperatures are warm after bloom, as in the central states.

Type

Type is a vague word that may refer to tree size, such as dwarf, or use, such as for cooking. In conjunction with cultivars, it generally refers to a sport or mutation that has been selected for better fruit color, fruit shape or texture, or other trait — disease resistance, for example — and clonally propagated. The word strain is employed in a similar fashion. Some apples with the most strains are 'Delicious', 'Fuji', and 'Gala'; somewhere between 40 and 100 strains of 'Delicious' alone have been selected.

You may see hybrids listed as types too. For instance, 'Macoun' is the result of a cross with McIntosh as a parent, and 'Liberty' is from a cross with 'Macoun'. Both may be listed as 'McIntosh' types. When looking at common cultivars in a catalog or at a nursery, they may differ depending on the type or strain being sold. If your 'McIntosh' apple is different from your neighbor's or from fruit you bought at the supermarket, they may be different strains.

'Jonathan' is a tart heirloom apple that dates to 1862.

Cultural Adaptation

When deciding what to grow, look for hardiness or suitability for your region, resistance to diseases, and flowering times. If you're just starting out, ask other gardeners or professionals which diseases are prevalent in your area and what cultivars are known to grow well there.

Remember to select cultivars with similar flowering times, which may be listed as a pollination group. If you don't see this information in cultivar descriptions, ask to make sure the trees you buy will cross-pollinate. Also note whether the trees bear annually or every other year (biennial-bearing or alternate-bearing), so you'll know what to expect, although you can modify this tendency with careful pruning. Some apples that tend to bear good crops annually and are easy to prune and care for are 'Empire', 'Golden Delicious', and 'Liberty'.

Taste and Use

Flavor is an important consideration in choosing fruits. Because flavor is a personal preference, recommending one over another is subjective. For eating fresh (sometimes called dessert apples), some people like soft fruit and others like their apples almost as hard as a rock. Some like a slightly sweet flavor; others claim to eat only the very sour kinds. Then there are those who hold out for juicy over dry, mealy instead of crisp, and have an opinion about all sorts of textures, aromas, and other qualities they feel make an apple perfect. Surveys have shown that consumers value both flavor and crispness. If you'd like to sample an apple before buying a tree, many cultivars are available at country roadside stands and farmers' markets in the fall. A large variety of apples is also available for tasting and evaluating from Applesource (see Resources).

Try to determine ahead of time how you'll use the apples, as some are best eaten fresh, others are great for baking (see chart), still others are well suited for making cider. The words cider and juice are often used interchangeably, although growers use the term cider to refer to the liquid from pressed apples, no sugar or water added. For a tart, tangy cider, consider 'Cortland', McIntosh, and 'Idared'; crab apples impart more astringency. For a sweet cider, try 'Red Delicious' or 'Golden Delicious' and 'Empire'. 'Jonathan' and 'Baldwin' make a more aromatic cider. If you grow or have access to some of these cultivars, try different combinations for a cider with more depth of flavor.

Each fall, our homebrewing club (in northern Vermont) teams up with a local orchard for a special apple pressing. Although their goal is fermented hard cider, I find it some of the best tasting fresh cider without this next step. Some of the club experts got with some of the top cider makers in the region to devise a formula, a key being lots of cultivars. The recipe has varied over the years, but in general it's 2 or 3 parts each (by volume) of 'Liberty', 'Northern Spy', 'Ida Red', 'Cortland', and 'McIntosh'. Many other cultivars have been used, including crab apples and heirlooms, but in general each year has had in addition at least 1 part each of 'Tolman', 'Greening', 'Empire', 'Jonagold', and 'Russet'.

Perhaps one of the easiest ways to use up a large apple harvest is to make cider.

Apples baked with raisins, walnuts, and maple syrup make for a simple, wholesome dessert.

Apple Cultivars

In the following chart you'll see information about some of the many apple cultivars now available. Check catalogs and online sources for more details on these and hundreds more. Note: Fruit color refers to the skin. Here are other explanations for the information in the chart.

Pollination Group. Which cultivars bloom at the same time for cross-pollination: early (A), midseason (B), late (C). Blooms times usually overlap, so one from group A likely will pollinate one from group B but not from group C. Self-fruitful (SF) cultivars will produce some apples if you plant a single tree, but will yield better with cross-pollination. Some apples have sterile pollen (SP); these can't be used to pollinate another cultivar.

Comments. Usually refer to uses. Most of these are multipurpose apples, good for eating fresh or in baking. You may come up with other ways to utilize them: for example, some listed for baking may make better pie fillings; others are better for applesauce.

Regions. All varieties are hardy to Zone 5 unless noted otherwise. Most apples will do well in many locations, but some thrive in a particular climate or are more popular in a particular region. Where apples are prone to diseases, pay close attention to disease-resistant cultivars. N = Northeast and northern Midwest; M-A = mid-Atlantic; S = South; M = central and Lower Midwest and Plains; NW = Northwest and temperate parts of the West.

Cultivar	FRUIT DESCRIPTION	POLLI-NATION GROUP	RIPENING SEASON	BEST REGIONS	COMMENTS
'Arkansas Black'	dark red, firm tart, stores well	B, SP	late	S, M, NW	Good for cider; heirloom
'Baldwin'	red, stores well	C, SP	late	N	Good for cider; heirloom from 1740; the most widely planted in U.S. until 1920s
'Braeburn'	red, large, firm, sweet-tart	B/C	late	N, M-A, M, NW	Good for baking and pies
'Cortland'	red, large, soft; slow to brown when cut	A/B	mid	N, M-A, M	Good for baking, cider, apple butter, sauce; heirloom from 1898; Zone 4
'Empire'	red	A, SF	mid	N, M-A, NW	Resistant to rust, fire blight; good for baking, cider; Zone 4
'Freedom'	red, tart	A	mid	N, M-A, NW	Disease resistant; good for cider; Zone 4
'Gala'	red or yellow, sweet, crisp, juicy	B, SF	early	N, M-A, S, M, NW	Most uses
'Ginger Gold'	yellow, crisp, juicy	B	early	N, M-A, S, M	Good fresh and for sauce and pies
'Golden (Yellow) Delicious'	yellow, large, sweet; popular	B, SF	mid	N, M-A, S, M, NW	Good for baking, sauce; Zone 4
'Granny Smith'	green, firm, crisp, tart	B/C, SF	late	M-A, S, M, NW	Rust resistant
'Gravenstein'	yellow/red stripes	A, SP	mid	M, NW	Good for cider; heirloom to U.S. around 1790; sterile pollen; Zone 4
'Honeycrisp'	yellow/red, crisp, juicy	A	mid	N, M-A, NW	Stores well; slow to brown when cut; Zone 3

Cultivar	FRUIT DESCRIPTION	POLLI-NATION GROUP	RIPENING SEASON	BEST REGIONS	COMMENTS
'Idared'	bright red, crisp	A	late	N, M-A, NW	Stores well; good for baking, sauce; trees bear at an early age
'Jersey Mac'	red	A	early	M-A, S	An early McIntosh type
'Jonafree'	red, tart	A	mid	M-A, S	Resistant to scab, rust, fire blight
'Jonagold'	red/yel-low, large; sweet-tart	B, SP	mid	N, M-A, S, M, NW	Good for sauce and pies; 'Golden Delicious' will not pollinate
'Jonamac'	dark red	A	mid	NW	Rust resistant; good for sauce, baking, apple butter
'Jonathan'	red, striped, tart, stores well	A,SF	mid	M-A, M, NW	Good for cider, apple butter, baking; heirloom from 1862
'Liberty'	red/green, tart	A, SF	mid	N, M-A, NW	Disease resistant; good for baking, apple butter; Zone 4
'Lodi'	green	A, SF	very early	M-A	Scab and mildew resistant; Zone 3
'Macoun'	red, sweet, juicy	C	mid	N, M-A, NW	Stores well; many uses; Zone 4
'McIntosh'	red/green, tart	A	mid	N, M-A	Rust resistant; good for cider and smooth sauce; heirloom from 1798; Zone 4
'Mutsu' ('Crispin')	yellow-green, large, juicy, sweet-tart	B/C, SP	late	M-A, S, M, NW	Non-browning flesh; sweetens in storage; good in sauce
'Northern Spy'	green-yellow, red blush; firm, tart	C	late	N	Stores well; fire blight resistant; good for baking, cider; heirloom from about 1800; Zone 3
'Paulared'	red	A	early	N, M-A, M	Rust resistant; Zone 4
'Red Delicious'	red classic apple, sweet	B	mid	M-A, S, M, NW	Resistant to rust, mildew, fire blight; good for cider; heirloom to 1870; Zone 4
'Redfree'	red	B	early	N, M-A	Scab and rust resistant
'Rome' ('Beauty', 'Red Rome')	red, firm; drooping habit	C, SF	late	M-A, S, M, NW	Good for cider; heirloom to 1848; Zone 4
'Stayman Winesap' ('Stayman')	red, tart; fruit cracks after rain	C, SP	late	M-A, S, M	Seedling of 'Winesap'; heirloom from 1866; good for pies and baking
'Winesap'	dark red, tart	B, SP, SF	late	M-A, M	Heirloom from 1817
'Yellow Transparent'	yellowish white	A	early	S, M-A, M	Short shelf life; one of best for sauce; heirloom from 1870; trees bear at an early age; Zone 4
Zestar!	red blush, crisp	A	early	N, M-A	Long storage, Zone 3

Low-Chill Apples for Warm Climates

These apples are especially suitable for many parts of Florida, southern California, the hills of the Southwest, and similar climates, although many will grow well elsewhere too. Most are good for both fresh eating and baking; 'Winter Banana' and 'Yellow Bellflower' are also good for cider. Note: The chill requirement (hours below 45°F) is approximate.

Cultivar	FRUIT DESCRIPTION	POLLINATION GROUP	RIPENING SEASON	CHILL REQUIREMENT (HOURS)	COMMENTS
'Anna'	large, green with red blush; sweet	A	early	200	High yields; pollinate with 'Dorsett Golden' or 'Ein Shemer'
'Dorsett Golden'	golden with red blush; medium to large; crisp, sweet	A, SF	early	100–250	High yields; trees bear at an early age
'Ein Shemer'	golden, large; sweet-tart	A, SF	early	150–250	From Israel; good yields
'Fuji'	red, medium size; sweet	B/C	late	200–400	Stores well; tends to bear every other year
'Pettingill'	green/red, thick skin, large; moderately tart	A, SF	mid to late	100	From Long Beach, California, in 1949
'Pink Lady' ('Cripps Pink' variety)	yellow/pink blush, medium to large; sweet-tart; flesh resists browning	A, SF	late	200–400	From Western Australia; stores well
'White Winter Pearmain'	yellow/red blush, medium to large; juicy, good flavor	B, SF	late	400	Very old English variety; all-purpose; stores well
'Winter Banana'	yellow blushed pink, large, tough skin; mild banana flavor	B, SF	late	300–400	Stores well; best for fresh eating and cider; trees bear at an early age
'Yellow Bellflower'	yellow blushed red, medium size; crisp, slightly tart but sweetens in storage	B	late	400	Stores well; good for hard cider

Crab Apples for Eating

One or two crab apples are a good addition to any home orchard, not only for their fruit and beauty, but because they're excellent pollinators for apple trees. For cross-pollination, most any will do, as long as they bloom at the same time as your apples. If you want to use the fruit, however, you'll have to be more selective. Most edible crab apples are ornamental as well. Ornamental crab apples have small fruit with less pulp and tend to be much tarter.

The fresh fruit of most cultivars is a bit sour for most people's taste, but it makes the most beautiful jelly, spiced apples, and juice (cider). The cultivars listed below as good for fresh eating are the least tart. Crab apples also make nice apple butter. The process was quite a full-day ordeal until the advent of slow cookers.

When choosing crab apples, look for disease resistance. Being close relatives of apples, they get the same diseases. A susceptible crab apple can serve as a reservoir for a disease that will affect your apple trees. Plant apple trees at least 100 yards from ornamental crab apples. If you are planting a crab apple that will also serve to pollinate apples, you'll need to plant them closer, so make sure to choose a disease resistant cultivar.

Our favorite crab apple is 'Dolgo', which was imported from Russia in the late 1800s and is sometimes described as the perfect fruit tree. Not only is it beautifully shaped, vigorous, pest resistant, regular bearing, and likely to fruit early in life, but it's also quite hardy. The flowers resist frost better than do those of most fruit trees, and the tree is a prolific producer. Like the other crab apples, 'Dolgo' is a good pollinator, although it may start blooming a few days ahead of some of the large apples. The large white blooms of our 'Dolgo' are so abundant that they hide the leaves, making the tree a mass of white beauty in the spring. In early fall, it's red with ripening fruit.

Here are a few popular crab apples grown for their fruit. Some not noted as resistant may still tolerate a particular disease.

Crab Apple Cultivars

Cultivar	FLOWER/SEASON	FRUIT	COMMENTS
'Callaway'	pink/white, early	red	Good for cooking; low chill requirement, so good in the South; disease resistant
'Centennial'	white, mid	yellow/red	Good for cooking and fresh eating; rust resistant
'Chestnut'	white, early/mid	green-yellow, red stripes; large; early	Good for fresh eating and cooking; resists scab, rust, and fire blight; stores well
'Dolgo'	white, early	red, tart, red flesh; early	Good for cooking; popular in the North; disease resistant
'Transcendent'	white, early	yellow with red blush; early	Good for fresh eating and cooking
'Whitney'	pink/white, early	yellow/red stripes; late	Good for cooking; resists scab and fire blight; popular heirloom (1865)

It may be easier to manage a harvest of pears than any other kind of fruit; they're picked green, stored, and can be ripened as they're needed.

CHAPTER 10

Pears

Two days after Christmas one year, I found a partridge in the pear tree in our backyard. Even though three French hens and two turtledoves never did appear, it seemed like a special holiday happening, and another of the many unexpected delights of growing your own fruit.

A soft, juicy, ripe pear is one of the finest fruits. I consider it the perfect dessert fruit, and a fruit salad or bowl without it is missing something. Not only is it delicious raw, but it's also one of the few fruits that taste nearly as good canned as they do fresh. In fact, unlike most other fruits, it tastes better canned than frozen.

Most pears (*Pyrus* species) grown in North America originated in southwestern Europe. They came to America with the earliest settlers and were grown in Salem, Massachusetts, as early as 1635. They grow best in cooler climates on heavy soils. If you aren't blessed with well-drained soils or you garden on clay, take heart: Your soil may still grow great pears!

Now that many fire blight–resistant cultivars are available, pears are easier to grow than apples. It's easier to produce quality fruit without spraying. Plus, you can get by with less pruning. On the other hand, if you like pruning, pears are easy to train as espaliers. The trees are attractive in the landscape, with pretty spring blossoms and glossy leaves.

Pears are hardier than peaches but some are less hardy than apples. Cultivars sold in nursery catalogs are generally suitable for Zones 5 through 8, although a few will grow in Zones 3 and 4. Almost all pears need a period of low temperature during the winter (generally 500 to 800 chill hours below 45°F). Only a few are suitable for the nearly frost-free areas of Florida and California; Asian pears are better for these areas.

Two Distinct Types of Pears

EUROPEAN PEARS are what most people think of when they think "pear." These fruits give us the description "pear-shaped" and when ripe have a juicy, buttery texture and sweet flavor. Unlike other fruits, these should be picked before they're fully ripe and must complete their ripening off the tree.

The delicious and versatile 'Bartlett' is still the most popular pear in North America as well as in Europe, where it's known as the Williams pear after the English nurseryman who originally introduced it. It accounts for 75 percent of commercial production throughout the world. Some cultivars take a long time — sometimes 8 years — to bear their first crop, but others tend to bear when quite young.

Asian pears have become increasingly popular. Like other pears, they make nice ornamental trees growing to about 20 feet tall, with large, shiny green leaves that turn a nice purplish red in fall. Asian pear trees start bearing after just a couple of years and produce more fruit than others do. Unlike European pears, pick these when they're fully ripe; they'll store quite well.

Their fruit is generally larger and more rounded, with crisp flesh and a sweet, juicy flavor. (Another name for them is "apple pears"). Japanese cultivars may have a smooth or russeted (rough with

Pear Fast Facts

USDA Hardiness Zones: (4)5–8, depending on cultivar

Height: Standard, 15–30 feet; dwarf, 6–8 feet

Spacing: Standard, 15–20 feet; dwarf, 8–10 feet

Pollination: Need two different cultivars

Pruning: Late winter, central leader; may switch to modified leader when 8–10 feet tall

Special requirements: Thin young fruits; harvest before fully ripe

Years to bearing: Standard, 4–6; dwarf, 3–5; Asian, 2–3

Yield per tree (bushels): Standard, 2–8; dwarf, 1–2; Asian, 5–10

Differing Traits of European and Asian Pears

Trait	European Pear	Asian Pear
Years to bearing	4–6, some cultivars sooner	2–3
Yield (bushels per plant)	2–8	5–10
Fruit shape	Pear	Generally rounded
Fruit weight	7–9 ounces	7–32 ounces; average 9–14
Fruit texture	Soft and juicy	Crisp and juicy
Picking stage	Before ripe	When ripe
Picking period	Once or twice over 1 week	Four to six times over 2–3 weeks
Storage (in refrigerator)	1–2 months	3–5 months
Skin, need to peel	Usually only for cooking	Generally tough, so peel

browning) skin. Some of the Chinese types produce smooth, greenish fruits with a mild flavor and more of a pear shape; they also tend to have better resistance to fire blight.

Standard or Dwarf?

When you go shopping for pears, you'll find that they're available as either standard or dwarf trees. Standards produce much more fruit per tree than dwarfs do, but dwarfs begin to bear earlier, need less room, and are easier to care for. Usually, dwarfs are grafted on quince rootstocks, which results in a mature tree 30 to 50 percent of normal size. These dwarfs are not as hardy; in cold climates, check hardiness before you buy. Standard trees are grafted onto pear seedlings (usually either 'Bartlett' or Callery pear, *Pyrus calleryana*). Callery rootstocks impart good resistance to fire blight.

Pollination Matters

It is safest to assume that all pears need cross-pollination for maximum yield. A few, including 'Bartlett' and 'Flemish Beauty', are somewhat self-fertile. These are good choices if you want to plant just one pear. 'Magness', on the other hand, has sterile pollen and can't pollinate other pears.

Even pears that are self-pollinating produce more fruit when they grow near a different cultivar. In general, if two different cultivars bloom at the same time, they'll cross effectively. 'Bartlett' and 'Seckel' are an exception to this rule; apparently, they're socially incompatible and need a third kind to pollinate them when planted together. Asian pears appear to mate best with other Asian kinds, or with an early-blooming standard pear.

Because pears bloom early (1 to 3 weeks before apples), poor pollination is not uncommon, especially during cold, wet springs. Some years I've had to resort to hand-pollination in order to save our crop when the bees failed to appear during bloom time. In addition to weather interference, bees may neglect pear blooms because the nectar has less sugar than that of plums or cherries, and this is particularly critical because the blossoms stay on the tree for a very short time. Orchardists who keep bees often place a few pear blooms inside a hive to encourage the bees to visit their trees. A strong hive in the neighborhood in spring is an invaluable asset to any orchard and is especially beneficial for pear growers.

Planting and Care

PEAR TREES can tolerate more moisture in the soil than either apple or peach trees can, but they don't like their roots underwater for more than 2 or

These pears have been pruned and trained to grow up over an arbor, so that the developing fruit hangs down for harvest from below.

3 days. They thrive in cool, moist, cloudy weather, which is why they do so well in the Pacific Northwest. They also love a thick organic mulch such as shredded bark. Except for 'Bartlett' and 'Seckel', they don't care for sandy, light soils.

Plant pears as for other fruit trees (see chapter 16). Care is similar, but pears are vigorous growers, so go lightly on the fertilizer. An excess of nutrients, especially nitrogen, promotes lush growth that invites fire blight and aphid infestations.

Pruning

At first, pear pruning is similar to apple pruning. In their early years, train trees to a central leader, then switch to a modified leader as they mature (see page 246). Pear trees trained to a central leader will yield more and sooner than one trained to a modified central leader. Being taller, though, they will be more difficult to manage. When there are sufficient scaffold branches and trees are a good height (8 to

TIPS FOR GROWING PEARS

- Select a site with good air circulation. Pears tolerate less-than-perfect soil drainage.
- Choose fire blight–resistant cultivars; plant at least two different cultivars that will pollinate each other.
- In early years, train to a central leader; spread upright branches so they'll grow horizontally.
- At 8–10 feet tall with good scaffold branches, head back the leader to begin a modified leader shape; don't over-prune mature trees.
- Thin fruit clusters when fruits are ½ inch wide.
- Harvest before fully ripe (except Asian pears); ripen in a cool spot at for at least 1 week, as needed.

Train young, flexible branches to grow at a wider, stronger angle to the trunk by attaching small weights or using wooden spacers. This will encourage vertical branches to grow at more of a 60-degree angle.

10 feet tall), cut back the leader to the uppermost lateral to begin the modified-leader shape. When selecting scaffold branches on young trees, in addition to having them spaced around the trunk, allow a foot vertically between branches on dwarf trees and 2 feet between them on standard trees.

After the trees have begun to bear, pears need less pruning than apple trees do: remove only a moderate amount of branches each year. Bearing on spurs, as 3- to 10-year-old apples do, pears are a common fruit tree for training as espaliers (see page 253).

If you're growing cultivars that aren't resistant to fire blight, prune even less to reduce the risk of this disease. Thin limbs as needed, but minimize heading back; this results in a profusion of tender growth more susceptible to fire blight. Some growers leave multiple leaders, to have replacements in case the central leader succumbs to fire blight and must be cut off.

As pears tend to grow more upright than apples, in early years you may need to intervene to encourage side branches to develop wide, strong angles. In later years the weight of the fruit will do this. To spread branches, hang weights from them, use notched sticks to separate branches from the trunk, or use clothespins on young and flexible branches as you might for cherries (see page 187).

Thinning is especially important to get pears of a decent size. Otherwise, too many will form, resulting in small fruits, excessive weight that may break branches, and a low yield the following year (alternate or biennial bearing). As codling moths prefer to lay eggs in fruits that are touching, this task will reduce damage from this pest. Thin out the fruits when they're small, about ½ inch wide. Allow only one fruit in a cluster to remain, leaving one fruit every 5 or 6 inches along a branch. It's especially important to thin Asian pears, as their fruits are

Thin young pears for the largest mature fruit, to avoid branches breaking, to lessen insect damage, and to promote fruiting every year.

heavy. 'Seckel', a small-fruited European pear, seldom needs thinning.

Diseases and Insects

By far the most serious trouble encountered by pear trees is fire blight. This strikes the flowers, limbs, and fruits, all of which turn black, as though they had been burned. If you plant resistant cultivars, you probably won't have to worry about this disease. Light pruning and minimal fertilizer go a long way to decreasing the risk of infection.

Bacterial blossom blast can be a problem on pears in cold, wet springs in the Pacific Northwest. It shows up under cold, wet conditions elsewhere, too, and can also affect apples. Blossoms turn brown, shrivel, and cling to the trees. It can kill the tips of shoots, causing symptoms similar to fire blight, but damage does not extend as far down the shoot. Affected bark is tan and papery, unlike the dark shoots that are the result of fire blight, and it doesn't produce the oozing sap that fire blight causes. This disease is interesting in that its presence makes flowers more susceptible to freeze damage, and once flowers are frost damaged the disease can spread more easily. Frost protection is about the only control.

Other common pear diseases are anthracnose, canker, crown gall, leaf spot, powdery mildew, and scab. For descriptions of these diseases and their remedies, see chapter 18.

The insects that attack the pear are similar to those that bother other fruits. Codling moth is common, as are San Jose scale and spider mites in some areas. The pear slug, which is actually the larva of a sawfly, may also pay a visit to your pear trees; control as for other types of sawflies. These insects are also discussed in chapter 18.

Pear psylla is perhaps the most bothersome pear pest. A gang of these small, aphidlike insects can soon coat a tree and its fruits with the sticky honeydew secretion, on which black sooty mold grows. If severe, shoots wilt and leaves drop. Natural parasites in an unsprayed orchard may provide good control. Otherwise, you may need to use a dormant oil spray before leaves emerge in spring, or spray an insecticidal soap after bloom (follow label directions).

Fire blight

Pear psylla

Harvesting Pears

UNLIKE OTHER FRUITS, European pears must be picked early and never allowed to ripen on the tree. If you wait to harvest pears until they're perfectly ripe, they develop hard, gritty cells in the flesh and begin to rot inside, as they ripen from the inside out. Many homegrown pears are lost because people wait too long before picking them.

Days from bloom to picking vary depending on the cultivar, ranging from 110 to 130 for 'Clapp's Favorite' and 'Bartlett', 120 to 140 for 'Seckel', and 170 to 190 for 'Kieffer'. Those such as 'Bartlett' and its sports that are picked in summer in California are called summer pears; those picked in early fall for use then into winter are called winter pears. Examples of the latter are 'Anjou', 'Bosc', 'Comice', and 'Seckel'.

Begin to harvest as soon as the fruit is well developed, separates easily from the tree with a gentle upward twist, yet isn't quite ready to eat. Leave the stem on the fruit. Pick pears with extreme care, because if you damage the delicate skin of European pears, the fruit will spoil quickly. A sharp fingernail can be devastating.

Pears lend themselves to all kinds of desserts: in tarts and crumbles, or simply poached with a pinch of saffron. They can also be preserved in butters and chutneys and as pear sauce.

Early cultivars may need a couple of pickings over a week; mid- and late-season cultivars can usually be picked all at once. 'Colette' is unusual in that it ripens over a long period, similar to Asian pears.

Because you'll be harvesting Asian pears when they're fully ripe, watch for a gradual color change, and taste a couple of times a week. Asian pears don't ripen all at once, so you'll need to harvest several times over 2 to 3 weeks. If you pick before they're ripe, they'll develop a spongy texture in storage.

Pears keep best in home storage if you wrap each one in tissue paper or a sheet of newspaper and store them in a cool place (30–45°F is ideal) free of odors (as from onions). They'll be ready to eat anytime from a week to a couple of months later, depending on the kind. Winter pears often have better flavor and texture with longer storage, and will keep in the fridge for at least a month; 'Bartlett' and other summer pears store well for 2 to 3 weeks.

For the best full, mellow flavor, allow them to ripen at room temperature for a few days after you remove them from cold storage. If you push on the stem end with your thumb and it makes a slight dent, the fruit is ready to eat. Summer pears turn lighter as they ripen; winter pears don't change color. Once fully ripe, pears last for about 5 days in a cool spot.

From a mature standard tree, expect anywhere from 2 to 8 bushels of fruit; from a dwarf tree, 1 or 2. A bushel of pears yields 20 to 25 quarts canned or 40 to 50 pints frozen; figure on about 2½ pounds of pears for a quart canned or frozen.

In addition to canning and freezing, the buttery-flavored pear can be processed in many delicious ways. A typically southern use is pear "honey," in which pears are combined with pineapple juice, lemons, limes, ginger, or coconut and cooked down until the mixture has the look and feel of honey. Then there are tasty pear conserves, chutneys, pickles, butters, and nectars. We like to peel and cut fresh pears into halves and top with vanilla ice cream, chocolate, whipped cream, and a fresh cherry. In Europe, large amounts are pressed into an alcoholic cider called . . . what else? Perry! This is becoming more popular in North America now, so look for it, or if you like making wine or apple cider, try this in addition.

Pear Cultivars

The following list contains some of the more popular cultivars. 'Kieffer', 'Orient', and 'Pineapple' are low-chill European pears for mild climates. 'Flemish Beauty' and 'Luscious' are among the hardiest, for Zone 4 and perhaps Zone 3. Others are generally suitable for growing in Zones 5–8. Asian pears generally grow well in Zones 5 to 9.

Cultivar	FRUIT DESCRIPTION	SEASON	COMMENTS
EUROPEAN			
'Bartlett'	large, golden; juicy, spicy flavor	early	Most popular; partly self-fertile; good fresh or for canning; susceptible to fire blight
'Flemish Beauty'	large, creamy yellow, red blush	mid	Hardy; partly self-fertile; Belgian heirloom
'Kieffer'	yellow, red blush; juicy, musky aroma	late	A standard; self-fertile, low chill requirement; long-lived; blight resistant
'Luscious'	medium size, yellow; more intense flavor than Bartlett	mid to late	Hardy; blight resistant; best fresh
'Magness'	greenish brown with light russeting; not gritty	mid	Vigorous, spreading; good blight resistance, tough skins resist insects; won't pollinate other pears
'Moonglow'	yellow, red blush; mild flavor, not gritty	early	Great disease resistance; productive; good pollinator
'Orient'	large, rounded, yellow with red blush; sweet, firm but juicy	early	Vigorous; low chill requirement; good fresh or canned; blight resistant
'Pineapple'	large, yellow with red blush; unique pineapple flavor	early	Self-fertile; low chill requirement; blight resistant
'Seckel'	small, yellowish brown; one of the sweetest	mid	Vigorous; fresh or canned
ASIAN			
'Chojuro'	medium size, shiny brown	mid	Productive; attractive fall foliage color; stores well
'Hosui'	large, golden russet bronze; very sweet	mid	Vigorous, spreading, and good quality
'Shinko'	large, golden brown; very sweet	late	Productive; blight resistant
'Shinseiki' ('New Century')	large, yellow green; very sweet	early	Self-fertile, vigorous; disease resistant; stores well

Unusual Tree Fruit: Quince

Although the quince (*Cydonia oblonga*) is a less common tree fruit, it has admirers who praise it highly. From colonial times through the early twentieth century, home landscapes often had one of these natives of Persia. It should not be confused with flowering quince (*Chaenomeles* species), an ornamental shrub whose small seedy fruits are good only for jelly. The well-behaved trees are small — usually under 15 feet tall — and have a rather twisted habit of growth. Their large white spring blooms, interesting form, and bright yellow fruits make them an attractive addition to the home landscape.

You can plant just one, as quinces are one of the few tree fruits that are truly self-pollinating. Though they bear more with a partner nearby, the trees are so productive that one tree can easily supply all the fruit that an average family needs or wants. This fruit tree is usually hardy into Zone 5, but needs a long growing season for fruits to ripen; fortunately, a light frost won't harm them. Quince trees bloom after the apples, so if they'll grow in your climate, there's not much danger of spring frost damage to flowers.

Quince fruit resembles either a large pear or a cross between a pear and an apple. The flesh is quite firm, and the skin is covered with a slight fuzz. It has an unusual flavor and scent, somewhat resembling pineapples or a floral perfume. Outdoors, the odor makes it attractive to wildlife. The odor is so pronounced, in fact, that it's never wise to put it in the refrigerator or leave it near other fruits because they'll soon take on the same smell. Perhaps that is why it's little grown commercially and rarely found in stores or fruit markets.

Grow quince much as you would pears. Unlike most other fruit trees, quince can grow and produce well year after year with little pruning, although you should remove crossed limbs and any dead or diseased wood. The trees thrive in soils similar to those enjoyed by pears and are bothered by the same diseases and insects, with the same susceptibility to fire blight. They're naturally slow-growing trees, so don't be tempted to overfertilize them, as this makes them even more vulnerable to fire blight. Although slow, they have a long life, usually 50 years or more.

Quinces ripen so late that many cold-climate gardeners can't get them to the edible stage before a killing frost. The fruits should stay on the tree until they have turned deep yellow, developed their strong odor, and can be snapped off easily. Ripening takes place as early as mid-October in some areas but is more often well into November. Handle the fruits with great care; they bruise easily. They'll keep in a cool place for about a month; at room temperature, only about a week. Store them in shallow trays, one layer deep so there won't be any weight resting on them.

The astringent fruit is seldom eaten raw, as few cultivars are sweet enough. They're usually cooked into jellies, preserves, and marmalades or added to apples in applesauce. Because of their high pectin content, they're often combined with berries or grapes that are low in pectin to make jellies without added commercial pectin. Rinse off the fuzz, peel, and scoop out the seeds before cooking, as you do with apples. One pound (two or three fruits) will yield about a cup of pulp or about 2 cups of juice. The juice tastes good combined with apple cider. Some people are devotees of the quince custard pie they remember from childhood. Others enjoy quince ginger, quince "honey," or quinces baked and served with whipped cream. The fruits also are delicious canned or spiced.

Quince Cultivars

Cultivar	FRUIT DESCRIPTION	CHILL REQUIREMENT (HOURS)	COMMENTS
'Cooke's Jumbo'	very large, yellow, oval; white flesh	100	Fruit about twice the size of other cultivars; from California
'Orange'	rounded, bright yellow; orange-yellow flesh	300	Turns red when cooked; an older cultivar
'Pineapple'	large, golden, pear-shaped; white flesh; pineapple flavor	100	Cold hardy yet low chill requirement; good fresh or in jellies
'Smyrna'	large, lemon yellow, oval; white flesh; mild flavor	100	One of best for cooking; good for colder areas

Nothing tastes quite like a juicy peach that has been allowed to fully ripen on the tree.

CHAPTER 11

Peaches, Nectarines, and Apricots

What a different taste a tree-ripened peach has, compared to the hard, sour ones from the store. That difference is why most of us who grow fruits in our home gardens want very much to include some peach trees. They're attractive in landscapes as well, beginning with their early-spring pink flowers on the bare branches. The leaves are long and drooping, like a wide willow leaf. Where they can be grown, dwarf cultivars are good for small spaces and large containers.

The peach is a challenge to grow, though, and it brings out the competitive spirit in gardeners, like growing the biggest tomatoes or the best roses. Just as those plants are a step more difficult to grow than radishes and marigolds, so the peach is slightly more difficult than apples and plums, unless your soil and climate are just right. Compared to pears and apples, peaches and their kin are not long-lived trees (10 to 20 years), so plan on having to replace trees eventually. Plant only the number of peach trees you can care for easily. Of all the orchard fruits, they are perhaps the most demanding in their pruning and climate needs, and their susceptibility to pest problems. Even a partly neglected tree can be a disappointment.

Peaches (*Prunus persica*) and nectarines (also *P. persica*, basically a non-fuzzy peach), like their close relative the apricot (*P. armeniaca*), are among the most "foreign" of the temperate-zone fruits. These were grown in China at least 4,000 years ago. It's amazing that today's cultivars originally came from ones grown in southern China that long ago, in an area whose climate resembles that of the southeastern United States (where much commercial production goes on now). From China, these fruits accompanied the silk trade west to Persia, where they were extensively cultivated. Peaches and apricots were originally thought to have originated there (*persica* means "from Persia" and *armeniaca* means "from Armenia"). From about 400 BCE, the Greeks and Romans distributed them widely, including throughout Europe. The Spaniards planted peach trees in Florida soon after their first settlement there.

By the early 1700s apricots were thriving in Virginia. Only in recent years, however, has the apricot become popular as a homegrown fruit. The noted horticulturist U. P. Hedrick scarcely mentions them in his well-known *Fruits for the Home Garden* (1944). Now that their growing range is so enlarged with newer cultivars, many amateur orchardists are enjoying their own tree-ripened apricots.

As with any fruit cultivated for so many years in so many areas, regional variations and groups have arisen. The two most important for the apricot are the European and Central Asian groups. Most apricots grown in North America are from the European group; these are derived from the Central Asian ones, and are less sweet and drier and so better adapted to commercial shipping. The Central Asian apricots bloom later, so they're not as subject to spring frost damage to flowers. The pits of the Central Asian are referred to as sweet pits, as the seeds can be broken apart and the nuts roasted, often used as an almond substitute. Don't eat European apricot seeds, though, without consulting a medical professional (some people believe apricot kernels help cure cancer, and they've long been used in alternative medicine), as most contain a highly toxic compound (the cyanogenic glycoside amygdalin).

In addition to their lighter-colored flesh, white peaches tend to have a sweeter, more floral, and somewhat less complex taste than yellow peaches do.

'Peento' is a cultivar of "flat peach" or "donut peach." This type was originally bred in the 1800s and has once again become popular among consumers.

'Red Haven' is one of the most widely planted peach cultivars; it is cold hardy and resistant to peach leaf curl.

Peach, Nectarine, and Apricot Fast Facts

USDA Hardiness Zones: peaches and nectarines, 5–9 (varies with cultivar); apricots, 5–8

Height: peaches and nectarines, standard, 10–15 feet; dwarf, 5–7 feet; apricots, 15–20; dwarf, 8–10

Spacing: standard, 18–20 feet; dwarf, 7–8 feet

Pollination: many cultivars are self-fertile (only one tree needed to produce fruit)

Pruning: open center (modified central leader for apricots); prune in late winter

Special requirements: somewhat demanding in climate and soils; mature trees need heavy pruning

Years to bearing: peaches and nectarines, standard, 2–4; apricots, 3–5; dwarf, 2–3

Yield per tree (bushels): peaches and nectarines, standard, 4–6; apricots, 3–5; dwarf, 1–2

Choosy about Climate

ALTHOUGH BREEDERS have developed peaches that are hardier and of higher quality, the growing range is still much smaller than that of pears, plums, apples, and cherries. Nectarines may be even more susceptible to cold injury. And even in places where branches and leaf buds of peaches are winter hardy (to –17°F), their flower buds may not be as hardy (–13°F). If you have great leaves but few if any flowers or fruits, this may be why.

In addition to its aversion to cold temperatures, the peach tree needs a long growing season to harden its new growth and develop the fruit buds for the following year. For this reason, peaches can sometimes withstand low temperatures for a short time but are unable to survive where the frost-free season is less than 5 months. The flower buds and blooms are very susceptible to spring frosts, as well.

Commercial peach growers like to plant trees on a well-drained slope with sandy soil just above a fairly large lake or river, so the water will moderate the temperature, keeping it more uniform. Peaches grow well on the Niagara peninsula of Ontario and even along coastal regions of British Columbia, for example.

Even though they prefer a warm climate, like all temperate-zone fruits peaches need a chilling period — a certain amount of cold weather — in order to survive. Most require between 500 and 900 hours below 45°F. Those listed as needing at least 750 chill hours are best in Zones 5 to 7. Gardeners in Zones 8 and 9 must be careful to plant only those varieties that require very little winter chilling; some, such as 'Red Baron' and FLORDAPRINCE, can get by with about 300 hours.

Apricots bloom very early; they're often the first tree fruit in bloom. As a result, their flowers are often damaged by spring frosts. This is often the limiting factor in growing them in cold-climate regions, more than winter hardiness, even though there are cultivars hardy to Zone 4 and a few to Zone 3.

Try to find a somewhat protected location for your apricot trees if you live in such an area. Mulching under the trees helps keep the soil cooler, which in turn slightly delays growth and flowering in the spring, as can planting on an east or north-facing slope. Watering the soil the day before a freeze may help; the wet soil will absorb more heat to radiate back at night.

Apricot buds may be dried out by winter winds or damaged by fluctuating temperature extremes in winter. Even a few warm days during a winter thaw can cause apricot buds to lose hardiness. The ideal climate for apricots is moderate winter cold for chilling, fairly hot summers for fruit ripening, and low humidity to decrease the incidence of disease. This is the climate in the mountainous parts of Turkey and Iran; a third of the world production is from these two countries.

Selecting Plants

MOST PEACH TREES and their cousins are self-fertile and don't need a partner to produce fruit; in most cases you can plant a single tree. There are exceptions: 'J. H. Hale' is a common peach that needs a mate, and the apricots 'Moongold' and 'Sungold' require cross-pollination. Most catalogs spell out the pollination needs of each cultivar. When in doubt, or to ensure a heavier fruit set, it's always best to plant two kinds of peaches unless your neighbor has a peach tree just over the fence. You'll end up with a better spring flower show, and by choosing appropriate cultivars you also extend the harvest season.

Although most peach trees are self-fertile, they'll have a heavier fruit set if they're pollinated by another cultivar, so consider planting more than one.

Rootstocks

Because of the strong demand for small trees, many nurseries supply peaches grafted onto dwarfing rootstocks to produce trees that grow only 5 to 7 feet tall and 7 feet wide. Some may be genetically dwarf with no grafting (see chapter 1). Dwarf trees are easy to care for and bear at an early age, so they're ideal for pot culture and for home gardeners with a small lot. As with all dwarfs, the trees are less vigorous and less hardy than standard (full-size) trees grafted on seedlings. Being shallow-rooted, they may need staking to prevent leaning when they're loaded with fruit. Their crops are smaller than those of standard trees, of course, but you can fit more trees in the same space. Sometimes grafted dwarf peaches sucker badly. They may begin declining even sooner than standard peach trees, often after only 7 years; many recommend just pruning a standard tree heavily if you want a smaller tree — peaches will tolerate this.

Pillar peaches. Some suppliers sell columnar, "pillar," or vertical cordon peaches, which grow upright and seldom more than 5 feet wide. These are a good alternative to dwarf cultivars for gardeners with a small yard. Popular for commercial growers to simplify harvest and maximize production in a given space, they work equally well as landscape novelties, for allées, to define garden spaces, and in containers. SWEET-N-UP is a midseason peach that spreads to about 8 feet; early ripening CRIMSON ROCKET spreads to about 6 feet; and SUMMERFEST is a late-ripening freestone that spreads about 6 feet.

Other specialized rootstocks. Peaches and nectarines are usually budded or grafted onto seedling peach tree roots, which grow rapidly and vary widely in habit. Peaches have also been grafted onto rootstocks of the botanically related plums, almonds, and cherries in an attempt to get them to adapt to heavier soils. Perhaps most widely used is the peach seedling Lovell. It supplies some cold hardiness, tolerates wet soils better than most rootstocks, provides good anchorage and disease resistance, produces few suckers, and is resistant to nematodes on all but sandy soils. FLORDAGUARD is a hybrid developed in Florida for resistance to nematodes

TIPS FOR GROWING PEACHES, NECTARINES, AND APRICOTS

- Choose appropriate cultivars for your climate: hardiness for cold climates, chilling hours for mild climates, long frost-free season.
- Plant in well-drained soils, not in low areas or frost pockets.
- Use minimal fertilizer to keep peaches and apricots less vigorous (use normal fertilization for nectarines); prune minimally in early years so you don't delay fruiting.
- Prune heavily once trees bear, keeping an open center or vase shape.
- Thin fruit clusters 4–6 weeks after bloom, leaving 5 or 6 inches between fruits.
- Check trees for problems starting in early spring and continuing throughout harvest, and use appropriate remedies.

and with a low chill requirement. Nemaguard and Nemared are two other popular nematode-resistant rootstocks.

Rootstock for apricots. Although apricots grow easily from seed and many of the seedlings produce very good fruit, unless you're willing to wait many years it's better to buy grafted trees. A small grafted apricot tree starts producing a few fruits in as little as three years; a seedling will take many years and grow quite large before it produces a single fruit. Apricots are usually grafted onto peach, nectarine, or apricot seedlings. Sometimes plum seedlings are used to make apricots more suited for growing in cool, northern soils. The Manchurian hardy apricot is often used as a rootstock, but it grows best in light and sandy soils.

Most nurseries offer only standard-size trees, although a few sell dwarf apricots grafted onto *Prunus besseyi*. This is the same dwarfing stock used for plums and peaches, and as with those dwarf trees, it tends to produce sucker growth.

Planting and Care

PEACHES, NECTARINES, and apricots are so alike that culture is the same for all of them, from planting to insect and disease control, as well as pruning and harvesting. Unless noted otherwise, comments made for peaches apply to nectarines as well.

The fussy peach tree is particular not only about temperature but also about soils. It's never happy in the cool, heavy soils that pears and plums tolerate. Peaches will grow well in ordinary garden soil if it's fairly light. Dry, sandy soils that warm up thoroughly make the best possible home for your peach trees.

Apricots aren't as fussy. They don't need sandy soils and will tolerate more alkaline soils than most other fruits. Once established, trees also tolerate drought better than most tree fruits. Watering during extended dry periods, though, will improve yields.

The basics of planting and follow-up tree care are similar to what's required for other tree fruits. Use the guidelines in chapter 16 except for fertilizing. Unlike some other fruits, peaches and apricots tend to be in a hurry to grow up. In fact, they're often in too much of a hurry, so fast growth should be discouraged. It usually results in a weak tree that breaks easily, gets winter injury, is more susceptible to insects, and is short lived. Fertilize a peach or apricot tree only if it needs it, and then only early in the spring; follow the 12–18 rule described on page 224. Nectarines aren't quite as vigorous, so they may need a bit more compost or fertilizer.

A small grafted apricot tree starts producing a few fruits in as little as three years

Pruning

Because of its vigorous growth habit, a peach tree requires severe pruning when mature, more than most other fruits. All this growth makes it a good candidate for getting a nice-looking espalier sooner than with other fruits. Clingstone peach trees may need less pruning than freestone ones. Start pruning early, right after planting, to develop an open center shape (see page 247).

Apricots have a shape more like cherries so they're often pruned to a modified leader shape. Some growers, though, use an open center for these too.

Prune peach, nectarine, and apricot trees minimally in the early years, as heavy pruning may delay bearing. Prune only to remove small branches blocking light and air flow from the interior of the tree for the open-center system; unlike heavier pruning, you can do this until midsummer.

Once trees begin to bear fruit, prune more heavily. In late winter or early spring remove any winter-killed branches. Also remove top limbs and head back scaffolds; such cuts will stimulate more new, fruit-bearing growth. Unlike apple trees, peach trees bear on 1-year-old shoots and apricots on these and 2-year-old spurs (short shoots on branches); this wood must be renewed by pruning. Don't prune in early winter or within a week of expected extreme cold, as this can result in winter injury. Cut off older limbs that aren't supporting new growth, perhaps a third of the older wood each year that has already borne fruit.

It's also important to thin the developing fruit clusters. Nature likes to hedge her bets against flower-bud losses, so trees may produce 10 times the number of flowers than are needed to produce a good fruit crop. Some of these young fruits drop or get blown off naturally, but usually not enough, so you must help out with further thinning by hand. Annual pruning and judicious thinning not only produce larger and better-quality fruit, but also prevent limb breakage from too-heavy loads, promote good crops each year rather than on alternate years, and aid in keeping trees healthy so they live longer.

A few weeks after bloom you'll see some fruits getting larger, but not all. The small ones don't have a pit forming inside; they won't mature and will fall off in what's called June drop. The time to thin is about 4 weeks after bloom in warm climates (6 weeks in cool climates), when peaches and nectarines are larger than a dime. This is often shortly after June drop. With peaches and nectarines, leave 5 or 6 inches between fruits to help them develop to their best size and quality. Each fruit needs two to three dozen leaves to support its growth. Apricots are smaller, so thin to leave 1 or 2 inches between them.

To avoid diseases that may plague overcrowded fruit, and to allow individual fruits to grow large, be sure to thin young fruits (like these nectarines) early on.

Diseases and Insects

As with other tree fruits, you can minimize most problems that affect peach trees with regular scouting for pests and diseases and employing similar controls (see chapter 18). Apricots tend to have fewer problems, so practicing good sanitation may be all that's needed. You may see more problems with nectarines, as their skins are more vulnerable to insects and diseases. Watch out in particular for brown rot on nectarines in humid climates and for plum curculios on all three fruits east of the Rockies.

These fruits are susceptible to brown rot, powdery mildew, peach scab, bacterial spot, and X-disease (see chapter 18), as well as some of the other diseases that affect plums and other stone fruits. Find out whether bacterial spot is prevalent in your area; if so, look for resistant cultivars and forgo nectarines, as they can be quite severely infected. Nematodes are a problem in some areas, especially hot climates and sites where peach trees have been grown previously. Under these conditions, choose peaches with a nematode-resistant rootstock.

Peaches also have a few of their own diseases. The ones you're most likely to encounter are peach leaf curl and peach split pit.

Peach leaf curl is a fungal disease that overwinters on tree twigs and spreads rapidly in the spring. Infected leaves turn yellow, curl, crinkle, and thicken; eventually they fall off. Look for cultivars resistant to peach leaf curl, such as 'Frost' and 'Redhaven'. Standard peaches in general are less susceptible to this disease than nectarines and genetically dwarf trees. To prevent peach leaf curl, apply a fungicide in the spring, before the buds begin to open. A lime-sulfur spray has long been used to control this ailment, but newer fungicides are more effective.

Oriental fruit moth larva inside a peach

Peach leaf curl

Peach split pit is just that: the pit is split when you cut open the peach. Fruits with this problem may be misshapen, have a shortened storage life, and often quickly develop rots that may then spread to healthy fruits. If severe, fruits themselves may split, making it easy for insects to enter. This is not a disease; it's a physiological disorder with no specific causes. It may be the result of fluctuating moisture levels while the pits are forming, or perhaps freeze damage during flowering and early fruit development. This disorder often occurs when the season is dry, then suddenly turns wet prior to harvest. Mulching trees to conserve moisture and watering during dry spells can help prevent it. Heavy watering near harvest and overfertilizing encourage split pit, so cut back on fertilizer if this has been a problem. Some cultivars, particularly ones ripening early, are more susceptible.

Most insects are not a great threat to these fruits. That's lucky, because the delicate peach and the thinner-skinned nectarine are less able to resist insects than other fruits. Some to watch for are borers, plum curculios, Oriental fruit moths, San Jose scale, and tarnished plant bugs. Descriptions and remedies are discussed in chapter 18.

Harvesting

AS A YOUNG BOY growing up on a Vermont farm, the only apricots I ever saw were dried and came from white paper boxes. They were one of the few foods we bought at the store and, like raisins, salmon, and cornflakes, were treats and a welcome change from our homegrown diet.

Not everyone likes the taste of the apricot, perhaps because many people have never eaten one that's fresh and tree-ripened. Commercially grown apricots are raised on the West Coast and canned or dried before they're shipped to the rest of the country.

If you grow your own peaches, nectarines, and apricots, you can especially revel in your harvest because by picking them at the best possible time you'll get better-flavored fruit than you would from stores (unless you're lucky to have a commercial grower nearby). Although peaches are often picked slightly green for cooking, like plums they're best when fully ripe, as I found out when I ate my first perfect peach. The same applies to nectarines and apricots, whose sugar level stops increasing once picked, even though they'll soften a bit if picked slightly unripe.

When the fruits come off the limb with a slight, gentle twist, peaches and nectarines are ready, and after a little experience you'll pick each one like a connoisseur. Apricots have a beautiful blush when ripe but are still firm to the touch. Always handle peaches and nectarines carefully — never yank them from the tree. Because they're tree-ripened they bruise extremely easily, and damaged fruit rots quickly. Apricots are firmer than peaches, but handle them with care too. As with other tree fruits, leave the stems intact on the fruit.

You should get 4 to 6 bushels of fruit from a standard mature peach or nectarine; a mature apricot will yield 3 to 5 bushels. Dwarf trees usually yield 1 to 2 bushels. A bushel of fruit will turn into 18 to 24 quarts canned or 32 to 48 pints frozen. For 2 pints of sliced frozen fruit, you'll need slightly more than 2 pounds fresh.

Store your peaches, nectarines, and apricots in a cool place, such as a refrigerator, and in a plastic bag for humidity. Peaches may last 5 or 6 days cool, 3 or 4 days at room temperature. Don't wash them until you're ready to eat or process them.

Perhaps one of the best ways to preserve apricots is to simply slice them in half and dehydrate them.

Each of us has a favorite peach dish. Shortcake, pie, cobbler, and salads abound when peaches are in season, and I don't know of anyone who would refuse a fresh peach pie, sundae, milkshake, or ice cream. Nobody wants to be without peaches for long, so we preserve them in jams, conserves, butters, chutneys, and pickles. Some people even dry them. Though most cultivars can be frozen, their flavor and consistency are usually better when canned.

Ripe apricots are delicious to eat right off the tree or cooked in any number of ways — from marmalade to mousse. They're sometimes frozen raw, but freezing toughens the skin, so peel them first. More often they're canned in syrup or dried. They're one of the best fruits for drying and make a good winter snack, or use them in granola, breads, or the paper-thin confections called leathers. They also make outstanding preserves. One of the best spreads we've ever had on toast is homemade apricot jam.

Choosing Cultivars

MANY CULTIVARS are developed for commercial growers, then gradually make it to the home market. Beware of large retailers that buy plants from outside your region and don't have trained professionals who know which cultivars are appropriate for your area. Check local nurseries and nursery catalogs that grow trees suitable for where you garden. Also study online and print publications supplied by your state Cooperative Extension Service (see Resources).

In addition to dwarf versus standard tree size, there are a few choices you'll need to make concerning the fruits. Peach and nectarine cultivars generally have either white or yellow flesh. Those with white flesh are more popular in Asia, and for fresh eating; those with yellow flesh are more popular in America. Cultivars with yellow flesh are more acidic, their tart flavor mellowing as they ripen, while the white-flesh ones are sweeter. The white-flesh cultivars may be slightly hardier. An unusual peach is 'Indian Blood', which has red skin and white flesh heavily streaked with red.

Then there are the freestones and the clingstones. These names just refer to whether the central pit clings or is easily removed when fruits are cut in half from the stem end to the bottom. Clingstone peaches and nectarines generally ripen earlier and have firmer flesh; they are superior for canning if you don't mind the extra work of freeing the pits. Freestones are popular for both fresh eating and canning due to the easy removal of the pits. You may see the terms "semi-clingstone" and "semi-free"; both are usually lumped together as clingstones.

You may have seen small, flattened novelty peaches called donut peaches. There's even a donut nectarine. Maybe you thought they were just misshapen normal peaches, but they're a separate group that was grown in this country back in the 1800s and has recently become popular. They have firm flesh and small (or no) pits. These also go by the names Peento peaches, bagel peaches, Chinese flat peaches, and Chinese saucer peaches. Although the original donut peaches had white flesh, newer cultivars may have yellow flesh (more appealing to American buyers).

Nectarine Cultivars

Many new cultivars are easier to grow than the older nectarines. Most nurseries don't offer many kinds of nectarines, and there isn't much overlap between those offered by one nursery and those from another.

Ripening season begins in June (early cultivars) in the West and South and July in the Midwest and mid-Atlantic states. Chilling requirement is the number of hours needed below 45°F for flowering and fruiting. Many nectarines are freestone, including all those below except 'Hardired'.

Cultivar	FRUIT DESCRIPTION	FRUIT SEASON	CHILLING REQUIREMENT (HOURS)	COMMENTS
'Arctic Fantasy'	white flesh, mostly red skin, very large	mid	400	Good for mild climates; in the 'Arctic' series; susceptible to leaf spot
'Fantasia'	yellow flesh, mostly red skin, very large	late	600	Some frost tolerance, good for warm winter climates; good for freezing
'Flavortop'	yellow flesh, mostly red skin, large	mid	700	Susceptible to leaf spot and cold
'Goldmine'	white flesh, sweet	late	400	Popular on the West Coast
'Hardired'	yellow flesh, semi-clingstone	early	850	Bears at a young age; good disease resistance; may grow into Zone 4
'Redgold'	yellow flesh, large	late	850	Popular and well known; good hardiness; stores well, best for areas without leaf spot
'Sauzee King'	donut type, white flesh	early	500	Bears at a young age, compact habit
'Snow Queen'	white flesh	early	300	Good for mild climates

Apricot Cultivars

Apricot cultivars don't vary greatly; they're generally golden with orange or yellow-orange flesh. Most are suitable for planting only where summer seasons are long and winters are relatively mild (Zones 5 to 8). Many cultivars are at least somewhat self-fertile, but nurseries usually advise planting at least two kinds for better crops. Ripening season begins (early cultivars) in June in the West and South and in July in the Midwest and mid-Atlantic states. Chilling requirement is the number of hours needed below 45°F for flowering and fruiting. Pits of those listed here are freestone.

Cultivar	FRUIT SEASON	CHILLING REQUIREMENT (HOURS)	COMMENTS
('Royal') 'Blenheim'	early	400	One of most popular in California; good for the South
'Chinese' ('Mormon')	early	700	Late bloom resists frosts; a "sweet pit" type; may grow in Zone 4
'Goldcot'	early	800	Disease resistant
'Harcot'	early	700	Late bloom resists frosts; disease resistant; may grow in Zone 4
'Harglow'	early	800	Good in the coastal Northwest and the East; late bloom resists frosts; disease resistant
'Harlayne'	late	700	Late bloom resists frosts; disease resistant; one of most hardy (to Zone 4)
'Katy'	early	300	Good for mild climates
'Moongold'	early	700	Self-unfruitful, pollinate with 'Sungold'; disease resistant; may grow in Zone 4
'Moorpark'	long	600	A long-time favorite; self-fertile; may grow in Zone 4
'Puget Gold'	late	600	Good for the Northwest; naturally semidwarf; some resistance to brown rot
'Sungold'	early	700	Self-unfruitful, pollinate with 'Moongold'; hardy, upright habit; may grow in Zone 4
'Tilton'	early	600	Late bloom resists frosts; good pollinator; self-fertile; one of the best for flavor and for canning and drying

Peach Cultivars

The following chart shows some of the more popular peaches for the home garden, to help you to choose from among the thousands that have been developed worldwide. Chilling requirement is the number of hours needed below 45°F for flowering and fruiting. Ripening season begins in June (early cultivars) in the West and South and July in the Midwest and mid-Atlantic states. Occasionally in catalogs you'll see a number with a plus or minus sign following the name of a peach cultivar, such as 'Reliance' (-3). This refers to the number of days the cultivar ripens before (-) or after (+) 'Redhaven', a popular cultivar. Those before or around this time are early-season, those a couple weeks or so after 'Redhaven' are midseason, and those at least 3 weeks later are the late-season cultivars. Often, though, you'll see peaches referred to as early to late, or in relation to another well-known cultivar, as in "at the same time as 'Loring'." Unless noted, fruit skins are yellow with a red blush of varying degree.

Cultivar	FRUIT DESCRIPTION	FRUIT SEASON	CHILLING REQUIREMENT (HOURS)	COMMENTS
'Babcock'	white flesh, freestone	early	400	Heirloom, bears fruit at an early age
'Belle of Georgia'	white flesh, freestone	early	850	Heirloom; heavy producer; good in colder areas
'Contender'	yellow flesh, freestone, large	mid	1000	Late to bloom, may grow in Zone 4
'Early Red Haven'	yellow flesh, clingstone	early	800	Earlier-to-fruit sport of 'Red Haven'
'Elberta'	yellow flesh, freestone, large	mid	850	Best-known freestone; good for canning and freezing; disease resistant
FLORDAKING	yellow flesh, clingstone, large	early	400	Good for mild climates, as in Texas and Florida
FLORDAPRINCE	yellow flesh, clingstone, small	early	150	Good for mild climates, as in Texas and Florida
'Frost'	yellow flesh, freestone, tangy flavor	mid	700	Resistant to leaf curl
'Galaxy'	donut type, white flesh, freestone, large	mid	450	Larger and more firm than Saturn
'Hale Haven'	yellow flesh, freestone	mid	900	'J.H. Hale' and 'Red Haven' cross, good for canning and freezing
'Indian Blood'	white, streaked red flesh; clingstone; red skin	mid	900	Resistant to leaf curl
'J.H. Hale'	yellow flesh, freestone, light skin fuzz, large	late	800	Classic and still popular, needs another to pollinate (but not 'Elberta')
'June Gold'	yellow flesh, clingstone, large	early	600	Popular in Texas and around the Gulf Coast
'Loring'	yellow flesh, freestone, light skin fuzz	mid	750	Resistant to leaf spot, good in Texas
'Madison'	yellow flesh, freestone	mid	850	May grow in Zone 4
'Red Baron'	yellow flesh, freestone, mainly red skin, large	early	300	Double red flowers, good in mild climates
'Redhaven'	yellow flesh, freestone, large	early	800	The standard for comparisons; world's most planted; good in colder areas; good for canning and freezing; resistant to leaf curl
'Redskin'	yellow flesh, freestone, large	late	750	'J.H. Hale' and 'Elberta' cross
'Reliance'	yellow flesh, freestone	early	1000	May grow in Zone 4
'Saturn'	donut type, white flesh, freestone, large	early	300	Resists bacterial leaf spot; good for mild climates; dark pink double flowers

Store-bought plums have nothing on the juicy sweetness of their tree-ripened cousins.

CHAPTER 12

Plums for Every Region

Plums picked before they're ripe and shipped hundreds of miles can never compare with those that are sun-ripened on the tree. One year, I got impatient for ours to ripen and in a weak moment went out and bought a package of plastic-wrapped, commercially grown plums. They were much larger than ours and a beautiful deep burgundy color, but the taste was disappointingly flat.

In some areas of the West, plums practically grow themselves with minimal care. But only a few parts of the country are considered perfect plum-growing regions. The rest of us have to settle for less than perfection and expect a year now and then when there will be a light crop or none at all.

Nevertheless, I believe every home fruit grower should include plum trees because the fruit is so delicious. When I was growing up, there were none in our family orchard, unfortunately, but our neighbors always had them. The old trees got no care whatsoever, but they bore fruit nearly every year. And how we missed them when they didn't!

'President' is a late-ripening European cultivar that is resistant to black knot.

'Green Gage' is a small, sweet heirloom variety with amber flesh.

Lots of Colors, Shapes, and Uses

POSSIBLY BECAUSE PLUMS originated in so many different places, few fruits vary as widely in size, shape, color, and flavor. The range is more varied than that of apples — from small, native American types to large European prune plums and giant Japanese cultivars. Despite their differences, each type is recognizable as a plum, both by taste and by appearance. Similar to its peach cousins, plum cultivars may be either freestone (with a pit that separates easily from the flesh) or clingstone (with flesh that clings to the pit). The dried prunes we buy are made from European prune-plums that when fresh contain less moisture and more sugar than other plums.

If you intend to grow a few plum trees in your orchard, you should know about the three main groups, their variations, and the crosses with plum fruit relatives. Although the trees and fruits of each species look similar, they're different enough that they usually won't pollinate each other. This, of course, causes trouble for growers who plant two unrelated plum trees.

European Plums

The first group consists of cultivars of the European plum (*Prunus domestica*). These are the most widely planted, with much of the commercial production going for dried plums (made from cultivars with a higher sugar content). Dried plums were formerly, and still are by many, known as prunes — a name that changed because of its negative reputation as a laxative. Oval, dark blue forms of European plums such as 'Stanley' are often called prune plums from this use. European plums got their start in the southern regions of Europe and were brought to the New World by the English settlers in the East and the Spanish missionaries in the West.

Being around for so many centuries, this plum species has many cultivars and variations. European plums have been grouped in various ways, so

Plum Fast Facts

USDA Hardiness Zones: European, 5–9; Japanese, 6–9; American hybrids, (3)4–8

Height: Standard, 12–25 feet; semidwarf; 12–15 feet; dwarf, 5–8 feet

Spacing: Standard, 18–20 feet; semidwarf, 10–15 feet; dwarf, 6–8 feet

Pollination: Two different cultivars of the same plum type needed for fruit

Pruning: Late spring, central or modified leader for European and upright types; open center for others

Special requirement: Early bloomers susceptible to late-spring frosts

Years to bearing: Standard, 4–6; semidwarf and dwarf, 3–5

Yield per tree (bushels): Standard and semidwarf, 2–6; dwarf, 1–2

in catalogs, you'll find them listed in different and sometimes confusing ways.

The original European plums were rounded and dark purple (as is often seen in the bullace types of plums). From these came the popular Damsons; at one time these were considered a separate species, but now they are generally considered a European type. Damsons withstand harsher growing conditions than most other plums. The blue Damsons are popular for jams and preserves. The oval fruits may be an inch long and half an inch wide, with large freestone pits and green flesh that starts sour but becomes sweet when ripe. Damsons probably originated in what is now Syria, as the name comes from Damascus. Seeds have been found from the prehistoric era, and the fruit was mentioned in records dating back to Mesopotamia and the Greek poets.

Related to the Damsons are the 'Mirabelle' and the 'Green Gage' plums, both originally from France. Oval, dark yellow 'Mirabelle' and its cultivars are popular for fresh eating, jams (main use), pies, and even wine or brandy. The 'Green Gage' cultivars (also known as 'Reine Claude') are some of the sweetest plums; they are small and oval, and when ripe are green both outside and inside. They're grown for fresh eating and canning. Once candied in a thick syrup of sugar and cornstarch, 'Green Gage' plums were used as decorations, made famous by reference to the sugar plum fairies in the Nutcracker ballet.

Japanese Plums

The second group is the Japanese plum (*P. salicina*) and its cultivars and hybrids. As the cultivars very likely originated in China, they're sometimes called Asian or Oriental plums. These are the plums most often sold in stores. Excellent for fresh eating, they come in a variety of flesh and skin colors. Often they're round and juicy. They were introduced into this country from Japan more than a century ago. Although some cultivars are fairly hardy, most are best suited for warmer regions, and some can be grown as far south as Florida. A different species of Asian plum is called Chinese plum or Japanese apricot (see Gallery of Uncommon Tree Fruits, pages 193).

American Plums

Species and hybrids of the American plum (*P. americana*) comprise another group. Most are crosses of native wild plums and other foreign species, mainly the hardiest Japanese, so they're sometimes known as the Japanese-American hybrids. They produce fruits that are generally small, rounded, and with a range of flavors. These hybrids are often the best choices for growing in the colder zones, and on soils that are too wet and heavy for other plums, provided they're grafted onto American plum rootstocks.

Rootstocks

Full-size plum trees never get very large, and most people prefer them, so dwarf plums are not as readily available as are dwarf apple trees. If you want a shorter tree, pruning may be a better option than planting a dwarf. Dwarf plum trees are usually grafted onto the Midwest sand cherry (*Prunus besseyi*) and the sand plum (*P. angustifolia*). These rootstocks are hardy, so if you choose hardy cultivars as well, these dwarf trees should grow in Zone 3. The downside is that your selection may be limited because these aren't compatible with many cultivars, so trees may die after only a few years. Dwarf plums are a good choice for large containers.

Almost all European and Japanese plum trees are grafted onto either peach seedlings (such as Lovell) or the roots of the Myrobalan or cherry plum (*P. cerasifera*), a hardy Asian species. For areas with nematodes, consider either the Marianna plum or the Nemaguard peach rootstocks. The Marianna is a cross between a native American species and the Myrobalan plum. The Marianna plum isn't well anchored, though, and the Nemaguard peach is less tolerant of wet soils than plum rootstocks. Some newer, semidwarfing rootstocks are the Krymsk plum from Russia, which is very hardy, and St. Julien, which is used for slightly dwarfing rootstocks that tolerate a range of soil types.

Climate Considerations

AMERICAN HYBRIDS are the hardiest of the plums, so these are the trees for those who garden in the cold parts of North America (Zones 3 and 4). European and Damson cultivars are less hardy than American hybrids but are still possible in some cold-climate areas. The Japanese are the least hardy of all, so most are best in mild climates. There are cultivars in each group that can withstand subzero temperatures, though. The Japanese cultivars generally require fewer chilling hours than the European.

Plums bloom early, usually a week or two ahead of apples, which makes them a special target in the frost belt. The Japanese hybrids bloom earliest, so these aren't good choices where late- or heavy spring frosts are common. If you're lucky to have enough

How Plums Differ

	European Plums	Japanese (Asian) Plums
TREES	More upright form, smooth bark; susceptible to more diseases; less vigorous	More spreading form, rough bark; more disease resistant; more vigorous
CLIMATE	Best for colder regions, Zones (4)5–8	Best for warmer regions, Zones 5–8(9)
SOILS	Tolerate heavier soils	Need well-drained soils
PRUNING	Central (or modified) leader, need little thinning when mature	Open-center training, need heavier pruning young and mature
BLOOM TIME	Later, so better for areas with late-spring frosts; fewer flowers	Earlier, so more susceptible to spring frosts; more flowers
CHILLING REQUIREMENT (HOURS)	800–1,000	250–700
FRUIT	Oval, sweet, fragrant; small, soft, less juicy; usually freestone; often blue skin with golden flesh but may have green, gold, pink or red skin; ripen later	Rounded (or heart-shaped), large, tart or sweet, firm; clingstone; often red skin with red or yellow flesh; ripen earlier
MAIN USES	Fresh eating, dried (prunes), jam	Fresh eating, juice, jam

Yellow 'Mirabelle' and purple 'Damson' plums are so small, they can be eaten by the handful.

American hybrid plums like these tend to be hardier than European or Japanese types.

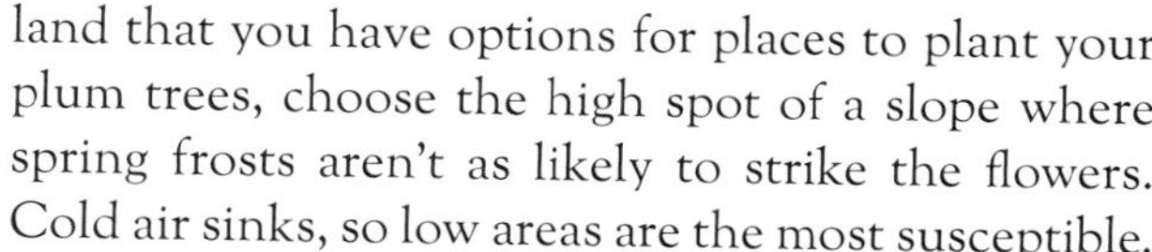

land that you have options for places to plant your plum trees, choose the high spot of a slope where spring frosts aren't as likely to strike the flowers. Cold air sinks, so low areas are the most susceptible.

Once the trees are in bloom, if the temperature drops into the mid-20s, there's little you can do to save the blossoms. We've tried everything from wrapping blankets and plastic sheets around limbs on cold spring nights to running sprinklers, with little success.

A heavy mulch helps to keep the roots cool, which may delay blooming for a few days. But in cold climates, this precaution doesn't always help: frost patterns are unpredictable, and occasionally early blooming is good. Some years our trees have bloomed during a warm spell and set little fruits. Then, a few days later the temperature dropped to the low 20s, but no damage was done to the crop, apparently because the forming fruits are more resistant to cold than the flowers.

Pollination Matters

LOTS OF GARDENERS plant a few plum trees without considering the pollination factor and have wonderful crops every year. Others have a terrible time, and we continually hear grumbling from people whose plums bloomed heavily and set lots of tiny fruits that then fell off.

There are numerous reasons for crop failure — poor soil, shortage of bees, and frost damage — but lack of pollination is the most likely cause. To get fruit, two different cultivars of the same plum type are necessary. For example, if you have only one tree, or one Japanese, one European, and one American, fruit will probably be missing because of improper family planning. Often descriptions of plums will suggest suitable pollinators. If choosing your own, make sure they'll bloom at the same time. Make sure the trees are close enough for bees to transfer pollen. Keep different cultivars of the same plum type within 80 feet of each other, half that distance if they are planted in landscapes with other pollen sources.

A Japanese-American hybrid should be pollinated by the native species that was its parent or by a Japanese plum. These hybrids usually pollinate Japanese plums blooming at the same time. Hybrids with other species (pluots, nectaplums, apriums) should be pollinated with the predominant parent — a Japanese plum could be used to pollinate a pluot, for example. A similar principle applies to hybrids of American species; for these, a native species should be included for pollination. Descriptions will usually give this information.

To add further confusion, the viability of the pollen of certain plums varies considerably, depending on where they're grown. In some areas, the cultivars of different types cross-pollinate with no problems. In other areas, however, two kinds that should mate perfectly will not, either because of weak pollen or because the trees don't bloom at the same time.

A few plums, such as 'Methley', a Japanese plum, are self-fertile. The Damson, 'Green Gage', and 'Stanley' European plums are often self-fertile; the 'Santa Rosa' is partly self-fertile. You may see some European plums listed as self-fertile. For the best yields, and to ensure that your trees get pollinated, plant a partner for these as you would for most other fruit trees.

Don't be discouraged by the complexity of plum pollination. If you have space, plant three different cultivars of the same plum type for insurance. If you don't have room for that many, try a self-fertile cultivar, or perhaps you can talk nearby neighbors into the advantages of diversified fruit growing. If your garden center or nursery catalog recommends a plum cultivar that is an especially good pollenizer for your area, incorporate one of those in your orchard or landscape. 'Compass', a small cherry plum, produces so much vigorous pollen that you may want to plant it as a pollenizer for American hybrids.

Planting and Care

IF YOU START with the kinds best suited for your region, you'll find plum trees easy to grow. Their relatively small size makes pruning and harvesting simple (also spraying, if necessary). They start producing early in life and are seldom subject to blights and other epidemics that can wipe out large numbers of other fruit trees. Aphids, mice, and deer don't bother them as much as they do apple and pear trees. Try to buy trees that are certified disease-free, and plant them several hundred feet from any other plum or cherry trees to reduce the chance of infection by disease or a virus. This will help your plum trees live to a ripe old age.

Follow the same basic soil preparation, planting, and after care as for other tree fruits (see chapters 15 and 16). Like pears — but unlike most other tree fruits — plums will tolerate heavy (clay) soils with less-than-perfect drainage. They grow best in well-drained soils, though, so try to plant in good soil in a spot that gets adequate drainage. European plums are the most tolerant of heavy soils; Japanese types prefer a loamy soil with good drainage.

TIPS FOR GROWING PLUMS

- Choose a site with abundant sun and well-drained soil. (Some plums tolerate less-than-perfect drainage.) Plums bloom early, so look for a site on a slope to minimize risk from a late spring frost. Try for a site away from wild plums and cherries, which could spread diseases to your new trees.
- Select a type, and cultivars, suited to your area. To assure cross-pollination, buy at least two cultivars of the same type (three is better), and plant within 40 feet of each other.
- Fertilize yearly in spring.
- Provide ample moisture throughout the growing season. A thick mulch helps conserve soil moisture.
- Train European and upright cultivars to a central or modified leader form, open center for other types of plums.
- Prune in late spring according to type: Japanese and American hybrids need more pruning than European selections do. On upright cultivars, spread young limbs so they grow at a 60-degree angle to the trunk.
- Thin fruit on Japanese hybrids when the size of a dime, so they're 4 to 5 inches apart; thin others only if too crowded, and then to 2 to 4 inches apart.

Because plums produce a large amount of fruit on a relatively small tree, adequate amounts of fertilizer and moisture must be available throughout the growing season. A thick mulch and a generous dose of organic fertilizer around each tree every year help to provide this.

Prune According to Type

Several years ago I found two articles related to plum growing in the same issue of a garden magazine. One expert wrote that plums need little if any pruning. The other said they're one fruit that should be pruned severely every year. Probably the writers had different types of plums in mind, because the Japanese and the fast-growing American hybrids certainly need more pruning than the slower-growing Europeans.

As with the other tree fruits, prune plum trees:

- to let in more sunshine (for healthy and better-colored fruit)
- to shape into a stronger and more attractive tree
- to prevent branches breaking under heavy fruit loads on Japanese types

Small-fruited plums. There's no doubt that certain small-fruited plum trees produce well with no pruning at all, but I've found that most varieties greatly benefit from pruning. Proper pruning results in fewer but larger fruits, encourages annual bearing, and helps prevent breakage by eliminating bad crotches and weak limbs. Prune so that the tree becomes nicely shaped, easy to work with, and productive.

European and Japanese plums. The European types may need only light pruning; they produce annually on older spurs (mostly 2 to 6 years old), so there's less need to stimulate formation of new branches. The Japanese types, which produce fruit on both spurs and 1-year-old stems, need heavier pruning to stimulate new growth in order to keep fruits coming yearly. In the arid West under good growing conditions, heavy pruning will help reduce some of the crop load to a manageable level for you and the tree. Light pruning to shape the young plum tree when still small will save you a great deal of corrective surgery later on, and will be less of a shock for the tree.

Plum trees bear their fruit on short, stubby spurs (like apples, pears, and cherries), so be careful not to cut off too many of these when you're pruning.

Prune According to Habit

Like apples, all plum trees don't grow in the same fashion. Try to adjust your pruning style to the particular growth habit of each type. The European and Japanese grow more like trees, European types often more upright than the Japanese. Modified-leader training (see page 246) is usually recommended for the upright European plums and for any upright Japanese cultivars, such as 'Santa Rosa'. Lower semi-dwarf or dwarf trees may be fine trained to a central leader if they won't be too high for your maintenance and harvesting. Most Japanese plums are spreading trees that do best pruned to an open-center (vase-shaped) style. American species and Japanese-American hybrids are also spreading and shrubbier, so an open-center pruning style is more appropriate for these as well.

Certain plums, such as 'Santa Rosa', tend to grow skyward — even the outside branches turn up. If young limbs on these are too vertical, you need to spread them, as with pears (see page 150), to create the strong horizontal branch angles needed to support heavy loads of fruit. Occasionally cut back the tops of upright trees, when needed, to encourage a more spreading, lower-growing tree that's easier to maintain and pick. Other varieties spread so wide that the outer branches become weepy and hang to the ground. Prune back all branches that are spreading too wide before they begin to trail.

Avoiding Water Sprouts

Heavy pruning, coupled with lots of fertilizer, will cause lots of water sprouts from the base of plum trees. Pruning less each year and pruning annually rather than waiting a few years to do a heavy pruning will help decrease the number of water sprouts. If the new growth is too vigorous, slow it down by bending branch tips into a weeping shape. Either hang weights from branches near the tips, or tie flexible ends of branches to weights on the ground. This practice, called festooning, is common in Britain.

Thinning Fruit

Some plums produce more fruit than the plant really needs. As with peaches, you'll need to manually thin the immature fruits when they're between the size of a dime and a quarter, leaving fruits 4 to 5 inches apart for Japanese plums. Thinning may not be needed for European cultivars; if it is, space fruits 2 to 4 inches apart. Damsons and native plums need no thinning unless they have a crop too heavy for their limbs to support. Thinning, along with pruning, will encourage annual bearing on those trees prone to bear more heavily every other year.

Diseases and Insects

Most plums grow well in the arid West because there they aren't troubled by diseases. Although the list of plum diseases is not as great as it is for other fruits, be on the lookout for black knot, bacterial spot, brown rot, and scab. Some cultivars, such as 'President', 'AU Roadside', and 'Santa Rosa', are resistant to black knot. In hot and humid climates, nematodes may be a problem, in which case look for nematode-resistant rootstocks, mentioned earlier. If your trees are grafted onto a peach rootstock, don't plant in wet or poorly drained soil, as peach rootstocks are susceptible to root rots that plum rootstocks won't get.

Another reason plums are easier throughout the West is that gardeners don't have to worry about the plum curculio. This is the main insect pest to watch for east of the Rockies. For descriptions of the curculio and plum diseases and their controls, see chapter 18 (page 279).

Harvesting Plums

PLUM TREES are extremely productive, and they're long-lived — often to 30 years for standard trees. If all goes well, the large-fruiting kinds should bear 2 to 6 bushels per tree (20 to 120 pounds). The fruit is ripe when it's well colored and has a powdery "bloom" (a white waxy coating). At this time, it should separate from the branch easily and be sweet and juicy to eat. Only Japanese plums may benefit from picking a short time before they're tree-ripe; allow them to ripen in a cool, but not cold, room for a few days before eating.

Many plum cultivars ripen over a fairly long season, so they're an excellent home fruit. They'll keep for a few weeks in a refrigerator or other cool place, but check them occasionally and use before they get mushy.

Besides eating them right off the tree, we enjoy our delicious plums in dessert sauces, pies, and coffee cake. We preserve plum conserve for winter treats, and freeze plums both raw and cooked. Sometimes we freeze the tangy juice for a punch base — chilled and mixed with ginger ale, it's our traditional Christmas cocktail. Figure on 1 bushel of plums yielding 24 to 30 quarts canned. For 1 quart canned, it takes just over 2 pounds of fruit.

Plums can be dried in a dehydrator, either cut in half with pits removed or sliced. If cut, first soak for 10 minutes in ascorbic acid or a similar product from the store to prevent browning. Then figure on 6 to 10 hours in the dehydrator for slices, 24 to 36 hours for halves. You can also dry plums whole (crack the skins first by dipping in boiling water for 30 to 60 seconds), but the process takes a lot longer.

Pluots and Plumcots

Plums are closely related to apricots, as well as to peaches and nectarines, so clever breeders have come up with some crosses among the various species. These crosses are sweeter than either parent, with similar hardiness (generally Zones 5–9).

The pluot is a cross between an apricot and a plum, with more plum heritage. Fruits have smooth a skin, like their plum parent, and a sweet flavor. They require 400 to 500 chilling hours. Plant with an aprium or Japanese plum to ensure pollination. Trees are attractive, three-season landscape plants with nice spring flowers, summer fruit, and fall leaf color. Some cultivars are 'Dapple Dandy', a freestone with maroon skin and creamy red flesh; 'Flavor King', with red-purple skin and red flesh; and 'Splash', with red-orange skin and orange flesh.

The plumcot has about the same amount of apricot and plum heritage, with a plumlike shape, an aroma of plums, and the slightly fuzzy skin of an apricot. The flavor has been described as a blend of fruit juices. As with pluots, plant with an aprium or Japanese plum to ensure pollination. The cultivar 'Flavorella' has yellow skin and flesh and a sweet-tart flavor; it ripens early. Plumcots have a low chilling requirement, 250 to 400 hours.

Other hybrids are less common. Apriums have more apricot than plum in their background, so fruits more resemble apricots with just a little fuzz on the skin. Plant with an apricot to ensure pollination. 'Tri-lite', a peach-plum hybrid that ripens early, has a unique taste with a flavor first of peaches and then a plum aftertaste; it's good for canning as well as fresh eating. 'SpiceZee' is a nectaplum, which is a nectarine-plum hybrid with a spicy sweet flavor. It makes a nice ornamental tree with spring blooms, and reddish leaves in spring turn a reddish green in summer.

Pluot

Plumcot

Plum Cultivars

It would be a hopeless task to try to list all the many plums grown in North America, and new ones appear each year. Here are few widely available cultivars that are tasty and good for fresh eating as well as other uses. Fruiting season ranges from late May to late August in warmer climates, mid-July to mid-September in colder climates.

Cultivar	FRUIT DESCRIPTION	FRUITING SEASON	CHILLING REQUIREMENT (HOURS)	COMMENTS
EUROPEAN				
'Green Gage'	light green with amber flesh, very sweet; small	mid	500	Old heirloom; may get brown rot; tends to bear every other year
'Italian prune'	purple with amber flesh, very sweet; large	late	800	Vigorous; amber flesh turns red when cooked; partly self-fertile
'Mount Royal'	blue with yellow flesh	mid	800	Naturally semidwarf; grows in Zone 4
'President'	blue with amber flesh	late	800	One of the last to ripen; resists black knot
'Shropshire' ('Damson')	blue-black with green flesh; small	late	800	Very old heirloom, vigorous, heavy yields, late bloom, bears at an early age
'Stanley'	blue-black with green flesh, large	late	800	Late bloom, popular in eastern states; resistant to bacterial spot; self-fertile
'Yellow Egg'	golden with yellow flesh, very sweet; large	late	800	Old heirloom; naturally semidwarf
JAPANESE				
'AU Roadside'	dark red with red flesh	early	700	Good disease resistance; blooms later; good for the South
'Burbank'	red-yellow with yellow flesh; large	mid	400	Bears at an early age; naturally semidwarf; semi-freestone
'Elephant Heart'	red-purple with red flesh; heart shaped; large	late	500	Long harvest season; popular in the West
'Inca'	golden skin and flesh; sweet-tart flavor	mid	300	Good for warm climates
'Methley'	dark red with red flesh	early	250	Self-fruitful; heavy yields; good for warm climates
'Santa Rosa'	dark red with amber flesh; large	mid	300	Bears at an early age; resists black knot; popular in the Southwest
'Shiro'	yellow with yellow flesh; large	early	500	Heirloom; productive
AMERICAN HYBRIDS				
'Bruce'	yellow-red with red flesh; small	early	450	Japanese and Chickasaw plum cross; partly self-fertile; early to bloom; good in the South; best in Zones 6–8
'Superior'	red with yellow flesh; clingstone; large	mid	800	Bears at an early age; hardy to Zone 4
'Waneta'	red with sweet yellow flesh; clingstone; large	mid	800	Bears at an early age; needs cross-pollination; hardy to Zone 3

Wild Plums

Beach plum

Several native plums grow wild in various parts of North America. They produce vast amounts of small fruits that birds and animals devour and people collect to make into tasty jams and jellies. Those that make small bushes are good landscape plants in beds, along foundations, or as a windbreak.

One of the best known of these native plums is the beach plum (*Prunus maritima*), found growing along the shores of the north Atlantic coast. If you deduce from its name that it tolerates sand and salty soils and air, you're correct. But it will grow equally well away from the beach, in Zones 3 to 7, as long as it grows in full sun and well-drained soil. Masses of white (sometimes pink) flowers in spring make this 6-foot shrub a great ornamental. Unless it's grafted onto an upright-growing understock, it will tend to grow suckers and spread, and it can be quite thorny. You can train it with some yearly pruning into a hedge or shrub. Few problems bother it.

Yields are variable, lots one year and little another. Two seedlings or cultivars are needed for cross-pollination. Fruits are small, generally less than an inch across, and reddish to deep purple. Because they're a bit tart, they're best in jellies. Cultivars were popular in the middle part of the last century but are difficult to find now. What you'll usually find are plants grown from seedlings.

Hybrids of western sand cherries (see page 184) and standard plums are known as chums in Canada and as cherry-plums in the United States. They've been around for a century, and originally came out of the Great Plains. They produce a small plum, not as good in quality as a true plum, but they tolerate severe winters and drought for those who can't grow plums otherwise.

The arrival of ripe, sweet cherries marks the beginning of summer in many parts of the country.

CHAPTER 13

Cherries, Sweet and Sour

In school one year we read a book about some English children who had a great many adventures, most of which, I'm sure, were exciting. But the only thing I remember about their exploits is that on summer mornings, the boys climbed out the upstairs window of their big house into a monstrous cherry tree and ate the giant sweet cherries. That made a big impression on me, and I decided that someday I would have a tree just like that.

The cherry trees those English children climbed to such great heights were sweet cherries. Because we couldn't grow those in our climate, I raised sour cherries, which are naturally smaller trees; most never grew more than 8 feet tall. Even a small child couldn't climb to the second floor in one of them.

Although I never did climb a cherry tree, I do love the taste of ripe cherries, sweet or sour. They have the added benefit of being beautiful ornamental trees, although their spring flowers are not as showy as those of the flowering cherries that don't fruit.

Cherries are an ancient fruit; pits have been found in European caves dating to the Stone Age. They were brought to America in the 1600s by early settlers. Today, most of us are familiar with some sort of cherry, if not from cherry pie and the maraschino cherries topping sundaes then from the wild species that grow in almost every region of North America.

Sweet, Sour, and Bush Cherries

WHEN YOU SHOP for cherry trees, you'll find two main groups — the sweet (*Prunus avium*) and the sour or tart (*P. cerasus*). The two types have different growth habits and thus different pruning needs, as well as different uses for their fruit.

Sweet Cherries

The sweet cherry group includes many more cultivars than the sour. These are more popular because of their sweetness. They grow well in the same areas as the peach (Zones 5–8), except they don't grow well in summer heat. Spring frosts can damage the early-to-bloom flowers; once their chilling needs are met, a mild spell in winter can inspire them to start to grow even earlier. Trees generally grow tall and more upright, 20 to 30 feet high and 20 to 25 feet wide if not pruned or grafted onto a dwarfing rootstock. They're more particular about growing conditions than sour cherries are. They grow best in cooler, western regions, where there are fewer diseases and pests to bother them, and in drier soils. At the end of the season, wet weather can cause fruits to crack and become diseased. Newer cultivars bear fruits with more elastic skins that are resistant to this cracking and splitting.

Heart types and Bigarreau cultivars. Sweet cherries are divided into two groups, based on fruit shape. Heart types have, as you might guess, heart-shaped fruit. The Bigarreau cultivars are more rounded. Because they have firmer flesh, and thus a longer shelf life, they're the ones you find in stores. Within each of these groups, cultivars that produce dark, reddish juice are known as dark sweets and those that produce pale, almost colorless juice are the light sweets.

Sour Cherries

In catalogs, sour cherries are often called pie cherries, as that's where so many of them are destined. They have the widest range, generally growing well in Zones 4–7. (In Zone 4 they may get trunk damage from the cold, and that will lead to their demise.) Flowers may be damaged by late-spring frosts, so commercial orchards are often located near bodies of water, which moderate the climate. One such is Lake Michigan, which is why the state of Michigan produces about 75 percent of the nation's sour cherries. Sour cherries need a few weeks' chilling in order to flower and fruit (see chilling hours, page 192). If you garden in a frost-free or nearly frost-free part of the country, you're likely to have trouble

Sweet cherries (left) have dense, sweet flesh. Sour cherries (right) have a lighter, more translucent appearance and tend to be somewhat smaller than sweet cherries.

growing them. Where they grow well, they'll be shorter than the sweet cherries — 15 to 20 feet tall and wide — with a more spreading habit.

Amarelle and Morello types. Sour cherries also fall into two distinct groups. More common in North America are the amarelle types, which include 'Montmorency', the most popular pie-cherry cultivar. Cherries in this group have bright red fruits with yellow flesh, flattened on the ends, and produce a clear juice. More common in Europe are the Morello sour cherries, which grow on smaller trees. Their fruits are rounded with bright red flesh and produce a dark red juice. A famous Morello cultivar, 'Marasca', was used in Italy to produce a liqueur called maraschino. This liqueur gives its name to the candied cherries we buy today, which are actually other sour cherries, bleached, then colored and sugared, with nothing much left of the original except the cherry shape.

Bush Cherries

Members of still another group, the bush cherries, are quite different from orchard cherries, even though the fruits are somewhat similar. These are small, very hardy shrubs. Though listed as hardy in Zones 4 to 6 or 7, some can be grown in Zone 2, especially where deep snow provides good winter

Nanking cherry is a beautiful flowering shrub that produces bright red berries in midsummer.

Cherry Fast Facts

USDA Hardiness Zones: Sweet, 5–8; sour, 4–7 (varies with cultivar); bush (2)4–6(7)

Height: (Standard trees) sweet, 20–30 feet; sour, 15–20 feet; bush, 4–10 feet

Spacing: (Standard trees) sweet, 20–25 feet; sour, 15–20 feet; bush, 3–6 feet

Pollination: Sweet generally need cross-pollination; not essential for sour or most bush cherries

Pruning: Late spring; modified leader for sweet; modified leader or open center for sour; cut older branches to ground for bush cherries

Special requirement: Be prepared to share crop with birds, unless trees are small enough for netting

Years to bearing: Sweet, 5–7; sour 3–5; bush, 2–3

Yield per standard tree/bush: Sweet and sour, 60–80 quarts; bush, 2–4 quarts

Rootstocks: Standard, Semidwarf, or Dwarf?

Cherries, like the other tree fruits, are grafted, and the height of your mature cherry trees will depend on which rootstock was used. The plant label (or your supplier) will tell you what to expect for the mature height. Dwarf trees are only half the height of a standard cherry tree, sometimes shorter. But rootstocks control more than just height, so it's worth finding out more before you buy your trees.

Cherries, like the other stone fruits, can be grafted interchangeably on roots of other cherries or on those of plum, peach, and apricot trees. Rootstocks impart many characteristics in addition to height, such as shape, vigor, soil adaptability, nematode resistance, age when trees begin to bear, and hardiness. When buying cherry trees, especially from a catalog, you may be faced with a choice of two or three different rootstocks for a particular cultivar.

Dwarfing. A good selection for sweet cherries in the home garden is Gisela, one of the newer dwarfing rootstocks. The Gisela series is widely available and produces shorter plants than a Mazzard rootstock does (see below), either semidwarf or dwarf, depending on the selection. They can also be used for sour cherries and may provide some disease resistance. Gisela rootstocks result in heavy crops, so fruit thinning is especially important for such trees.

Nematode resistance. The most common rootstock is Mazzard, a wild European sweet cherry (*Prunus avium*) that's believed to have been used for a couple of thousand years. Most commonly used for sweet cherries, Mazzard will work with most sour cherries too. It provides resistance to root-knot nematodes in the soil, good anchorage, and more tolerance of less-than-perfect soil drainage.

For sandy soil. Mahaleb is a wild semidwarf European sour cherry (*P. mahaleb*) used mainly for sour cherries. It results in a shorter, hardier tree, and one more tolerant of sandy soils and drought. Trees on Mahaleb rootstocks don't tolerate poorly drained soils, however. When used for sweet cherries, Mahaleb may produce a tree with a more spreading growth habit.

Other dwarfs. You may encounter two other dwarfing rootstocks; both are relatively new and compatible with all cherries. Those in the Krymsk series from Russia don't sucker, and they lead to fruiting at an earlier age (precocious is the technical term for this). Colt results in a shorter plant than a cherry grafted onto Mahaleb, and it provides some disease resistance as well as better tolerance of less-than-perfect soil drainage.

protection. In spring, if a late frost threatens flowers, plants are short enough that you can spread row covers over them for frost protection.

Nanking cherry. The popular Nanking cherry (*P. tomentosa*) makes a gorgeous flowering shrub in spring, 6 to 10 feet tall with white to pinkish flowers. The half-inch, bright red berries, which ripen in midsummer, have a good flavor between sour and sweet cherries. This shrub is often used as a windbreak in Zone 3, as well as in landscapes, and sometimes for a rootstock. Plant at least two for cross-pollination.

Western sand cherry. The western sand cherry (*P. besseyi*) is native to the Great Plains. It forms a suckering shrub 4 to 6 feet tall and is often used as a dwarfing rootstock for peaches, apricots, and plums, which then may develop its suckering habit. Clothed in fragrant white flowers in late spring, it bears dark purple cherries in midsummer. The bitter fruits sweeten as they ripen; although they're edible, they're more commonly used for jellies. Glossy green leaves turn orange-red in fall. The western sand cherry grows best in well-drained soils but will tolerate rather unfavorable sites in Zones 3 to 7, including alkaline, sandy (as the name indicates), and clay soils. It's seldom bothered by insects and disease, and will tolerate drought once established. Plant at least two bushes for cross-pollination. 'Hansen's', with large, dark purple fruits, is the most common cultivar.

Interspecies crosses. Other bush cherries are crosses between species, or even with plums (these are known as chums or cherry-plums). 'Carmine Jewel', developed in the Canadian prairies in the 1940s, is a cross between the sour and Mongolian cherries (*Prunus cerasus* × *P. fruticosa*).

Unlike most varieties of sweet cherry, 'Sweetheart' is a self-fertile cultivar. It doesn't need to be pollinated by another cherry tree.

Picky about Pollination

SOUR CHERRIES are one of the few fruits that almost always self-pollinate well, so one tree is all you need. In most cases sweet cherries will need another cultivar for successful fruiting. A few sweet cherries are self-fertile; seek out cultivars such as 'Lapins', 'Stella', and 'Sweetheart' if you have room for only one tree.

Pollination for sweet cherries is more complicated than for most other fruits. Pay attention when getting sweet cherries not only to buy at least two different cultivars, but also to make sure that they'll cross with each other. Descriptions should provide this information; some references have a table to help you match cultivars compatible for cross-pollination. Sour cherries are not good as pollinators for sweet cherries because they seldom bloom at the same time. Nor can cherry plums and the other stone fruits satisfactorily pollinate cherries.

How Sweet and Sour Cherries Differ

	Sweet	Sour (Tart, Pie)
FRUIT USES	Fresh, freezing, canning	Cooking (pies, cobblers)
YEARS TO BEARING	5–7	3–5
WHERE FRUIT IS PRODUCED	On 2- to 10-year-old spurs, some at base of 1-year-old shoots	1-year-old shoots, some on 2- to 3-year-old spurs
POLLINATION	Most need cross-pollination	Self-fertile
MATURE HEIGHT AND SPREAD	20–30 feet	15–20 feet
HARDINESS ZONES	5–8 (9)	4–7 (9)
BEST CLIMATE	Drier, western U.S.	More humid, eastern U.S.
SOIL REQUIREMENTS	Good drainage	Tolerate heavier (but not waterlogged) soils
GROWTH HABIT	Upright	Spreading
PRUNING STYLE	Central or modified leader	Modified leader or open center (vase)

Planting and Care

ALL CHERRY TREES fruit best in full sun. Sweet cherry trees must have well-drained soils, although some rootstocks are more tolerant of occasionally damp soil. Sour cherries can withstand a heavier, cooler soil as long as it's reasonably well drained.

When planting, make sure the graft union is 1 to 3 inches above the soil level. As this union may be weak in cherries, it's important to stake trees directly after planting, so winds don't break off the tops (see page 238).

All fruit trees need careful planting (see chapter 16), but cherries require special care because their roots dry out so easily. Never let the roots get dry when you're planting, and keep new trees adequately watered until they begin to grow well. Because cherry trees are shallow-rooted, droughts are hard on them, particularly those growing in sandy soil. They thrive under a thick, cool mulch.

Cherry trees need very little fertilizer. If the soil is in good condition, you may not need to add anything other than compost each year. Overfeeding will produce a tree that grows too fast, bears poorly, and is more susceptible to disease. Underfeeding, on the other hand, may reduce the amount of fruit you get. Cherry trees need some nutrients, especially nitrogen, to produce enough shoot growth to support formation of fruit buds.

Let your tree guide you in how much to fertilize. Follow the 12–18 rule on page 224 for young, nonbearing cherry trees. Once they begin to bear fruit, sweet cherries may be expected to produce slightly more growth (10–15 inches) a year compared to sour cherries (8–10 inches a year). If your cherry trees produce more than these amounts, don't fertilize them; if they produce less, you need to fertilize.

Prune According to Type

Sweet, sour, and bush cherries have different pruning needs to match their different growth habits. Follow the basic guidelines in chapter 17, but adjust pruning based on your trees' vigor (especially as influenced by the rootstock), the amount of fruiting of a particular cultivar, and to promote larger fruits.

Cherries, like plums and apricots, bear their fruit on spurs, short blunt growths off branches. When pruning, take care not to remove these spurs unless they look old or, on older trees, are too numerous. Flowers of sweet cherries, and thus their fruits, are formed mostly on 2- to 10-year-old spurs on older branches, although some also appear at the base of 1-year-old branches. The largest, and best, cherries are produced on new branches and younger spurs (1 to 3 years old); to stimulate such new growth it's important to prune your trees every year. The flowers and fruits of sour cherries form mostly on 1-year-old branches, though some will appear on 2- to 3-year-old spurs, too.

Timing. The timing for pruning cherry trees depends on your climate. Cherries, particularly sweet ones, are quite susceptible to bacterial diseases that are most active during cool, wet weather. In arid regions such diseases aren't much of a problem; prune in early spring to stimulate vigorous growth, or if trees are already producing vigorous growth you can prune in early summer. Everywhere else, though, you should prune mature cherry plants after flowering

When pruning cherry trees, be careful not to remove too many fruiting spurs, or that season's harvest will be diminished.

in late spring. That's when temperatures are warmer, conditions are a bit drier, and pruning wounds heal faster, which will minimize the chance of infection. If cankers and other diseases are known in your area, try not to prune 2 or 3 days before rain is predicted — this will lessen their spread.

Training sweet cherries. Sweet cherries generally grow upright, so often they're trained to a central leader. If you have a standard tree and want to keep it shorter, use the modified-leader system instead (see page 246). Try to leave about 12 inches between scaffold branches. (This is twice the distance for sour cherries, as sweet cherries are usually more vigorous than sour cherries.)

On young sweet cherry trees, prune back the main scaffold branches as well as the central leader. Also remove a third to a half of the tip growth on future fruiting shoots (those formed the previous year). These heading cuts will promote more branching and reduce the eventual crop load to a level that can be supported without limbs breaking under too much weight. Also prune back, or even remove, the more upright branches and those that are overly vigorous and threaten to dominate others.

To promote wider, stronger, 45-degree branch angles, spread branches at an early age, as you would for pears (see page 150). This is often needed on sweet cherries, which grow more upright than the sour cherries. The simplest means is to use clothespins for a few weeks when branches are only a few inches long. Attach a clothespin to the trunk, just above a branch, to hold the branch at a more horizontal angle.

Once your sweet cherries have been bearing for a couple years, start heading back about a fifth to a quarter of the fruiting branches each year. This will promote development of new spurs that will form better-quality fruit, and it will reduce some of the heavy crop load. On upper branches, leave 3- to 5-inch stubs; leave longer ones lower in the tree, where they receive less light. Continue to thin out new shoots that appear weak or too upright.

Training sour cherries. Sour cherries have a more spreading habit than sweet cherries, so usually they're trained to a modified leader (page 246). You may train to an open center if you want to keep trees shorter, but such plants may not bear as heavily. Don't prune as heavily as sweet cherries in the trees' early years; too much pruning of young sour cherries each year will result in stunted trees.

When the branches of a cherry tree are young and flexible, clothespins can be used to train branches so that they have a wider angle from the trunk.

Identify four to six main "scaffold" branches to allow to develop and prune out the rest. These scaffold branches should be about 6 inches apart and spaced evenly around the trunk, not directly above each other or directly across from each other. Don't prune these scaffold branches, and don't cut back the leader, as you might for other fruits, as you don't want to stunt trees.

Once sour cherries begin to bear, cut back the leader to a lateral scaffold to begin modified-leader training. (Or, to keep trees shorter, switch to open-center training.) Also prune out some older stems (3 to 5 years old) each year to stimulate new growth. Because these trees tend to be top-heavy, with upper limbs shading the lower ones, you may need to thin out some upper branches, too, each year.

Pruning bush cherries. Bush cherries need less pruning than other types. They grow as shrubs with new shoots each year sprouting from the base. Most fruit is produced on shoots less than 5 years old, so cut older shoots right to the base of the plant in late winter or early spring. This will keep newer fruiting shoots forming each year. Also remove suckers growing out into areas where you don't want them, and thin shoots that are getting too crowded. This will let more air and light into the center, which results in better fruit and less chance of disease.

Birds, Insects, and Diseases

Birds love cherries more than any other orchard fruits, and are probably the grower's biggest problem. You may be able to use netting on smaller tart cherry trees. On larger trees, try "scare-eye" balloons and similar devices (see pages 189 amd 298). Some people try to outwit the birds by planting yellow cherries, thinking the birds will wait for them to ripen and turn red. But birds are no fools, at least not for long. And deer may browse young trees and growth, resulting in loss of fruit and stunted trees (see page 295).

Cherry leaf spot

Diseases. Although cherries are subject to several diseases (most of the same ones that affect plums), many home orchardists never spray their cherry trees and have no problems at all. Keeping dead or infected fruit and leaves picked up, removing and destroying infected branches, and cutting down infected nearby wild cherries will greatly reduce disease problems.

The most common diseases of cherries are black knot and brown rot. Other potential diseases, particularly of sour cherries, are verticillium wilt and powdery mildew. In early summer, verticillium (a fungal wilt) causes leaves to become dull and light colored. The fungal perennial canker that infects cherries forms blackened wounds on stems. In summer, X-disease of stone fruits can cause the sudden death of cherries grafted onto Mahaleb rootstock. For trees on Mazzard rootstock, X-disease may cause a slow decline over several years. A clue that the disease may be present is scattered small and pink fruit that taste bitter. See chapter 18 for more on these diseases, and their controls.

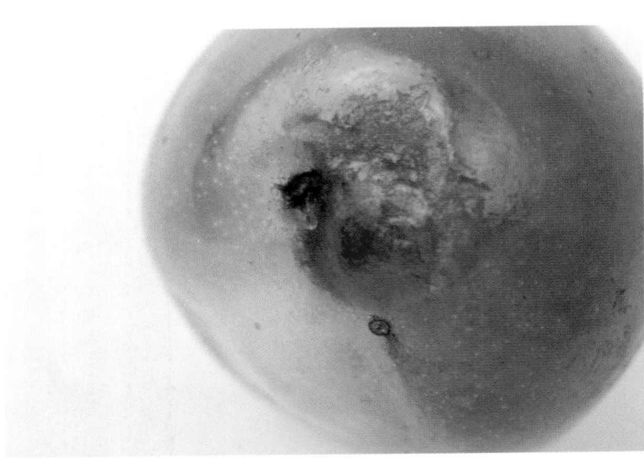

Cherry maggot hole

Cherry leaf spot is a fungal disease that becomes noticeable in spring, shortly after petal fall. Small purplish spots appear on upper leaf surfaces, later turning brown and sometimes merging to form brown patches; in severe cases leaves yellow and then drop prematurely. This defoliation will weaken trees over a period of years, reducing fruiting and leading to winter injury in cold climates. Although all cherries are at risk, sour cherries are most susceptible, plus it's more difficult to control the disease on sour cherries. In the fall, clean up fallen leaves from infected trees; this may be all the control you need.

Black knot fungus

If you have just a few birds to scare away from your cherry tree, a scare-eye balloon may be the answer.

Netting provides the best protection against birds. Install the netting just before cherries begin to color.

Otherwise, apply fungicide sprays as needed, beginning after petal fall and continuing up to harvest; you may need to spray a couple of times after harvest as well. You can alternate between spraying one side of the tree one week, the other side the next. As always, follow the specific directions and timing on the label of any product you use.

Viruses. Leaves that become mottled or distorted may have a virus, which usually comes from infected rootstocks or from infected trees nearby. The virus spreads throughout the tree and by the time a tree has produced for a dozen years or so a few limbs begin to wilt and die. Often within 2 or 3 years of this stage, the tree is dead. Fungicides aren't effective on viruses. Buy virus-resistant or virus-free trees if at all possible, and isolate your plantings from wild and infected trees.

Physiological issues. Bark splitting may be mistaken for disease but is actually a physiological problem common on many fruit trees (see page 267). Another physiological problem, one unique to some sweet cherries, is fruit cracking. As the fruits ripen late in the season, rainy weather may cause them to absorb more water than they can handle. The flesh inside swells but the inelastic skins are unable to expand, so fruits crack or split. This may be worse when the weather is quite warm. If fruits aren't yet ripe, rot disease may set in and ruin them. To enable split fruits to ripen without rotting, a protective fungicide spray may be required. Or grow cultivars resistant to cracking such as 'BlackGold', 'Lapins', and 'WhiteGold'.

Insects. The same insects that may affect plums can also strike cherries: plum curculios, peach tree borers, San Jose scale, and mites. Luckily for us, the tent caterpillar is about the only insect that has ever attacked our sour cherry trees. For ways to manage any of these pests, see chapter 18.

The cherry maggot, or cherry fruit fly, is a serious pest in some areas. It operates in much the same way as the apple maggot: adult flies lay eggs inside the fruits, and these hatch and cause wormy cherries. This insect also lays eggs in wild cherries, so keep your cultivated trees away from their wild cousins. Removing any cherries remaining on trees after harvest and raking up fallen cherries on the ground may provide some control too. Maggots spend up to 10 months a year in the soil, about 2 inches deep; adults ultimately emerge in late spring to early summer. Watch for the emerging adults. If you plan to use a pesticide, it's important to spray during the few days when the adults have emerged but before they lay eggs. Once the eggs are inside the fruits, they — and later the legless maggots — will be protected from sprays. Instead of a chemical spray, you can hang red ball sticky traps (see page 263) in the trees; they'll attract and entrap many adult flies.

TIPS FOR GROWING CHERRIES

- Choose a site with full sun and well-drained soil; sweet cherries prefer a lighter, sandier soil; sour cherries tolerate heavier soils.
- Stake trees after planting.
- Don't let roots dry out; keep well-watered until established; water regularly in dry climates, and on sandy soils.
- Don't overfertilize; annual compost application may be all that is needed.
- Prune back the main branches of young sweet cherries by one-third to one-half; don't prune back young sour cherries.
- Only prune mature sweet cherries to thin or remove broken branches; prune out older branches of mature sour cherries.
- Use bird protection, if needed.

Harvesting Cherries

CHERRIES ARE DELICIOUS right off the tree. Their size, color, taste, and ease of "pull" from the branch will tell you when cherries are ready to pick. Generally the sour cherries ripen 2 to 3 weeks later than the sweet cherries. The longer you leave sour cherries on the tree, the sweeter they'll become, but be sure to pick them before their skins crack.

Picking cherries is easy and fun. Leave the stems on the fruits. You can pile them in a container without harming the fruit, but use them soon after picking because they keep for only a short time. In a refrigerator, the firm sweet cherries should keep from 2 to 3 weeks, but the soft sweet kinds and the sour ones last only about a week.

Unless the birds beat you to the fruit, your trees will produce lots of cherries. Figure on 60 to 80 quarts, or 25 to 100 pounds, from either a sweet or a sour cherry tree.

If you have a surplus of cherries, there are 101 different ways to use them! There are few people whose mouths don't water at the mention of fresh-baked, homemade cherry pie. Cherries can also be frozen, canned, and dried or made into relish, juice, and preserves. Rather than use a mostly artificial maraschino cherry in drinks and on sundaes, try a real, tasty, and healthful cherry fresh from your yard.

Dark cherries are the easiest to freeze, as their flesh won't darken; those with light flesh need treatment with ascorbic acid to prevent darkening. Pit first, then freeze whole on rimmed baking sheets prior to packing. This way, you can remove them as needed, and they won't be frozen into a block. You can also freeze with sugar or in syrup; using ascorbic acid in the syrup will prevent browning of the light cherries. If drying, pit first and cut large ones in half before putting in the dehydrator. When canning, figure on 2 to 2½ pounds of cherries to make a quart of canned fruit.

There are few people whose mouths don't water at the mention of fresh-baked, homemade cherry pie.

Cherries can be pitted (above) and used for pies and jams, or they can be pressed for juice or syrup (left).

Cherry Cultivars

Thousands of cherry cultivars have been developed and named, though only a few are now available in grocery stores and produce markets. Although new cherry cultivars do not appear as frequently as new apples and peaches, there's still a good selection. The following chart describes some of the best cherries for home gardens. Most grow best in Zones 5 to 8, unless noted, and require between 700 and 1,000 chilling hours.

Cultivar	FRUIT DESCRIPTION	FRUIT SEASON	COMMENTS
SWEET			
'Bing'	dark red skin, dark sweet flesh	mid	Most well-known sweet cherry, the one usually seen in markets
'BlackGold'	dark red skin and flesh	early	Late to bloom; some disease resistance, crack resistant; self-fruitful; good pollenizer
'Black Tatarian'	dark red skin and flesh	early	Early blooms; productive and vigorous; good pollenizer
'Brooks'	dark red skin and red flesh	early	Low chill requirement (400 hours); good for mild climates but best in dry climates; semi-freestone
'Lapins'	dark red skin, light red flesh; large	mid	Similar to 'Bing'; requires 700 chilling hours; split resistant; self-fruitful
'Rainier'	yellow skin with red blush, yellow flesh; very sweet	mid	Very popular; productive
'Stella'	dark red skin, dark sweet flesh	late	The first self-fruitful sweet cherry; requires 700 chilling hours; some crack resistance
'Sweetheart'	dark red skin and flesh	late	Self-fruitful; crack resistant
'WhiteGold'	yellow skin and light flesh	mid	Late to bloom; crack resistant; self-fruitful; good pollenizer; may grow in Zone 4
SOUR			
'Balaton'	large, firm, dark red skin; red flesh; unique sweet flavor	late	Good for fresh eating; fruits over a long period; productive; bright red juice
'English Morello'	very dark red skin and flesh	late	Morello type; naturally small tree; heirloom; low chill requirement (500 hours); Zones 4–9
'Montmorency'	red skin and amber flesh	early	Amarelle type; most common and best-known sour cherry; heirloom; Zone 4
'North Star'	light red skin, red flesh	early	Morello type; resists brown rot and leaf spot; naturally dwarf; Zone 4

Gallery of Unusual Tree Fruits

In addition to those listed below, some trees grown as ornamentals have edible fruits. Among these are cornelian cherry (*Cornus mas*), hackberry (*Celtis* species), and strawberry tree (*Arbutus unedo*). To find the fruits listed here, you may need to seek out specialty fruit nurseries and catalogs, and rare-fruit organizations. Recommended regions are only general; some fruits may grow in other areas depending on local conditions and microclimates. This is especially true of the West, where some fruits prefer warmer regions and others the cooler Pacific Northwest.

Korean Mountain Ash (*Sorbus alnifolia*)

USDA Hardiness Zones: 4–7

Best regions: North, Midwest, West

Height: Up to 45 feet

Spread: 20–30 feet

Plant description: Leaves divided into many leaflets

Fruit description: Clusters of small, bright reddish pink to purple berries in late summer and early fall

Culture: Avoid too dry and too wet soils, also alkaline; prone to fire blight disease

Uses: Good fresh when fruits are fully ripe and soft; also good for jam, jelly, and juice

Chinese Date

Jujube (*Ziziphus jujuba*)

USDA Hardiness Zones: 6–9

Best regions: South, Midwest, West (warmer sections)

Height: 15–20 feet

Spread: 10–15 feet, depending on cultivar

Plant description: Small yellow flowers in midsummer with a fragrance like grape soda; can spread with suckers from roots; good ornamental; attractive bark with spines that fall off with age

Fruit description: Reddish when ripe; wrinkled like a small date, 1 to 2 inches across; tastes like an apple

Culture: Needs summer heat; low chill requirement; some cultivars are self-fruitful but bear more with cross-pollination; few problems or pruning needs; once established, tolerates drought and saline and alkaline soils; won't tolerate shade, severe cold, and poorly drained soils

Uses: Pick in fall when ripe; eat fresh, candied, or dried (use as you would raisins and dates); minced, they're used in confections

Japanese Apricot

Ume (*Prunus mume*)

USDA Hardiness Zones: 6–8

Best regions: South and West

Height: 10–20 feet

Spread: 10–15 feet

Plant description: Pink to white, single to double spring flowers with spicy fragrance

Fruit description: Yellow; 1 inch across; summer; usually self-fruitful

Culture: Tolerates many soil types, including acidic; problems similar to those of apricots

Uses: Can be candied, boiled, used for a liqueur or a sour jam, or preserved with sugar; preserved with salt, they're known as salt plums or *umeboshi*, for sushi and Asian cuisine

Loquat

(*Eriobotrya japonica*)

USDA Hardiness Zones: 8–10

Best regions: South, West (warmer sections)

Height: 10–15 feet

Spread: 10–20 feet

Plant description: Evergreen tree or large shrub with large leaves and creamy white, fragrant fall flowers

Fruit description: Yellow; fuzzy; pear-shaped; 1–2 inches long

Culture: Low maintenance; plant at least two to ensure pollination; may tolerate part shade; drought tolerant but fruit better with ample moisture; avoid overfertilizing; thin some terminal shoots after harvest; plants will tolerate severe pruning

Uses: Often grown as an ornamental in subtropical and Mediterranean-type climates, as a shrub or espalier; may grow in a zone colder but not bear fruit; ripe fruits eaten or used fresh, unripe ones best in jams; avoid eating seeds and young leaves, as these are slightly toxic

Medlar

(*Mespilus germanica*)

USDA Hardiness Zones: 5–8

Best regions: South, Midwest, West

Height: 10–25 feet

Spread: 8–15 feet

Plant description: Large leaves; large white flowers in early summer; very long lived

Fruit description: Odd appearance, resemble apples but with flared ends opposite stems; chestnut brown, ripen to dark brown in fall; 1 inch wide; flavor of applesauce and spices

Culture: Doesn't tolerate extreme heat or cold, unlike other fruits; if grafted, plant so the union is below soil line

Uses: Uncommon in North America, popular in Europe for centuries; too sour and difficult to eat when picked after first frost, so let ripen in cool and light for 2 to 3 weeks (a maturing process called bletting)

Mulberry

(*Morus* species)

USDA Hardiness Zones: Black (*M. nigra*), 7–10; red (*M. rubra*), 3–9

Best regions: Varies with species

Height: Black to 30 feet; red, 40–70 feet

Spread: Black, 20–30 feet; red, 40–50 feet

Plant description: Flowers not showy; drooping catkins in spring as leaves emerge

Fruit description: Resembles blackberries on trees in late summer, with similar taste

Culture: Plant away from paved surfaces to avoid staining by fruits; without male trees, females produce seedless fruit; can be kept shorter with pruning (fruits are produced on new wood); prune while dormant and only branches less than 2 inches in diameter (large wounds may not heal); don't overfertilize

Uses: Black are best choice for fresh eating (sweet and less acidic); eat only ripe fruit of red; also used in jellies and syrups; good shade tree for landscapes; some cultivars make effective windbreaks. Note: Check with state agencies or local horticulture professionals before planting white mulberry (*Morus alba*), which has become invasive in many areas

Pawpaw

(*Asimina triloba*)

USDA Hardiness Zones: 5–8

Best regions: South, Midwest, West

Height: 15–25 feet

Spread: 8–10 feet

Plant description: Elongated oval leaves; spring flowers maroon and downward-facing, up to 2 inches in diameter

Fruit description: Green to yellow skin, orange to yellow flesh; tropical flavors; late summer to fall ripening, depending on cultivar; 3–6 inches long and ⅓ to 1 pound each; fewer fruits in colder climates

Culture: Likes cold winters and hot summers once established (protect from full sun the first couple of years); can be kept shorter with pruning, which also promotes younger growth where fruit are borne; cross-pollination needed, so plant two; if heavy fruiting, support branches to prevent breakage; doesn't like transplanting; tolerates many soils except waterlogged; with few problems; needs 400 chilling hours (below 45°F) and 160 frost-free days; doesn't grow well in dry and windy climates

Uses: Eat or use the pulp fresh, or freeze; heat from cooking (into jams, for example) can change its flavor

Note: Some people are allergic to this fruit

American Persimmon (*Diospyros virginiana*)

USDA Hardiness Zones: 5–9

Best regions: Most, varies with cultivar; native to the East, southern United States
Height: 35–60 feet

Spread: 10–30 feet

Plant description: Leaves to 5 inches long and 2 inches wide; light yellow, fragrant, bell-shaped flowers late spring to early summer

Fruit description: Yellow to pale orange; at least 1 inch in diameter; rounded; soft and dry texture; astringent; in fall, persists on trees for some time after leaves drop

Culture: May need cross-pollination (two plants yield better fruiting), trees usually male or female; tolerates colder climates but won't fruit; fruit is attractive to wildlife

Uses: May sucker to form thickets; may tolerate part shade; tolerates drought once established

Oriental/Asian Persimmon Kaki (*Diospyros kaki*)

USDA Hardiness Zones: 7–10

Best regions: Southeast and Southwest

Height: 15–35 feet

Spread: 15–20 feet

Plant description: Leaves to 7 inches long and 3 inches wide; inconspicuous flowers in early summer; often bright red fall foliage

Fruit description: Red, orange, or yellow; rounded to oblong or flattened; jellylike texture; some cultivars are astringent

Culture: May need cross-pollination (plant two for better fruiting); trees male or female or both, which may vary yearly; prune similar to apples; remove fruit from young branches to prevent breakage

Uses: A major crop in their native Asia where the fruit is found in stores; firm, astringent kakis, when peeled and dried whole, become sweet with texture of dates.

Note: If you've had recent gastric surgery or complications, don't eat large quantities

One mature walnut tree can produce a harvest of 60 to 75 pounds of nuts a year.

CHAPTER 14

Nuts

Nearly every region in north America once had an abundance of wild nut trees. It used to be an annual event for country folks to take burlap bags into the woods on a crisp, fall day and race the squirrels to the tasty treats hidden among the newly fallen leaves. Back home they'd dump out their sticky treasures onto the attic floor to dry for winter cracking. Unfortunately, blights, weather, and heavy cutting of the nut trees for their valuable lumber have taken their toll. Nutting, as it was called, is mostly a thing of the past.

Most nut trees get too large for a small suburban lot. Though pruning can keep them shorter, small-space gardeners will need to limit themselves to the two that grow on bushes — filberts and hazelnuts. For those with space, nut trees are ornamental and easy to grow, and provide shade and food for wildlife as well as humans. They require less in the way of care and chemicals than most fruits. And unlike fruits, you can easily store them for months or even years without processing.

Nuts differ from other tree fruits as they produce a single seed enclosed in a hard, woody casing that must be removed before eating. Nuts are an excellent source of protein and other nutrients. Several nuts (almonds, hazelnuts, pecans, and walnuts) are rich in heart-healthy oils, with more than twice as much polyunsaturated fats as saturated. Most are a rich source of omega-3 fatty acids, too.

Eating nuts is one of the most enjoyable ways to use them, of course, but they are prized too for the many uses of their lumber — from fine furniture to sports equipment. Even before the chestnut blight struck North America, most of the great chestnut forests of the East had already been cut for their fine lumber.

Getting to Know the Nuts

MOST NUT TREES need a partner, and to be compatible, the partner must be of the same species. The two should be within 100 feet of each other, because almost all nuts are pollinated by wind rather than bees. Any that are self-fertile will be listed as such by nurseries. Although a single black walnut or butternut tree should produce nuts, even these benefit from having a companion.

Filberts and Hazelnuts

Filberts have the advantage of maturing to a size that fits well into most home landscapes. The trees grow from 10 to 15 feet tall or about the size of a semidwarf apple. Plant them about 20 feet apart, yet be aware the European filbert can spread. Unlike most other nut trees, they don't have a long taproot, so they're easy to transplant. Soils suitable for fruit trees usually suit filberts, but fertilize them only lightly so they don't grow too quickly. Filbert trees root easily from layers and root suckers, so even cultivars are seldom grafted. If you buy a tree, you can propagate it in this way to increase your plantings.

The round European filbert (*Corylus avellana*) is familiar to everyone who has ever bought a bag of mixed nuts. It's native to southern Europe, probably originating in Italy. Most of North America's commercial filbert production is in the Pacific Northwest, although they can be grown in areas where peaches do well. They begin bearing at an early age. The nuts are flavorful, nutritious, and easy to crack, and they drop free from the husk.

An American cousin of the European filbert, the hazelnut, or American filbert (*Corylus americana*), is slightly hardier (Zones 4 to 9) and grows wild in hedgerows all over the northern United States and southern Canada. The small nuts are favorites of chipmunks and squirrels, and as children we used to gather them, too. It always seemed hardly worth the effort to take off the prickly burrs and dry and crack the nuts to get the tiny sweet meat. Over the decades, breeders on the West Coast, Canada, and the northern United States have worked to get better fruit and resistance to a blight disease.

Other hazel species generally grow in Zones 4 to 7, perhaps 8. The Turkish hazel or filbert (*Corylus colurna*) may reach 90 feet tall. It's good for landscaping, with attractive mottled bark. This was crossed with the European to make the Trazel, which is shrubby when young but when older makes a tree to 60 feet tall. The Chinese tree hazel (*C. chinensis*) and the India tree hazel (*C. jacquemontii*) also have attractive mottled bark. The beaked hazel (*C. cornuta*) grows only to about 12 feet tall as a large, multistem bush. Its unique fruits have nuts with husks protruding in beak shapes. This native American hazel was crossed with the European filbert to make a filazel, or a hazelbert, of which several cultivars have been selected.

TIPS FOR GROWING NUTS

- Choose a site that allows enough space for the mature tree spread.
- Unless listed as self-fertile, plant at least two of the same nut type (but not the same cultivar) for cross-pollination.
- Plant in well-drained, deep soil.
- Place tree guards on the trunk to protect from mice; where sunscald is a problem, first coat the trunk with white latex paint diluted to half strength with water.
- The first year, make sure trees get the equivalent of 2 inches of rain each week.
- Refrain from fertilizing the first year; subsequently, feed as for fruit trees in the spring.
- Prune minimally to promote a strong form, following the appropriate system for each type of nut. If grafted, remove any suckers that arise from the base.

Fast Facts for Nuts

Nut	USDA HARDINESS ZONES	MATURE HEIGHT (FEET)	SPACING (FEET)	YEARS TO BEARING	YIELDS (MATURE TREE, POUNDS)
Almonds	5–8	20–30	15–20	3–4	10–20
Black walnuts	4–7	50–75	35–50	4–7	60–75
Butternuts	3–7	50–75	35–50	3–4	60–75
Chinese chestnuts	4–8	40–60	30–40	4–7	60–75
Filberts	5–8	15–18	15	4–5	20–25
Hazelnuts	4–9	15–18	15	4–5	20–25
Hickories	4–9	70–100	35–50	10–12	60–75
Nut pines	4–7	30–40+	20–25	5–10	10–30
Pecans	5–9	70–100	3–50	5–8	60–75
Walnuts	5–8	40–60	40–50	4–5	60–75

NOTE: Most nut trees need to be pollinated by another cultivar or native tree to produce nuts; even the few self-fruitful ones will yield more if another cultivar is nearby.

Because of their small size (10 to 15 feet) and range of hardiness (Zones 4 to 9), hazelnuts are one of the easiest nuts to work into the home landscape.

Chestnuts

The American chestnut (*Castanea dentata*) was an important part of colonial American life. Its lumber was greatly prized for paneling and for export to Europe. Holidays were never complete without chestnut dressing for the turkey or goose. When in the early 1990s blight wiped out almost every chestnut tree, a search began for blight-resistant varieties. Trees were introduced from China, Japan, Manchuria, and Spain, and some were successfully crossed with the few remaining American species. Many of the resulting hybrids are now producing quality nuts in American backyards.

The Chinese chestnut (*C. mollissima*), introduced by the USDA, is the chestnut usually sold in nurseries and garden centers. There are several cultivars that have been developed, with good but not total blight resistance. Some have nuts that can be eaten raw; others bear nuts that need roasting over a fire or in a microwave for about a minute. The Chinese chestnut is quite ornamental, with long leaves and sweetly fragrant flowers. A similar species, the Japanese chestnut (*C. crenata*), has even better blight resistance.

Chestnuts are borne inside large, spiny burs (called involucres); the nut is ripe when the involucre splits open.

Almonds

Almonds (*Prunus dulcis*) are closely related to peaches (and often grafted onto peach seedling rootstocks), but they're much more particular in their climate requirements. They need low humidity and don't tolerate wet soils. Though listed for several hardiness zones, they require mild winters and hot, dry, and long summers, as is typical in the Mediterranean and the Central Valley of California. In fact, some three-quarters of the world almond production comes from California. They've been cultivated for more than 5,000 years, and were first brought to California by Spanish padres in the 1700s.

Their attractive flowers are fragrant and light pink or white. Trees bloom quite early (February), making them susceptible to frosts in many areas where the plants are otherwise hardy. Rainfall during bloom can destroy the crop as well. Trees can get 20 to 30 feet tall, a little over half that wide, and if pruned to a modified central leader can be kept even shorter. Prune back vertical branches so they they'll branch outward. Since almonds fruit on one-year-old wood, prune off some of last year's fruiting branches. The almonds we eat come from the nuts or pits (similar to a peach pit), which in turn are encased in a fuzzy husk.

Trees are best planted in January or February. Almonds generally require between 250 and 500 hours of chilling over winter to flower and fruit. They need 180 to 240 days to mature. Nuts are harvested between early August and late September, depending on the cultivar.

Bad Company?

Nut trees have some bad habits. Both black walnut and butternut roots give off a toxic substance (juglone) that eliminates their competition by killing certain nearby plants, especially evergreens. Fortunately, they don't have this poisonous effect on grass, or on some annual flowers (such as impatiens), and many herbaceous perennials. Most of these and the few resistant vegetables you wouldn't want to plant under a tree anyway, as they'd get too much shade. Remember when choosing which, if any, nut trees to plant that some people are very allergic to nuts.

Nut Pines

Though people on the East Coast might not think of growing their own pine nuts, in the West the nuts of native pinyon pines are well known. Many, especially native and Hispanic peoples, collect them in the wild. Often the pine nuts you see in stores come from pinyon pines. Pine nuts are slightly smaller than pistachios and are an excellent source of protein. Nut pines are self-fertile, so you can get nuts if you plant just one tree. Like most fruit trees, though, you'll get higher yields from each tree if you plant two for cross-pollination.

Perhaps most common of the 20 or so pines grown for their edible nuts are the Korean pine (*Pinus koraiensis*) and the Swiss stone pine (*P. cembra*). Although cones take 3 years to mature, once they reach bearing age (5 to 8 years) there will be mature cones each year to harvest. Both species are hardy in Zones 4 to 7 and make nice ornamental plants. They have provided food for thousands of years, since the Paleolithic era.

Pinyon pines have long been utilized as a source of nutritious pine nuts.

As you might guess, the Korean pine is native to northeastern Asia. It has blue-green needles, and its branches droop almost to the ground. It has a pyramidal shape and reaches 30 to 50 feet tall. Space Korean pines 25 to 35 feet apart.

The Swiss stone pine is the main edible pine nut in Europe, along with the Italian stone pine (*P. pinea*). This pine, native to the mountains of Europe, has dark green needles and grows slowly. When young, it has a pyramid shape; it becomes more rounded as it ages. The Swiss stone pine reaches 30 to 40 feet tall at maturity; space them 15 to 20 feet apart.

The pinyon pine is a native you may encounter in the West and the central United States, and in Mexico. There are three main species, the Colorado pinyon (*P. edulis*), the single-leaf pinyon (*P. monophylla*), and the Mexican pinyon (*P. cembroides*). American pinyon pines grow quite slowly. If started from seeds, they will reach just a couple of feet tall in 10 years, and they begin to bear cones in 10 to 12 years from sowing seeds. Eventually — in 60 years or so — trees may reach 20 to 60 feet tall and 16 feet wide. These trees grow in Zones 5 to 8 (sometimes colder). This is a good drought-resistant landscape tree in the West.

Hickories and Pecans

There are several species of hickories. Pecans (*Carya illinoinensis*), the most common, are our only major native nut crop. Pecan cultivars can be grouped into those for the East, West, and North. Eastern pecans are those traditionally grown in, and adapted to, the warm and humid southeastern states and have resistance to diseases found there. Western pecans don't have such resistance. Those for the North are generally hardy to Zone 5 but produce nuts only to Zone 6 and warmer, and don't require as long a season to ripen. They're often listed as "northern strains," or similar wording. The main factor limiting pecans in the North, where they're hardy, is a warm-enough summer and late-enough fall for the nuts to ripen fully. Pecans keep for only a few months at room temperature, but store well for a year or more at temperatures below freezing.

You need more than one cultivar or seedling type for cross-pollination; three is what's generally recommended. Unlike other nuts, the best

Often thought of as a southern crop, a few cultivars of pecan are hardy to Zone 6. They need a long, warm summer for nuts to mature.

yields come from mixing cultivars from two different groups, often called types 1 and 2. Some pecans shed pollen early, before the female flower is ready for it (protoandrous, or type 1). On others the female flower is receptive before the pollen is shed (protogynous, or type 2). Don't let the botany confuse you; nurseries and catalogs will tell which tree will pollinate another.

Unlike most North American nuts, the pecan has been cultivated commercially for many years, and many cultivars have been developed. These have more disease resistance, better yields, and earlier maturing nuts than the species.

Although hickories are seldom offered commercially, they're much appreciated by those lucky enough to live where they grow, in Zones 4 to 9. The shagbark hickory (C. *ovata*), the best of dozens of native species, has the disadvantage of a very tough shell and a small meat that usually breaks in cracking. If you can find a cultivar or selection from wild trees, it should bear nuts at a younger age that are larger and easier to crack. The hardiness of the new kinds isn't always known for sure, however, and thus far not many are being grafted and offered for sale. Shellbark hickory (C. *laciniosa*) is slightly less hardy (Zones 5 to 8) than shagbark. Both have attractive, shaggy bark and make good ornamental trees.

In an effort to combine the flavor of pecans with the hardiness of hickories, horticulturists have created hybrid hicans. These hybrids can be grown farther north than pecans, but the different cultivars vary widely in hardiness.

Walnuts

Persian walnuts (*Juglans regia*) are often called English walnuts in English-speaking countries because they've been grown in Great Britain for centuries. They were considered far too tender for most of North America until a missionary discovered a strain growing wild in the cold mountains of Poland. He brought several thousand seeds to Ontario in the 1930s and found they grew well there. They succeeded so well, in fact, that within only a few years the cultivar he introduced (*J. regia* 'Carpathian') was being grown in Zones 5 and 6. Since then, some nurseries have selected their own strains from plants originating in the Carpathian mountains of Poland, even though the plant is native as far east as Korea. Most walnut trees you see for sale are the more hardy Carpathian strains. The hardiest of these will survive in more protected parts of Zone 4. The walnuts you usually find in stores, however, are from much less hardy strains grown in California.

English walnuts are by far the most popular kind of nut in this country. Originating in the Middle East (and often called "Persian walnuts"), they grow best in warm, dry climates.

Walnuts are without doubt the most popular of all nuts both to eat out of the shell and to enjoy in countless appetizing baked goods. Unfortunately, some people get canker sores from eating them and thus have to sacrifice a real delicacy. As with butternut and black walnut, roots of this plant produce juglone, which is toxic to some other plants if grown nearby.

Walnuts prefer a slightly sweeter, more alkaline soil than most nuts. Avoid planting them in frost pockets, as they're susceptible to spring frosts.

Japanese walnuts (*Juglans ailantifolia*) have a spreading growth habit. On average they grow 35 feet tall and spread 30 to 50 feet. Their flavor is between that of the English walnut and the butternut. The species has larger leaves than the butternut, with rounded nuts slightly more difficult to crack than English walnuts. As you might guess, the fruits of heartnut, a variety of Japanese walnut (*J. ailantifolia* var. *cordiformis*), are heart-shaped. Trees are productive, early to bear, rapid growing, and hardy in Zones 5 to 9, sometimes colder.

The black walnut is a multipurpose tree: in addition to producing unusually flavored nuts, it's also a good source of lumber.

Butternuts and Black Walnuts

Like dried corn, beans, and smoked meat, butternuts were one of the staple foods that helped the Iroquois Indians to live well through the hard northern winters. The early settlers soon learned to store and use them too, and they've been a winter treat in the Northeast ever since.

The butternut (*Juglans cinerea*) is one of the hardiest nut trees (Zones 3 to 7; 5 to 7 for grafted plants), and its oily meats are some of the most flavorful nuts. Even the wild ones crack easily if you pour boiling water over them, let them stand for 15 minutes, then drain. With one easy hammer blow you can then pop the halves apart intact. This works for black walnuts too, although you may need a few blows with the hammer.

Butternut blooms are easily damaged by late-spring frosts. The trees are likely to bear abundantly one year and then take a few years off, so it's lucky for us butternut lovers that the nuts store well. Unfortunately, butternut decline, or canker disease, has almost wiped out native stands in some areas, so the tree is considered threatened or endangered in places.

Butternuts have been crossed with heartnuts to result in the buartnut. This tree is vigorous and hardy, has good yields and disease resistance, and often produces unusually shaped nuts. Seedlings will grow in Zones 4 to 7; grafted plants, in Zones 5 to 7.

The black walnut (*Juglans nigra*) does well throughout most of Zones 4 through 7. Hardier strains survive in Zones 3 and 4, and you'll find them occasionally into Zone 8. Native to the eastern United States, it is valued more for its timber than for its hard nuts. Not everyone cares for the black walnut's unusual flavor (smoky and strong with a taste of wine), but its fans use it to flavor cakes, ice cream, and other desserts. The green outer husks covering the nuts produce an almost indelible black stain, so wear gloves and protective clothing when removing them.

In addition to the different strains of seedlings, which vary widely across the country, there are several cultivars with nuts that are easier to crack and contain larger and better-flavored kernels. Cultivars tend to be less hardy, however. Hind's black walnut (*J. hindsii*), native to northern California in Zones 7 to 9, has a good flavor and is used as a rootstock for the Persian walnut.

Starting from Scratch

Unlike most fruits, you can grow nut trees from seed. Either plant a nut where you want the tree to grow permanently or start it in another part of the garden and transplant to its final spot after 2 or 3 years.

Fall is the time when the squirrels do their planting, and it's the best time for us, too. Most nuts sprout well only if they have been frozen for a few days first, so if you forget to plant them in the fall, you can still do it in the spring, after freezing each nut for a week inside a container of water kept in the freezer. They may not sprout quite as quickly as when shells had time to soften in the ground during the winter, however.

It may be midsummer before your new little seedling finally bursts through the soil. As soon as it does pop up, it will grow rapidly, however, and may be 2 or 3 feet tall within 6 or 8 weeks. The nut itself carries enough nutrients to get the tree off to a good start, so don't feed it anything or it will keep growing too late in the season and be winter-killed.

If you plan to move your tree, don't wait until it gets big. Most grow tremendous taproots that head speedily toward the center of the Earth, so don't attempt to move them after they get much more than 3 feet tall. If you should break or bend the taproot in the process of transplanting, the tree is likely to die. The best time to transplant is in early spring.

Dig a small hole and bury the nut an inch or so deep.

After you plant, protect the nut with a wire screen, particularly if you have squirrels or chipmunks around. They may forget where they've hidden their own nuts, but they'll have no trouble finding yours and hauling them away.

Planting and Care

NUT TREES take a long time to bear, so most people buy a tree already started to get a head start. Often you'll find strains from a particular nursery sold as the species, with claims for some feature such as growth rate or hardiness. Some of the new cultivars are as superior to wild nuts as named apples are to the sour wild ones, so if the cultivars will grow in your climate, consider planting them rather than seedling trees. Grafted cultivars take much less time to produce their first crop than do seedling trees, which may require 8 years to bear their first nut.

Pollination

Plant two different cultivars or a few seedling trees of the same species for cross-pollination. If you plant a hazelnut cultivar such as 'Santiam', plant another such as Jefferson, or some wild filberts, to pollinate it. Two 'Santiam' hazelnuts will not pollinate each other because they both originated from the same tree. Each seedling tree is different, however, so a seedling will pollinate any other seedling or hybrid of the same species.

Site Selection

When choosing a location, keep in mind the eventual size of the tree. Filberts remain nicely within fruit tree dimensions, but most other species attain a height of at least 50 feet and grow almost as wide. Give them enough room, and don't plant them beneath overhead wires or too close to your house. The falling nuts can become a nuisance, too, so plant away from streets, sidewalks, roofs, and any lawns that will be mowed in late fall. Nuts are tough on mowers and can be a safety hazard when mown over.

In cold climates try to avoid low areas, which could be subject to late-spring frosts. Frost-nipped flowers won't produce nuts. Planting on a slope is safer.

Planting

Like fruit trees, nuts grow best in well-drained soil, but most will tolerate heavier soil (as long as it's not constantly wet). Most prefer a slightly acidic soil pH (6.0 to 6.8), slightly more acidic for Chinese chestnuts and slightly more alkaline for walnuts. Chestnuts will grow in sandy soils and in quite acidic soils.

Nut Problems

Diseases and insects seldom infest backyard nut trees. This is fortunate, because spraying such large trees is no simple matter. Keeping leaves and nuts raked up in the fall helps to minimize diseases by removing overwintering spores and bacteria.

Nut Problem	Possible Causes
Fail to develop, drop	Spring frosts, pollination problems, excess fertility
Start growing, then drop	Insect damage, too little fertility, too little water, root problems (disease, poorly drained), leaves damaged by insects or disease
Kernels inside shriveled	Too much shade, too cool a season, also same causes as growing and then dropping
Kernels have dark spots	Insect or disease injury
Nuts with holes, eaten, drop	Insects (pecan weevil, pecan nut casebearer, hickory shuckworm, and others)
Nuts black, fall off (walnuts)	Anthracnose
Shells and kernels stained, rot (walnuts)	Codling moths
Velvety olive-brown to black spots	Pecan scab

Most nut trees develop a long taproot as they mature, which makes them difficult to transplant once they become established.

Planting a nut tree is much the same as planting a fruit tree (see chapter 16). During the first year, it's important to provide sufficient water — at least 2 inches a week if rain doesn't supply this amount. This may mean 5 gallons for a small tree and 10 for a large one. (More is needed on sandy soils.) Once trees mature, they are fairly drought-tolerant.

Fertilizing

Hold off on fertilizer the first year. After that, feed in spring as for fruit trees but use a balanced fertilizer that's higher in nitrogen (such 5-3-4 or 10-4-10). Nut trees need more nitrogen than fruit trees to grow well. As a tree grows, slightly increase the amount of fertilizer you apply.

For proper nut formation, trees in some areas (and particular seasons) may need applications of the element zinc to supplement what is normally present in soils or what is found in complete fertilizers. Zinc may be needed particularly for pecans, in cool and wet spring seasons, and on alkaline soils. If the leaves on your nut trees appear oddly distorted (curled or wavy edges, or bunched near branch tips), contact your Cooperative Extension Service for information about zinc products, and their application, to apply to correct a deficiency. A soil test for nut trees may provide this information as well.

To imitate the conditions of the lush forest floor, apply a thick organic mulch when the tree is still young. Mulch helps keep weeds from competing with the young tree for nutrients and water.

Pruning Nut Trees

Because even a hybrid nut tree still closely resembles its wild relatives, it needs no special pruning. Too much pruning can actually delay fruiting for a few years. On a grafted nut tree, remove any suckers that arise from the base of the plant.

For most nuts, prune to one central trunk when the trees are young to promote a strong structure. If a tree you buy has not already been cut back, head back the main stem the first year, removing about a third of the top growth. This will develop a stronger leader than the initial whip (seedling); it also promotes formation of side branches. Remove existing side branches just below the cut to direct energy into making a stronger central leader.

The next few years, thin out branches only to create well-spaced branches spiraling up the trunk in different directions. These branches (scaffolds) should be about 18 inches apart. Remove those that form a narrow crotch (less than 40 degrees from the trunk). Also remove any upright limbs that could compete with the central leader. When there are 10 to 15 good scaffold branches, cut back the central leader to one of these laterals, and train the tree thereafter to a modified leader shape. (See chapter 17 for more on pruning.)

Once trees reach maturity, little pruning is needed except to remove dead and damaged branches. For mature trees 20 to 30 years old, thin out a few of the upper scaffold branches to let more light to the interior.

Hazelnuts are an exception; grow these as bushes with five to seven main shoots. Thin out weaker shoots, cutting them off at ground level. Also remove some of the center shoots so more light can reach the center. The related filberts are usually trained to grow as small trees; it's important to remove the suckers that sprout from the base on young plants to encourage a more treelike form.

Harvesting Nuts

WHEN THE NUTS begin to fall off a tree, this means they're mature and ready to pick. They often change color, usually from green to yellowish, and some can be dented with a fingernail. Squirrels don't always wait for them to drop, however, so it's best to begin collecting as soon as the squirrels do. If you're careful not to damage the limbs, you can shake most nuts from the trees. In fact, walnuts and pecans are often harvested commercially by mechanical shakers. The entire crop of most nut trees can be gathered at one time, although some, like walnuts, will need several pickings. Don't let nuts stay on the ground for any length of time; after they fall they deteriorate rapidly.

Nuts must be dried thoroughly before their meats are ripe enough to eat. Spread them out, one layer deep, on benches in a greenhouse or garage, on a warm attic floor, or, best of all, on raised screens where dry air can circulate around them. Turn them occasionally so they'll dry on all sides. (On our attic floor, the playful kittens turned them for us.) After drying the nuts completely, store them in burlap bags, boxes, or barrels in a cool place, making sure the storage area is mouse-proof and squirrel-proof. Shelling, then freezing, is another option used to store nuts up to several years.

You'll likely need a heavy-duty nutcracker for the hard shells of nuts such as black walnuts. Some use a hammer, others a shop vise. Peel Chinese chestnuts with a knife. The nuts of black walnuts and butternuts are covered with hulls or husks that will stain fingers and clothing dark brown. These husks have been cooked into dyes for fabric and woodworking, even hair dye. Hickories and walnuts have hard husks as well, which are more easily removed when ripe and somewhat spongy — when nuts fall naturally from a tree rather than from picking.

Although butternuts and black walnuts may need a good soaking and a hammer to open, for most nuts a simple nutcracker is all you need.

Nut Cultivars

As nuts take so long time to bear, breeding has developed less rapidly than for fruits and berries. The most progress has been made with those grown commercially: almonds, filberts, pecans, and Persian walnuts. Newer cultivars are hardier, bear younger, and produce nuts that are larger, tastier, and crack more easily than their wild ancestors. Many nuts are grown as the species rather than cultivars; even when cultivars are planted, the species may be planted for cross-pollination. The nut trees you'll find at a nursery are often simply seedlings from ordinary wild trees (as for pinyon pines), but a few cultivars are listed here.

Hardiness may vary among cultivars as well as among plants originating from different regions. The number of years to first harvest varies with climate, culture, and cultivar.

Nut	Cultivar	Comments
Almond	'All-in-one' 'Garden Prince'	Self-fruitful, semidwarf hardy yet requires hot summer, 400 chill hours (below 45°F) Self-fruitful, semidwarf productive, bears at a young age, 250 chill hours
Black walnut	'Thomas Black'	Widely available, very large nut
Butternut	'Beckwith' 'Craxezy'	Medium-size nut bears annually Cracks easily, productive
Chinese chestnut	'Eaton River' 'AU Leader'	Large nuts, early maturing Productive, good in the South
Filbert	'Butler'	Medium-size nuts, easy to shell
Hazelnut	'Santiam' 'Jefferson'	Immune to filbert blight, productive Immune to blight and mites
Hickory, shagbark	'Grainger' 'Weschcke'	Thin shells easy to crack Early maturing, good in the North
Hickory, shellbark	'Fayette' 'Henning'	Self-pollinating, thin shells Fast growing
Pecan	'Major'	Heavy annual crops, cracks easily, type 1
	'Mohawk'	Thin shells, type 2, good for lower Midwest and Southwest
	'Pawnee'	Good for smaller spaces (30 feet high and wide), thin shells, type 1
	'Stuart'	One of most common, strong and upright, type 2, may grow in Zone 6
	'Desirable'	Good pollinator for most, self-fertile, type 1
	'Warren'	Early maturing (145 days), type 2
	'Mahan'	Prefers arid climates and warm winters, type 2
Nut pines	Sold as species; cultivars not available	Pinyon pines generally wild-collected in the Rockies
Walnut	'Hansen' 'Lake'	Self-fruitful, hardy, 30 feet tall Heavy yields at an early age

PART FOUR

Growing Healthy Fruits, Nuts, *and* Berries

Provide your fruiting plants with a well-prepared site, appropriate pruning, and sufficient water, and you'll be rewarded with delicious fruit for years to come.

WHEN YOU PLANT A FRUIT TREE, BERRY plant, or vine, keep in mind that with proper care and a little luck with weather, it will provide you with ample fruit in its lifetime. Growing good fruit starts with good soil, but proper planting, pruning, and pest control are equally important.

A deep, fertile soil is essential for the future health of your fruits, especially fruit and nut trees. If you hit a rock ledge or hard clay when you dig a hole, seek out another location. The tree or shrub roots can find their way around small rocks, but if the soil is too shallow, your planting will be doomed from the start. Attempts to break up subsoils with an iron bar, a pickax, or a tractor subsoiler are usually so frustrating that you should resort to one of these only if no other location is available. You can plant strawberries in raised beds if you have poor soils.

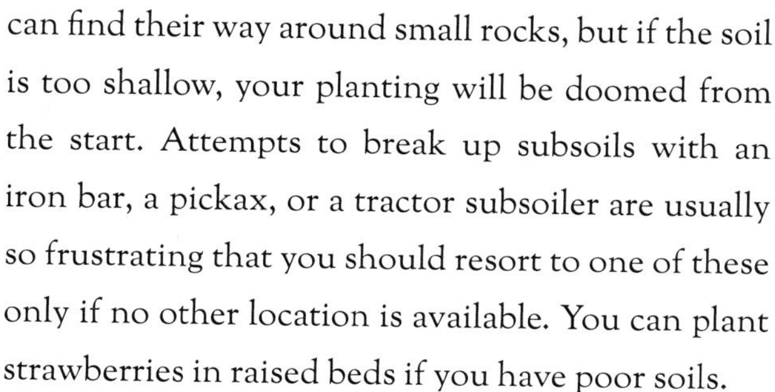

Sometimes gardeners hurry the planting operation too much. When a tree they've ordered in the leisure of winter arrives during the spring rush, its new owner unwraps it hastily by pulling away the strings and packing, scraping off bark in the process. They let the defenseless tree lie in the sun and wind while they dig a hole that's too small. Then they cram the roots in the hole as best they can, heap the soil over part of them, and leave the tree to its own devices. "Why did my tree die?" the owner puzzles. A few simple steps will ensure that your newly planted trees survive and thrive.

Proper pruning helps a plant to produce better fruit and, even more important, it conserves its strength for a longer, healthier life. This is especially important for young trees. Just as many adult habits are set in childhood, so is the mature tree structure established in the first years. Fruiting bushes need pruning also. Even strawberry plants need "pruning": removing the blossoms on young plants improves yields and helps plants live longer.

In recent decades there's been a shift away from the spray-for-every-pest mentality. Many of the trees now being sold are surprisingly disease resistant. With good sanitation, you should be able to get by with very little spraying, especially if your plantings are located some distance from a neglected orchard or infected wild fruit trees. If you don't mind a blemish or two, you may be able to get away with no spraying at all. When intervention is necessary, there are now many products that even organic gardeners can use with a clear conscience. There are combination sprays, often of insecticides and fungicides, to make your pest control simpler.

Most of us who toil over trees and berry bushes, however, hope to keep at least a small part of the fruits of our labors for ourselves. Fences and repellents are some of the means to keep away unwanted wildlife.

Adding generous amounts of organic matter is a good way to improve the quality of your soil.

CHAPTER 15

Improving Your Soil

How was your diet this past week? If all you had was a little weak tea, chances are you don't feel too much like an evening of vigorous square dancing or painting the spare bedroom. If you had healthful meals each day, you're much more likely to be feeling energetic and ready to take on anything. Nobody considers a steady diet of weak tea to be sensible, but a great many would-be gardeners act as if their fruit plants can get by nicely on such, or even less. Often people tell me their trees are looking poorly and ask what could possibly be wrong. "What do you use for fertilizer?" I ask. "Fertilizer?" they say, looking puzzled.

Though there are gardeners who over-fertilize their plants, often ending up with more leaves than fruit, many more neglect fertilizing altogether. Because the soil around a tree is the repository for the nutrients it needs, you'll want to understand that soil and how to treat it properly.

What Is Soil?

GOOD SOIL IS something special. It's full of life and provides the right conditions for plants to grow and thrive. It contains mineral nutrients; clay, sand, and other rock particles; and humus formed from decaying plant life plus moisture and air. Good soil also has an abundance of beneficial bacteria that break down the organic matter, and it contains earthworms that loosen the soil and add fertility. There are fungi that help roots absorb nutrients, and a whole host of other microorganisms without which your plants would grow poorly.

If you have ever dug a hole, you already know that soil is found in several layers, usually of varying colors. Most of the action takes place in the dark topsoil layer, and that's the most important to gardeners. Good topsoil contains humus and fertility and is loose in texture. Subsoil, the next layer down and often lighter in color, is usually quite hard. It contains mostly minerals and possibly traces of organic material from long ago. Often it's filled with lumps of clay, veins of gravel or sand, and large rocks. Roots of trees, particularly deep-rooted trees, penetrate this subsoil and absorb many mineral nutrients from it. Farther down is the hardpan, which is a thick layer of clay and bedrock. Roots can't penetrate hardpan, except in spots where breaks or faults occur, and water cannot move through it freely.

SOIL LAYERS

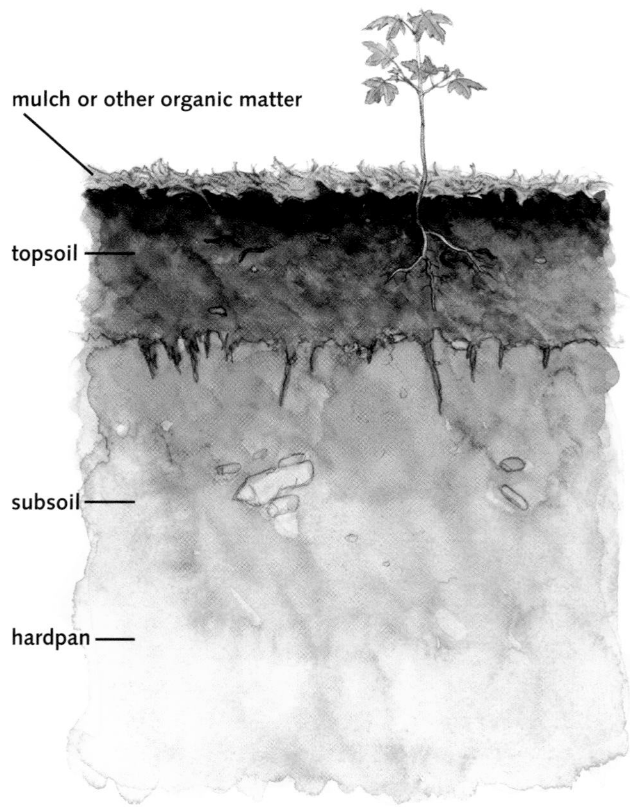

The depths of both topsoil and subsoil vary greatly from place to place. Very few spots on the earth are still blessed with deep fertile topsoil of just the right texture, moisture-retaining ability, and proper soil acidity for good plant growth. Most of us have to doctor up our soils in some way, and it's very important to diagnose soil problems and correct them, not only before you plant, but also frequently thereafter.

If your soil is good enough to grow a nice lawn, you can usually get it into shape for berries and fruits. To help understand what's going on beneath the surface of your orchard or berry patch, let's divide the properties of soil into three important components: texture, pH, and fertility.

Sand, Silt, or Clay?

Soil texture can be defined loosely as the general makeup of the soil, whether it's sandy, clay, rocky, or worn-out powdery dust. (Some people refer to this as soil type, but "type" is a more involved classification system.) Soil structure refers to how these particles clump together: soil with good structure forms crumbs of various sizes that break apart easily. Because trees in particular need considerable room to spread their roots, neither rocks nor heavy clays nor wet mucky soils provide adequate growing conditions. Nor does sand or gravel, as these dry out so quickly.

Soil texture is more difficult to improve than pH or fertility. If you're stuck with a thin layer of soil over solid rock, there's little you can do, short of hauling in many loads of topsoil. Owners of new homes may have this problem, because builders usually scrape off all the good topsoil and later put back

Beyond Chemicals

Some gardeners regard soil as something that holds up a plant and acts as a temporary repository for nutrients and moisture. They learn which nutrients a plant needs, mix the chemicals in correct proportions, then pour the concoction over the soil to feed the plant.

Organic gardeners have a different viewpoint and consider soil a living thing. They believe it should be loose, spongy, and full of life, containing an abundance of decaying organic matter as well as additional minerals in natural form. To protect soil, they cover it with mulch or a living crop, such as grass. They believe that when soils contain an abundance of nutrients in natural form, soil microbes will make them available gradually, as plants need them. Synthetic nutrients, they argue, disturb and may kill soil life. Synthetic fertilizers are often highly soluble. This means they can wash out of soils in a heavy rain, and they can cause flashes of growth that are more susceptible to insect and disease attack. Gardening organically, there is less chance of excess chemicals washing into and polluting a watershed.

Organically managed fruit plantings have a better chance of continuing to produce good fruit if, for any reason, they must be neglected for a season or two. A planting that is chemically dependent can suffer withdrawal and decline when the applications are discontinued for any length of time.

There is a third group who feel that the best way to garden falls somewhere in between. A great many gardeners belong to this group. They believe in good, healthy organic soils, in deep mulches, and in recycling garden wastes, but they feel no guilt about adding a little chemical fertilizer if a plant seems to lack nutrients. They know that soils well stocked with organic matter will make better use of any additional fertilizer, organic or synthetic. Organic matter (humus) is like a sponge; it can absorb and hold on to nutrients so they won't wash away in the first heavy rain and yet are available to plants.

only a few inches for a lawn. If plants are already established, don't add too much soil or compost on top, as this will smother trunks and lower branches and cause shallow rooting near the surface.

Enhancing Soil Quality

Nevertheless, there are measures you can take to enhance poor soil. Create more moisture-holding capability in a sandy soil by tilling in copious amounts of shredded bark, manure, leaf mold, peat moss, or compost. If you're planting in an area that was previously gardens, you may need only an inch or two spread on top, then tilled in. Otherwise, add 4 to 5 inches of compost. In addition to helping soil texture, compost provides slow-release nutrients and helps buffer against pH and nutrient imbalances. Compost also feeds the soil microorganisms that help the plants; good-quality compost may even help prevent some diseases. Adding compost to soils provides your plants with a healthful, gourmet meal.

Mulches, too, can perform miracles when you're trying to improve your soil, but they take time. Another way to improve soil is to plant and plow under crops of growing plants, such as clover, oats, and winter rye, a process called green manuring. This requires planning ahead, as it takes several months, but it's an excellent way to reduce weeds in planting areas and to add organic matter over a large area.

Heavy clay soils can be improved by generously tilling in copious amounts of shredded bark, manure, leaf mold, peat moss, or compost. You'll still see sand often recommended to lighten heavy soils but, in fact, adding sand may make the structure worse. To break up clay subsoils, plow deeply or use a backhoe, although probably neither of these methods is feasible if you own only a small piece of land. If you do have poor heavy or rocky soil and use a backhoe for some other reason (such as I did to build a stone wall, or a neighbor did for a septic system), take the opportunity to remove and replace your future fruit garden soil.

Mulching not only keeps down weeds and increases moisture retention in the soil, it also improves the soil quality over time.

Good growth can't take place in soil that is packed hard. Compacting may be caused by heavy machines or by excessive foot traffic through the area, and it is most common in soils lacking in organic matter and in areas after new construction. Spreading compost around plants will help over time, as will mulching and not walking or driving near plants.

Acidity and Alkalinity

Soil pH indicates the alkalinity or acidity of the soil and is measured on a scale of 1.0 to 14.0, with 7.0 considered neutral. Below this midpoint, soils are acidic ("sour"); above it they're alkaline or basic ("sweet"). On the pH scale one point is 10 times the previous one, so a soil with a pH of 5.0 is 10 times as acidic as one with a pH of 6.0. Most soils range between 4.0 and 8.0.

The pH is caused by the balance in the soil of positive and negative ions (element particles with a charge). Hydrogen and aluminum ions, with positive charges, cause acidity, and often relate to the parent material from which the soil is formed. Soils from weathered granite are generally more acidic than those from limestone. Soils from evergreen forests and under pine trees, for instance, tend to be acidic. A wet climate, as in the eastern states, tends to produce more-acidic soils, as rains have leached away alkaline elements such as calcium and magnesium. Acid rain intensifies this leaching process.

Why pH matters. When soil becomes too acidic or too alkaline, plant roots can't absorb the fertilizer and the nutrients remain locked within the soil. Plants have a certain pH range over which they can best utilize soil nutrients. For most fruits, the ideal is 6.0 to 6.5; for blueberries it's 4.5 to 5.5. Don't worry if your soil pH is not quite in the preferred range, as most plants are not too fussy as long as it's close to the desired range and not extreme.

Similarly, plant nutrients are most available within a certain soil pH range. Nitrogen is most available when soil pH is 6.0 to 8.0; potassium is most available between a pH of 5.5 and 10.0. In general, the pH range for best availability of all nutrients, and thus best plant growth, is 5.5 to 6.8.

Soils with ample amounts of organic matter, such as compost and manure, are less likely to have pH problems. Organic matter has the ability to absorb lots of ions to counteract both acidity and alkalinity, buffering changes in the soil chemistry. Two forms of organic matter, sawdust and especially peat moss, are acidic and will reduce the pH of soils that are too alkaline. If you plan to use sawdust, just make sure that it's old and partially decomposed or rotted, as otherwise it can take away nutrients from plants as it breaks down.

Testing soil pH. To determine your soil's pH, you can purchase an inexpensive, simple-to-use soil acidity test kit in a garden store. For somewhat more money you can get a complete testing kit that will also show your soil's fertility, and for a bit more you can get an electronic tester that will analyze soil pH instantly. We've used such a meter in our nursery for many years, but for most small gardens the chemical kits are adequate. Most state Cooperative Extension Services offer a soil-testing service; it tends to cost more than the simple pH kits but is cheaper than the complete kits. The results are much more accurate than from a home kit, and give recommendations for adjusting pH and nutrients based on your region's soils.

A handheld pH meter is one way to make sure your garden soil is neither too alkaline nor too acid for the fruits you'd like to plant.

Altering your pH. Soil pH is easy to improve; see the box on page 221. Make acid soils more alkaline by adding lime or wood ashes. You can simply spread lime evenly on top of the soil and let rain dissolve it, but because it moves through the soil slowly, for faster results it's better to till it in. Clay soils have a greater capacity to absorb calcium and so require more lime than sandy ones. Don't be tempted to add more than is directed, because too much lime, like too little, locks up the fertilizer and stops plant growth. Too much lime also causes fruit trees to drop large numbers of fruits before they mature. Always test soil pH before you add anything.

Lowering the pH is seldom necessary in the eastern states, except when you're growing acid-loving plants like blueberries. If you're planning to use a synthetic fertilizer containing ammonium ingredients, be aware that these will lower the pH. Many western soils are overly alkaline, and due to their specific nature may have specific needs for amendments to lower the pH. Aluminum sulfate is a commonly used, and quick-acting, amendment to lower soil pH. Use it with caution: it will burn plant roots if overused, and some gardeners feel that it spoils the flavor of blueberries. Better alternatives to create and maintain acidity are cottonseed meal and peat moss. Oak leaves and pine needles, although they start off acidic when fresh, lose their acidity over time and have only a small effect on soil pH in all but very sandy soils. For severe alkalinity, use elemental sulfur to lower pH. More is required to neutralize clay soils than sandy ones, and it's slow acting over months or even a year.

Soil Fertility

Soil fertility is determined by the amount of readily available nutrients. Soils are depleted by both erosion and use, so orchard and berry crops are likely to need some additional fertilizer every year. The three main elements needed for plant nutrition (major or primary nutrients) are nitrogen, phosphorus, and potassium. These three are included in any balanced or "complete" fertilizer. Those needed in lesser amounts (secondary nutrients) are calcium, magnesium, and sulfur. Don't apply these unless a soil test shows a deficiency; too much of any one can make other nutrients unavailable and create a new deficiency. Then there are some elements needed in very minute amounts. These micronutrients (sometimes called trace elements) are boron, copper, chlorine, iron, manganese, molybdenum, and zinc.

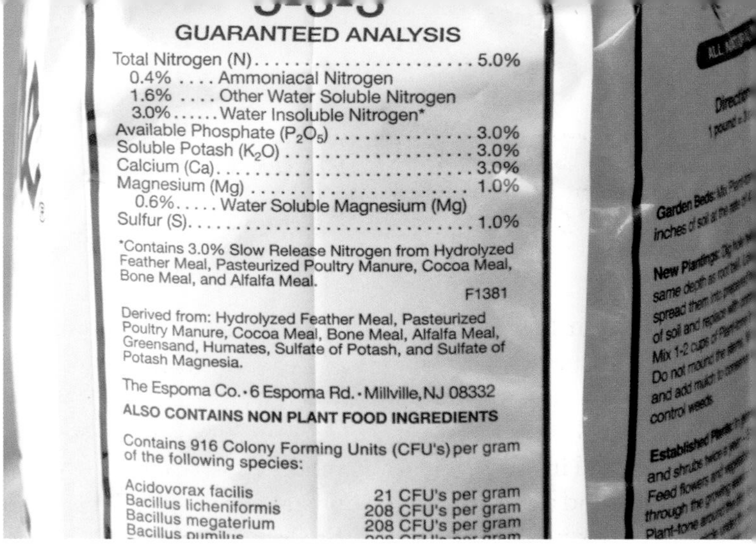

If you use abundant amounts of organic matter and your soil pH is in the right range, usually you need be concerned only with supplying the major nutrients. Secondary elements, necessary in smaller amounts, may be present or may be supplied through regular fertility, but they're sometimes out of balance. Boost calcium and magnesium levels with dolomitic lime, which contains both, but don't use where magnesium levels are adequate. Calcitic limestone supplies only calcium and not magnesium. Boost low levels of sulfur with elemental sulfur (for alkaline soils), sulfate of potash magnesia (langbeinite, for soils also lacking magnesium and potassium), or gypsum (for soils also low in calcium).

Micronutrients are present in almost all soils and are supplied by compost, but particular soils in some parts of the country or specific locales may have too much or too little of one or another. If you grow nut trees, zinc is important for good nut formation. A soil test from your state university Extension Service is the best way to tell. Don't guess. These nutrients are needed in very small amounts. Adding an excess can result in plant toxicity symptoms such as stunted growth and leaf browning.

Any fertilizer, whether organic or synthetic, should clearly show the N-P-K analysis, as well as the source of each nutrient.

The Basics of N–P–K

Nitrogen. This is necessary for good fruit tree growth, and it is lacking in most soils. Organic gardeners who use greensand, wood ashes, granite dust, and rock phosphate may not realize that these don't supply nitrogen. This element is absorbed from the air in small amounts by the soil, and thunderstorms provide some. Nitrogen in its pure form is a gas, so it can be volatile (can evaporate from the soil). In some nitrate forms it will burn plants if used in excessive amounts.

If you don't use a balanced fertilizer, you can supply nitrogen by applying synthetic sources such as nitrates or organic sources such as manures and blood meal. Most organic forms release nitrogen slowly and so provide safer feeding for longer periods than the chemical ones. (Bat guano and poultry manure are exceptions; fresh and uncomposted, both are strong enough to burn plants.) Excessive amounts — more common with synthetic sources than with organic sources — can stimulate production of shoots and leaves at the expense of fruits, and make plants more susceptible to some insects (especially aphids) and diseases.

Phosphorus. A nutrient used by plants for roots and early growth in particular, phosphorus doesn't move well in soil, so mix it in before planting if a soil test shows it's needed. Often you may find a sufficient amount already present, if the site was previously lawn or garden. Too much can wash into and pollute waterways, especially when applied in the form of superphosphate or triple superphosphate. A balanced fertilizer blend should supply all the phosphorus you need, or you can use rock phosphate, bonemeal, manures, or compost, to supply it. When your soil test shows plenty of phosphorus already present, look for a fertilizer with less or no phosphorus (one with a low middle number of the three in the analysis, such as 10-4-10 instead of the more common 10-10-10). This is important to reduce phosphorus pollution of waterways.

Potassium. This element is necessary for healthy roots and fruit, and it increases disease resistance. Again, a balanced fertilizer blend should provide all the potassium you need. Greensand, seaweed-based fertilizers, and wood ashes also supply this element. Some sources found in synthetic fertilizers are various potash salts, such as potassium sulfate.

Preparing Soil for Fruiting Plants

FIRST, TEST YOUR SOIL'S PH; if this is way off, plants won't be able to make use of fertilizers. Either buy an inexpensive testing kit, or send a sample to a soil laboratory (see Sources and Resources; the lab will instruct you how to collect a sample). If possible, send a soil sample to your state university Extension Service or a soil laboratory (see Resources, page 307) for a complete soil test, which will show nutrient levels as well as pH. Levels of soil nitrogen are difficult to measure, but the test will tell you if your soil is out of balance or deficient in other nutrients.

If the pH is higher or lower than the desired range for the fruits you're growing, amend as needed. Because limestone is slow acting — it takes several months to affect pH — it is usually added in the fall, so the soil will be ready by spring. If you must raise or lower pH by more than one point, do it in stages (ideally over 2 years). Apply the amounts below, wait a few months, and test pH again before adding more.

Avoid hydrated or "quick" lime, which is caustic and can burn plants. Instead, use finely ground or pelletized limestone. In general, use calcitic limestone; dolomitic limestone is appropriate only if the soil test indicates low levels of magnesium.

Amending Soil pH

Listed below are the approximate amounts of lime (to raise) and sulfur (to lower) to adjust soil pH one point for 100 square feet of garden. Use half these amounts for half a point on the pH scale. Clay soils will need more than sandy soils to achieve the same change in pH. Note: Don't apply lime or wood ashes at the same time as a nitrogen fertilizer, as the lime will cause much of the nitrogen to evaporate.

Soil Type	LIME (POUNDS)	SULFUR (POUNDS)
Sand	6.0	1.5
Loam	8.0	2.0
Clay	10.0	3.0

How to Fertilize

If you're just starting out or putting in a new row of strawberries, you can amend and fertilize prior to planting. It's best to mix any fertilizer into the planting area ahead of time to avoid the potential of burning sensitive new roots (there is less chance of burning with organic and less-concentrated fertilizers). For existing plantings, you'll need to topdress — apply to the surface — then either work in with a bit of raking or, better yet, water into the soil.

New plantings. For new plantings, you may need little or no additional fertilizer the first year if you tested your soil and prepared it properly before planting with adequate nutrients and compost. Strawberries are an exception; they often need some additional nitrogen a month or so after planting, particularly if leaves are yellowish. In mild climates, with vigorous crops you may need to fertilize strawberries monthly until mid-September. (See page 54.)

If you didn't incorporate nutrients before planting, you will need to apply a balanced fertilizer to fruit trees and bushes a month or so after planting, or when new growth is 4 to 6 inches long.

Established fruit gardens. For existing plantings, late winter or early spring is the best time to fertilize in most areas, when growth is beginning. In very mild climates (such as much of California), you may fertilize during spring bloom and fall harvest. Don't fertilize after midsummer in all but the mildest climates, so new growth can harden off for winter. (Again, strawberries are an exception: midsummer — after renovation — and early September are the most important times; don't fertilize before harvest.)

If a soil test during the season shows the need for phosphorus or potassium, you can add it in late fall after growth stops and before the ground freezes. Apply nitrogen earlier in the growing season; it moves through soil rapidly and so should be supplied while the plants are growing and able to utilize it. Let your fruit trees tell you if they're getting enough fertilizer (see The 12–18 Rule, page 224).

Around the Tree's Dripline

Trees are large, so the way you fertilize them is important. There's approximately as much of a tree underground as there is above: the area covered by the tree's root system is at least the same size as the spread of the branches, and likely much wider if the topsoil is shallow. The largest roots are near the trunk; the small, fibrous hair roots that absorb the soil nutrients are farther away. With a young tree, they're in a circle beginning a foot or two from the trunk and continuing to the outside spread of the branches — the dripline. With older trees, all the feeder roots will be farther from the trunk, and any fertilizer placed close to the trunk or much outside the branch area is going to be wasted.

Bulky fertilizers such as compost and manure should be spread on top of the soil. If you mulch regularly, pull off the mulch and spread the fertilizer directly over the soil beneath the branches. Then replace the mulch and add to it as necessary. Dry fertilizers work more effectively if they're put in the soil; they lose nitrogen readily when exposed to air. Cut a slit with a spade, or punch a hole with an iron bar, and put the fertilizer a few inches into the soil. If you have many trees, you may want to invest in a tree feeding probe, the kind professionals use. You attach this to a hose, add fertilizer to the reservoir, and simply insert the probe (which has holes in the tip) into the ground where you want to fertilize. Fertilizer tree stakes and similar products also work: simply press them into the soil around the tree according to product directions. If you live in the North, don't spread lime, manure, compost, or any kind of fertilizer on frozen ground unless it will be covered with mulch. Otherwise, melting snows and rains will wash it away before it has a chance to work.

Don't overfertilize! If in doubt, don't — or use less. Too much fertilizer delays bearing on young trees and causes poor fruit color and delayed ripening on mature trees.

Choosing Fertilizers

Each gardener has his or her favorite source of plant nutrients. Compost provides many nutrients, but generally in low concentrations. Manure also supplies most nutrients, but be careful that you aren't introducing millions of weed seeds. I have a friend who loves to boast how he got a "deal" on some free manure from a farmer, but then wonders why each year he has so many weeds. Horses and cows may be fed hay that contains weed seeds, which then pass into the manure. Buying composted manures in bulk or in bags should eliminate the weed problem.

If you want to use raw manures, all except rabbit manure are best composted or aged at least 6 months; fresh manure can damage plants from high levels of ammonia and may contain human pathogens. For strawberries, fresh manure should be composted at least twice to 140°F to kill potential food pathogens.

Commercial fertilizers. When you buy commercial fertilizer, whether synthetic or organic, the guaranteed analysis is printed on the bag, as required by law. It's listed in numbers, such as 5–10–10. The first number indicates the percentage of nitrogen (N), the

Many natural amendments supply the necessary macronutrients (N–P–K), along with small but important amounts of micronutrients.

PROPER FERTILIZER APPLICATION

Spread fertilizer over the entire area where the feeder roots are located. On trees (A), spread at least to the dripline, below the outermost branches, begining at least a foot away from the trunk. For berry bushes (B), spread over the entire bed but keep fertilizer at least 6 inches away from stems. Liquid fertilizers (C) offer an easy alternative to granular fertilizers.

second of phosphorus oxide (P_2O_5), and the third of potassium oxide (K_2O). Thus, a 50-pound bag of 5–10–10 fertilizer contains 2½ pounds of nitrogen and 5 pounds each of compounds of the other elements (not of the individual elements). Most of the other weight is filler, which consists of inert ingredients.

A "complete" or balanced fertilizer such as 9–5–4 or 5–10–10 contains at least some of each of these three primary nutrients, but if it's from synthetic sources, it may contain few if any micronutrients. An "incomplete" fertilizer contains only one or two of the primary elements (such as superphosphate, 0–20–0, or bonemeal, 4–12–0), even if it contains a wide range of minor nutrients. Some synthetic complete fertilizers are now available with reduced levels of phosphorus (the middle number of the three), which reduces the chance of excess washing into waterways (where phosphorus has become a serious pollutant). Although organic fertilizers often have a lower analysis — that is, lower numbers — than synthetic fertilizers, their effect is still significant, as they generally break down slowly and release nutrients over a much longer time, supply micronutrients, and aid soil microbes.

Whatever fertilizer you use, read the label carefully and follow the recommended application rates for your particular plants and according to soil test results. Don't think that overfeeding your trees and bushes will give you faster growth and more fruit. You may end up with lots of leaves and no fruit or plants that are prone to insects and disease. Like overfeeding ourselves, it isn't a good idea, and twice as much is never twice as good.

Many gardeners have good luck using blended fertilizers, which consist of two or more dry fertilizer products. Organic blends are now widely available, as well as synthetics. You can make up your own blend using the nutrients listed in the chart opposite.

The 12–18 Rule

Let your trees tell you if they need fertilizer. Look at the most recent growth at the tips of branches — the tender, often light-colored and thin growth that comes from a hardened ring of wood where the previous year's growth ended. If this is 18 to 24 inches for young trees, 10 to 12 inches for mature trees (that is, those of bearing age), they're getting enough nutrients. This is called the "12–18 rule." If a mature tree produced less than 12 inches of growth in the past year, fertilize more. If you see 12 to 18 inches of new growth, fertilize the same as before. If your trees produce more than this, don't fertilize at all. In some areas, you may expect 4 to 6 inches more than these for cherries, plums, and peaches.

Liquid products. Specific liquid fertilizers are useful to help transplants get established and to get them growing quickly. Many synthetic formulations now come with their own hose attachments, so you simply hook them up and water. They're so easy that it may be tempting to overuse them. Resist! As with all chemicals, use according to directions and never after midseason, so you won't encourage late-summer growth.

Fish emulsion, liquid seaweed, and blends of the two are organic liquid fertilizers. You can make a fast-acting manure tea with composted manure. Just mix manure and water in a large garbage can, let soak, dilute to the color of weak black tea, then pour the "tea" over the soil and even the leaves for foliar feeding. Avoid spraying it on developing fruit.

Slow-release fertilizers. Slow-release (now often called controlled-release) synthetic fertilizers release their nutrients slowly over a period of weeks or months, similar to organic ones, ensuring a long season of even feeding. They also reduce the likelihood of burning plants from excess fertilizer, and are less likely to leach away in rains than ordinary chemical fertilizers. Some are available in a pill form that you bury near a tree or plant. On the downside, unlike organic fertilizers many don't supply trace elements, and they're much more expensive than many other blended fertilizers.

Although slow-release synthetic fertilizers give long-term and consistent feeding under ordinary conditions, when the temperature rises unusually high, the release in some products is faster. For this reason, in warm climates it's better to apply two smaller feedings per year, rather than one heavier one in the spring.

Organic Nutrient Sources

You can use the organic sources here to supply a nutrient that's deficient in your soil, or blend them to make your own balanced fertilizer. For example, mix blood meal with greensand in combination with bonemeal or rock phosphate for a complete fertilizer. Follow rates listed on the labels or recommendations with soil tests.

Alfalfa meal. Dried pellets from alfalfa plants provide nitrogen and potassium (about 2–1–2); also add trace elements; good for compost.

Blood meal. Dried animal blood, typically 12–0–0. Good source of nitrogen; acts as a deer repellent.

Bonemeal. Finely ground animal bones, generally steamed, typically around 4–12–0. The odor may attract skunks digging in the soil looking for the buried bones.

Cottonseed meal. Good for acid-loving plants such as blueberries, typically 6–0–1.

Fish products. Derived from fish processing; available in various forms, often with fishy smell (deodorized have less); complete fertilizer (5–2–2) also add trace elements.

Greensand. Material from ocean deposits. May contain only 0–0–3 analysis, but is valuable for many additional trace elements.

Poultry manure (composted). So strong smelling that some gardeners think trees grow just to get away from it. More powerful than cow and sheep manure. To avoid disease issues and risk of burning plants, make sure it's composted. Fresh, it may be as high as 56–45–34.

Other manures. Analysis will vary depending on whether manure is fresh, dried (dehydrated), or composted, and from what animal. Dehydrated cow manure is widely available. Although the analysis is low (often in the range of 1–1–1), it also supplies trace elements, lots of organic matter, and is safe to use in quantity (unlike more concentrated fertilizers). Dehydrated poultry manure may be double or more than these numbers. Check the label on bags of dehydrated manure for usage rates.

Fresh manures are problematic: they are very high in nitrogen and may burn plants, and they may contain pathogens harmful to humans. Fortunately, composting for at least a month before using will eliminate these hazards. Turn the pile every few days with a shovel, and wear gloves to protect hands from pathogens.

Rock phosphate. Natural phosphate rock that has been ground very fine, usually 0–3–0. Becomes available to trees extremely slowly, but should last for at least 3 years.

Seaweed. From kelp and sea plants, in various forms; minimal major elements but adds micronutrients and other beneficial compounds; apply to the soil or leaves.

Soybean meal. Dried pellets from soybean plants provide nitrogen and phosphorus (about 7–2–1).

Wood ash. Ashes make soil more alkaline, so use only on acidic soils. Typically 0–1–3, up to 8 percent potassium. Don't apply at the same time as a fertilizer containing nitrogen in the form of urea or ammonium, as either will release ammonia gas when combined with such an alkaline material. One rule of thumb is a gallon of ashes per square yard of soil, with half that on sandy soils, or no more than half an inch top-dressed on soil.

Mulches Are Labor-Savers

ORGANIC MULCHES offer such great advantages that it would be a mistake not to use them on your orchard and berry plants. In addition to enhancing the structure of the soil and providing fertility as they rot, they suppress weeds and grasses that steal soil nutrients, prevent erosion from wind and rain, keep soils cooler (which may be good in hot climates, and helps delay spring bloom in cold climates), and help retain soil moisture by greatly decreasing evaporation. They also encourage earthworms and other soil organisms, and guard against rapid freezing and thawing of the ground in cold climates.

Some gardeners like the clean appearance of a nonorganic mulch such as crushed rock around their plantings, and some spread black plastic between rows. Nonorganic mulches last for years but add no humus or nutrients to the soil.

Don't overdo mulches, however, or mound them up around a trunk, creating a "volcano" effect. Mulches that are more than 2 inches deep after they settle can have the same effect as burying a tree too deep: smothering the roots, which need exposure to air, and resulting in too-shallow roots (these are sensitive to drying out and don't anchor plants well). Deep mulches also make it difficult for rain and watering to reach the roots.

Mulch provides a convenient nesting place for rodents, who will thank you during winter while they feast on the tree bark. If you mulch your

Mulch "volcanoes" like this one have the same effect as planting the tree too deeply in the soil, and also provide a place for bark-gnawing rodents to nest right up against the trunk of the tree.

Spreading mulch in a ring around the base of the tree, on the other hand, will help direct water to the tree's roots.

Mulch Material

Organic Materials	Nonorganic Materials
Burlap	Black plastic
Cardboard (remove any adhesive tape)	Commercial landscaping fabrics
Cocoa shells	Crushed rock or gravel
Compost, composted manure, composted bark	Flat rocks or paving blocks
Evergreen needles (pine are best for blueberries)	Marble or granite chips
Lawn clippings (let dry slightly before using)	Avoid recycled rubber mulches (they are highly flammable and may release toxic contaminants)
Newspaper (use multiple layers for weed control)	
Shredded leaves	
Shredded bark	
Straw	

fruit trees, install tree guards or hardware cloth to protect trunks from nibbling mice and voles (see page 238).

My favorite way to mulch fruit trees is to spread a layer of manure or compost around each tree from the trunk to the outside spread of the branches and then cover this with a thick layer of newspaper or cardboard. This smothers the grass and weeds very effectively. Then I add a layer of wood chips or shredded bark a couple of inches deep to hide the not-too-attractive paper or cardboard, and to keep it from blowing away. Each year I reapply these layers, adding a little fertilizer first. This practice is called sheet mulching. For wide rows in the orchard, mown grass is easiest.

Mulches also are good for berry bushes. Besides all the other advantages, mulches keep rains from spattering dirt on ripening strawberries. Don't use slow-to-rot wood chips on strawberry beds if they'll be plowed back into the soil within a year or two. Straw, dried lawn clippings, and shredded leaves make better mulches for them.

For narrow aisles between rows of strawberries and mature bushes, I use a combination of a commercial landscaping fabric on the bottom and wood chips or bark on top. Landscaping fabric allows air

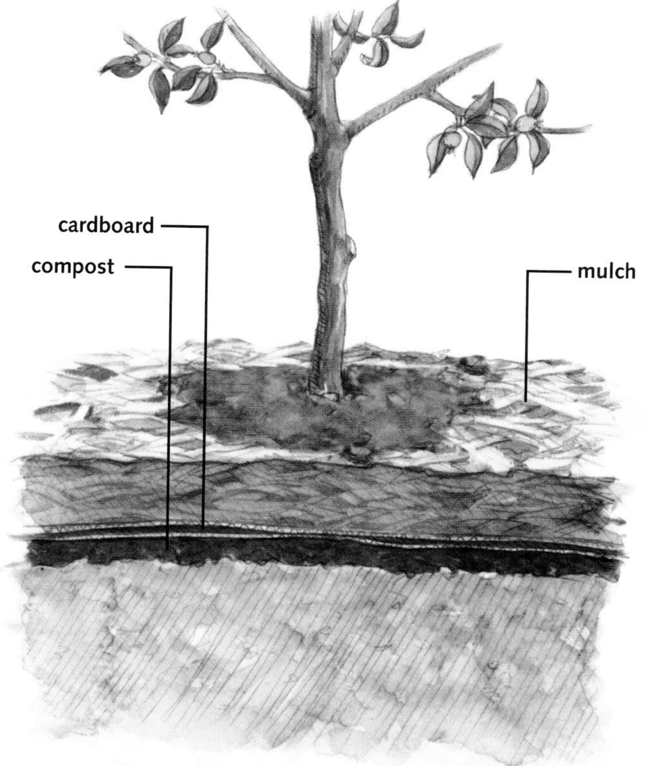

Sheet mulching around trees or bushes is a good way to smother grass and weeds, but keep mulch away from base of trunk.

Three Ways to Use Leaves for Soil Improvement

1. Shred and add immediately to the soil. Run a lawn mower over a row of raked leaves to shred, or put through a shredder.
2. Compost for at least a year before you incorporate them into the soil. Leaves compost into leaf mold, which is one of the best soil amendments and fertilizers.
3. Use shredded leaves as a mulch around fruit trees and berry plants. Check the soil underneath in a year, and you'll find earthworms galore and hundreds of little root hairs exploring the composted leaves for nourishment.

Make Your Own Compost

COMPOSTING DOES, in a faster and more manageable way, what nature does all the time in gardens, fields, and forests. The rotting of trees and plants over millennia has provided us with the humus in the soil that makes it possible to grow our plants and trees. Gardeners and orchardists can speed up the natural process by building compost piles. Piling waste material in heaps increases the heating process and speeds decomposition. The easiest way to get a good mix of ingredients in your compost pile is to alternate layers of dry "browns" and fresh "greens" and soil. Browns include fallen leaves, straw, shredded newspaper and cardboard, and sawdust (not from pressure-treated wood). Greens include manure, grass clippings, coffee grounds, crushed egg shells, fruit and vegetable trimmings, green garden trimmings, and sod

and water to pass through but prevent weeds as long as it doesn't get punctured. (Weeds seem to find any hole and edge.) Each spring I simply peel back the layer, add some compost, then put it back, replacing any torn areas of fabric. Don't use weed fabrics around bushes that spread, such as raspberries, or you'll prevent needed growth of new shoots.

One of the best mulches I've ever found is also one the least expensive: leaves. If you're lucky enough to live in an area where they lie in large heaps on the ground every fall, consider them a gift from nature and scoop them up. I have friends, not so fortunate, who make fall pilgrimages to the recycling center to collect others' bags of leaves. The only problem they report is that you have to get there early, as the competition for leaves is heating up. Got a friend or neighbor with lots of deciduous trees? Make a deal to haul them away for free.

Leaves are an excellent soil conditioner, and offer a double benefit as nature's own fertilizer. The roots of large trees reach far into the subsoil to bring up nutrients and trace elements that shallow-rooted trees and plants never reach, and these end up in their leaves.

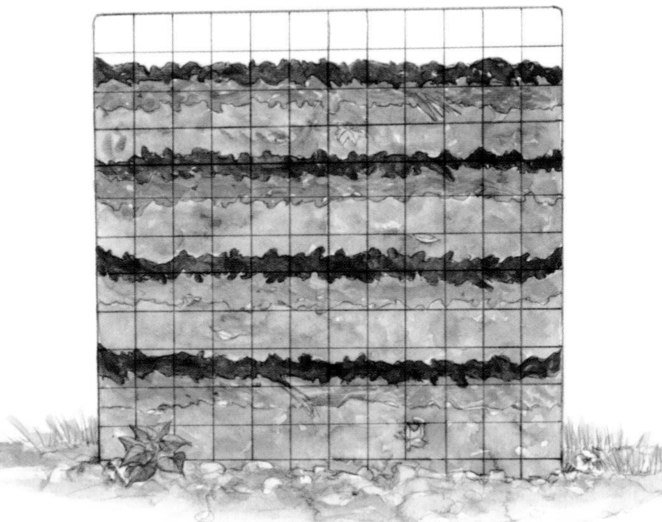

A good compost pile will have alternating layers of dry organic matter (such as leaves or straw), green organic matter (such as fresh lawn clippings or kitchen waste), and soil or composted manure.

Finished compost will be dark and crumbly, and will have a deep, earthy aroma.

(broken into small pieces). Although all these are ideal for compost, don't worry and skip composting if you're short on an ingredient. Composting will save adding such decomposing materials to landfills, if nothing else.

Organic matter that you can add to a compost pile can be most any natural material that decomposes. Just make sure you don't add diseased or weedy plants to your compost, or weeds that have gone to seed. Never add meat scraps, pet wastes, or yard trimmings with pesticide residues. Examples of plants and products that decompose most rapidly are shredded leaves, shredded paper, eggshells, coffee grounds, fruit peels, vegetable scraps, and fine wood shavings. Slow to decompose, taking 2 years or more, are wood chips, corncobs and cornstalks, and nut shells. Breaking up or shredding these slower materials or adding extra nitrogen will help speed things up.

Microorganisms are responsible for breaking down materials to form compost. Adding soil or manure to the compost pile supplies them. Manure and other "greens" supply the nitrogen (N) they need. The plants and other "brown" products are the carbon (C) sources microorganisms use for food, and the result is compost. Although you can get rather technical with ratios of C:N and how the various components contribute to the total ratio, you can make good compost with about 2 to 3 parts of brown materials to one part of green.

Troubleshooting

If the compost is decomposing slowly, you may have too much organic matter or carbon source — the "brown" materials mentioned above. To balance this, add more "green" matter — the nitrogen source. If you don't have manure, try adding some fresh grass clippings or nitrogen fertilizer (about 1 cup per layer for a 4-foot-by-4-foot pile).

If you smell ammonia, you have too much nitrogen and need to add more brown materials as a carbon source. If you need lots more carbon, sawdust and chopped leaves are good choices. Some like to add a sprinkling of lime to counteract the acidity of most fresh materials in compost. Compost microorganisms need a neutral to slightly acidic environment to work best.

TIPS FOR COMPOSTING

- Use a compost bin or make a pile at least 4 feet by 4 feet and 3 feet high after settling.
- Chop or shred coarse materials such as large leaves and wood chips to hasten their breakdown.
- Alternate layers of carbon-rich "browns" 5 to 8 inches deep with nitrogen-rich "greens" 2 to 3 inches deep, topping each double layer with soil or composted manure 1 to 2 inches deep. Browns include leaves, straw, wood chips, shredded newspaper and cardboard; greens include composted manure, grass clippings, fruit and vegetable wastes, and green garden trimmings.
- Moisten layers as you go. Materials should be about as wet as a wrung-out sponge.
- Turn the compost every few days or weekly to aerate.

Build your pile in the open, or enclose it in a commercially made box or bin or one constructed from stones, boards, or cement blocks. Some bins are quite attractive. I like the mounted barrel type that you can easily rotate to turn and aerate the compost. Some towns forbid open compost piles, so check your local bylaws. If necessary, you can make compost in covered garbage cans in a garage or shed; just make sure to open them daily and turn to mix in enough air. If your compost smells rotten (whether in a bin or out the open), it's too wet or isn't getting enough air. Covered bins, or a tarp over the pile, will keep excess rain off and the compost from being too wet.

If not in a bin, compost piles should stand about 3 feet high after settling has taken place. Keep the top of the pile flat or slightly concave so rain can soak in. If rains are lacking or you garden in a dry climate, water every few days. Turn the heap occasionally to provide air and to speed up decomposition. An active and ideal compost pile should heat up inside to 110° to 140°F within a couple of weeks, which you can measure with a special compost thermometer available at garden stores or from catalogs. Don't worry if yours doesn't heat up quickly; just make sure you have the right ratio of ingredients, turn periodically, and be patient while the compost organisms work.

If a pile is properly made and turned, there won't be any unpleasant smell either when the compost is rotting or while it's being used. If your compost pile is near a field or source of weed seeds that may blow in, keep it covered with a plastic tarp. Remove plastic when rain is forecast or you need to water, and to turn the contents every few days.

Compost is finished when it's dark and crumbly and smells earthy sweet. In areas with normal precipitation, it may take a full year to rot an outdoor compost heap properly, but turning and keeping the heap moist during dry weather will speed things up. You can also add activators, available at garden stores, for even faster decomposition. Large piles tend to decompose faster than small ones; those in warm climates faster than those in cool climates.

Most gardeners like to have three compost piles: one that's being made, a second in the process of rotting, and a third actively in use. I usually have at least two bins. I fork the compost from one bin into the other to turn it. Growing up, I had one large bin made of concrete blocks, with enough room inside to fork the compost from one side to the other.

Planting well, mulching properly, and keeping weeds to a minimum will help ensure that your fruiting plants get off to a good start in life.

CHAPTER 16

Getting Plants off to a Good Start

Each spring, we observed Arbor Day at our little one-room country school. The tree-planting ceremony was quite impressive. After a salute to the flag, someone especially chosen for the honor would dig the hole, a decree that had gone out from the governor would be duly read, and a child always recited "Trees," by Joyce Kilmer. Finally the group sang an appropriate song, quite off-key. Then we would plant the tree.

The ceremony was well organized and the poetry more than adequate, but we were all deficient in our planting ability. No one considered that the tree might be planted too shallow or too deep. No one thought it might be suffering more than we were, as the poems and readings went on and on and both they and the tree were getting drier and drier. No one ever thought to cover the little tree's roots or to bring a pail of water. If we'd paid as much attention to the trees as we did to the ceremonies, more of those Arbor Day trees would have survived.

Compared to other fruit crops, fruit trees take the biggest investment of your time and money to get good fruit and big yields. So it pays to get them off to a good start. Berry bushes and vines may cost less, but you'll be investing your labor in them, so give them a similar good start. This chapter discusses bushes and trees; for strawberries, see chapter 4.

Care Starts before Planting

THE TREES AND BUSHES you purchase at a nursery or a garden center are probably in containers. Larger specimens may be balled-and-burlapped. Both have the benefit over bare-root plants, in that they can be held through the season until you're ready to plant. Just make sure to keep them well watered, often daily unless there's a good rain, especially those with roots encased in burlap. For these, if you're not going to plant right away, it helps to mound mulch or wood chips around the ball of soil.

Most mail-order trees are shipped bare-root, packed in some sort of moisture-retaining wrap. Treat these like fish: they can't live long without lots of moisture. Bare-root trees are the least expensive and usually offer more variety than those balled-and-burlapped or in containers. Nurseries dig them in the fall, store them in controlled temperature and humidity sheds during the winter, then wrap and ship them in the spring. They're likely to be quite dry when they reach your doorstep, so your first, and very important, step should be to unwrap them upon arrival and soak the roots in a pond or tub of water for 3 to 6 hours (but not over 24 hours). Don't worry if the trees arrive on a cold day. Even if the roots are frozen, there's no problem as long as you let them thaw slowly by leaving the package in a cool basement or garage for half a day before you soak them.

You can set out balled or container-grown trees and bushes successfully at any time of the year when the ground isn't frozen, but it's best to plant bare-rooted trees in the spring, before growth starts in cold-climate areas (Zones 5 and colder), so the trees will have a full season to get established and well rooted before winter. If you live in Zone 6 or warmer, however, you can safely plant in the fall.

Soak bare-root trees and bushes in a tub of water for several hours before you plant them.

Try to keep the rootball intact, disturbing roots as little as possible, when removing the wrapping of balled-and-burlapped plants.

Remove any plastic wrapping or container from a balled or potted tree, but keep intact the soil ball surrounding the roots. If you disturb it, you'll break all the little feeder roots that make a balled or potted tree superior to one that's bare-root. Any roots that are broken should be pruned off at the break. If, in spite of your best efforts and care, the soil easily falls off the roots when you remove the pot or burlap surrounding the rootball, treat it like a bare-root tree. If that happens with a container-grown specimen, chances are the tree was potted only recently. I've seen this in some garden stores that don't grow their trees and from retailers that don't specialize in plants. Buy your tree later in the season in a pot and it will likely be well rooted, but then the selection is rather poor.

Presumably you've already chosen a good location with plenty of sun (at least 8 hours a day) and well-drained soil, not in a low area where late-spring frosts could damage spring blooms. Allow enough room for the mature size of the tree. Figure on a space about as wide as trees are tall, so for a 10-foot-tall tree, space at least 10 feet apart from other trees. Follow the spacing recommendations listed on the plant label, or the general recommendations at the beginning of each fruit chapter.

Best Sites for Fruit Trees, Bushes, and Vines

- At least 8 hours of sun a day
- Deep, well-drained soil
- Away from wild fruit trees and bushes
- Good airflow, but not too windy
- Avoid low areas, as these are frost pockets and soil drainage may be poor

Planting Well Pays Off

PLANTING A ROW OF BERRIES or bushes differs from planting an individual bush or tree. If you're planting a whole row, begin a year ahead by adding plenty of compost or other organic matter on top of the soil and tilling it in deeply. If the row is weedy or covered in sod, plant a cover crop the season before to help enrich the soil and control weeds. This is the time to add lime, if called for by a soil test.

For a tree or a single bush, dig the hole much wider than you think is really necessary — one as wide as a bushel basket should be adequate for a 6-foot tree. Put all the soil that you remove into two heaps, the good topsoil on one side and the poorer subsoil on the other. Pour a pail of water into the hole and let it soak in. Don't dig the hole deeper than you'll spread the roots or place the rootball. Unless the soil underneath is firmed properly, it will settle and the tree will end up planted too low. This smothers the bark and forces roots to grow too near the surface. Planting too low increases the possibility of rot setting in around the base and may result in the decline and even death of the tree over time.

For trees and bushes, no fertilizer is needed in the hole at planting (it may burn the tender roots). If possible, till or fork some compost into the area around the planting hole, which is where future roots will grow. A suggestion in the past was to mix generous amounts of compost, peat moss, or manure with the topsoil before backfilling. Most recommendations now call for little or no added organic matter. You can probably incorporate up to 25 percent by volume with no problem, but studies have found that the roots tend to stay in such a rich soil and don't grow as well out into the surrounding soil. This stunted and reduced root growth is reflected in less top growth and trees that aren't anchored well. If the soil is poor, try to find a better site, or choose a fruit or cultivar that will tolerate poor soil. Some apple rootstocks, for example, are better than others in poor soils.

Set the bush or tree at about the same level as it grew in the field or pot. On a bare-root tree, you can find this level easily on the bark just above the roots. When digging the hole, I like to first measure the roots or pot with a yardstick or tape measure, then make sure the hole I dig is the same depth. If you plant a tree too deep, the roots will be smothered, which is likely to kill it; if you set it too shallow, the roots will dry out. (For the correct depth to plant strawberries, see page 53).

PLANTING A TREE

1. When planting, dig a hole more than wide enough to contain all the roots without crowding. For grafted trees, make sure the graft union is 2 to 4 inches above the soil level. Put the better topsoil on one side of the hole and the poorer subsoil on the other.

2. Slowly pour a whole watering can full of water into the hole.

3. Backfill the better topsoil around the roots, either watering in as you go, or firming. If you run out of topsoil near the top, add plenty of compost to the subsoil before finishing. Fill the hole almost to the top with the remaining subsoil-compost mix.

4. Leave a slight depression in the soil around the trunk to catch rain and water from the hose. Water in well, supplying 2 or 3 gallons. You can use a dilute liquid fertilizer if desired.

If the bush or tree is in a container, remove the container and then loosen the outer roots with your fingers, trowel, or garden fork. When roots are thick and tight or circling the pot, make three or four vertical cuts with a sharp knife. This will stimulate new roots to grow outward once planted, rather than around and girdling the trunk.

For a grafted tree, plant so the graft union will be 2 to 4 inches above the soil. At the higher end of this range, you'll get more of the benefits from the rootstock, such as hardiness and height control. If the union is below soil level, the top or scion will root and you'll lose the benefits of the rootstock. If it's too high, sucker growth may come up yearly from the rootstock base. If you know the rootstock, and that it's prone to suckers or burr knots, plant the tree with the graft union at or just above soil level.

Hold the tree straight (a partner to hold the top while you work on the bottom is helpful), spread out the roots (if bare-root), and put back enough of the soil to barely cover the roots. Gently move a bare-root tree up and down to help settle this initial soil around the roots. Gently tamp the soil down to remove air pockets, or add some water.

Now add some more soil and water, and continue until the hole is filled. Alternatively, firm the soil as you add it back around the roots with gentle foot tamping; packing as if you were jumping on a trampoline will harm both soil and roots. Be careful not to damage the tree with your shovel during the process, because the bark is tender and can't stand rough treatment. It may be necessary to use a little of the subsoil you've dug up to fill the hole completely, but most of it should be used elsewhere, such as for filling a low area, or mixed in with some of the better topsoil.

Leave a slight depression in the soil around each plant, beginning a few inches from the main stem or tree trunk, to catch rain and water from the hose so the water will soak into the ground and root zone. (If you have extra subsoil, you can use it to build up a berm.) Water the tree or bush well once it's planted. Wait until growth starts (usually 2 to 4 weeks) to fertilize bare-root plants.

Unless it rains hard, water newly planted trees and bushes thoroughly each week for the first month. If the weather stays hot or you have sandy soil, you may need to water more often. Pour slowly, so all of it reaches the bottom of the roots.

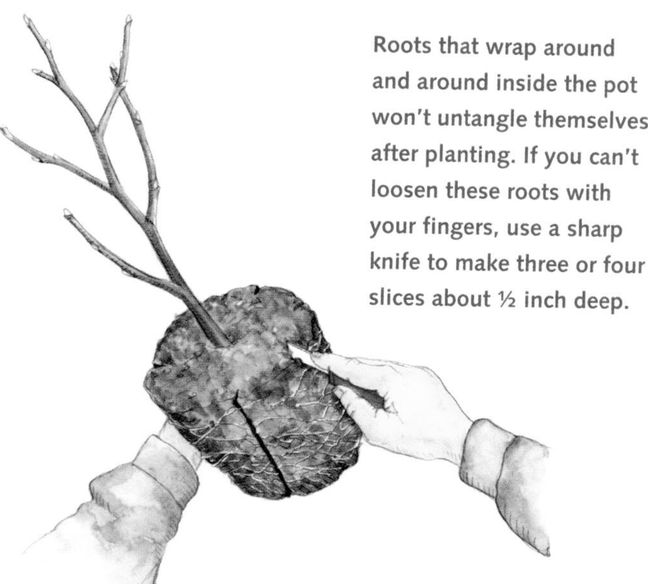

Roots that wrap around and around inside the pot won't untangle themselves after planting. If you can't loosen these roots with your fingers, use a sharp knife to make three or four slices about ½ inch deep.

This step of watering cannot be emphasized too strongly. It's the least expensive and most dependable way to help a little tree get off to a fast start. Don't overdo either the watering or the fertilizing, though, especially if you have a heavy and poorly drained soil. One of our neighbors accidentally left the hose running on a small tree for an entire weekend. Not only was this hard on his well, but by Monday morning his poor tree had drowned. Figure on using 3 to 5 gallons of water each time for a new tree 4 to 8 feet tall.

Pamper after Planting

CHECK TO MAKE SURE there are no labels wrapped around, or tied to, limbs or the trunk that will strangle the tree as it grows. If you buy a bare-root tree through the mail, it has probably already been cut back before being shipped. If not, it's a good idea for you to prune right after planting to help compensate for the loss of roots at the time of digging. Do this too if you move your own small tree from elsewhere. Even if it was cut back, or if the tree was balled-and-burlapped or potted, you may need to prune selectively to start shaping its structure (see chapter 17).

A tree guard will help protect the trunk of a young sapling from mechanical damage caused by weed trimmers and mowers. Taller guards are needed to protect against winter bark splitting, sunscald, and mice feeding in areas with snow.

Mulch and Protect

Spread a layer of mulch around trees after the planting. As explained on page 226, a mulch helps hold moisture, suppresses grass and weeds, and improves the soil structure over time. The mulch should not be more than 2 inches deep: more than that will smother the roots and lower trunk or stems, similar to planting too deeply, as well as prevent water from reaching them; less and it will provide little benefit. Even when you're planting in a well-kept lawn, remove the sod a couple feet out from the trunk. This will reduce competition for the new tree roots from grass, will provide an area for mulch, and will keep away errant weed trimmers and mowers. Keep mulch a couple of inches away from the trunk, and definitely don't pile it up against the trunk, as is commonly seen in landscapes in some regions; otherwise, it provides a home for trunk-munching voles over winter.

Once you've mulched but before you've staked the tree, install a tree guard (see picture). This protects the young, tender bark from splitting, caused when the bark temperature changes rapidly, such as from the sun heating it quickly after a cold winter night, or temperatures plummeting at night after a warm and sunny afternoon. Tree guards also protect against mechanical injury (weed trimmers, mowers), and from winter feeding by small mammals such as voles. You may need additional protection from large mammals — specifically, deer. These love to browse the young growth and then future buds in winter (see page 295).

Staking

Newly planted, standard-size fruit trees seldom need staking if you set them in carefully. In a windy area, however, they may lean with the prevailing winds unless you give them some help in their early years. Young dwarf trees, which are extremely shallow rooted, will need staking unless you've put them in a sheltered location. Most growers use a 10-foot section of 1-inch-diameter electrical conduit pipe, as it's relatively inexpensive, sturdy, and easy to handle. Place this 4 to 6 inches out from the trunk. Push or pound it 2 feet into the ground, leaving 8 feet above. Then secure the tree to the post with strips of cloth, special twine for just this purpose, or wire enclosed in pieces of garden hose. This keeps the wire from cutting into the bark.

If you only have a few trees and they're in a landscape, you can use more attractive wooden posts or stakes. Pound these in the ground beginning 12 to 18 inches from a tree and angled slightly outward. Place three equally spaced around the trunk. Attach the tree to them as above, making sure the fastening material isn't too tight around the trunk.

Check at least annually to make sure the wrapping still isn't too tight. When the trees are 3 or 4 years old and well anchored, remove the stakes. The exception is a dwarfing rootstock that by nature doesn't provide good anchoring for the tree — keep plants that are grafted on that type of rootstock staked.

Fertilize

Two to four weeks after planting a bare-root tree, when it starts to show new growth, fertilize with a low-analysis or slow-release fertilizer. If you purchased the plant in a container or balled-and-burlapped, you can fertilize after planting. If growth is vigorous, or if you're planting after midsummer, don't fertilize. It may be best to wait longer to feed blueberries, as they are sensitive to too much fertilizer at this point. See the individual fruit chapters for specific fertilizer recommendations.

Scatter dry blends several inches away from the plant to avoid burning the newly forming roots. Many gardeners use a soluble liquid fertilizer, such as fish emulsion, or one specifically for transplanting that's a bit higher in phosphorus (good for root growth, such as 3–10–3). If using a dry fertilizer on strawberries, try to keep it off the leaves; water after fertilizing to wash the product off leaves and into the soil.

Document

Labels soon fade and fall off, so in a chart record plant names, dates, and any other pertinent information, such as where you bought the plants. A simple spreadsheet or database program on a computer is what many use. A record of your plantings will not only identify the fruits when they start to bear, but will also help you if you need to replace any trees. Make sure any labels on trees are loose and will not strangle branches as these grow.

Don't Harvest Too Soon

AS A BEGINNING FRUIT GROWER anxiously awaiting my first crop, I was always delighted to find a tree blooming the first or second year after planting. As the little fruits grew, it was even more exciting to see how many of them a tree was producing. Actually, as I found out later, this wasn't at all good for the young tree.

If your tree is growing extremely well and is in good, rugged condition, it probably won't hurt it to bear a fruit or two the second year after planting. For most fruit trees, though, you should pick off all fruits until the third year. It may be difficult to do, but it's for the tree's own good and to ensure better fruiting in the future. A young tree doesn't have sufficient roots and enough resources to support both new growth and fruit. Removing fruit in early years is especially important for cultivars that have a tendency to bear far too soon ("precocious") and too heavily, which can weaken them so much that they won't produce another crop for several years. Such a tree can easily become infected and die an early death.

Even after a tree is mature, control overbearing by annual pruning and by thinning out the fruits when small (see page 257). Otherwise, the tree may bear large crops of small-sized fruit every other year (alternate bearing), or branches may break under the weight of too many fruits.

Similar treatment to postpone the first crop will improve your yields with other fruits as well. For grapes, remove flowers the first two years so vines bear no fruits; this will direct the plant's energy into good root growth and new canes. Remove the first strawberry flowers so those plants too will put energy into growing more leaves and roots to support fruit production. Do this the entire first year for June-bearing strawberries; remove only the first bloom cluster for everbearing types.

Removing flowers for the first two years will help ensure the health of the vines and abundant harvests in future years.

Annual pruning should be a part of any fruit grower's maintenance schedule.

CHAPTER 17

Pruning: Not Just for Trees

Years ago, when I was in the nursery and landscaping business, I often pruned other people's fruit trees, shrubbery, and hedges. I soon learned that the job went best when the owners were away. Everyone seemed to like the finished results but, to many people watching, the procedure seemed a bit like slaughtering a steer: "You'll kill that tree!" or "How can you be so ruthless?" A few people look happy as larks when they're cutting away at their trees and dreaming of harvests to come. Many others prune far too cautiously, with just little snips here and there.

Pruning a fruit tree for maximum production is different from pruning it for beauty. A properly pruned orchard tree is not beautiful to all eyes, especially in winter, when the leaves are off and it looks butchered. A tree that is important in the landscape should have less pruning. We have an apple tree in our backyard and enjoy both beauty and good crops of fruit by pruning it only moderately every year.

Heading vs. Thinning

Any description of pruning ends up talking about two types of cuts. Thinning or a thinning cut refers to removing whole branches (large and small) by cutting them back to a larger branch. Heading back or a heading cut refers to removing just part of a branch (also called tipping and tipping back). The reason you need to know this is that the different cuts cause a bush or tree to grow in different ways afterward. Heading back a branch stimulates more growth from just behind the cut. If you don't want to stimulate more growth, then remove the branch at its point of origin (another branch or the tree trunk) instead.

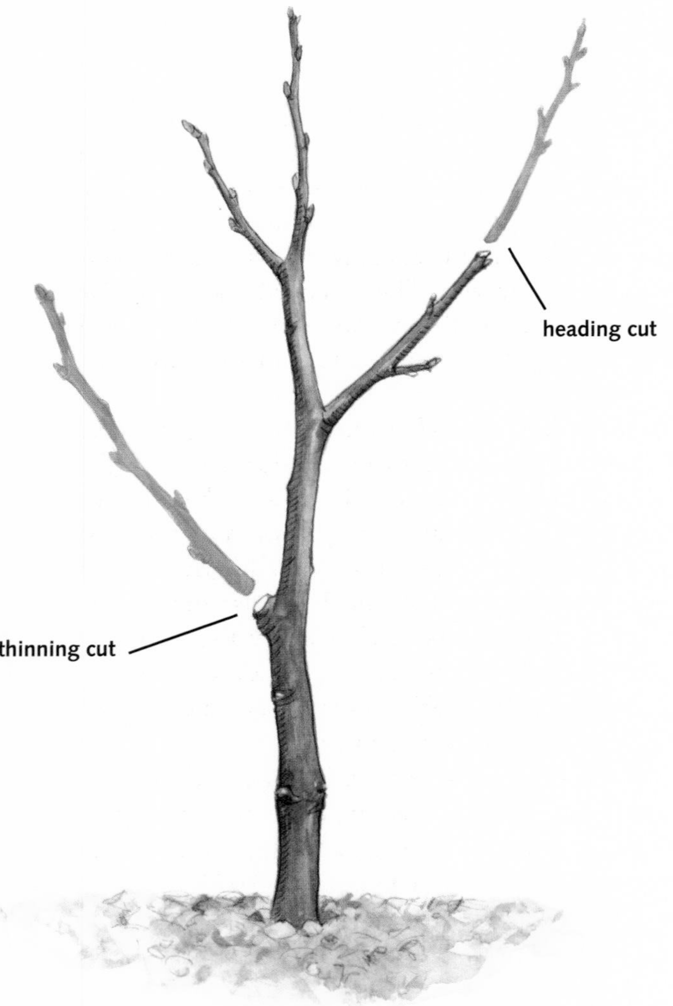

Why Prune?

PROPER PRUNING HELPS a plant to produce better fruit and, even more important, it conserves its strength for a longer, healthier life. This is especially important for young trees. Just as many adult habits are set in childhood, so is the mature tree structure established in the first years. Without this initial shaping of fruit trees, several years of dormant pruning may be needed to correct the shape, and fruiting may be delayed during this period. Fruiting bushes need pruning also (see individual chapters for specific details). Even strawberry plants need "pruning": removing the blossoms on young plants improves yields and helps plants live longer.

Pruning is not at all difficult when you understand the reasons and procedures. First, keep in mind that there's no one right way to prune a tree or bush. Then, as you approach your bushes and trees, saw and clippers in hand, remember the reasons for pruning:

- To train a plant to grow into a good shape and be strong enough to hold up its fruit load.
- To keep it at a size that's convenient to prune, spray, and harvest. Our standard fruit trees would grow to 25 feet tall, but we keep them cut back so we can reach almost all the fruit from the ground. Some brambles are easier to manage if cut back to 4 or 5 feet tall.
- To remove broken branches, those suffering from winter injury, and any infected by disease or insects. Harvesting all brambles is easier when dead canes are removed each year.
- To decrease the amount of bearing surface. By thinning out the limbs, a smaller number of fruits will result, but they'll be larger and the total yield will be greater. Trees that naturally bear in alternate years may begin to bear every year.
- To remove any crossed limbs. Limbs that rub against each other in the wind open wounds through which disease can get a foothold.
- To open up the bush or tree so that more sunlight can reach into the inner branches. An open plant allows fruit to ripen even in the interior, and helps control diseases by allowing more air circulation.

- To renew bearing wood. You can renew most of the bearing surface of a tree every few years by removing a few of the older limbs that have lost vigor. New, healthy limbs will replace them. This is important for bushes, too.
- To remove any weak tree limbs that will split when the tree is loaded with fruit or ice. Branches that grow at a narrow V-shaped angle with the trunk can't support as much weight as can more horizontal branches.

Summer pruning is good for directing new growth in espaliers. Make heading cuts to just above a bud, thinning cuts back to a branch or trunk.

When to Prune

LONGTIME ORCHARDISTS love to argue about the best time to prune. A few maintain that they prune whenever their tools are sharp or whenever it fits their schedule. In cold climates, most prune on warm days in early spring, while it's still cold but the temperature is above freezing. (This is before any growth begins or buds begin to swell.) Working when it's above freezing is easier on the pruner and also on the plant, as cuts made to frozen branches may result in cold damage and dieback on some fruits. In warmer climates, you can prune safely all winter, as long as the trees are dormant. This is referred to as dormant pruning.

In all areas, it is best not to prune when trees start to leaf out in spring because this can interfere with flowering. Plums and cherries are an exception; prune these trees in late spring after bloom. Don't prune in late summer, as this often stimulates new growth that won't have time to harden before fall. Nor is fall pruning good, as the wounds won't heal and diseases can enter the cuts. Early winter pruning should be avoided in cold climates; this could result in winter damage.

Pruning in early summer, appropriately termed *summer pruning,* is used to train growth on young trees, let more light into the interior, thin heavy fruiting, remove water sprouts and suckers, and get rid of broken branches. Because summer pruning doesn't stimulate as much growth as does dormant pruning, it's also essential for espaliered fruit trees (see page 253).

You may see references to Lorette, or Modified Lorette, pruning, which was developed in France early in the last century and named after its inventor. These systems use only summer pruning (no dormant pruning) to encourage less-vigorous and more-upright growth. The practice is more popular in Europe and Britain. In this country Lorette and Modified Lorette pruning are rarely used, except for espaliered fruit trees.

We prune our orchard in early spring, because it's much more pleasant to work during the bright spring days, and I find it easier to see where to cut when there are no leaves or fruits on the branches. After a long northern winter, I relish the excuse to work outside. At that time I can also nip off any branches that have been chewed by the deer and those broken by snow and ice. I find, too, that it's easier to check for problems such as fire blight, black knot, and sunscald (see chapter 18).

I also carry a pair of small, handheld pruning shears whenever I walk through the orchard during the growing season. Frequent light pruning is ever so much better for a tree than cutting off large limbs later. It also conditions the orchardist to the pruning habit and helps develop both the right attitude and the skill.

Pruning Bush Fruits and Grapes

THE SHOOTS OF RASPBERRIES and blackberries grow for a year, fruit the next, and then they're done. Prune away the spent canes to keep new ones coming, and so the patch doesn't become too crowded, which reduces fruiting and can lead to disease. This also simplifies picking. Everbearing raspberries can be cut to the ground each spring to get a new heavy crop each fall (see page 70).

Blueberries need less pruning than most other fruits. For the first 5 years or so (longer in cold climates) little pruning is needed except to remove broken and rubbing branches. This may be all that's ever needed for lowbush types. Otherwise, when plants reach 5 or 6 feet tall, cut to the ground shoots that are 5 years old or more, and those more than an inch thick. Prune to keep plants at a maximum of 6 feet tall. This will make picking easier, and will let in more light to ripen berries and reduce disease (see page 83).

Currants, jostaberries, elderberries, and other bush fruits need minimal pruning as well. On currants, remove the less productive shoots that are at least 3 years old — these are the dark gray to blackish ones. Wait a year later to remove those on gooseberries. On elderberries, once the plant is mature with 6 to 8 upright stems, prune away older stems as new ones develop, keeping in mind that fruit are formed on new growth — both on new shoots and on new branches on 2-year-old stems (see page 95). Without such pruning, elderberries will form a thicket with lots of old stems that are weak, and will fruit poorly or not at all. (See chapter 7 for more on pruning these fruits.)

Grapes by nature produce more top growth and flowers than their roots can support, so vines require extensive pruning for good fruit production and quality. Remove 70 percent or more of the top growth each year in later winter, and thin new fruit clusters to leave just two bunches per new shoot. Follow one of the training systems in chapter 8, and you should get plenty of good-quality grapes.

Bush fruits need minimal pruning; thin growth and remove some of the oldest stems to improve crops. Remove canes of brambles after they've fruited.

Match Pruning Style to Your Tree

SOME FRUIT CULTIVARS grow naturally into a nice shape with little care. The 'Dolgo' crab apple, for example, shapes itself beautifully. On the other hand, the 'Yellow Delicious' apple and most pears seem bent on growing as many tops as possible. For such trees, you'll need to cut back all but one central trunk ("leader") to encourage a strong form and a wider tree. Also, many plum trees grow so wide that their outer branches hang on the ground unless you snip them back occasionally.

If you turned a dozen orchardists loose on your trees, no two would trim them quite alike, yet each might do a good job. The three main styles for fruit trees are the leader, the modified leader, and the open vase. Some refer to these three pruning styles as training systems, using the word pruning only to

Cut back unbranched whips to 30–36 inches; cut just above a bud.

On branched trees remove all but three to five wide-angled branches. Prune off branches growing at narrow angles to the trunk or too close together; head back main branches by half.

refer to cuts made to maintain a tree's existing structure. The ultimate example of training is espalier, in which branches are trained to grow into certain shapes on a vertical plane (see page 253).

Pruning Young Trees

If you buy a bare-root tree that wasn't already cut back (ask your supplier if unsure), you should prune it at planting time, depending on the fruit and habit you want (see below). Then until fruit trees begin to bear, they need relatively little pruning compared to later in their lives, except to remove unwanted branches and begin the important tree shaping. Overpruning at this stage can cause excessive growth, which in turn can delays bearing. As your tree grows, you'll need to correct any bad crotches and remove extra tops, branches growing in the wrong direction, and any suckers or water sprouts coming from the roots or below the graft.

Common Training Systems

- **Central leader.** Has a strong central trunk, creating a cone-shaped tree; often used for standard, semidwarf, and even dwarf apples, European pears, plums, sweet cherries, nut trees
- **Modified central leader.** Like the central leader, but with the leader cut back; often used for apples, cherries, pears, apricots (semidwarf), plums, persimmon, pecans, walnuts
- **Open center, vase shape.** Limbs growing out around an open center; used for peaches, nectarines, apricots, pomegranates, Japanese plums, almonds, figs, filberts

The first summer and at the end of the first winter are when you should begin steering growth toward the desired form for each type of tree, as described below, by selectively removing branches. Although a gnarled, spreading, twisted old fruit tree may look picturesque, if you want maximum fruit production, this early shaping is essential. After the tree begins to bear fruit, you should get more serious and prune more heavily each year.

Central-Leader Training

Pruning to a central leader simply means keeping a strong, single trunk in the middle of the tree. Vertical branches that could compete with this central trunk are removed, but horizontal branches are allowed to grow from it. The result is a cone-shaped or Christmas tree–shaped habit. This system can make dwarf and semidwarf apples stronger and earlier bearing, and it's excellent for weak trees and for those growing on poor soil. It's the most common system for standard, semidwarf, and dwarf apple trees; European pears; plums; sweet cherries; and large nut trees.

If your tree was not pruned before purchase, after planting remove any shoots below about 18 inches up the stem, then cut the top off at about 3 feet (2 feet for pears, 1 foot above the top branches on trees with lots of them). Cut just above a healthy bud or shoot. Cutting off more will stimulate excessive growth; too little results in a whorl of weak growth near the top with little below.

The first summer is the time to establish a central leader in young trees. Once a main stem starts growing from a bud near where you cut back the main stem, train this as the central leader by removing the shoots just below it. During the summer, remove any vigorous side shoots that are growing upward, as these would compete with the developing leader.

The first summer also is the time to choose the main scaffold branches you'll want to keep. Scaffolds are branches that are horizontal or slightly upright; these are stronger than vertical ones and produce more and better fruit. Side branches for future scaffolds should be 3 to 4 inches apart up the stem on dwarf trees, 8 to 12 inches apart for others. (This may vary slightly depending on the fruit or nut tree; see specific chapters.) They should be spaced evenly around the trunk, with no two directly across from each other or directly above each other. Choose three to five well-spaced branches as scaffolds and remove other side branches. Especially in sunny climates, if the lowest scaffold is on the southwest side it can shade and prevent sunscald damage to the trunk.

In subsequent years in late winter, prune off about a quarter of the leader if it grew over 18 inches the previous year. This will result in a new top bud taking over as leader, as in the first year, and the formation of more scaffold branches. If the leader grew less than 18 inches last year, cut back both it and the scaffold branches by about a third to stimulate more growth. You can skip cutting back the leader if you want an upright tree more quickly, or earlier fruiting on dwarf trees (at the expense of fewer branches and so less fruit.) Remove any upright branches that could compete with the new central leader.

In areas where fire blight is a problem, you can allow more than one upright central leader to develop, in case the disease girdles the main leader. This multiple-leader system is often used on European pears.

Modified-Leader Training

Training for a modified leader means keeping a central stem partway up the trunk (about 6 feet), then allowing it to branch more freely into several scaffold branches. The modified-leader habit is not as tall or as conical as the central leader, but it's more upright than the vase shape described below. If you prefer to grow standard trees or you garden where dwarfs or semidwarfs aren't hardy, you can keep a standard-size tree at a manageable size for an indefinite period with a modified-leader approach, if you begin early enough and are persistent. The modified leader is also recommended for especially vigorous trees. In addition to apples, it's often used on sour cherries, figs, persimmons, and walnuts. In areas where fire blight disease is prevalent, this is the method used to keep apple trees more open in order to reduce susceptibility. In hot climates with strong sun, as in the Southwest, it can be used on peaches to provide a bit more shade to the fruit. You may see the same fruits placed variously in this or the central-leader group, depending on the region or purpose.

Train young trees to a central leader, as described below. Once you have four or five well-spaced horizontal scaffolds, cut off the leader. As soon as the tree is about 7 feet tall, selectively cut back the tops to about 6 feet. The tree will grow back during the summer, so repeat the cutting back each spring. Don't shear straight across the top (giving a tree a crew cut is called topping). Topping stimulates the growth of shoots at the top that will shade the lower branches on which fruits form and take the tree's energy from fruit production.

Open-Center (Vase) Training

Pruning to an open-center or vase shape means keeping the center of the tree open and letting limbs grow around this open space. The result is a lower, more spreading habit. This arrangement allows the maximum amount of sunlight to penetrate the tree's interior. Peaches are the common subject for this type of pruning, and it's also used on nectarines, apricots, pomegranates, Asian pears, plums, almonds, figs, and filberts. Even apples, sweet cherries, and plums may be pruned to an open center in some regions, such as on the West Coast, to keep plants lower, or for more spreading apple cultivars such as 'Golden Delicious' or 'Freedom'.

CENTRAL-LEADER TRAINING
Pruning this apple tree to a central leader means removing competing upright shoots to leave a single vertical trunk.

OPEN-CENTER (VASE) TRAINING
To prune peaches or plums to an open-center tree, the first year remove the most upright branches in the center and leave three to five main scaffold branches.

After planting (if not already pruned), prune back the main stem to about 30 inches high. If the tree has lateral branches, select three to five to be the scaffolds and remove the others. As with the central leader, good scaffold branches should be spaced evenly around the trunk and 8 to 12 inches apart up the stem (3 to 4 inches on dwarf trees). If few or no laterals are present at planting, wait until the end of the first winter to select scaffolds. At this time, also prune off any upright shoots from the inside of the main scaffolds, then cut back upright shoots on the ends of scaffolds to just above a outward-facing bud (prune off other upright shoots on the scaffolds). Repeat this pruning of upright shoots in subsequent winters or early each spring.

Unlike most other tree fruits, stone fruits (peaches, cherries, plums, and apricots) can be pruned right after bloom. This helps reduce the risk of canker disease and can be used to remove wood damaged by late frosts. Prune stone fruits minimally for several years, until the trees are bearing and somewhat mature. Peaches usually then need more pruning to keep them to a manageable height (8 feet or so) than do cherries, plums, and apricots. For these latter fruits, thinning out some inner branches and removing broken or rubbing limbs may be all that's needed.

What to Cut on Trees

Before pruning, learn the fruiting habits of each tree. This will determine what branches you should remove and which to leave. Peaches and nectarines produce their fruits only along the branches of the previous year's growth, and not at the tips. These need heavy pruning each year to stimulate the formation of new fruit-bearing branches.

Most other fruits tend to bear mostly on short, stubby spurs (short wrinkled stems under 4 inches long). Apples and pears produce fruit mainly on spurs, but these spurs generally don't produce flower buds until the second year, and most don't fruit until the third. Spurs on apple trees can live more than 10 years. You don't have to prune apples and pears as heavily, as you don't want to stimulate lots of branch growth. You do want to be careful when pruning and harvesting not to break off these spurs, or you'll reduce next year's crops.

Cherries, apricots, and plums bear along stems and at the tips of stems as well as on spurs on older wood. Spurs on sweet cherries produce for a decade or more, those on sour cherries produce for only half as long. Yet cherry spurs produce fruit when only 1 year old. Similarly, plums produce fruit from year-old spurs, but they produce only for 3 years.

When deciding how much to cut, remember that the more severe the pruning, the more growth the tree will produce in reaction. If a tree is vigorous already, don't prune as much. Perhaps you need to reduce fertility instead if you want the tree to grow more slowly. If a tree is weak (not producing abundant growth), prune more severely to stimulate growth, but don't get carried away. A mistake of beginning tree-fruit gardeners is to cut off too much of the previous year's growth, which results in no fruit.

Horizontal branches bear more fruit than vertical ones, and they're stronger as well. In general, keep the more horizontal branches and remove the more vertical ones (except the leader). If your tree doesn't naturally produce horizontal branches, you'll need to bend branches at an early age to make them less vertical. (See page 150.) Some use clothespins for young branches (see page 187); they use flat sticks with forked ends for older branches and wider angles. Commercial growers use short, thin wood sections with nails on each end (sharp points sticking out) to bend branches. Others hang weights from the branches. (Lowering branches by tying or weighting them is also done to slow vigorous growth on plums.)

Different cultivars of the same fruit grow in different ways, so try to determine the growth habit of each cultivar. 'Red Delicious' apple trees tend to grow more upright, for example; trees of 'Jonagold' and 'Liberty' have a spreading habit. Most pears and sweet cherries tend to grow upward and produce many upright branches. Although you can prune away some of the branches with narrow angles, you'll need to spread at least some to give you more horizontal branches.

In heavy snow country, don't let trees branch too close to the ground. Settling snow can break the lower ones. As a tree grows and begins to bear heavy loads of fruit, branches that formerly grew upright tend to hang downward. Because these are likely

BRANCHES TO REMOVE ON MATURE FRUIT TREES

(A) Dead or diseased branches. (B) Broken branches. (C) High branches that are difficult to reach and that shade the interior and lower branches. (D) Vertical branches that compete with a central-leader or vase shape. (E) Crowded branches. (F) Branches that rub, which wear away the bark. (G) Water sprouts. (H) Suckers. (I) Branches growing at narrow angles to trunk (less than 45 degrees); will break from winds and under the weight of fruit.

to be in the way, eventually you'll have to remove them. By cutting off such growth when it's still small, you can avoid much heavy pruning later on.

Making the Cuts

IN PRUNING, how you make the cut is as important as when. Always cut small limbs back to another branch, bud, or the trunk without leaving a lifeless stub. Such a stub will rot and often invite canker or other diseases that can kill the tree. You want to cut back to the branch collar — that raised area on the trunk from which the branch emerges and from which the growth that heals the wound will grow. Cut back to, but not into, this collar. If you're cutting a large limb and the cut is horizontal, make it at a slight slant so water will run off instead of settling and rotting into the wood.

When removing the top or end of a branch, cut on a slant about a quarter of an inch above the bud. Also, always cut above a bud that's on the outside of a branch, so a spreading tree will result. Branches growing from inside buds will turn inward and created a pyramid-shaped tree that's too dense for the tree's health and fruiting.

Make all large cuts in three stages. The limbs of fruit trees are heavy and when partially sawed off are likely to split into the main trunk with a big ragged wound. Lighten the load by cutting off the main part of the limb first. Make undercut A first, then overcut B, and when the weight of the branch is removed, you can finally make cut C to remove the stub back to the branch collar. If necessary, smooth over any rough spots with a rasp or chisel. Covering wounds with a tree paint was once recommended, but studies have shown that this doesn't help the healing process and may even be harmful, trapping disease and moisture inside.

LARGE CUTS

Make all large cuts in three steps. First, make an undercut at A, so the limb won't split from its own weight when you make your next cut. Then cut off the limb at B. Once the limb is out of your way, make the final smooth cut at C, just outside the branch collar.

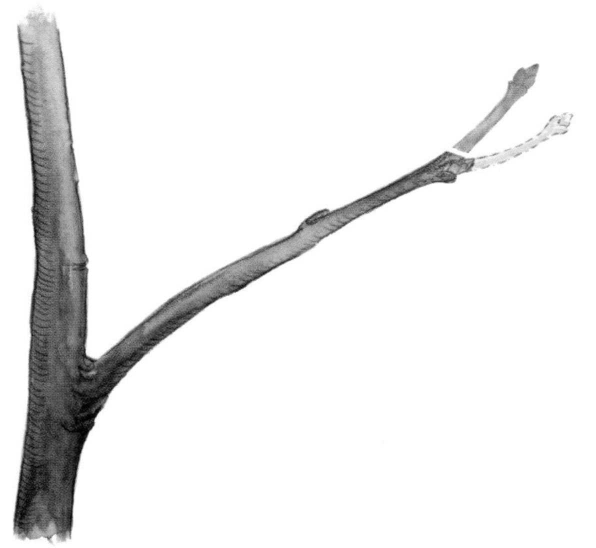

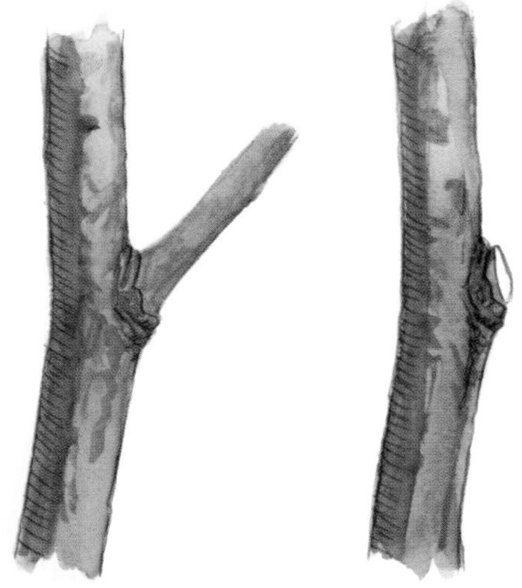

CUTTING ALONG A BRANCH

When cutting along a branch, always make the cut just above an outward-facing bud; this type of pruning encourages spreading branches and a more open tree. Pruning above an inside-facing bud causes ingrown limbs and crossed branches.

CUTTING FLUSH

When cutting off an entire branch, don't leave a stub, but also avoid cutting off the swelling at the branch's base (the branch collar). Cuts will heal fastest if flush with the outermost edge of the collar.

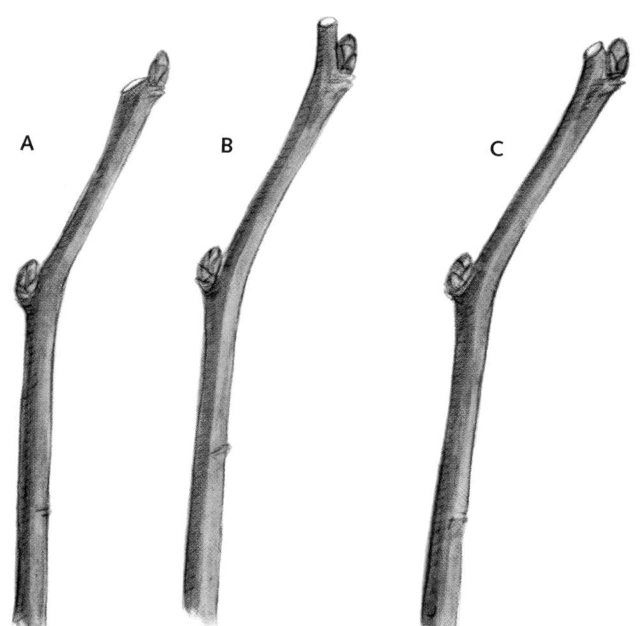

WHERE TO CUT ON A BRANCH

(A) is too close; the bud will die. (B) leaves too much of a stub and should be more angled. (C) shows the right way to cut.

Prune a Lot or a Little?

- If a tree is already vigorous, don't prune too much. If it appears weak, prune more severely to stimulate growth.
- Fruits to prune heavily: non-spur apples, Japanese plums, nectarines, peaches; blackberries, raspberries; kiwis, grapes; weak trees
- Fruits to prune lightly: spur-type apples, apricots, cherries, pears, persimmons, plums and plumcots, quince; nut trees; blueberries, currants, elderberries, jostaberries; vigorous trees

TIPS FOR BETTER PRUNING

- Keep your tools clean and sharp, so that you can make smooth cuts. These will heal faster and the job will go much quicker. Have a sharpening stone on hand.
- Sterilize tools after cutting diseased wood. (See Disinfecting Pruning Tools, page 273.)
- Prune every year. A tree suffers far less stress if you prune it moderately every year instead of cutting off a lot of wood every few years.
- Be careful when working in tall trees. Use a sturdy ladder, well supported, and ask another person to help steady it. If branches are too high, as they may be on standard trees and nut trees, pay an arborist rather than risk paying the hospital if you fall.
- When you prune, don't butcher the tree, but don't be stingy, either. Just as in thinning the fruit, my Scottish blood kept me from doing a good job at first. Now I have a very effective method. I go out one day, cut off all I dare to, and haul off the prunings. I then return the next day and cut off more — about as much as I cut the first day — and that appears to be about right. Use the adage that the tree should be open enough that a bird could fly through it without hitting any branches.
- Prune each tree according to its growth habit. Determine if your fruit tree needs to be pruned to a central leader or to an open center. In addition, every fruit tree grows differently; adjust your pruning to each tree's natural habit. With a spreading tree, you may occasionally need to cut back the ends of branches so it tree won't get too wide. With an upright-growing trees, prune out branches with weak (narrow) crotches, and prune or spread limbs to force the limbs to spread out more.
- Remove the wood and trimmings. After you've finished pruning, always take away the branches you've cut off and either burn them or bring them to a landfill, so you aren't providing a place for insects and diseases to spend the winters.
- Don't use a chain saw for pruning. Tempting as it is, I would never use a chain saw, even to make large cuts, unless it is to take out a dead or unwanted tree. Even a small power saw is difficult to control when you're doing precision work, and it's too easy to cut into a nearby branch that you don't want to harm.
- Don't prune neglected trees too heavily. It's a shock for an old tree to be pruned heavily if it hasn't been touched for many years. (See Reviving Old Trees, page 259.)
- Prune with confidence. This can't be overemphasized. As you prune, keep telling yourself it's for the good of the tree. If you still have doubts about the advantages of severe pruning, drive past a commercial orchard after it's been pruned to see how much wood was cut out.

Espaliers: Pruning as Art

THE MOST INTENSIVE FORM of pruning is that required to train a fruit tree (and some shrubs and vines) as an espalier. In this technique, a plant is trained to grow in a vertical plane, usually flat against a building, wall, or fence. Espaliers are widely used in Europe, where gardens are small and land is scarce; in North America, gardeners use them primarily for their ornamental value.

You might guess that an espalier is more difficult to train than a regular fruit tree, as it means forcing a tree to grow in a manner completely different from how it otherwise would. Naturally, an espalier requires some extra care, but the training isn't at all complicated and not nearly as exacting as bonsai. The simplest espalier, the vertical cordon (an upright trunk with no branches), may need little or no pruning if you buy a cultivar bred for this habit. Although these "pillar trees" are being developed for efficient commercial production, they are wonderful for small properties or people with little time for pruning.

You can save a great deal of time and effort by buying a tree with the shaping already started. Because the more complicated preliminary work has already been done, it's a simple matter to continue the training. A dwarf or semidwarf variety will need much less pruning.

Pear, apple and crab apple trees are good choices, because they're easiest to train. Peaches, nectarines, and apricots are only a bit more difficult. It's possible to use cherries, plums, and quinces, too, but their bushy habit of growth makes training trickier. I've seen grapes, blueberries, trailing blackberries, and even the taller-growing varieties of currants and gooseberries espaliered in small, cottage-type gardens.

Common Espalier Patterns

Vertical cordon (columnar). Simplest: basically a central stem with side branches kept pruned off, permits you to grow many trees in a small space; often seen with apples. A few apple cultivars are naturally columnar, such as 'Golden Sentinel' and 'Northpole'.

Tiered. Sometimes known as horizontal cordon or horizontal T: horizontal wires and stems on two or three levels; similar to vineyard systems, also good for apples and pear trees; good starting point for other shapes; some of the others, such as candelabra (see below), are actually the same shape in successive tiers or levels.

Fan. Branches trained in a spreading, fan-shaped, upright pattern, with straight lines/stems; good for apricots, peaches, and figs.

Candelabra. Series of U shapes, each larger than the one above as you go down the trunk; good for small or narrow spaces and tall walls; good with apples and pears; easiest is the simple U shape.

Informal. Branches upright but in no regular pattern; lines/stems often not straight; easy with figs, persimmons, and pomegranates.

Vertical Cordon

Fan

Candelabra

Tiered

Avoid planting an espalier under a wide roof overhang, as the tree will need both sunlight and rain, and ice and snow falling from the roof could be a problem. Choose a spot where it can get at least half a day of sunshine, preferably full sun. A south- or west-facing wall is ideal (except in hot climates). In addition to using espaliers against buildings and walls, you can plant them in a freestanding row.

Apples and pears are some of the easiest fruits to espalier. Be patient, as an espalier may take 5 to 10 years of training to reach its final shape.

Choose a Design

The first step is to decide on the design you want. Then, go to a nursery that has a good choice of trees, so you can find one you can train with the least amount of trouble. Be sure to select a variety that bears on spurs rather than branch tips (as some apples do), otherwise you'll end up cutting off most or all of the bearing wood. Select a small tree with branches that are already growing in the right directions, if possible. For a candelabra, a U-shaped tree that would be unsuitable for an orchard may be perfect, because you can spread out the two tops to start the design. If you find nothing candelabra-like, choose a tree with two branches that are almost opposite each other and prune back the center stem, leaving only the two branches and start with that.

Planting and Training

Set the tree so the trunk is about 18 inches away from the building or wall. Install supports for training. Bamboo stakes are often used initially to train stems in the right directions and to keep them straight. Secure the branches to the bamboo or other supports with plastic ties or cloth strips. Don't use string or wire; either will cut into the tender bark. Tie every 6 to 8 inches along the branches to prevent a curved or bowed shape. Add more fasteners as the tree grows.

Supporting with wires. You'll need horizontal wires to support the stems and their bamboo stakes. Install a post 7 or 8 feet high at each end of where the espalier will ultimately grow; set each 2 feet deep. Be sure the posts are well braced so they won't tip from the pull of the wires. Staple strands of 9-gauge wire to run between the posts to make a "fence" of four or five strands. Place the bottom wire about 2 feet from the ground and the top three wires each about a foot apart. Make the wires taut and securely anchor them to the posts so they won't sag.

Guiding the branch direction. As the branches begin to grow, snip or pinch off all that are growing in the wrong direction (such as perpendicular from the desired plane) and overcrowded, crossing, and main branches less than a foot apart. The direction the bud is facing is the direction the future branch will grow. Choose upright buds for more vertical growth, buds facing downward or sideways for more horizontal growth. Always prune back to the main trunk, to a branch, or to just above a bud, and don't leave stubs. Remove flower buds the first couple of years to promote better shoot and root growth.

Pruning

Prune leader(s) until the desired height is reached, usually just below the top wire, then top; dormant-prune one quarter of the previous year's leader

Some Useful Pruning Tools

Hand clippers, long-handled pruners, and a pruning saw for large cuts are all the tools you need to grow fruit on a small scale. A good pair of gloves will save you many a blister when pruning lots of limbs. If you have large trees, pole pruners that reach up into the canopy will also be useful.

Hand clippers come as either bypass pruners (blades cut like scissors) or anvil pruners (the blade contacts a solid bar). Most have replaceable blades. These are good for small branches, but you'll need long-handled pruners for thicker branches.

Use **ratchet loppers** or a **pruning saw** for heavier branches. A curved or short saw is useful for small limbs and tight clearances; folding models are available. A bow saw makes pruning larger branches easier.

Resist buying bargain tools: they become dull quickly and break easily. Even with good tools, you may want to keep a spare handy. It's a nuisance to stop in the middle of a pruning job to find another pair of clippers.

Sharp blades make the work go a lot faster and are better for your plants. Many garden and hardware stores carry a carbon stone or something similar for sharpening tool blades.

growth, more for weaker shoots; Once the leader reaches the desired height, usually just below the top wire, cut back each year (dormant-prune) to one inch above last season's growth. When the lateral branches are long enough, pull them in the desired direction and fasten them to the bottom wire. Allow branches to grow from this bottom branch. As they grow, fasten them to the upper wires to direct them toward the desired shape. Leave at least 12 inches between main horizontal branches, or leaders in a multiple-leader design.

Pruning fruiting shoots is similar to the method used for traditional pruning (see specific fruit chapters). When plants are young, prune during the dormant season to stimulate growth. As plants mature, do most of your pruning during summer (not after midsummer in cold climates) to slow growth and prevent undesirable water sprouts. Branches that are more upright (45 degrees or less from vertical) grow faster; you can slow their growth by bending them when young (flexible) in a more horizontal direction. Check every week or so to make sure the branches are growing the way you want and not sneaking out in the wrong direction. When the tree is sturdy, rigid, and well shaped, you can remove the wire trellis — though you may prefer to leave it in place, especially for dwarf cultivars.

Taking shape. Be patient. It may take more than two seasons before the espalier begins to take on its shape, so don't be discouraged if it doesn't look like much the first year. Achieving the final shape can take 5 to 10 years. As these are plants, each will be different with its own character; don't expect a perfect geometric shape. Even when mature, the plant's natural tendency is to grow branches in all directions each year, so you'll need to check throughout the season and prune to keep the shape, also to stimulate some new growth for fruiting.

Watch the buds. When cutting off new growth, watch for the fat flower buds that are forming. Don't clip off too many, or you'll have few fruits the following year. Lack of fruit on an espalier may also be due to improper pruning (see specific chapters for how to prune each fruit to ensure fruiting wood), or other factors such as poor pollination. (See Why Doesn't My Tree or Bush Have Fruit?, page 268.)

Thinning Fruits

One of the most important types of pruning requires no tool at all: Use your fingers to pick off developing fruits. Mature apple trees, nectarines, peaches, pears, and plums all produce better-quality fruit when you thin before their fruit matures. In a productive year, you may have to pick and throw away about 80 percent of the crop. The tree's energy is then diverted to the remaining fruits, allowing them to grow larger and resulting in better color and quality. Often the crop will add up to more bushels than if you'd kept them all. If you don't thin, a tree may use up all its energy to produce the crop and spend the following year recuperating, bearing few if any fruit (this is called alternate or biennial bearing). Though young trees usually don't produce enough fruit to need thinning, the procedure is essential for mature trees.

The time for thinning is early summer, right after the June drop, or 2 to 3 weeks after bloom. The fruits should be between the size of a dime and a quarter. The June drop is the natural thinning that many trees undergo as a result of producing more flowers than they need. Don't worry if you see fruits the size of large marbles under your tree; it just means the tree is doing some of your work for you. It's a signal that it's time for you to help out. Thin so that each fruit is at least 6 inches from any other (4 inches for plums) and only one fruit is left in each cluster.

Thin so that each fruit is at least 6 inches from any other (4 inches for plums), and only one fruit is left in each cluster.

Reviving Old Trees

THERE'S SOMETHING MAJESTIC and nostalgic about a gnarled old apple tree. It exudes character. Old fruit trees are beautiful, but are they worth saving? If your trees are badly broken, hollow inside, and falling apart — or if the fruit is hard, bitter, or sour even when ripe — well, let's face it: The practical thing to do is to turn them into firewood and start over with young, healthy trees.

On the other hand, if trees appear to be in sound condition and the fruit is of good quality even though small, they may well be worth the considerable work of renovating. Old orchards often contain some fine antique cultivars that today are difficult to come by.

Before you decide, examine your trees. If they have more than one trunk or are growing in tight clumps, they may be new sprouts from the wild rootstock — relatively worthless specimens that produce inferior fruit. These probably aren't worth saving. Trees growing much too close together and in a haphazard manner rather than in orderly rows are probably seedlings from fallen fruit. Unless you're convinced the fruit is good, better take the saw to these, too.

Wild and domestic animals often browse the lower branches of trees in an abandoned orchard. This forces the growth upward and makes the trees grow tall. If trees are more than 18 feet tall, with few lower branches, you're better off replanting.

In reviving an old orchard, as in starting a new one, a small number of well-cared-for trees will be far more productive and much more satisfying than a large orchard of even partially neglected ones. Limit your orchard to a size that fits the time you can spare for it, and save only the trees that are worth the effort.

Should you plant new trees in bare spots among the older kinds? The soil of an old orchard may already be full of roots from living or long-gone trees. It will be many years before the roots of a large tree completely return to the soil. Furthermore, a little-understood affliction commonly called replant disease is often prevalent in new plantings in old orchards. For these reasons, you're better off planting in a new spot. If that's not possible, before you order any trees, get the soil in as good a condition as possible.

The first step is to get rid of those trees that aren't worth saving. Burn or chip all the branches and wood you remove. Tackle the pruning next. Resist the temptation to remake your trees all at

Renovating an Old Orchard

once; instead, spread the operation over at least 3 years. Although a young, vigorous tree can stand having up to a third of its limb area pruned away, this would be far too much shock for an elderly one. This is especially important in areas where the growing season is short. If heavy pruning doesn't kill a tree outright, it's likely to stimulate an abundance of new growth that will be killed during the winter.

First cut out all the broken limbs, dead and diseased branches, and sucker growth at the base of the trunks. You can do this at any time of the year, but don't remove healthy branches until the tree is dormant. Remove whole limbs rather than just cutting them back. Cutting limbs only partially back will stimulate growth of unwanted water sprouts. This limited pruning is about all the tree can stand the first year. Although you shouldn't cut off bearing wood the first year, you can improve the quality of the fruit immediately by thinning it (see page 257).

The year after cleaning out the orchard, fertilize the remaining trees at half the usual recommended rate for healthy specimens. Test the soil pH and amend if needed. Soils in old orchards may be worn out, and for many years the weeds and brush have competed with the trees for what little fertility was available. Don't overfertilize, as this will stimulate unwanted growth. Unless the area around the trees is to be mowed weekly throughout the growing months, use a mulch.

The second year, begin to thin out the regular wood when the tree is dormant but the weather is above freezing. Prune to let sunshine into the tree's interior; thinning out some of the bearing wood will increase fruit size and quality and encourage annual bearing. Remove whole limbs, as in the first year. Aim to leave branches that grow slightly upward (at a 60° angle), rather than horizontal, vertical, or hanging down — these latter ones are candidates for pruning out. Also cut back a few of the tallest branches. By the third year, it should be safe to prune more heavily. In the years that follow, prune in the usual way.

Diseases and insects may be problems in old and neglected orchards because both thrive on broken limbs, loose bark, and weakened trees, as well as on dead leaves and decaying fruit on the ground. Orchard sanitation will solve many problems (see chapter 18).

1. Remove unwanted trees: those that are weak, too close together, badly broken, or hollow inside, and those with few or poor-quality fruits. Burn or haul away tree prunings to eliminate pests and diseases.
2. Thin out remaining trees, if needed, so trees don't touch each other. Cut out broken limbs, dead and diseased branches, and all sucker growth at the base of trunks.
3. **YEAR ONE:** When trees are dormant, prune lightly to remove rubbing/crossing limbs; prune off whole limbs rather than heading back. Avoid removing bearing wood. Thin fruits in early summer.
4. **YEAR TWO:** When trees are dormant, thin out some limbs to allow more light into the center, removing weak and very old limbs first.
5. **YEAR THREE:** Prune more heavily.
6. **SUBSEQUENT YEARS:** Prune as you would any other fruit tree.

Diseases, pests, and physiological problems in fruiting plants can often be avoided with routine maintenance and a watchful eye.

CHAPTER 18

Diseases, Insects, and Other Fruit Problems

Small home orchards, fruit gardens, and edible landscapes with a mix of fruits are not as inviting to bugs and diseases as are plantations consisting of acres of all the same kind of fruit. Still, if you grow fruit year after year, sooner or later there's a good chance that a few pests will locate your plants and decide to make them a summer project. Fruits have been grown for so many centuries and in so many places that they've accumulated a huge number of pests. Yet with these have developed a huge number of natural enemies for these pests. It's truly a bug-eat-bug world out there. Minimize your orchard spraying as much as possible to avoid killing off these good bugs and thus inviting more pests.

Diseases and insects are not the most exciting subjects to read about for most people, so just get familiar with what follows in case you need it. Like a medical reference, these descriptions are here to help you cope with those little surprises nature occasionally tosses at us to make life more interesting. Remember that usually your fruits will tolerate some of these problems, and won't even experience most of them.

Nonchemical Controls

ONE OF THE ALL-AROUND best pest controls is to plant cultivars resistant to a particular disease or pest. These minimize or eliminate problems before they appear. Many are now available, and some produce fruit of superior quality. Each fruit chapter gives a few recommendations. Contact local experts and/or your state university Extension Service for the best cultivars for your climate and particular pest problems.

Pest control begins at the planning stages of fruit growing. Locate your planting as far away as possible from wild fruit trees or a neglected orchard. Remove any wild fruit trees and brambles you aren't maintaining; they may harbor disease. If there are other small orchards in your area, try to coordinate your pest-management strategies. Mix up your plantings. Large growers need all the same cultivars together, but small growers don't. As one of our friends put it, "If a bug finds one of my plum trees, I'm not going to make it easy for him to hop to the next one."

Good Sanitation

Good sanitation around your fruit bushes and trees will reduce or eliminate many problems. The following practices are simple yet surprisingly effective.

- Pick up all dropped fruits. Bury them in the compost pile if they're healthy; if they're diseased, destroy them (bury them in the ground or dispose of them in bags with yard waste). Many bugs and diseases overwinter in old fruit.
- Prune your trees regularly. Thin out the branches to allow more sun to enter and permit

To remove sites for overwintering insects and diseases, pick up all dropped fruit and rake up leaves under fruit trees.

Wildflowers can welcome beneficial insects and pollinators into the orchard.

better air circulation. This will help control fungal diseases in particular. Also, prune off diseased branches and any mummified fruit. Burn the prunings if they have disease or dispose of them with yard waste.

- Rake up and compost fallen leaves, as these are favorite overwintering spots for scab and other diseases. The heat from the composting process will destroy many fungi and insect eggs. If your trees and bushes have had diseases or your compost pile usually doesn't heat up much, burn or bury the leaves instead.
- Carefully trim loose bark from older trees so insects can't overwinter there.
- Remove tree wraps from younger trees during the summer; insects may hide there.
- Keep the grass mowed around bushes and trees to discourage field mice and voles and to eliminate breeding places for insects and disease. Remove sod in a 2-foot area around trees, especially if they're growing in a lawn. (As a side benefit, this will prevent possible girdling of trees from a string trimmer.) Replace sod with mulch — wood chips or bark mulch; and install tree guards for rodent protection.

Traps

Some pests can be reduced to manageable levels with simple traps, or these can be used to monitor for pests. Combining pheromone lures (chemicals to attract pests, available from many suppliers) increases the effectiveness of such devices. These are some of the more common traps:

- Gallon glass jugs with a pint or so of vinegar in them will attract and trap large numbers of fruit flies.
- Paper cups with a bit of molasses in the bottom, hung among the limbs of apple trees, trap egg-laying codling moths in the spring.
- Red artificial apples (available commercially), covered with a sticky material, attract and trap egg-laying apple maggots in early summer. There are various other "sticky traps" or cards that professionals often use to monitor which insects are about.
- Japanese beetle traps have powerful hormonal attractants that will draw in beetles from all around. Place traps far away from your berry bushes and fruit trees, as only about 70 percent of the beetles will end up in the trap, and those that do will probably have a last supper on your plants on the way to their end.

Keeping insect-eating birds like chickens is an effective way to minimize insect pest problems.

Natural Predators

Enlist the aid of natural insect enemies to help you with pest control. Birds, bats, toads, and turtles consume enormous quantities of insects. Chickens are famous for their pest-control prowess in orchards.

A hedgerow provides protection and nesting places for insect-eating birds. Birdhouses, feeders, and bird baths also encourage residency. Just make sure the hedgerows aren't surrounding your bushes and trees. If they act as windbreaks, keeping down airflow, you may encourage diseases.

Toads eat vast quantities of those insects that spend part of their life cycle on the ground. Encourage these beneficial and friendly fellows by laying out inverted clay pots with a hole broken on one side and providing pans of drinking water.

Beneficial insects can be a great ally. Because the use of toxic sprays might kill them, as much as possible avoid spraying and urge your neighbors to avoid spraying, too. If you must spray, follow the precautions for minimizing harm to your insect allies. To attract flying beneficials to your yard, dedicate even a small patch of your garden or orchard to creating a habitat for them. Use cover crops, such as buckwheat, clovers, and hairy vetch, between plantings and on fallow ground. Plants flowers such as those in the daisy family, or herbs such as caraway, dill, and fennel. You'll get more beneficials from a diverse planting of species, including short and tall plants, and both annual and perennial species. You can even buy seed mixes designed to attract a wide variety of insect predators.

Some of the more common beneficial insects are:

Ground beetles. These large, iridescent brown or dull black insects have bodies ridged lengthwise. They run rapidly but don't fly. Both the beetle and its larvae eat caterpillars of all types.

Lacewings. These pale green insects with lacy, netted wings lay eggs on leaves, each tiny egg on the end of a delicate threadlike stalk. They feed voraciously on many pests such as aphids, the crawler stage of scale insects, spider mites, and even small caterpillars.

Syrphid fly

Ladybugs. These beetles, sometimes called ladybird beetles, feed on aphids, scales, and spider mites. Unfortunately, imported ladybugs may not stay around all summer unless you have a large supply of aphids, although they usually stick around long enough to be helpful.

Parasitoids. These are small flies or wasps that feed on or in other insects. The adults can be seen, but it's more common to see the eggs or larvae on the host. The attacked pest may have holes or be rigid and mummified. Tachinid flies have iridescent wings and are gray-black, and resemble big houseflies. They're some of the more important predators, as they attack so many of our fruit moth and beetle pests.

Praying mantis. The size (they're big!) and strange appearance of these creatures make them a little frightening at first glance, but they're well-known consumers of aphids and other unfriendly insects. Their huge brown egg cases are a welcome sight to the gardener in the fall. Mantids don't survive the winter in very cold areas, but they thrive in the regions where they're most needed. Like ladybugs, they're often listed for sale in the classified columns of garden magazines.

Syrphid flies. These brightly colored insects with yellow and black stripes, resembling bees, hover as they fly and so are also known as hover flies. They feed on aphids, scale, and caterpillars by sucking their fluids.

True bugs. Not all bugs are bad. Damsel bugs and assassin bugs in particular are desirable predators that use their front legs to grab and hold their prey.

Determining What's Wrong

DIAGNOSING THE PROBLEM correctly is essential in order to figure out what steps to take. First rule out physiological problems (see box on page 268, Why Doesn't My Tree or Bush Have Fruit?). If a plant's problems are not caused by its environment or by mechanical damage, check for insects on the leaves and bark. Some, such as tent caterpillars and Japanese beetles, you can spot easily. Others — mites and scale, for example — are tiny and difficult to identify (even with a 10-power hand lens), but you can recognize them by their damage. Still other insects spend the daylight hours out of sight and do all their mischief at night. Some moths lay their eggs inside the blossoms or under the skin of the fruit. The eggs then hatch and the larvae work inside the fruit, invisible until you take that fateful bite. The chart on page 288 will help you diagnose what's wrong.

Diseases are easier to identify. Whoever named many of them used terms so descriptive that almost anyone seeing the problem for the first time can recognize them. How could you not identify brown rot, powdery mildew, leaf curl, scab, sooty blotch, fire blight, black knot, or rust? Others may not be quite as obvious. If the leaves are yellow, for example, any number of things could be wrong. You may need to call in an expert for help. Start with trained professionals at a garden store, the local Cooperative Extension office, or master gardener programs. Most state universities have a plant diagnostic clinic that can provide definitive answers. (See Resources.)

Some insects are tiny and difficult to identify, but you can recognize them by their damage.

Physiological Problems of Fruit Plants

PLANTS CAN APPEAR UNHEALTHY for a variety of reasons, and the trouble is not always caused by insects or disease. Many times it's physiological — created by environmental conditions or culture, not a disease organism. If a fruit plant is unhappy with its climate, moisture, soil, fertilizer, or light conditions, or if it's competing with weeds and grass, it will not do well, and no amount of spraying or praying will help. Poor soil and too-deep planting are common causes of unhealthy trees, often resulting in death over the long term (see chapter 15). Likewise, if a tree has been damaged by animals, chemicals, salts, or machinery, it's almost certain to look less than thrifty. If a bush or tree isn't growing or producing well, consider whether one of these may be the cause.

Lack of sun. Fruit trees and bushes require almost full sun to grow well and to produce good fruits. If plants are shaded by buildings or large shade trees, they won't produce abundant blooms or fruits. If possible, remove limbs (or even trees) that shade your plants.

Too much sun. Sometimes in the South, or in the West where temperatures are high and skies clear, fruits and berry plants get stressed by more heat than is good for them, especially under drought conditions. Pears and apples may develop off-color patches, European gooseberry plants may collapse, plums and apricots may develop pit burn (see below). To avoid damage, choose cultivars suited to such climates. For peaches, use a modified-leader system for pruning to provide some shade to inner branches and fruit (instead of the usual open-center pruning designed to let in light).

Too much water. Fruit trees need good soil drainage. Their roots should never stand in soil that is constantly wet or where pools of water stagnate for hours after a heavy rain. They'll grow poorly, their roots will rot, and the trees will eventually die. But if your soils are only periodically wet (for a day or two), look for rootstocks that will tolerate such conditions; plums often tolerate periodic wetness.

Too little water. In dry seasons, berries and trees can suffer from lack of water, especially in poor or sandy soils. Leaves will wilt, turn brown on the edges, and, if severe, turn yellow. To help plants tolerate dry spells, incorporate extra organic matter (such as compost) into the soil before planting, use a heavy mulch, and water deeply.

Over-limed or under-limed. Too much lime or too little locks up nutrients in the soil and causes fruit drop and poor growth. Test your soil every few years to determine the pH, and take steps to make any necessary corrections.

Overfertilized. Fertilizer burn shows up as a brown, scorched appearance ("burned") on leaves and may even kill a tree. Moderate overfertilizing can cause a young tree to grow too fast and delay bearing for years. It can also cause a mature tree to produce fruits with poor color and with less flavor.

Underfertilized. When a tree makes weak growth and the leaves appear yellowish or pale green (chlorotic), lack of nutrients may be the problem. Test the soil fertility and pH. In alkaline soils, iron may not be available, causing yellowing between the veins of leaves. Other factors that keep a plant from taking up the nutrients it needs are cold and wet soils and very dry soils. Adding more fertilizer under such conditions probably won't do any good. Similar symptoms can be caused from viruses, or damage from pesticides and herbicides.

Spring-frost injury. Buds that fail to open or blooms that fail to set fruit may have been killed by a late frost. An early-spring frost, when leaves and buds are just appearing, may cause browned leaves and buds. In areas prone to spring freezes, choose cultivars that bloom as late as possible and don't plant in low frost pockets.

Animal damage. When bark is rubbed or chewed, or twigs snapped off, wild or domestic animals may be the culprits.

Mechanical damage. If you see that bark is scraped from the trunk, especially at ground level, suspect the careless use of a mower or similar equipment. A thin cut into the bark at the ground line, as from weed trimmers, may be not as noticeable.

Road salt. In cold climates, melting snow and salt runoff from roads and driveways can cause drying out of leaves, weakening of a tree, and browning of leaf edges. The symptoms are similar to those of fertilizer burn. Reduce the amount of salt if you use it on a driveway or walkway. If plants are young, consider moving them away from the road.

Oil burn. Spraying horticultural oils for pest control at the wrong times or temperatures, and when trees are stressed, may burn leaves, cause bark to be spotted or darker overall, result in water-soaked areas on fruit, and cause russeting. Don't use older-type dormant oils during active growth; at that stage, use only summer-weight horticultural oils.

Pit burn. On plums and apricots in hot climates, the inner fruit tissues turn gray, then brown. This occurs during periods of unusually hot temperatures during fruit development, when fruits don't get enough oxygen to mature normally.

Salt burn

Catfacing on strawberry

Catfacing. This refers to fruit that is scarred, puckered, and deformed. It's more common on strawberries and stone fruits. Insects such as the tarnished plant bug can cause this, as can poor pollination and environmental factors.

Fruiting varies year to year. This is usually not a disease, but rather the alternate- or biennial-bearing nature of many tree fruits, particularly apples. Moderate annual pruning helps minimize this. If poor or no fruiting is random from year to year, another cause, such as poor pollination or climate stress, may be responsible.

Excessive suckering. Some rootstocks send up lots of little plants below the graft union. Wounding the trunk, as from sapsuckers or insects, can stimulate this unwanted growth as well. Remove these plant suckers regularly to direct the energy into the grafted part of the tree.

Water sprouts. If trees produce too much new upright growth around a recently pruned limb, try pruning earlier in spring. Do a moderate amount of pruning annually rather than severe pruning every 2 or 3 years to help prevent water sprouts.

Sunscald/bark splitting. Sunscald results when warm sunshine in a cold winter strikes dark-colored bark, raising the temperature of the wood. The sudden drop in temperature as night falls, or when a cloud covers the sun, can cause rupturing of the plant cells in the bark, making it split. The hot days of summer may cause a similar injury in the South. Drought followed by lots of rain, as

Why Doesn't My Tree or Bush Have Fruit?

This is probably the most frequent question asked by fruit growers. Usually it's a physiological problem. Among the possibilities:

- pollination problems
- frost injury to flowers
- too much shade
- too much fertilizer (especially nitrogen)
- tree is alternate-bearing type
- improper pruning

well as too much growth stimulated by overfertilizing, may also result in bark splitting.

With a sharp knife, trim the flared bark edges around the split. Then keep tree watered during dry spells. A healthy tree will heal such wounds most the time on its own, leaving a ridge of bark. To prevent injury, you can coat the trunk of young trees on the east and south side with white latex paint diluted to half strength with water to reflect the sun.

Diseases

DISEASES ARE CAUSED generally by a fungus, a bacterium, or a virus. Most of the ones you'll see listed are fungal diseases, commonly spread by wind, rain, and insects, and are controlled by fungicides. Bacterial diseases are less common than are fungal diseases, but more difficult to control; they won't respond to a fungicide. Fire blight and root (crown) gall are good examples of bacterial problems. Viruses are spread in the same way and also are often passed on through an infected scion or rootstock. Most viruses greatly shorten the life of a tree, reducing vigor and yields, and are very difficult to eradicate; pesticides and fungicides are ineffective against viruses. About the only way to cope with them is to start with virus-free plants and isolate them from infected ones.

Disinfecting tools after pruning plants can help prevent the spread of many diseases (see Disinfecting Pruning Tools, page 273). Wear protective clothing (if using chlorine bleach) and don't use any of the solutions on pruned plants, as they can burn them.

Anthracnose. This fungus disease shows up as leaf discolorations, in contrast to leaf spots from other diseases, and dark and sunken spots on fruit. It's more common on strawberries, raspberries, and blueberries, less common on currants and other *Ribes*. Cut back any plants that show signs of infection, and destroy the diseased branches. To reduce chances of recurrence, keep weeds and grass out of the planting beds, and thin some branches to improve air circulation. Fungicides can be used, but keeping the disease out to begin with (exclusion) and looking for resistant cultivars may prevent this disease.

Bacterial blossom blast. This disease is primarily a pear problem occurring during cold, wet springs in the Pacific Northwest. It can also affect apples, and it can show up under cold, wet conditions elsewhere.

Bacterial spot. This is a serious disease of stone fruits. It appears as tiny, dark spots on the skin of peaches or water-soaked spots on smooth-skinned stone fruits. Leaves have angular spots, which turn brown, then fall out, leaving "shot holes." This disease is most often seen during rainy periods and in regions with lots of rainfall. Alternating copper and antibiotic sprays provides control, as does choosing resistant cultivars and not planting near infected trees.

Black knot. This one's easy to recognize by the thick, gnarled black mass on limbs of plum trees. It can be a serious problem on plums, and may be found occasionally on cherries, peaches, and apricots. This fungal disease begins in summer as sticky secretions but is most noticeable in winter, when the leaves are gone. It can girdle stems, killing them. Spraying is largely ineffective, so remove all diseased limbs in summer as soon as you spot them, and cut down any infected wild plums and cherries that are nearby.

Black rot. This fungal disease is particularly common on grapes but also found on apples, especially in eastern and midwestern states. It can occur any time during the season under warm and wet conditions. Leaves become covered with brown spots and black pimples, and fruits turn black, rotten, and shriveled. (These shriveled fruits are called mummies.) On apples, it starts as reddish brown cankers of various sizes on twigs and branches. Spores from these infect leaves, resulting in purple spots with concentric rings that give rise to its alternate name, frog-eye leafspot. Keeping bark healthy without wounds will help prevent cankers. Prune off any twigs and branches with cankers, disinfecting tools between cuts (see Disinfecting Pruning Tools, page 273). Good sanitation by cleaning up old fruit and leaves will help greatly by preventing disease spores from overwintering. Sprays for apple scab should control this on apples as well.

Anthracnose

Brown rot. This disease is also caused by a fungus. It attacks the flowers, fruits, and spurs of all stone fruits, plums and peaches especially. A fruit becomes a mass of mushy rot just before it ripens. Brown rot is probably the most common disease of cherries, causing fruit to become gray and fuzzy before it finally rots. Like scab, it overwinters in decaying fruit on the ground and is worse in wet summers. Cleaning up fallen fruit (drops) at the end of the season helps prevent infection. Regular spraying with a fungicide controls it.

Black knot fungus

Canker. In its many forms, canker can be caused by either a fungus or a bacterium. One or more forms will occasionally infect fruit and nut trees as well as berries and grapes. Apple blister canker, bleeding canker, blueberry canker, butternut melanconis dieback, camellia canker, currant canker, grape dead-arm disease, perennial canker of stone fruits, and nectria canker are only a few of them, but fortunately probably none will ever bother your orchard. Perennial canker can be serious in some areas such as the Northeast, particularly on peaches.

Canker manifests itself as a very noticeable diseased section of the woody part of a tree or bush, and may show as an open wound. In some cases, it spreads around the circumference of the trunk and kills the tree. Canker is often secondary, the disease coming about from an injury that has been left untreated such as sunscald winter injury on bark, mechanical injury, broken branches, or improper pruning.

Brown rot on plum

Apple canker

Fire blight

Generally the best treatment for canker is to prune off and burn diseased limbs before a rainy period. On large branches or the trunk, use a sharp knife to remove infected tissue. Create a pointed oval cut along the branch axis for the wound to heal quickly. Then disinfect all the tools you used (see Disinfecting Pruning Tools box on page 273). If you know that a particular canker is caused by a fungus, you can spray a fungicide for control.

Fire blight. This deadly bacterial disease attacks pears, apples, and quince; some cultivars are especially vulnerable. Fortunately many resistant varieties are now available, making this less of an issue even if fire blight is common in your locality. If you're strolling through your orchard and see some sick-looking leaves hanging on branches that look as though someone had held them in a flame, fire blight bacteria are probably at work. It's a mysterious disease because it can be bad in some years and then disappear entirely with no treatment.

At the first sign of the disease, prune away all infected parts and burn them. Fire blight bacteria are spread by wind, insects (including bees), and pruning tools. The first two are difficult to control, but you can prevent infection by the latter with good sanitation. Each year, prune all your uninfected trees first. Immediately after pruning the infected ones, disinfect all tools.

Fly speck. This fungal disease creates a black, speckled pattern of many shiny dots on fruit near harvest time, mainly on apples and pears. Fly speck is mostly an appearance problem. It may shorten the storage life of fruit but doesn't cause it to decay. Controls are similar for sooty blotch (see below), as when you find one, you often find the other.

Gray mold. Also commonly called by its scientific name, botrytis, this fungal disease is common under damp conditions and on old (overmature) fruit of most kinds, particularly strawberries, brambles, and grapes. Blossoms are infected first, and the disease is often worst when weather is wet during bloom. Keep plants pruned properly for good air circulation and keep ripe fruits picked to lessen or eliminate this disease.

Powdery mildew. This shows up as a white, velvety substance covering leaves, twigs, and fruits of grapes, currants, and tree fruits. It can be a major problem in warm and humid areas and seasons on grapes, especially on French hybrids and European cultivars. To prevent it, buy mildew-resistant cultivars, provide sanitary conditions, don't let plants get crowded, and prune rather heavily to permit good air circulation. Bordeaux and wettable sulfur have long been the standard treatments, but several fungicides now on the market give better control, including some organic ones related to baking soda. Some American grape cultivars, such as 'Concord', 'Chambourcin', 'Foch', and 'Leon Millot', are sensitive to sulfur sprays.

Root (crown) gall. This bacterial disease causes large swellings and fleshy growths on the roots of fruit trees, grapes, and brambles. Some cultivars and rootstocks appear to be more susceptible than others, and in some cases the gall doesn't greatly affect a plant or the crop. Because there is no known cure, plant only certified disease-free plants in soil not previously infected with diseased bramble plants, tree fruits, grapes, or related plants such as roses. If the disease gets severe, dig out all the plants, dispose of them, and start a new bed elsewhere with new plants.

Scab. Often called peach scab, black spot, or freckles, this fungal disease attacks peaches, nectarines, apricots, and plums. It can cause small (1/4-inch) round and yellowish spots on leaf undersides. These spots may fall out, leaving shot holes, and if severe, the leaves will fall off. It may start with even smaller, superficial olive green spots on half-grown to mature fruits; these spots enlarge to form velvety blotches. In severe cases, fruits will be stunted, misshapen, and crack open. If there are only a few spots, these will mainly harm the appearance and no control is necessary. To eliminate the need for a fungicide, avoid moist and low areas when planting, and prune away dead and potentially infected twigs in early spring. Mowing grass and weeds around trees, along with thinning branches and fruit, will reduce humidity and so may slow this disease. A separate fungal disease, apple scab, is a major problem on apples (see page 135).

Sooty blotch. Aptly named, this appears as sooty-colored or olive green circles to large patches on nearly mature fruits of apple and pear trees. Often this fungal disease is seen with fly speck during extreme wet periods, as both grow under similar conditions. Thin developing fruits and prune plants to increase air circulation and to reduce moisture around fruit. Weeding and mowing grass around trees also helps reduce moisture levels.

Verticillium. Caused by a fungus, this is one of the most common wilts (see below), attacking vegetables and shade trees as well as fruits. It is one of the most serious diseases of strawberries and brambles in some areas; other fruits are susceptible, including stone fruits. On raspberries, canes will suddenly droop and die, usually in midsummer. It is usually seen in cool weather, and is most severe in wet soils and after a cool, wet spring.

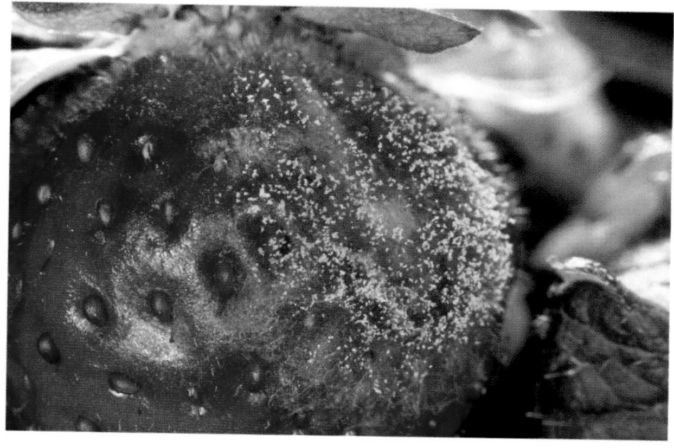

Botrytis on strawberry

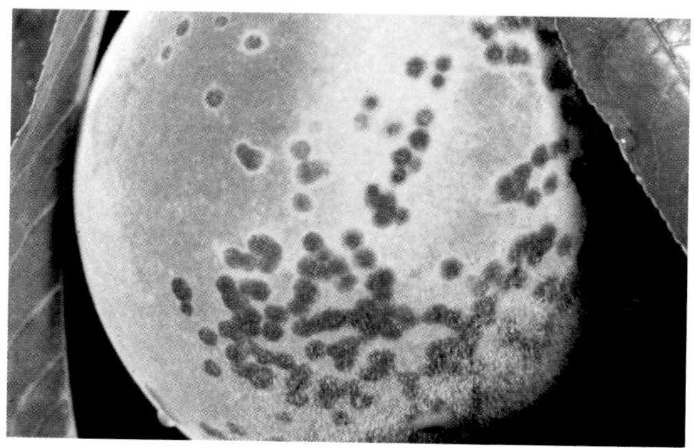

Peach scab

Verticillium on strawberry

Crown gall on raspberry

Blossom wilt on apple tree

Control of verticillium wilt is especially difficult; by the time you see the damage, sanitation is your only option. Cut out infected limbs or bramble canes and burn them at once; in the case of strawberries, dig out and destroy the entire affected plant. As a preventive, plant fruit trees and berries away from vegetables that may harbor the disease: eggplants, melons, peppers, potatoes, and tomatoes. Don't plant in soils that have grown these for at least 5 years — wait 10 years where the disease is already present. Keep away the weedy relatives of tomatoes, such as nightshade and horsenettle, that may harbor this disease; lamb's quarters is another host weed. Soil solarization (see page 274) greatly reduces this disease. Disinfect any pruning tools and shovels used on infected plants (see Disinfecting Pruning Tools box on page 273).

Viruses. A number of virus diseases affect fruits. Leaves on grapes and tree fruits may have spots or various discolored and mottled patterns, with symptoms more often seen during a cool spring. Bramble canes may be marbled green, with greenish yellow mottled leaves, or their berries may crumble. Raspberry and other bramble plants decrease in size each year until they perish. Viruses weaken trees and grapes and shorten their life. Fruit yields may be reduced up to 50 percent. At one time, most of the established apple trees in North America were infected with various viral diseases; existing older trees may still harbor such diseases and may serve as a source of infection. You may see various names for different fruit viruses such as plum pox and mosaic.

Viruses are difficult to control, as they aren't killed by pesticides. Thanks to new propagation methods such as tissue culture, many trees and bushes are now available virus-free. Replace infected plants with certified virus-free plants, and plant them 500 feet from similar plants (such as wild brambles, for virus-free brambles) to reduce chances of infection. Make sure your soil doesn't have nematodes, which can spread viruses. If you're pruning plants that appear to have a virus, disinfect tools before pruning healthy plants (see Disinfecting Pruning Tools, right).

Wilt. The name refers to any disease that causes a sudden drooping of a branch or the entire plant.

X-disease on a sweet cherry tree

That branch (or the entire plant) looks as if it's suffering from lack of water, even when the soil has plenty of moisture. Different wilts are caused by various viruses, fungi, and bacteria, and they trouble an assortment of tree fruits and berries. Verticillium wilt (see opposite page) is probably the most common on fruits.

X-disease. When a plant disease name isn't descriptive, this usually means that the cause isn't known, or at least wasn't initially. Such is the case with X-disease, which was once thought to be caused by a virus, and now is known to be caused by a different organism — a mycoplasma-like organism (MLO). The MLO is a parasite that lives in certain plant cells of stone fruits, especially peaches. What it does on peaches is to cause leaves to curl inward, with reddish spots that eventually drop out, leaving shotholes. Leaves and fruit drop prematurely. In cherries, trees can die quickly if grafted onto Mahaleb rootstock. This disease is harbored in wild chokecherries, so eliminating any nearby will help with control. It's spread by leafhoppers, which are especially attracted to red clover, strawberries, and blackberries. Controlling leafhoppers will help control X-disease, too.

Disinfecting Pruning Tools

After pruning infected plants, it's important to sterilize tools to prevent the spread of cankers, some fungi, fire blight and other bacterial diseases, and viruses. If you have a lot of trees, consider using a second pair of pruners while the first are soaking. A less-effective alternative is to wipe blades with one of the solutions below or to dip after each cut, to prevent spreading the disease elsewhere on a healthy tree.

First clean any dirt and debris from tools. Soak them, or at least the blades, for at least 5 minutes (longer for tools with rough surfaces), then rinse with water and dry.

If you prefer not to use chlorine because of its potential damage to plants, clothes, tools (it can be corrosive), and even your health should you get it on you and breathe the vapors, try one of the alternatives. Lysol has been found to be among the least corrosive to tools and to give the most consistent results.

The most common solution is 1 part chlorine bleach to 9 parts water. (Some use a stronger solution: 1 part bleach to 5 parts water.) Always add bleach to water, not the other way around; read the label and use caution when handling. Mix only as needed, because chlorine evaporates.

Nonchlorine alternatives include household disinfectants such as denatured or rubbing alcohol (full strength), also Listerine and Lysol (full strength or diluted, 1 part Listerine or Lysol to 5 parts water).

Solarizing Soil to Control Nematodes

A nematode isn't an insect or a disease, but a microscopic, eel-like roundworm. There are many species, but the root-knot nematodes are the most damaging to many crops, not just fruits. They're often worst in warm, sandy soils. They cause distinctive swellings, or galls, on roots, which damage them and also allow diseases to enter. These aren't rubbed off, as are the nodules on roots of nitrogen-fixing plants such as legumes. Aboveground, plants wilt and grow poorly. You'll need to rule out possible similar effects from too little water or nutrition, or from root rots. If you suspect nematodes, check whether your local Cooperative Extension Service will test for them.

Nematodes are usually introduced through infected soil. They're difficult to control, so avoid bringing them in through dirty tools and boots, or by moving infected plants with soil on roots between gardens or even within large plantings. Starting with healthy plants and minimizing stresses such as drought to keep plants healthy will go a long way. Look for resistant cultivars and rootstocks. If you know

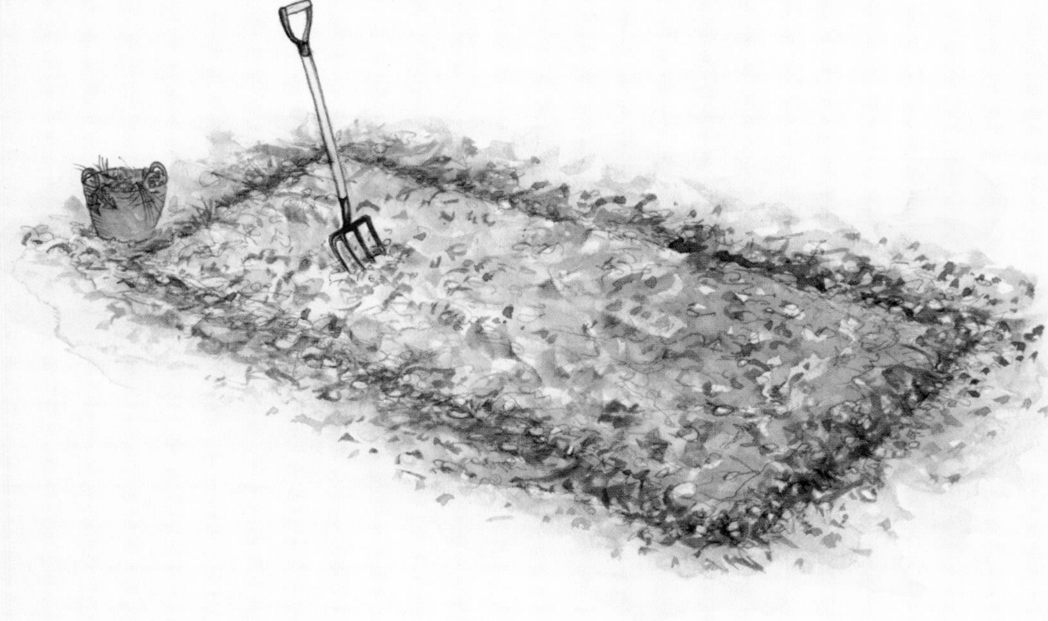

1. In May or June, weed the area and cultivate to loosen the soil (as for planting).

2. Moisten the soil, as moist soil when it's heated will destroy more pests.

nematodes are a problem in your area, consider leaving the ground bare (fallow), or plant a crop on which they can't reproduce before you plant your fruit trees and bushes. Plant an annual cover crop such as wheat or barley, or try resistant tomato and bean varieties. The marigolds 'Nemagold', 'Queen Sophia', and 'Tangerine' will suppress nematodes if planted over the whole area. Up to 4 years of such controls may be needed to rid an area of nematodes before you can plant fruit trees and bushes.

Soil solarization is often practiced in strawberry beds, providing prevention for a year or two until nematodes return. When done properly, it can kill many weed seeds and soil diseases such as verticillium wilt within the top 8 inches as well. This process involves covering the soil with a clear plastic sheet for 6 to 8 weeks and letting the sun heat the soil. Do it before you do any planting. It's best to do this in June and July, when the sun is hottest; otherwise you'll need more than 8 weeks for it to be effective.

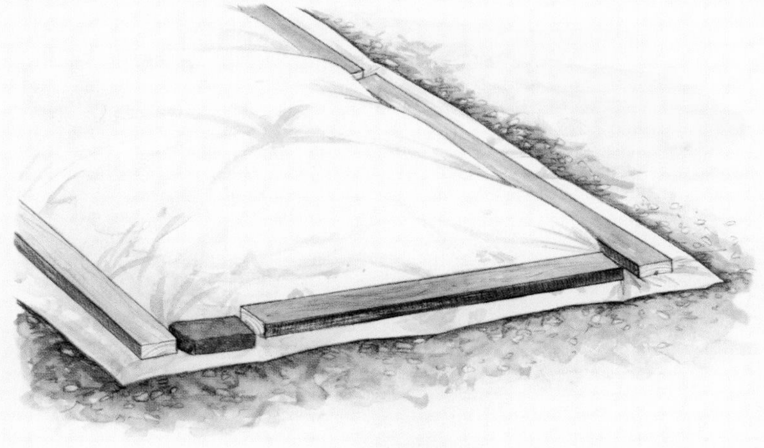

3. Cover with clear plastic sheeting; bury sides under 5 or 6 inches of soil or secure with boards or bricks.

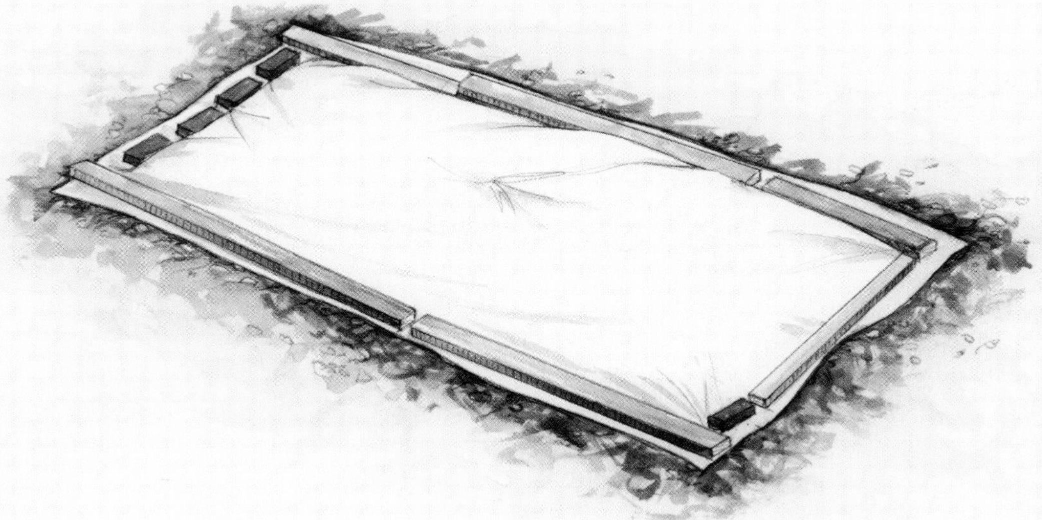

4. Leave for 4 to 6 weeks in hot climates; in cold climates, leave for 6 to 8 weeks.

Insects

ONE DAY IN HIGH SCHOOL biology class, our teacher confided in a hushed voice that a single insect could produce 100,000 descendants in a few weeks. While all of us were showing the expected degree of amazement, the boy sitting behind me whispered loudly, "Imagine what would happen if she ever got married!" That little remark stayed with me, and I think of it each spring as cocoons burst and larvae proliferate. No longer do I pretend to be amazed at the procreative ability of bugs. I really am amazed.

Early control of orchard pests prevents a great deal of trouble later on. Get in the habit of checking your plants at least weekly. The many types of insects attack fruit plants and trees in different ways. Some chew the leaves, some burrow into the trunk or a cane, still others suck nutrients from the leaves or through the bark.

Every insect you see in your orchard is not an enemy. Most are quite harmless, and some are important predators of common pests, so it's important to distinguish friend from foe before you load up that sprayer. Also follow the precautions on page 283 to minimize damage to beneficial species.

The pests described here are generalists and may show up on various types of fruits. Additional pests with more specific tastes are discussed in the fruit chapters.

Green apple aphids

Aphids. These are common, small insects, and may be green, pink, black, or white. Various kinds attack the bark, leaves, or fruit of almost every tree and plant, and although there's no visible damage at first, they suck out the juices and greatly weaken a plant; they can also transmit viruses. A tight curling of new leaves at the ends of branches on young fruit trees is a good indication that aphid colonies are at work. The sweet secretion they leave behind grows a black coating called sooty mold, which is another sign that aphids are at work. Ants too are a sign, as they're attracted to this sweet residue and may even protect aphids from natural predators in order to keep getting it. They're not after your fruit, only the by-product of the aphids.

You can knock out small infestations with a forceful stream of water. If that fails, insecticidal soaps will control them; repeat the treatment in 1 week to catch any that appear later. Be careful with all sprays; these can kill natural predators and leave plants more vulnerable to aphids. Decreasing the amount of fertilizer (especially nitrogen) may make plants more resistant, because overfertilizing makes for the lush growth that attracts them.

Borers. These are small larvae of some insects (moths and beetles in particular) that burrow into the trunks of trees, often near or just above ground level, but they may bore into other parts as well. The peach tree borer is one of the most common types, as are appletree, shothole, and dogwood borers. Most tree fruits are targets, as are nut trees. A pile of sawdust and some excrement, together with the weakened condition of a tree, indicate the presence of this alien invader. Even one borer can weaken a tree enough to cause it to break off at ground level. The most effective means of disposing of it is to brutally punch the fat grub with a wire inserted into the hole in the trunk, as sprays are not likely to reach it. Tree wraps help discourage this creature, but, unfortunately, trees from nurseries sometimes contain young larvae when you buy them. Inspect your trees frequently and look closely at the trunks of all new purchases. Because borers are attracted to trees weakened trees from stress, such as drought or disease, keeping them healthy is a good start toward prevention of this pest.

Peachtree borer moth

Earwig

Codling moth

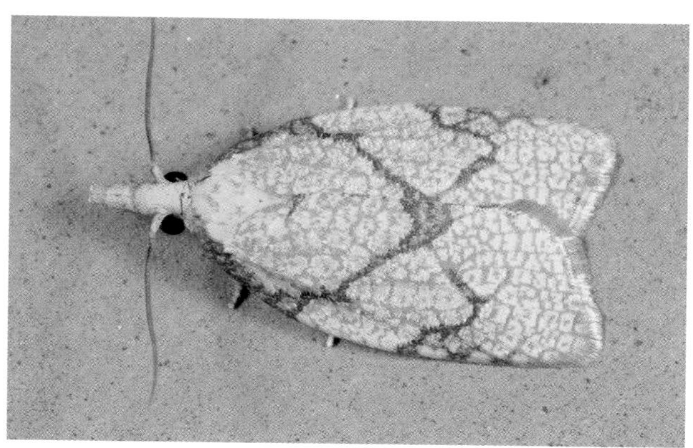
Fruitworm moth

Codling moths. "What's worse than finding a fat worm in your apple?" The answer is, of course, "half a worm." The larvae of codling moths are the culprits that cause those wormy apples. To a lesser extent this insect attacks other fruits, in particular pears, as well as English and black walnuts. The plump, white or grayish grub and its excrement around a hole in the fruit are solid indicators that this insect has been active. The codling moth lays its eggs in the flower at bloom time, so the best way to control it is to spray after the bees leave — directly after the petals have fallen — but before the new fruit has formed enough to protect the hatching eggs. Sometimes a second and third generation appear later the same year. Codling moths overwinter in sheltered spots, and a favorite one is under the loose bark on older fruit trees. Special triangular traps, often called Delta traps, are available for luring and capturing them. Thinning fruit helps prevent the moths from going between fruit, and allows better coverage if spraying.

Earwigs. If you see a reddish brown insect about ¾ inch long and with what appear to be dangerous pincers on the end as in a science-fiction movie, don't be alarmed — it's just an earwig, and it won't attack a human. In fact, earwigs are beneficial in many cases, eating aphids, mites, insect eggs, and other pests. They also feed on soft fruit, such as the stone fruits and berries, especially those with holes already in them from another pest. If earwigs become a problem, work to reduce their habitat where they rest by day — weeds, ground covers, and mulches. You can also trap them with rolls of moist newspaper or cardboard, or a short can (such as from cat food or tuna fish) containing half an inch of tuna oil or vegetable oil with a bit of bacon grease.

Fruitworms. These small caterpillars are often called green fruitworms, as the various types are basically green with white or another color stripes. These eat unopened flower buds, chew leaves and tie them together loosely with silky threads, and

Grasshopper

Grape leafhopper

gouge or eat fruit. They're not partial to any one fruit. Natural controls may keep them in check, or spray with Bt or another product that lists them on the label.

Grasshoppers. These familiar jumpers are mainly a pest on grains and herbaceous crops such as vegetables, but when populations are large enough, they'll feed on the leaves of strawberries, grapes, and fruit trees. Of the many species, only four or five are common. Usually they're a problem only in areas that get less than about 30 inches of rain a year — primarily parts of the western states — and when other food sources such as fields have been harvested. Sprays may not have much effect on adults in large populations. If you don't want to use a spray, focus on habitat instead. Keep some unmown grassy areas, even watered and fertilized, nearby for them to live in and feed on instead. Or plant some desirable trap crops such as zinnias to lure them to one area where they can feed and you can then focus your control efforts. Place row covers over strawberries to keep them out (they'll eat through lighter fabrics such as cheesecloth). Poultry are great predators, if they don't disturb your plantings as they scratch around. Finally, there are several natural controls you can purchase such as those containing Nosema (a single-cell protozoan, a disease-causing organism that is toxic only to grasshoppers).

Japanese beetles. These shiny bronze-and-green beetles can be found on most fruits, but they're particularly attracted to grapes and many members of the rose family, especially brambles. If you find them on your berry bushes, simply knock them off into a pail of soapy water. Traps are widely available, but they'll attract these beetles from afar. Milky spore, a biological control, works on the beetle grubs in warmer climates (Zones 6 and warmer). You must treat all the grass in the surrounding area with milky spore, as that's where the grubs live. If you want to turn lawn into a berry patch, grow corn for a year or two on the site to eliminate the Japanese beetle grubs before you put in the berry plants.

Leafhoppers. These are small insects that usually do little damage on their own, but they cause problems by transmitting viruses. You may find them on strawberries, raspberries, and grapes, as well as on apples and plums. They suck the fluids out of plant cells and leave behind a sticky excrement that darkens with age. In addition to this undesirable trait, leaves may yellow, be stunted or distorted, and even drop off if populations are high. If damage is extensive, or to prevent viruses, consider organic or synthetic controls. Otherwise, the many natural predators that feed on leafhoppers may keep levels tolerable.

Leaf rollers. Several species of caterpillars can roll leaves, often with webbing, and eat leaves and flowers. They may damage fruit (causing young fruit to fall off) and riddle mature fruits with deep gouges, often bronze colored. A few leaf rollers can be tolerated, but if you have too many, Bt and other sprays work on the caterpillars and dormant oil applied before flowers open will work on eggs.

Oriental fruit moths. Although this pest mainly attacks peaches, it can be found on other fruits, too. The larvae bore through tender terminal shoots, causing them to wilt (similar to the tarnished plant

Leaf roller moth

bug; see below). Later, the larvae, boring into them, cause young fruit to drop and mature fruit to be wormy. In apples, the difference between the Oriental fruit moth and the codling moth is that the former tends to tunnel at random and the latter tunnels directly toward the center and feeds on the seeds. In the wild, the Oriental fruit moth is controlled by more than 130 natural predators, but many of them aren't present in an orchard or are killed by sprays. A regular spray program should control this pest, as will pheromone traps, which disrupt its mating. The traps are simple twist ties, treated with the appropriate pheromone, that are attached to branches of fruit trees.

Plum curculios. These long-nosed weevils are a serious tree fruit pest east of the Rocky Mountains. Their name is misleading, as they attack apples and most other tree fruits and not just plums. They're most easily identified by the telltale crescent-shaped scar they leave on fruits. They create this small puncture just as a fruit is forming in order to lay eggs; the puncture often causes the fruit to drop prematurely or enables brown rot to enter. You'll find dark blotches around the punctures on the fruits that remain on the tree. Mature fruits may be knobby and gnarled. Treat with a spray after petal fall, when the adults are ready to lay their eggs. Begin looking for the curculios every few days before flowers open. Hold a white paper plate under a branch and shake the limb; especially on cold mornings, they'll fall onto the plate rather than fly away.

San Jose scale. This is neither a musical term nor a pest limited to San Jose; rather, it's an insect so tiny that you need a magnifying glass to see it. It lives under a hard film or scale it has built for protection and, along with its numerous relatives, sucks nutrients from the twigs in such quantities that entire branches often die. Bark may appear ash gray where scales mass. Few fruit trees are immune to this pest, but dormant oil controls it very well, as does a standard orchard spray program before bloom and after petal fall.

Sap beetles. These pests are small, only about 1/8 inch long, and brown. They're a problem primarily on strawberries, and in some areas on raspberries. Once strawberries start developing, these beetles may appear to feed on them. The result is soft,

Oriental fruit moth larva

San Jose scale

Sap beetle

Gooseberry sawfly larvae

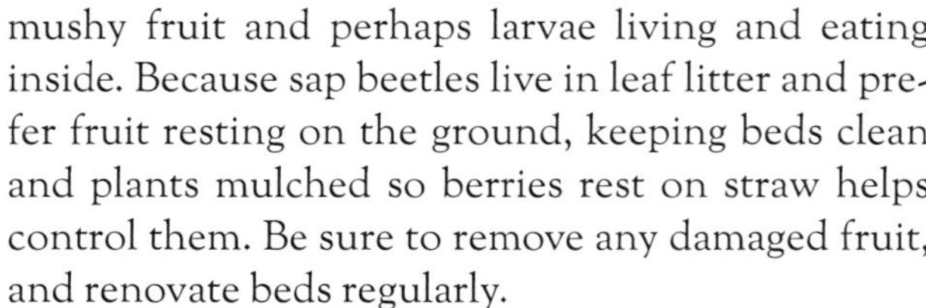

mushy fruit and perhaps larvae living and eating inside. Because sap beetles live in leaf litter and prefer fruit resting on the ground, keeping beds clean and plants mulched so berries rest on straw helps control them. Be sure to remove any damaged fruit, and renovate beds regularly.

Sawflies. The European sawflies and related sawflies can attack most fruits in summer, causing a circular raised ridge on the skin. Their larvae feed on leaves, skeletonizing them. The same controls suggested for apple maggots (see above) after petal fall are effective.

Spider mites. Often referred to simply as mites (although there are many types of mite pests), these are so small that you'll need a hand lens to see them. You can see with the unaided eye their characteristic fine stippling discoloration of leaves and their webbing on the undersides of leaves and between leaves and stems. They're more apt to show up when conditions are hot and dry and plants are stressed. Try hosing them off leaves; you may need to repeat this a couple of times in a week or two. Mites aren't true insects, so insecticides won't work on them; you need a specialized miticide unless you use an insecticidal soap

Spider mites

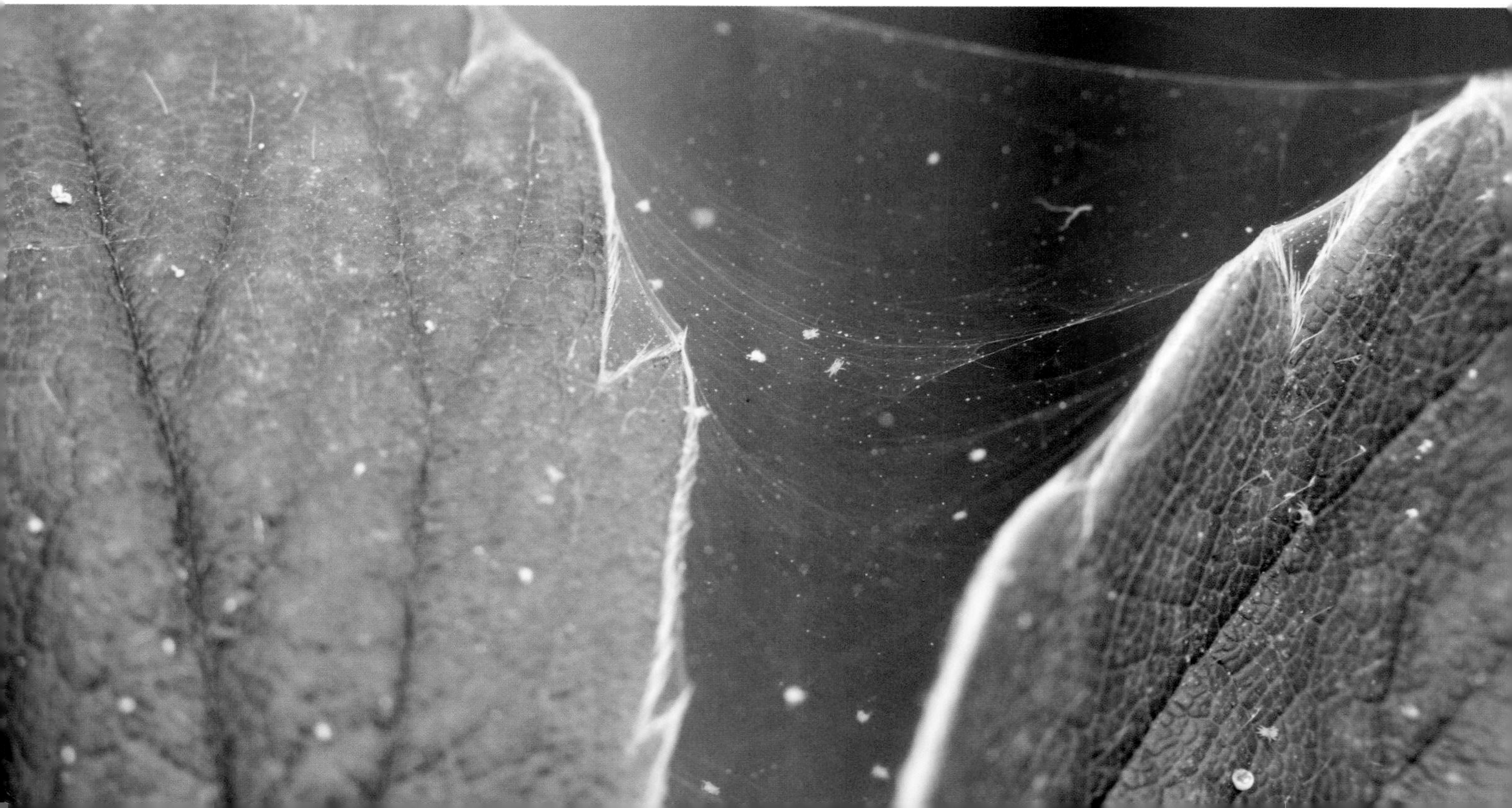

or horticultural oil. There are other types of mites, although spider mites are the most common. Some mites are even beneficial predators.

Tarnished plant bugs. These are true bugs that suck plant juices from flowers, stems, and fruits. (They also attack crop plants.) The results are tender young shoots wilting on peaches, punctures or deep dimples on young apples, and blemishes or scabs on mature fruit. Strawberries, one of the bug's favorites, can be misshapen, or hard green "buttons" can develop instead of fruit. Some damage on strawberries can be tolerated. Watch for this insect as strawberry plants begin to bloom. It's about 1/4 inch long with black and yellow markings. Monitor with white sticky traps. Natural enemies will provide some control, but keeping the bed free of weeds and away from overwintering herbaceous plants is perhaps the best way to limit their populations. Because this pest is quite mobile and active during bloom, spray controls are ineffective.

Tarnished plant bug

Tent caterpillars and webworms. These caterpillars create cobweb masses that are a familiar sight on fruit and nut trees. The webs protect the worms from birds as they consume large quantities of leaves during the summer months. Cut off and burn the webs to get rid of them, or spray the biological control Bt on leaves while young caterpillars are feeding. Learn to recognize the tent caterpillar's distinctive brown or gray frothy egg case, which wraps around branches. As you're pruning in late winter, prune off and destroy the small branches containing these egg cases, and you'll eliminate the problem.

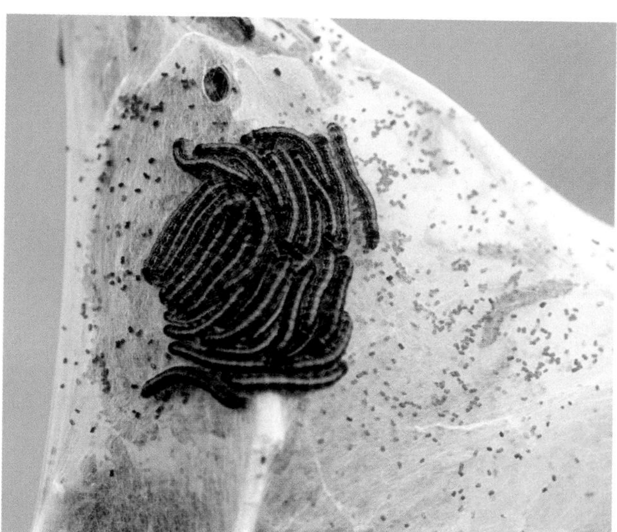

Tent caterpillars

Thrips. Thrips are tiny, slender insects that suck the fluids out of plant cells. They feed on many plants, including the small fruits. The evidence of their feeding is scarred flowers, leaves, and fruit surfaces and distorted plant parts. Damage from thrips usually isn't severe enough to merit spraying. There are many beneficial insects that feed on these pests, and you can exclude thrips with row covers over strawberries. An alternative is to surround plants with a reflective mulch, which confuses thrips and other flying insects such as aphids, leafhoppers, and whiteflies.

Pear thrip

Time Your Pest Patrol

Some key stages of stone and pome fruits are useful to know, as you'll hear or see them in relation to plant culture and in particular to scouting for insects and diseases. These stages respond to and vary with season and climate. Commercial growers monitor even more stages, but the following should be sufficient for the home fruit orchard. Apples and peaches are used as examples of pome and stone fruits; other fruits in each group are similar. Cornell University has a good visual guide for each stage online (see the appendix).

Here are the times to look for some common insect pests and diseases on fruit trees. Take heart: just because these are listed for a stage doesn't mean your tree fruits will get them.

- Dormancy until silver-tip stage: scales, plant bugs
- Silver-tip to tight-cluster stage: leaf rollers, aphids, scales, plant bugs, fruit worms, scab, powdery mildew, cedar apple rust, brown rot
- Pink stage to petal fall: plum curculios, leaf rollers, pear psylla, fruit worms, aphids, plant bugs, scab, powdery mildew, cedar apple rust, leaf spots, fire blight, brown rot
- The month after petal fall: codling moths, leaf rollers, apple maggots, sawflies, cherry fruit flies, mites, aphids, scales, plant bugs, scab, powdery mildew, leaf spots, fire blight, brown rot
- Midsummer until harvest: codling moths, leaf rollers, cherry fruit flies, apple maggots, Oriental fruit moths, mites, aphids, scales, borers, cherry leaf spot, brown rot

Apples	Peaches	WHAT HAPPENS
Silver tip	Bud swell	Buds swell and turn fuzzy silver from emerging leaves
Green tip	Bud burst	Green leaves begin to emerge from tips of buds
Half-inch green	Half-inch green	Specific amount of leaves are now visible, folding backward as they emerge, resembling the other name for this stage in apples — mouse ears
Tight cluster	(Not applicable)	Young apple leaves have emerged and are folded backward, revealing a tight flower cluster; buds are more sensitive to cold
Pink	Pink	Flower buds have grown sufficiently to reveal the petal color
Open cluster	(Not applicable)	Apple flower buds are now distinctly separate
King bloom	First bloom	The center, or king, bloom of apples opens first, before the several buds surrounding it; it usually produces the best fruit; first bloom opens in peaches
Full bloom	Full bloom	At least 80 percent of the flowers are open
Petal fall	Petal fall	Petals are raining down from the trees, carpeting the ground; when all the petals are off peach trees, the fruit is "in the shuck"
(Not applicable)	Shuck split	When the enlarging peach fruit splits the shuck — the dried remaining floral parts around the forming fruit
(Not applicable)	Pit hardening	You can't see this; cut a peach in half to see if the pit has become hard
Fruit set	Fruit set	Young fruit are visible; after fruit set growers measure other stages as fruits develop; for example, when apples are ¼ to ½ inch across (about the time of June drop) is the best time to thin for best fruit development
(Not applicable)	Red color	Peaches begin to change from yellow to red
Harvest	Harvest	This varies with the cultivar, season, and number of fruit on the tree; for peaches, this is divided into first harvest, then general harvest for multiple pickings

Spraying: How, What, and When

SOMETIMES GOOD SANITATION and culture is not enough. Many gardeners rely on a combination of organic and synthetic pest-control sprays to grow fruit. Some use only those products certified for organic growing; others resort to the latest and safest synthetic products, particularly for difficult-to-control pests. Remember that chemicals — whether organic or synthetic — don't discriminate; they kill good as well as bad insects, and can poison the birds that eat the sprayed bugs. In addition to ecological reasons for not using chemicals, many folks don't want to eat fruit that has been sprayed with materials that might be toxic. Keep in mind that with good culture, Integrated Pest Management, and a tolerance for some pests and diseases, you can usually get by with little or no spraying. The more blemishes you can tolerate on your fruit, the less you'll need to think about spraying.

Preventive Spraying

When diseases or insects are especially bad, preventive spraying may be necessary, because by the time symptoms appear, considerable damage may already have occurred. Whether you use synthetic or organic sprays, timing is very important. All diseases and insects have times when they're most vulnerable and other times when spraying is a waste of time and money. Diseases and insects can spread at an alarming rate, so knocking out the first wave saves much work, money, and grief later on. Your local Cooperative Extension office may be able to provide the dates of when insects hatch in your area. Often they supply specific climate information to help you evaluate the risk of a particular disease, such as scab, so you can decide whether spraying will be needed. There are times when you definitely should not spray, even if you use an organic pesticide. Never spray when the trees are blooming, because you'll kill the pollinating bees. Second, never spray closer to picking than the time recommended on the product label; many sprays must be stopped at least 2 weeks before harvest.

Dormant Oil

Though some may recoil at the very word *spray*, not all sprays are bad. One of the most common is an oil that works by smothering rather than poisoning. Many growers use a dormant oil spray on fruit trees before they leaf out. This one spray is sometimes all that's necessary if you've planted disease-resistant cultivars and follow good sanitation practices.

Many home gardeners spray only a small part of a tree, but for good pest control you must get thorough coverage at the top of the tree and also the inner branches. Choose a day with no wind for the job. I prefer to do any spraying in the early morning, when the air is usually quiet and it's not too warm for the protective clothing we all should wear. I choose a nice day, too, because rain within a few hours is likely to undo everything. Cold, rainy seasons are difficult ones for the orchardist.

Insecticides, Fungicides, Herbicides

Whether organic or synthetic, the chemicals used on fruits and berries fall into three categories: insecticides, fungicides, and herbicides. Insecticides are used to control insects, and include miticides for mites. Fungicides treat a wide variety of fungi, but will not help you control insect pests or diseases such as bacteria and viruses. Herbicides are those chemicals designed for eliminating unwanted weeds, grasses, and woody brush. Some gardeners prefer the convenience of a ready-mixed, commercial home-orchard spray containing both a fungicide and an insecticide, so one spraying will control most common orchard diseases and pests.

New pesticides are introduced every year that are safer and more effective than the existing ones. Because products and their labels continually change and availability varies, you won't find specific products listed here. Ask your Cooperative Extension Service, state or provincial agriculture officials, or a local farm or garden store for the most up-to-date, effective, and safest treatment for any problems in your area.

Garden sprayer

Spraying Equipment

Spraying equipment ranges from small trombone sprayers that spray from a pail and cost only a few dollars to large, power-driven machines. Don't buy a cheap model of whatever sprayer you choose. The trombone type is easy to clean, has few parts to wear out, is convenient to store, and is ideal for someone who has only a few bushes or trees. Trombone sprayers are not handy to use, however, so an easier-to-carry sprayer is better if you have more than a dozen trees. The compressed-air tank type works well and is perfectly satisfactory if you have low-growing trees, but the spray may not reach the tops of full-size trees. For larger trees and plantings, there are backpack sprayers, both power- and hand-operated, and even electrically powered mist blowers that can cover a tree with only a small amount of spray.

Always clean a sprayer after use. Leftover spray will corrode the tank and plug the small orifices. Replace worn gaskets immediately, so that the spray doesn't squirt out on you, and, for the same reason, never open a tank sprayer before the pressure is relieved (see Safety First, on page 287).

Organic Sprays

The following organic sprays are available at many garden stores and online. As with synthetic sprays, follow label directions carefully and completely.

Bt. Short for *Bacillus thuringiensis*, Bt is a bacterial biological control that kills the larvae of certain harmful caterpillar larvae, such as leaf rollers. It isn't as effective against those that attack fruit directly, such as the codling moth. Make sure you get the correct product for fruits, as there are several versions of Bt.

Clay. Clay-based products contain highly formulated kaolin clay, which when sprayed on plants serves as a barrier against insects and mites. (Don't try ordinary clay powder; it isn't very effective and can damage plants.) It dries to a white coating that confuses pests looking for host plants. Apply according to label directions, for the first half of the season for plum curculios and early codling moths and for leafhoppers on grapes. Apply through the season if there's a large population of pests (it's good for most major apple pests). Clay-based products are used in hot climates for sunburn protection. Avoid applying within a few weeks of harvest so you don't end up with white powder on your fruit; the fine kaolin clay is not harmful to humans but doesn't rinse off easily.

Dormant oil. Dormant and horticultural oils kill or at least suppress many insects. Applied just as the first bit of green shows in the swelling buds of fruit trees, the oils smother overwintering eggs of aphids and mites. For the best control, thoroughly

Apple coated with kaolin clay

Integrated Pest Management (IPM)

If you've gardened much, you've probably heard about IPM — the technique of controlling pests by using a combination of sanitation methods, physical and nonchemical controls, beneficial insects, and then, if necessary, some of the safer pesticides. It involves regular scouting for pests and diseases (which means knowing what you're looking for) and tolerating some of both, especially ones that won't cause significant damage. The least harmful control strategy is used for any problems that arise, taking care of them at the right stages. It minimizes the use of harmful chemicals, so the fruit produced is far less likely to have harmful residues.

coat the trunks and branches of dormant trees with the oil. Early versions were applied only during dormancy, as they were too strong to apply during the growing season, hence the name. Current versions of dormant oils are highly refined, though they still may be stronger than summer oils. Both dormant and summer oils are often called horticultural oils; now the words dormant and summer may be used to refer to the timing rather than the type of oil. Don't use summer oils at temperatures over about 80°F to avoid burning plant leaves. Also, don't use within a week of applying products containing sulfur, as the combination harms leaves and fruit.

Garlic. This is the basis for several products that repel a host of insects and may help prevent some

Even with organic sprays, it's important to wear a mask to avoid inhaling the fine mist. When spraying harsh chemicals, more protection should be worn, as indicated on the warning label of the product you're using.

diseases. Stronger formulas help repel birds from fruit. One popular product label says that it can be used up to harvest with no lasting taste or odor on fruit. If you make your own spray, try it on a small portion of the plant first to make sure it won't harm leaves, and don't spray right before harvest. Garlic sprays may repel beneficial insects as well, so don't overuse, and use only on infected plants.

Insecticidal soap. This controls aphids, mites, mealybugs, scales, and whiteflies, among other insects. Several brands are readily available. You may need more than one application for control.

Neem. Neem oil is from the neem tree (*Azadirachta indica*), a relative of mahogany. It acts against many insects, mites, and fungi by disrupting their molting and reproduction. Used as directed, it's safe around fish and wildlife.

Rotenone and pyrethrum. These are insecticides made from plants. Both have relatively low toxicity to humans but are highly toxic to fish; pyrethrum is also highly toxic to bees. They kill a range of insects, including beneficial ones, but as they biodegrade in a few days they're less damaging to beneficial insects than are many synthetic compounds. They must be applied frequently to be effective.

Sabadilla. This is a potent insect killer derived from a Latin American plant of the lily family (*Schonocaulon officinale*). It's especially good against flies and true bugs, such as the tarnished plant bug. It's toxic to honeybees.

Sulfur. Either by itself or in products such as copper sulfate and lime sulfur, sulfur is used as a fungicide for diseases such as scab, powdery mildew, and brown rot. These products often have to be applied regularly through the season on apples if diseases are present and when rain washes them off. The schedule is to spray beginning at green tip until 4 weeks after petal fall, then every 2 weeks if disease is still present. Stop the use of copper fungicides at the half-inch green stage to prevent damaging fruit (russeting). Use lime sulfur with caution, as it's caustic; apply right after mixing, and don't store it for more than a season. A common product that that been used for decades is Bordeaux mix, a combination of copper sulfate and hydrated lime. This and copper sulfate are of low toxicity to humans (unless used long term), but are toxic to fish and may endanger bees. Copper sulfate may also be poisonous to farm animals, and extensive use may kill soil life such as earthworms.

Synthetic Sprays

If you choose to follow the nonorganic or synthetic spray route, here's a schedule to follow. The first spray is the same dormant oil used by organic growers. All-purpose or multipurpose synthetic orchard sprays are available in hardware and garden stores. Most consist of a mixture of at least one insecticide and a fungicide, which enables you to control both insects and diseases with one shot. Follow label directions, even if they differ from the guidelines here.

1. Dormant spray. When tips of buds are swelling and turning green. Use dormant oil for this one.
2. Bud spray. When leaf buds are just beginning to open.
3. Pink spray. When blossom buds show pink and are almost ready to burst open.

Remember that chemicals — whether organic or synthetic — don't discriminate; they kill good as well as bad insects, and can poison the birds that eat the sprayed bugs.

Safety First

All pesticides must be handled with care. Even organic sprays, like the synthetic ones, may be harmful to humans, fish, pets, and beneficial insects. Make sure the label says that the product will control your target pest, and always follow the directions on the package carefully. Note all precautions, as some chemicals can burn plant leaves. Check the label of any product you use to see how close to harvest you can apply it.

Don't buy more than you can use within a year or so. Shelf life for many of them is limited, and their potency can change over time. Always store pest-control products in a dry, cool but non-freezing place, secure from children and pets, and away from all foodstuffs. Keep them in their original labeled containers, and don't put extra in jars or cans.

Use care when handling. Even with the safest spray, avoid breathing it in and getting it on your skin or in your eyes or hair. Wear a repellent raincoat and cap, goggles, and rubber or plastic boots and gloves. Label directions will advise whether any special protection is required, as well as whatever else you need to know for safe and effective control. Always stand well behind the spray. If you accidentally get any chemical on you, wash it off immediately and thoroughly. If you get a strong product or concentrate on you and have an adverse reaction even after washing, or get some in your eyes, seek medical attention at once.

It's best to use up any spray you've mixed, rather than dump it out. Make sure when rinsing the sprayer not to dump rinse water down a stormwater drain or where it could run off and end up in a waterway. When you're finished with a product or container, check with your local waste-disposal agency on how to get rid of it; do not discard in the trash unless you're told that it's safe to do so.

Do NOT spray any pesticides, organic or synthetic:

1. during bloom, to avoid killing bees pollinating flowers
2. within the recommended period before harvest
3. without reading, and following, label directions

4. Petal-fall spray. When almost all petals are off the tree. This is the most important spray of all. You may need to repeat this application 10 days later.

5. Summer sprays. Two or more additional sprays may be necessary in some areas, and in some years beginning midsummer. Space these 10 to 14 days apart to control mites, sawflies, apple maggots, and summer diseases such as brown rot and scab. Discontinue all spraying 4 weeks before harvest, or according to label directions on the product you're using.

Because trees bloom at different times, the second, third, and fourth sprays will have to be done according to the flowering period of each species. After that fourth application, you can spray the whole orchard at one time if more is called for.

If your spray doesn't seem to be providing control, perhaps you aren't putting on enough. This is a common problem of some home-fruit growers, especially for trees. Most sprays are meant to be sprayed to "runoff." That means until the spray is dripping from the leaves and stems. If you don't get the undersides of the leaves, insects may escape their doom.

Diagnosing What's Wrong

Don't give up on growing your own fruit when looking at this list of problems! You should see only a few if any of these. Many have similar symptoms, so if you're not completely sure, seek the help of a professional, your local Extension office, or a university plant diagnostic clinic (see the appendix). Also see Nut Problems on page 207.

Symptom	POSSIBLE CAUSES	FRUITS TO WATCH
PLANT TOPS		
Branch dieback, leaves fall off	scale, drought	most
Overall wilt, even with sufficient moisture	root damage as from wet soils; grape root borers (grapes)	most
Weak growth, spindly	too little sun	most
Tips wilt, leaf edges brown	drought stress	most
Bark missing	rodent damage (usually during winter)	most
Bark split	sunburn, winter injury	most tree fruits
Sunken areas in bark, off color, may be gummy	canker	most tree fruits
Bark peels off southwest side	winter injury	most tree fruits
Small holes near base, sawdust	borers	most tree fruits
Bark damaged at base	weed trimmer, mower, animals	most tree fruits
Poor overall growth under good conditions, stunted, damaged roots	root nematodes; cyclamen mites (on strawberries)	most, especially strawberries
Young shoot tips wilted	tarnished plant bugs; Oriental fruit moths; cane girdlers (grapes); cane borers (brambles)	most, peaches especially; grapes; brambles
Branch tips dead, black	fire blight, other blights	apple, pear, walnut
Shoots tips wilted on older canes with fruit	raspberry crown borers	brambles
Gray blotches with purple edges on bark	anthracnose	brambles
Canes with darkened areas at base, some dead	cane blight	brambles
Leaves yellow, old canes dead	spur blight	brambles
Canes die back	dead arm, phomopsis	grapes
ROOTS		
Warty tumors or growths on roots, becoming hard	root (crown) gall	most
Swollen, knotty areas	black knot	cherries, plums
Grape roots eaten	phylloxera	grapes
Rot from tips, reddish inside	red stele	strawberries
Strawberry roots eaten	white grubs	strawberries
Roots, plant base rotted	shoestring fungus	walnut

Symptom	POSSIBLE CAUSES	FRUITS TO WATCH
LEAVES		
Main-branch leaves wilted	verticillium wilt	most
Curled, puckered, sticky coating	aphids, leaf rollers	most; pecans
Mottled patterns, distorted	virus; herbicide damage	most
Speckled with tiny yellow dots, fine webbing	mites	most
Pale overall or along edges, or pale centers along veins	nutrition deficiency; improper soil pH; herbicide damage	most
Chewed, tied loosely with silk threads, rolled	fruitworms, leaf rollers	most
Skeletonized	sawflies	most
Eaten, lacy appearance	Japanese beetles	most; particularly grapes and brambles
Excessive basal shoots (suckers)	trunk wounds	most tree fruits
Fall off, webbing masses	tent caterpillars	most tree fruits
Excessive shoots (water sprouts)	improper pruning	most tree fruits
White "mold" on surfaces, beginning on lower leaves	powdery mildew	most, apples and cherries in particular; grapes
White specks, curled down, stunted shoots	leafhoppers	apples, plums, grapes, strawberries, raspberries
Eaten (dry climates)	grasshoppers	strawberries, grapes, fruit trees
Yellow-orange spots on undersides	rusts	apples, brambles
Olive velvety spots under leaves	apple scab	apples, occasionally pears
Frog-eyed spots, purple border	black rot	apples
Dark spots, leaves yellow and drop	leaf spot	cherries, pears
Gray fuzzy down on leaves and new shoots	downy mildew	grapes
Brown spots, black pimples	black rot	grapes
Swollen along midrib, puckered, then brown, drop	leaf curl	peaches
Small, black, velvety spots	pecan scab	pecans
Galls and knots, fall off	phylloxera	pecans
Water-soaked or angular dark spots below, shotholes	bacterial spot	stone fruits
Rolled, spots on edges, yellowed	bacterial canker	stone fruits, mainly cherries
Curl inward, reddish spots develop into shotholes	X-disease	stone fruits, especially peaches
Reddish pinpoints or blotches, curling and brown edges	leaf scorch or leaf spot	strawberries

Diagnosing What's Wrong *continued*

Symptom	POSSIBLE CAUSES	FRUITS TO WATCH
White foamy masses, eaten	spittlebugs	strawberries
Black except for midvein	leafhoppers	walnut
FLOWERS		
Blighted, gummy when warm/wet	brown rot	most, particularly cherries
Die suddenly, fail to open	frost in cold-climate regions	most
Turn brown, shrivel, cling on tree during cold, wet spring	bacterial blossom blast	apples, pears
Delayed	too little chilling over winter	most tree fruits, particularly apples
Unopened buds, blossoms eaten	fruitworms; flea beetles (grapes); rose chafers (grapes)	most, grapes
Withered, dead	fire blight	apples
Eaten, webbing	grape berry moths	grapes
Buds fail to open, fall	weevils	strawberries
FRUITS		
Few or none	too little sun; poor pollination; alternate bearing (tree fruits)	most
Chewed or mostly eaten	fruitworms	most
Gouged, deep bronze scars	leaf rollers	most
Drop in June or later	plum curculios	most tree fruits
Knobby, gnarly	plum curculios	most tree fruits
Circular, raised ridge in summer	sawflies	most tree fruits
Mature have blemishes, scabs, deformed "catfacing"	tarnished plant bugs; poor pollination; environment	most, particularly strawberries and stone fruits
Misshapen ("buttons")	tarnished plant bugs	strawberries
Small, misshapen ("buttons")	poor fertilization from stresses	most, particularly apples
Crescent-shaped cuts in skin, then drop	plum curculios	most, particularly stone fruits
Cracking, splitting	wet weather; scab	most tree fruits, particularly cherries
Gray mold, rotten	botrytis	strawberries, brambles, grapes
Worms, tunnels	apple maggots, Oriental fruit moths, coddling moths	apples, other fruits
Olive velvety spots	apple scab	apples, sometimes pears
Mature fruits warty, cracked	apple scab	apples, sometimes pears
Rings of dark rot on ends opposite stems	frog-eye leaf spot	apples, pears
Light patches, especially on south sides of fruit	sunburn	apples, pears
Small brown spots, dry rot, shriveled, black	black rot	apples, grapes

Symptom	POSSIBLE CAUSES	FRUITS TO WATCH
Black, sooty growth	sooty blotch	apples, pears
Black speckling	flyspeck	apples, pears
Scabs	anthracnose	brambles
Crumble when picked	poor pollination; cool summer; virus	brambles
Worms	cherry fruit flies/maggots	cherries
Reddish spots, worms	grape berry moths	grapes
Tiny spots or flecks	bacterial spot	peaches
Velvety blotches	peach scab	peaches, plums
Insides gray, brown	excess heat	plums, apricots
Tan or gray, mushy inside	brown rot	stone fruits
Dark, deep sunken areas	bacterial canker	stone fruits, mainly cherries
Cracked skin, sunken areas, water-soaked lesions	bacterial spot	glossy-skinned stone fruits
Soft, mushy, worms inside	sap beetles	strawberries, brambles
Eaten, irregular holes	slugs, snails, sap beetles	strawberries
Bronzed, scars, cracks	thrips	strawberries
Shells and kernels stained, rot	codling moths	walnuts
Nuts black, fall off	anthracnose	walnuts

Not only will deer help themselves to your fruit harvest, they'll also eat the foliage and strip the bark from your trees.

CHAPTER 19

Wildlife Friends and Foes

Over the years my attitude toward wildlife has changed quite a bit. When we had a flock of chickens, I thought of coyotes, bobcats, and fishers as villains. Since we've been raising trees and plants, I look at these former so-called varmints — along with owls, hawks, and weasels — in a different way. Those predators consume rabbits, mice, and woodchucks, which, along with porcupines and deer, have become the bad guys in my book.

Wherever you live, you may face unexpected, uninvited garden guests. In a few months under favorable conditions, mice can multiply astronomically to strip the bark of many fruit trees in winter, and deer can destroy many years' worth of growth in a few hours of feeding. As one who has tried to garden and grow fruits for four decades on the edge of a wilderness, I sympathize with any gardener who must battle wildlife.

Suburbia has spread, and our homes are now where wildlife homes once were. Nature has adjusted to today's changing world, and city and suburban gardeners often find woodchucks, skunks, raccoons, rabbits, and even bears in their gardens. Deer and even moose occasionally stroll down the streets of good-size cities. These have survived as their predators have moved on or died out. Often the most effective predators — humans — aren't allowed to kill or trap wildlife.

Of course, some people plant fruit trees and bushes because they want to attract animals and birds. This is one of the ways you can get your backyard certified as wildlife habitat by the National Wildlife Federation. Most of us who toil over trees and berry bushes, however, hope to keep at least a small part of the fruits of our labors for ourselves. Though I enjoy watching the cedar waxwings and other birds feast on the unripe fruit from my serviceberries, I'm always hopeful they'll leave a few to ripen for me.

Preventing Mouse Damage

MICE AND VOLES (field mice) are among the worst problems facing fruit trees, simply because of their sheer numbers. Particularly upsetting is their habit of chewing the bark from the trunks of trees beneath winter's snow, so you don't see what's happening until spring. Even though a girdled tree may leaf out, it will soon die, and there is usually no practical way to save it. If it's girdled only halfway around, it has a better chance.

Mice girdle not only newly planted fruit trees, but also those 8 inches or so in diameter. Some years the damage is worse than others, and because you can't predict when they'll strike in full force, it's best to be on guard at all times.

A good hunting cat is fine control, but in case she misses a mouse or two, it's more reliable to wrap young tree trunks in hardware cloth or heavy metal screening. You can leave them on the trees all year, but remove them before they constrict growth. If you need protection from sunscald (see page 267), paint trunks before you wrap them. You can also wrap the trunks carefully each fall with two or three thicknesses of aluminum foil, or use the plastic tree guards available at most garden-supply firms. Remove these in the spring, however, because insects like to work in the dampness they find here. Guards should extend at least 2 feet aboveground and be sunk at least 2 inches into the ground to provide adequate protection.

Plastic guards and those made with similar materials protect young trees from rodent damage.

Keep mulch and straw away from trunks and keep grass mowed to reduce mice damage by taking away their favorite habitats. For serious mouse problems, there are various snap-type traps; those with the mechanism enclosed in a case are much safer and don't endanger pets or other mouse predators. Some commercial orchardists spread poison corn or oats around their trees, but this can be toxic to pets directly, or indirectly if they eat a sickened mouse. Birds that feed on poisoned mice too will die.

Rabbits, Porcupines, Raccoons, and Squirrels

IN SOME PLACES, these small animals cause a lot of grief. Rabbits eat the lower branches and bark from trees. Porcupines chew the bark and sometimes cut off entire limbs, dropping them to the ground for easier nibbling. Several times these prickly creatures have invaded our garden, cutting down and consuming a whole long row of raspberry canes in a single night.

Raccoons and squirrels are more likely to eat mature fruit, and they often invade our barns to steal the nuts and fruits we've already picked. The raccoon doesn't wear his bandit mask for nothing! Gray squirrels often run merrily over a tree, taking one bite from each apple and ruining the whole crop.

Some dogs chase away these animals very effectively. Or try fencing them out; low electric fences are often used to keep away porcupines and raccoons.

Squirrels are especially troublesome in nut-tree orchards.

There are some smell repellents that may work, too. Hunting and trapping, where they're allowed, are an option; you can hire a licensed trapper. Some counties and states have laws prohibiting trapping and releasing wildlife. Before setting any traps, contact your local wildlife management office or state Fish and Wildlife agency to be sure it's legal to relocate trapped animals, and to ask about the best place to do so. The best defense, however, is to eliminate the habitats that attract these animal pests.

Dealing with Deer

IN COMPARISON WITH fighting bugs and mice, deer seem like monsters. They love both apple twigs and fruit, and also seem to get a kick out of scrubbing the bark off any valuable tree with their antlers. They like other fruits too, especially the new growth on brambles. (Apparently, thorns aren't an issue or a deterrent.) Blueberry plants and fruits may get a few nibbles, but they seem to be of little interest to deer, and serviceberries, chokeberries, and currants generally escape as well. Just as different humans prefer different foods, so do deer. This explains why some plants are resistant in one place and not in another. Although bear, moose, and elk occasionally damage fruit trees and bushes, deer are usually the only large wild animals that bother an orchard.

Not Tonight, Deer

Control of super-smart deer is difficult. But as they've become one of the main problems for gardeners in many parts of the country, controls have proliferated as well. Among them are repellents based on taste, sound, light, and smell. Except for taste, these work on a deer's sense of danger, either startling her or, in the case of smell, masking her ability to perceive a threat.

Taste. There are many taste repellents to spray on plants favored by deer. Many of the newer ones last much longer, through many rains, than either older products or home concoctions. Although a pepper-based spray may deter the casual deer, it won't have much effect on deer desperate for food.

Sound. A radio is effective for a while, but deer will become used to it if you don't move it around. Those who use radios swear by talk-radio shows, which may drive some family members away as well. Some orchards use sound cannons, but these aren't conducive to good neighbor or even family relations.

Light. Motion-detector lights, the same ones used for home security, are an option. These are usually available in hardware stores. I have one with a solar-recharged battery, mounted on a stand I can move around, and on a timer so that it goes off after a few minutes. It has been somewhat effective, except when I'm away or forget to move it regularly. (Similar to motion-activated lights are sprinklers, often sold for dog control, that squirt water about when they sense motion.)

Smell. Odor repellents for deer include some rather exotic products. Mothballs, hair from a barbershop or beauty parlor, dried blood, rotten eggs, lion or tiger manure (if you live near a zoo), sweaty underclothes, and human or predator urines have all been used with some success. Rotation of several of these, or with other types of repellents, is the key.

Many smell repellents formulated for deer are now available for purchase; these work better in winter and for longer periods compared to earlier products. Some have a scent pleasant to humans but unpleasant to deer and some other mammals, such as oil of peppermint, cloves, or lemon. Others are absolutely vile, made from slaughterhouse wastes. They definitely signal danger: something bad happened here and it's best to leave now. I figure if my deer are still around when I use one of these, they've lost their sense of smell.

The most popular odor repellent is bars of smelly soap, the more fragrant the better. Hang them, still in their wrappers, in trees and around bushes. Hang the soaps well away from a trunk so they won't drip down the bark as they dissolve; mice eat soap and also soap-saturated bark. You'll probably need several soap bars, closely spaced, for this method to be effective; I've found that my local raccoon prefers some brands to carry off and nibble on.

Fence Them Out

In addition to repellents, there are a number of fencing options. In fact, most gardeners have found that a high, tight fence is the only answer to a serious deer problem. In our experience, deer will give up on an orchard only when it's made impossible — not merely difficult — for them. A deer fence must be extremely well built, as deer can and will squeeze through the most unlikely places.

If you have only a few trees in a yard, or a small bramble patch, fence each individually with wire mesh 5 or 6 feet high. Just make sure the mesh is a small-enough weave that deer can't get their noses through and far enough away from a plant that they can't nibble the edges or reach the plant over the top.

Although a 5- or 6-foot fence seems adequate for a few bushes, a large orchard needs a fence at least 8 feet high. If the fence is solid (impossible for deer to see through), you can get by with one lower — perhaps 6 feet high. Although deer can jump this, they usually won't because they can't see what's on the other side and don't want to risk the unknown of getting trapped, or worse.

There are many types of fencing and configurations for deer control. The simplest and cheapest is a strand of cord or white clothesline, with flagging tape strips hung every 5 feet or so. Deer can't see well, so the flagging lets them know something is there. (Flagging helps keep you from walking into the line, too, though it may not be sufficient to keep kids from getting tangled if they play nearby.) A couple of single cords as above, or fences 4 to 5 feet high, parallel and 5 to 10 feet apart, will create a space they can't clear, and they won't want to get risk getting trapped inside it.

A single strand of electric fence (check local regulations before using) works well when it's installed at the height of a deer's nose and combined with bait. Spread peanut butter on aluminum foil and secure it to the wire every 3 feet or so. Deer smell the peanut butter and come to eat it. The resulting zap should scare them off.

Lower fences are effective only when they're too wide for the deer to clear. One type has strands of wire on a diagonal from the ground. The offset fence has three strands, creating a triangle in cross-section about 5 feet high and 5 to 8 feet wide.

The ultimate, of course, is the netted or mesh fence, 8 to 10 feet high. Plastic netting is now available that performs as well as wide-mesh wire and is less expensive, plus it's barely visible from a distance. Another version of this has posts installed with 8 feet aboveground and eight wire strands strung between them about a foot apart vertically. If you opt for fishing line or cord instead of wire, use flagging tape every 5 feet or so along the cord so the deer can see that something is there. As the flagging tapes flutter in the breeze, they may frighten the deer.

TYPES OF DEER FENCES

If you have only a couple of plants, installing a tall cage around them is one option.

In regions where deer are not persistent or habituated to humans, a simple taut clothesline tied with flagging may be enough to deter them.

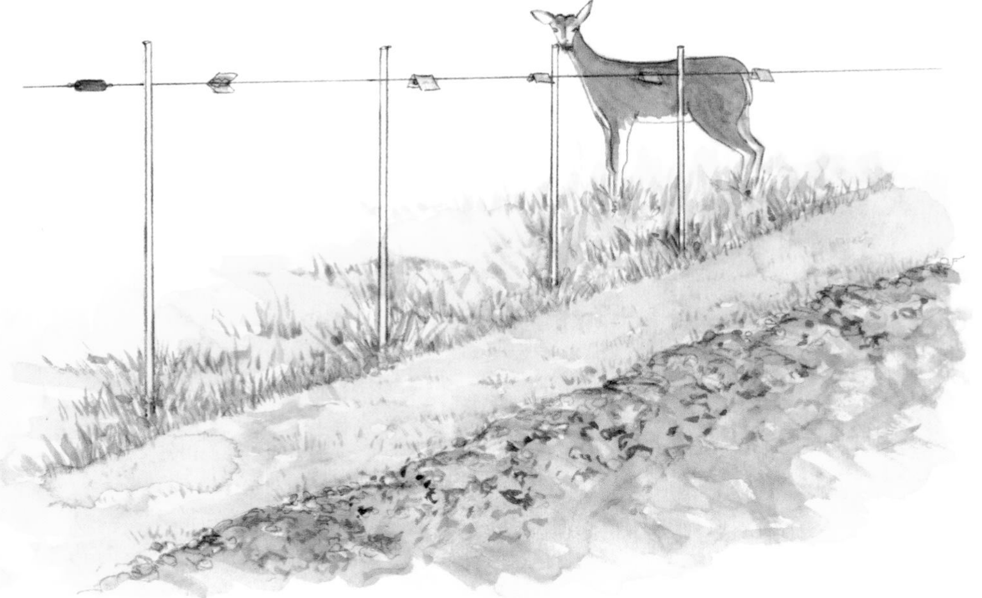

A single-strand electric fence, baited with peanut butter on pieces of aluminum foil, may train deer to avoid the area.

Where deer are a constant problem, more elaborate fences may be needed. An alternative to a tall fence is a series of diagonal wires, which needs to be 5 feet high and 5 to 8 feet wide to be effective.

Deer Facts

To understand why a plant listed someplace as deer resistant is favored by your deer, or why deer bother plants in your yard and not in your neighbors', or why a repellent works for a while but then stops being effective, or why it works for your neighbor and not for you, it helps to know a few deer facts.

1. Deer have great senses of smell and hearing, but bad eyesight. Their nose is what warns them of danger and tells them what's good to eat. Mess with this — as with smell repellents — and they get nervous and may go away.

2. Deer are quick learners. If they figure out a "deterrent" isn't a problem, they'll resume eating. This is why you must rotate not only the types of repellents but also their location to keep deer off their guard. One suburbanite kept a dog on a chain. The deer soon learned how long the leash was and resumed feeding only a few feet away from the growling canine. The message is, if you have a dog on a leash and deer are about, move or lengthen the leash every few days. Like children, teach deer early — both in the season and in age — that they aren't welcome, and your controls will be more effective.

3. Deer are creatures of habit, so if you find their main routes, block them or put repellents there to try to deter them.

4. Like most animals, deer don't like danger. Create a setting such as a sunken or walled garden where they think they might get trapped and they likely won't enter. This is how a couple of low parallel fences 5 or so feet apart can be just as effective as a single tall fence. They can jump over one, but if they aren't sure they can make both and might get trapped between, they may stay away.

5. Deer must eat to survive. When populations are high or the food scarce, they'll eat plants they wouldn't normally eat, in spite of foul smells and bad tastes. This is why a certain plant may be listed as resistant but in some areas it's eaten by deer, and why a repellent works in one yard and not another. In this case, the only real solution is a good fence.

Outwitting Birds

FENCES CAN'T KEEP OUT bird intruders, unless you build a cage or use a net. We welcome birds for their cheery songs and colorful ways, and because they're voracious insect eaters, we don't want to lose them. Still, some species, such as jays, waxwings, and blackbirds, can be a problem at harvest time. Not only do birds love cherries and berries, but they often ruin large amounts of apples and other large fruits as well. Fruit isn't all they may bother, either. Sapsuckers bore hundreds of orderly holes in the bark of the trunks of our crab apples during the winter and spring. I've been amazed at how many holes my chokecherry can be riddled with and still keep living.

Scare tactics. We've used all the ploys in defense of our crop — strips of fluttering aluminum foil, noisemakers, radios, scarecrows, cats, netting, and plastic snakes — and they all help, but only to a point. We've learned to install bird-scaring devices (see page 189) just before the fruit is mature. If we put them out too early, the birds get used to them; if too late, the feathery gourmets have already developed a craving for the delicacies and have no intention of giving up.

Nets. Netting is the best way to keep birds off strawberries and berry bushes. If you have just a few berry bushes, you can put netting directly on them. With strawberries, though, birds may be able to peck at fruit through the netting, so a lightweight white fabric (the same row cover used for insect control) will be more effective. Or erect some form of structure or frame on which to suspend the netting over the planting, especially if you have a large berry patch. Weight down the edges of the netting with soil or anything heavy, such as boards, rocks, and bricks. After covering the bushes, check them daily; despite your best efforts, some birds will find their way underneath and become trapped.

Some desperate growers use netting on fruit trees; others have even built large chicken-wire cages around their cherry trees. One easier variation on the net theme I've seen recommended is to throw a spool of black thread back and forth over a tree. All these threads "may" get caught up with the birds enough to reduce damage. More effective is to erect some form of tent made of threads, in a maypole or Christmas tree shape, over a tree.

Decoy plantings and sprays. I've heard that it helps to plant mulberry trees nearby, because some birds seem to prefer them, but I've never tried that; after all, it may just attract more birds. There are some garlic-based products that are touted as effective at repelling birds. When you harvest the garlic-coated fruits, simply rinse them with water; the taste is not absorbed into the fruit. Begin spraying when fruits start to ripen and birds begin to appear, and respray weekly or as the label directs.

Netting draped over a PVC cage is the best way to keep birds out of your berries.

Avoiding Other Hazards

BESIDES ANIMALS, we fruit growers have learned to expect other problems. In snow country, snowmobilers don't always bother to go around young orchards, especially at night. Trail bikers and horseback riders sometimes view a new planting as only a bit of brush. Children may thoughtlessly bend over and snap off a limb or even a small tree to use as a whip or cane. But probably the biggest mechanical threats to your trees are your own lawn mower and weed trimmer, so impress whoever mows the lawn or uses a tiller or any other machinery to exercise care around your trees. String trimmers will quickly cut through the bark of a fruit tree; cutting through the bark all the way around (girdling) will kill the tree.

Those of us who live in agricultural country can expect farm animals to break loose occasionally, and if they do, they're almost certain to head for your orchard or garden. In only a few minutes, a herd of cows or a few horses can devastate the best planting, as can wandering goats, sheep, and pigs. Puppies tend to try out their growing teeth on new trees, and cats like playing games in them. If any one of these hazards is likely in your backyard, maybe the best answer is a strong fence with a sturdy gate. Chickens, on the other hand, are a good partner for fruit trees as they'll eat many insects such as plum curculios.

Glossary

More-common terms can be found through the index.

alternate bearing (fruiting). The propensity of some fruits, such as kiwis and some apples, to produce heavily one year, then little to none the next, alternating between heavy and light yields.

apical bud. The bud at the tip (apex) of shoots; pruning out the apical bud promotes formation of side branches.

arm. Stem or shoot of grapes two or more years old; short branches off the trunk from which future canes develop. One-year-old shoots, called canes, produce the shoots (spurs) that bear fruit.

asexual propagation. See vegetative propagation.

axil. Where the leaf joins a stem.

axillary bud. See lateral bud.

balled-and-burlapped. Roots and the soil surrounding them are encased in burlap to hold them together; can be planted if not plastic coated, as burlap will decompose.

bare-root. Refers to plants sold with no soil around roots; common when ordering fruit trees from a catalog.

bench cut. Pruning a major upright limb back to where it joins a lower, horizontal limb; used sparingly to shorten trees that have gotten too tall.

berry. Type of fruit arising from one flower, with soft flesh around one or more seeds; often used to refer to small fruits that are usually eaten whole.

bilateral. Growing in two opposite directions, as with grape canes off the trunk along trellis wires.

biological control. A naturally derived chemical, predator, or nonchemical means of controlling pests.

bleed. When sap oozes from cuts or wounds in early spring on some plants, such as muscadine grapes. This doesn't hurt the plants.

bloom. With fruit, refers to a whitish coating as on plums and blueberries.

blush. A light red tint on skin of some fruits, such as apples, peaches, and yellow cherries.

botrytis. See gray mold.

bramble. A fruiting plant in the Rubus genus such as raspberry and blackberry, often with thorny stems.

branch collar. The region of a tree trunk from which a side branch emerges, often slightly raised. Prune branches flush with the outermost portion for fastest healing.

bud. Found in the axils, basically a dormant and compressed shoot that, given the right conditions, will resume growth.

budding. Vegetative propagation method of attaching a bud (scion) from one plant to the stem of another (rootstock); where they meet is the bud union.

buffering. Ability of soil to resist (buffer) changes in pH or fertility.

burr knots. Ugly, misshapen growths on some apple rootstocks (such as M.26 and MM.111), sometimes on branches, from the plant trying to grow roots aboveground. Cause is unknown; provides entry for borers and diseases.

bushel. Unit of volume, equal to 8 gallons; used mainly for tree fruits. A bushel of apples weighs about 42 pounds.

button. A small, misshapen fruit, as sometimes occurs with apples and peaches; often caused by poor fertilization of flowers.

callus. The growth of a stem or trunk over a wound or graft union.

calyx. In fruits, the opposite end from where the fruit is attached to stem. In flowers, a group of sepals below the petals.

cambium. The thin layer of tissue, often green or greenish yellow, between the bark and the wood; important in grafting, as the cambium of rootstock and scion must be aligned in order for the graft to be successful.

cane. The main stem of many plants with small fruits, such as the brambles and currants, that produce many stems; one-year-old stems of grapes; or woody stems that have buds after leaves fall.

cane pruning. A training system for grapes in which whole canes and most cordons are removed each year.

canker. A decayed or sunken area of bark, often discolored, caused by disease; may have sap oozing out.

canopy. In trees, the total area covered by leaves and shoots. In vines, the aboveground portions.

catfacing. Scarring and puckering of fruit; most common on strawberries and stone fruits.

central leader. Main upright trunk at the top of a tree; also refers to a system of training trees to one central stem.

chilling hours. The number of hours below 45°F required by some types of fruit in order to flower and bear.

chlorosis. Yellowing of leaves overall, generally from lack of an essential element such as nitrogen.

clone (adj: clonal). A plant genetically the same as its parent or another plant, created through vegetative propagation. Clones of many fruits are not able to pollinate each other.

collar. See branch collar.

compost. Soil amendment created by micro-organisms breaking down organic matter.

cordon. 1. One of the stems (long arms) of grapes that are horizontal, or almost so, and 2 or more years old, from which canes or spurs arise. 2. The grape-training system in which horizontal stems support fruiting spurs. 3. A form of espalier in which the tree is trained to a narrow column.

core. Central stem or stalk inside the fruit of raspberries and blackberries; also called receptacle.

cracking. When skins of fruits such as grapes and peaches split; also called splitting. Often occurs after heavy rains; shortens storage life and enables diseases to enter.

crotch. Angle formed where two branches meet or where a main limb joins the trunk. Narrow V-shaped crotches are not desirable, as they are weak and can break under a heavy load of fruit or snow, or from wind.

cross-pollination. The process in which pollen is transported from one flower to another, on the same plant or among flowers on different plants.

crown. The base of a plant, where the stem meets the roots. On strawberries, it is the shortened stem from which leaves emerge. On some brambles, it is the central area on the ground from which canes emerge. On trees, the crown refers to the entire branch structure with foliage.

cultivar. Short for "cultivated variety"; a closely related group of plants within a species originating not from nature but instead by humans through a process of selection or breeding. Most fruit selections are cultivars. Compare variety.

cutting. A small piece of plant stem, rooted to make a new plant.

day-neutral. A strawberry cultivar that continues to bear through the season and is not affected by the length of daylight hours.

deciduous. A shrub or tree that loses its leaves each fall.

dioecious. Producing male and female flowers on separate plants (from the Greek meaning "two houses"). Examples are hollies and dates.

division. Propagating plants by separating (dividing) them into smaller sections.

dormancy. Stage of growth during which a plant isn't growing, but is capable of resuming growth given the right conditions. Many plants go dormant during drought or over the winter.

dormant pruning. Trimming when plants are not actively growing, usually in later winter or early spring.

drip irrigation. Watering plants using soaker hoses or a system of hoses and tiny spouts (emitters) that place water at the base of plants rather than wetting leaves. This is the most efficient method of watering.

drip line. The area under a tree below the outside edge of branches. Many feeder roots are located just inside this line, so compost and fertilizer should be applied all the way out to the drip line.

drop. A fruit that falls on the ground, especially early in the season from insect damage or another problem.

drupe. Technical term for a stone fruit — that is, a type of fruit with a central pit such as cherry, peach, or plum.

ethylene. A gas given off by some fruits such as apples and bananas. Ethylene is used commercially to artificially ripen fruits; a ripe apple or banana can be put in a bag with unripe fruit such as kiwis to speed their ripening.

everbearer. A strawberry cultivar that fruits in early and late season; compare to day-neutral.

floricane. The second-year-old (fruit-bearing) cane of a bramble; compare to primocane.

girdling. Removing bark or damaging it, as with a string trimmer, around most or all of a tree's circumference, resulting in the death of the parts above the damage.

girdling root. A root that grows in a circular way around the root mass, next to the trunk, choking off the flow of nutrients and weakening and possibly eventually killing the tree; usually arises from not loosening roots of potbound trees at planting time.

grafting. Propagating by attaching a piece of stem (scion) from one plant to the stem of another (the rootstock).

graft union. The point where the stem (scion) meets the rootstock.

gray mold. Another name for botrytis disease.

grubs. Larvae of insects (mainly beetles, such as Japanese beetles); they are generally light colored with darker head and resemble a short fat worm. Grubs are most common in soil but are sometimes found in fruit (as with the larvae of plum curculios).

larvae, especially of Japanese beetles and similar insects, often found in soil.

hardiness. The ability of a plant to withstand temperature extremes; usually refers to the ability to survive cold temperatures.

head. The area on a grapevine trunk from which arms and canes are produced.

heading back (heading cut). Pruning back stems partway to promote side branching.

heel-in. To temporarily bury the roots of a bare-root plant in the ground or in a moist material such as damp sawdust.

hybrid. A plant formed from crossing or pollinating two different parent plants.

imperfect flower. A blossom with either male or female parts, not both; compare to perfect flower.

incompatibility. In pollination, the inability of one plant to pollinate another; in propagation, the inability of a scion and a rootstock to grow together.

internode. Part of the stem between the thickened areas where leaves or other stems join (nodes).

interstem. Piece of stem grafted onto a rootstock and onto which is grafted the cultivar scion; used to impart other properties to the tree from the rootstock; sometimes used on apples, but much less common than an ordinary single graft.

IPM. Short for Integrated Pest Management, controlling pests and diseases based on understanding and then interrupting cycles of problems, beginning with nonchemical methods.

larva (plural: larvae). The immature stage of some insects during which they don't look like the adult. The larvae of butterflies are caterpillars.

lateral branch. A side branch or shoot that grows off a main (scaffold) branch; often simply called a lateral, as in the case of grapes.

lateral bud. A bud in the axil, where leaves or branches join a trunk or a larger branch.

layering. Propagating by rooting stems of plants, still attached, on soil.

leaf burn. The browning of leaves, often at their edges; often caused by too much fertilizer, excessive salts in soil, or drought.

lime. A calcium material used to raise the soil pH, making it more alkaline and less acid. Dolomitic lime contains magnesium.

loam. Desirable soil texture with a balance of about $^2/_5$ sand, $^2/_5$ silt, and $^1/_5$ clay particles; loosely used to refer to good soil.

microclimate. A localized area with environmental conditions different from those of its surroundings, such as in the shelter of a building, on a south-facing slope, or at the bottom of a hill.

modified leader. 1. A system of training fruit trees that helps to reduce tree height. 2. A replacement shoot that sprouts when the central leader is cut off.

monoecious. Having separate male and female flowers (imperfect flowers) borne on the same plant.

mulch. An organic material such as pine needles or wood chips used on the soil around plants to help conserve moisture, control weeds, and keep soils cooler.

mummy. A fruit that is shriveled and dark with dry rot, as from the black rot fungus.

nematode. A microscopic, wormlike organism, also called eelworm or roundworm. Beneficial nematodes are decomposers that speed up the decay of organic matter, or provide natural pest control. Other species are harmful, such as the root knot nematodes that attack plant roots (especially strawberries), causing impaired growth or death.

node. Part of the stem (often thickened) where leaves or other stems join; the location of leaf axils, lateral buds.

nut. A single-seeded fruit enclosed in a hard, woody casing that must be removed before eating. Pecans and walnuts are examples.

open center. A method of training trees in which central branches are pruned away, creating a vase shape, to allow more light into the center.

organic matter. The part of the soil made up of carbon-containing substances such as decayed leaves and peat moss; important to feed soil microorganisms and create good soils.

ovary. The swollen base of the female part of the flower (pistil), which develops into the fruit.

overbearing. The propensity of some fruit trees, especially some dwarf cultivars, to bear too much fruit too soon, before they are fully grown and have sufficient roots to support their top growth and fruiting. Unless checked by removing or thinning fruit in early years, it can lead to weakened trees.

own-root. Refers to seedlings, plants not grafted onto a rootstock. Most standard fruit trees are grown on their own roots.

perennial. A plant that grows for more than 2 years (if hardy), producing new growth each year. Usually describes plants that die back to the ground, then regrow in spring.

perfect flower. One that has both male and female parts (bisexual); compare to imperfect flower.

pH. The scale used to measure acidity. A reading of 7.0 is neutral; lower values are acidic and higher values indicate alkaline. Soil pH affects the availability of nutrients to plants.

phenology. The study of the stages of plant development (usually leaves and flowers and fruit) that vary with season and climate. Recognizing phenological stages is important for controlling fruit pests and diseases.

pheromone. A chemical an insect uses to attract another, such as the powerful chemicals females use to attract males. Synthetic pheromones are used in pest control to disrupt mating or to lure pests into traps.

physiological. Refers to problems caused by an environmental condition, not by a disease organism. Examples are browned leaves from too much fertilizer and frost injury to flower buds. Also called abiotic, to distinguish from problems with a biological cause.

pinching. Removing the tip of a developing shoot, especially very tender growth that can be removed with fingertips.

pit. The hardened central casing around a seed, as in cherries, peaches, and plums (botanically a pyrene). May be called a stone, as in a stone fruit.

pollen. The fine powder or grains on the male portion of flowers (anthers) containing male cells that fertilize flowers to make seeds (and therefore the fruit that surrounds the seeds). Pollen is usually orange or yellow.

pollenizer. A plant or cultivar that produces pollen capable of fertilizing another plant or cultivar for successful cross-pollination and fruit production.

pollinate. To transfer male cells (contained in pollen) from one flower to another, generally on a different plant; important with many fruits. Pollination is the process.

pollinator. The agent that transfers pollen among flowers — bees and other insects, wind, a human — to bring about cross-pollination.

pome (pome fruit). A type of fruit, such as an apple, with a fleshy layer surrounding a core containing several seeds.

precocious. Bearing fruit at a young age relative to other plants. (The noun is precocity.)

primocane. A first-year cane or stem of a bramble, which doesn't bear fruit; compare to floricane. (First-year canes of fall-bearing cultivars do bear fruit, so these are sometimes called primocane-bearing cultivars.)

receptacle. See core.

renewal pruning. Removing older stems, usually at least 2 years old, to promote new shoots and growth. Examples are removing shoots of currants more than 3 years old and removing limbs of old apple trees.

renewal spur. On grapes, a cane cut back to a couple of buds in order to produce the future canes (renewal canes) for the following year.

rootstock. The plant onto which another is budded or grafted to impart vigor, hardiness, height, or other traits; also called understock.

runner. On strawberries, a stem coming off the main plant from which a new plant will arise at the tips. Also called a stolon.

russet. A reddish brown roughening of skin that occurs naturally on some apples and pears (resembling the skin of a russet potato). Russeting can also be caused by injury to fruit (as from a chemical burn).

sanitation. The removal of injured or diseased branches and fallen leaves and fruit to eliminate sites where insects and diseases could live or overwinter. Mowing grassy areas and weeding around plants are also part of good sanitation.

scaffold. A main or primary branch off a tree trunk that helps form the canopy and from which may arise lateral branches. Important in training fruit trees to a strong structure.

scion. The part of a plant (usually a small stem section) that is grafted onto another plant (rootstock).

seedling. A plant grown from seed (sexual propagation) rather than from a graft or cutting.

self-fertile. A plant that is able to pollinate itself and thus bear fruit without cross-pollination. A self-fertile plant may have male and female parts in the same flower, or bear separate male and female flowers on the same plant. Also called self-fruitful.

self-sterile. A plant that can't pollinate itself and thus needs another plant for cross-pollination in order to bear fruit; the opposite of self-fertile.

shoot. The green growth that arises from a bud; can be on branches, trunks, canes, or other plant parts. A shoot produces leaves and may also produce fruit.

side-dress. To add compost or fertilizer along the side of a row of plants.

skeletonize. The act by an insect such as a sawfly larva whereby it eats leaf tissue between the veins, leaving a skeletonlike appearance.

soaker hose. A permeable hose through which water drips along its length to provide water at the base of plants. See also drip irrigation.

soil type. See soil texture.

soil texture. The proportion or ratio of sizes of soil particles (sand, silt, and clay); see loam, for example. Sometimes incorrectly called soil type, but that refers to a more elaborate classification of soils.

splitting. See cracking.

sport. A mutation with a particular characteristic such as fruit color, tree shape, or leaf variegation. See also strain.

spur. A stubby side branch off a lateral or scaffold branch that bears fruit. Common in apples (some cultivars, such as 'Delicious', are available in both spur and non-spur types) and cherries; in grapes, a cane cut back to usually one or two buds to produce the fruit.

spur pruning. A system for pruning grapes in which fruiting canes are cut back each winter, leaving only two or three buds on each spur, and leaving the main branches (cordons) along wires.

stolon. See runner.

stone fruit. See pit and drupe.

strain. A mutation (sport) of a plant variety that is propagated as a clone (vegetatively) to maintain desirable characteristics such as fruit color, tree shape, and leaf variegation. All the variants of 'Red Delicious' and 'McIntosh' are strains — different from each other but not enough to be considered different varieties or cultivars.

strig. A delicate, drooping flower stem several inches long, on currants and gooseberries. Also, the fruit cluster on these plants.

sucker. A shoot arising from underground stems or roots. Suckers may be desirable on spreading plants, but they can be a problem if they sprout from the rootstock of a grafted or budded plant. Suckers may also arise from the base of a tree trunk; see water sprout.

tendril. A modified curling shoot that some vines such as grapes use to attach to and hang on to a wire or trellis. A tendril arises opposite a leaf on a stem.

thinning. 1. Removing or pruning out branches in order to allow more light and air circulation within a plant canopy. 2. Type of pruning cut in which a whole limb is removed at its point of origin rather than being cut back (heading back). 3. Removing some immature fruit in order to enable remaining ones to grow larger.

tissue culture. The propagation of a plant starting with only a few cells or a piece of tissue grown in a sterile medium of growth substances and hormones.

top-dress. To add compost or fertilizer to the soil surface around plants.

type. A vague term that may refer to tree size (dwarf, semidwarf) or use (such as cooking or dessert apples). When used with a cultivar, it generally refers to a sport or mutation of a particular cultivar that has been selected for better fruit color, fruit shape or texture, or another trait such as disease resistance.

understock. See rootstock.

variety. A botanical designation for closely related plants within a species that share similar a trait such as flowering or growth habit. Commonly but incorrectly applied to cultivars that arise from, or are maintained through, human action.

vegetative growth. The nonflowering growth of stems and leaves.

vegetative propagation. Creating identical plants (clones) using an asexual method such as tissue culture or cutting, a method that does not involve seeds and the combination of male and female cells. See also asexual propagation.

veraison. The stage of grape ripening when berries begin coloring and softening.

vigor. The amount and rate of growth. Plant vigor varies among cultivars and is also affected by such growing conditions as soil fertility.

water sprout. A vigorous upright stem that sprouts from a branch, often just below a major pruning cut; see sucker.

whip. A young tree with only a central stem; side branches pruned away to promote vigorous upward growth.

USDA Plant Hardiness Zone Map

Hardiness zones are areas that share similar winter temperatures. The United States Department of Agriculture (USDA) created this map (updated 1990) to give gardeners a tool for selecting appropriate plants for their climate. A zone on this map shares the same average minimum winter temperature. Zone 1 is the coldest; Zone 4 represents –20° to –30°F in winter. www.usna.usda.gov/Hardzone

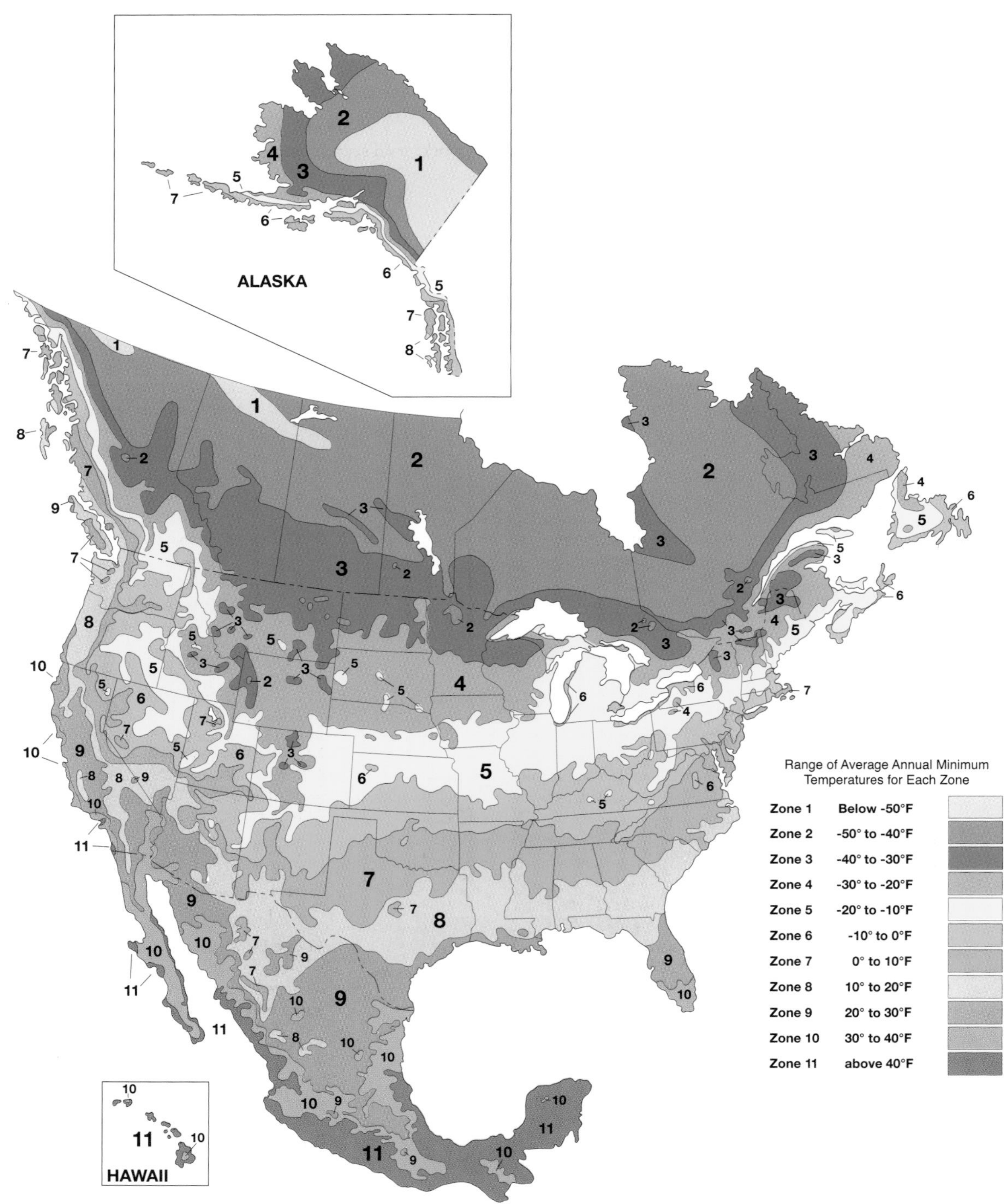

Resources

Sources and Resources

Don't forget to check your own local nurseries. Often nurseries are excellent sources of information in addition to plants. There are many other sources such as complete garden stores; those below mainly specialize in or have a very large selection of fruit. If a website doesn't work, try a search using the business name.

Regional Information

Cooperative Extension System
National Institute of Food and Agriculture
www.csrees.usda.gov/Extension

NORTHEAST

Cornell Gardening Resources, Fruit
Cornell University
www.gardening.cornell.edu/fruit

MID-ATLANTIC

Fruit Production for the Home Gardener
Pennsylvania State University
http://ssfruit.cas.psu.edu

MIDWEST

Ohioline Yard & Garden, Fruit
Ohio State University
http://ohioline.osu.edu/lines/fruit.html

SOUTH

Small Fruits
Clemson Cooperative Extension
Clemson University
www.clemson.edu/extension/hgic/plants/vegetables/small_fruits

WEST

Extension and Experiment Station Communications
Oregon State University
http://extension.oregonstate.edu/catalog

General Internet Resources

Some of the following may offer printed publications as well.

American Pomological Society
http://americanpomological.org
Since 1848, membership, publications

Dave Wilson Nursery
www.davewilson.com
Wholesale, but extensive information and fruit and nut tree descriptions

Home Fruit Growing
www.homefruitgrowing.info

Home Orchard Society, Inc.
www.homeorchardsociety.org

North American Fruit Explorers
www.nafex.org

Northwest Berry & Grape Information Network
http://berrygrape.org
Mainly commercial, but some good home garden information

Sandy Bar Ranch & Nursery
www.sandybarnursery.com
No plants but good information; list of apples for southern California

Nurseries

Many of these carry a wide selection of berries, trees, and minor fruits. Most also sell orchard equipment and other fruit-growing supplies.

Aaron's Nursery
888-652-7939
www.aaronsfarm.com

Adams County Nursery, Inc.
717-677-8105
www.acnursery.com
Fruit trees

Apple Art Espalier
707-795-0919
www.appleart.com
Apples, pears, other espaliers

Bay Laurel Nursery
805-466-3406
www.baylaurelnursery.com

Bottoms Nursery
770-884-5661
www.bottomsnursery.com
Specialty is muscadine grapes

Burgess Seed & Plant Co.
309-662-7761
www.eburgess.com

Burnt Ridge Nursery & Orchards Inc.
360-985-2873
www.burntridgenursery.com

Chestnut Hill Tree Farm
800-669-2067
www.chestnuthilltreefarm.com
Low-chill fruits, chestnuts

Cloud Mountain Farm
360-966-5859
www.cloudmountainfarm.com

Cummins Nursery
607-592-2801
www.cumminsnursery.com
Fruit trees, unusual cultivars, custom grafting

Daisy Farms
269-782-6321
www.daisyfarms.net
Small fruits

Edible Landscaping
800-524-4156
www.ediblelandscaping.com
Many unusual cultivars

England's Orchard and Nursery
606-965-2228
www.nuttrees.net
Fruit, nut trees

Fedco Seeds, Inc.
207-873-7333
www.fedcoseeds.com
Fruit plants and supplies

ForestFarm
541-846-7269
www.forestfarm.com

G. W. Allen Nursery Ltd.
902-678-7519
www.gwallennursery.com

Grandpa's Orchard
877-800-0077
www.grandpasorchard.com
Tree fruits

Green Barn Nursery
514-646-1340
www.greenbarnnursery.ca
Fruits for cold climates, permaculture; only ships in Canada

Greenmantle Nursery
707-986-7504
www.greenmantlenursery.com
Heirlooms, apple specialty

Gurney's Seed & Nursery Co.
513-354-1492
www.gurneys.com

Hartman's Fruit Tree Nursery
253-848-1484
www.hartmannursery.com

Hartmann's Plant Company
269-253-4281
www.hartmannsplantcompany.com
Many unusual cultivars, berries

Henry Field's Seed & Nursery Co.
513-354-1495
www.henryfields.com

Henry Leuthardt Nurseries, Inc.
631-878-1387
www.henryleuthardtnurseries.com
Espaliered fruit

Hidden Springs Nursery
931-268-2592
www.hiddenspringsnursery.com
Many unusual cultivars

Indiana Berry & Plant Co.
800-295-2226
www.indianaberry.com

Ison's Nursery
800-733-0324
www.isons.com
Muscadine grapes a specialty

Johnson Nursery, Inc.
888-276-3187
www.johnsonnursery.com
Many types of fruits, also pecans

Just Fruits and Exotics
850-926-5644
www.justfruitsandexotics.com

Maple Valley Orchards & Nursery
920-842-2904
www.maplevalleyorchards.com
Apples, pears, plums, heirlooms, scionwood for grafting

Mid City Nursery, Inc.
707-642-4167
www.midcitynursery.com

Miller Nurseries
800-836-9630
www.millernurseries.com
Many fruits, including grapes

Nourse Farms
413-665-2658
www.noursefarms.com
Small fruits

Oikos Tree Crops
269-624-6233
www.oikostreecrops.com
Edible natives, seed-propagated, less-common fruits

One Green World
877-353-4028
www.onegreenworld.com
Many unusual fruits

Pense Nursery
479-369-2494
www.alcasoft.com/pense
Berries, grapes

Raintree Nursery
800-391-8892
www.raintreenursery.com
Many unusual fruits and cultivars

Rolling River Nursery
530-627-3120
www.rollingrivernursery.com
Organic, fruits both temperate and tropical, nuts

Simmons Plant Farm
479-369-2345
www.simmonsplantfarm.com
Berries

Southmeadow Fruit Gardens
269-422-2411
www.southmeadowfruitgardens.com

Spring Hill Nurseries
513-354-1510
www.springhillnursery.com

St. Lawrence Nurseries
315-265-6710
www.sln.potsdam.ny.us
Great for cold climates

Stark Bro's Nurseries & Orchards Co.
800-325-4180
www.starkbros.com

Trees of Antiquity
805-467-9909
www.treesofantiquity.com
Fruits, heirloom fruit trees, many organic

Ty Ty Nursery
888-811-9132
www.tytyga.com
Nuts too

Whitman Farms
503-585-8728
www.whitmanfarms.com
Nuts, some hard-to-find fruits

Willis Orchard Co.
866-586-6283
www.willisorchards.com

Woodstock Nursery
888-803-8733
www.wallace-woodstock.com

Apple Information

All About Apples
www.allaboutapples.com

Apple Sources

Apple Luscious Organic Orchards
250-653-2007
www.appleluscious.com
Whips and apples to eat, shipped in Canada

Applesource
800-588-3854
www.applesource.com
Apples to eat, apple fruit tools

Big Horse Creek Farm
oldapple@bighorsecreekfarm.com
www.bighorsecreekfarm.com
Southern heirlooms

Strawberry Information

California Strawberry Commission
www.calstrawberry.com
Strawberry recipes

Fraises des Bois
www.fraisesdesbois.com
Alpine strawberry information

"Strawberries: Safe Methods to Store, Preserve, and Enjoy"
University of California, Division of Agriculture and Natural Resources. ANR Publication 8256, by Linda J. Harris and Elizabeth Mitcham, 2007
http://anrcatalog.ucdavis.edu/pdf/8256.pdf

Strawberry Sources

Krohne Plant Farms, Inc.
269-424-5423
www.krohneplantfarms.com

Sakuma Bros. Farms, Inc.
360-542-1299
http://shop.sakumabros.com

The Strawberry Store
www.thestrawberrystore.com
Alpine, heirloom

Strawberry Tyme Farms, Inc.
519-426-3099
www.strawberrytyme.com

Blueberry Information

Cooperative Extension: Maine's Native Wild Blueberries
University of Maine
www.wildblueberries.maine.edu

U.S. Highbush Blueberry Council
www.blueberry.org

Wild Blueberry Association of North America
www.wildblueberries.com

Blueberry Sources

Bluegrass Blueberries
270-432-5836
www.angelfire.com/biz/kyblueberry

DeGrandchamp Farms
888-483-7431
www.degrandchamps.com

DiMeo Farms
609-561-5905
www.dimeofarms.com

Finch Blueberry Nursery
800-245-4662
www.danfinch.com/berrys.htm

Jericho Croft Farm and Nursery
270-908-0703
www.blueberrycroft.com

Waters Blueberry Farm
True Vine Ranch
913-441-0005
www.watersblueberryfarm.com

Information on Brambles

Oregon Raspberry & Blackberry Commission
www.oregon-berries.com

Brambles Sources

Bramble Berry Farm
479-369-1705
www.alcasoft.com/winfrey

Burnside Greenhouse & Berry Farm
Shadoan Enterprises, Inc.
606-561-4884
http://somersetflorist.net

Grape Information

Cold Hardy Grapes
University of Minnesota
www.grapes.umn.edu

National Grape Registry
http://ngr.ucdavis.edu
Extensive cultivar listing

UC Integrated Viticulture
University of California
http://groups.ucanr.org/iv/

Grape Sources

California Rootstock
800-595-3754
www.californiarootstock.com

Double A Vineyards
716-672-8493
www.rakgrape.com

Ecce Vineyards & Nursery
763-498-4782
www.eccevines.com

Grafted Grapevine Nursery, LLC
315-462-3288
www.graftedgrapevines.com

Great River Vineyard/Nursery
877-345-3531
www.greatrivervineyard.com
Cold-hardy, Minnesota cultivars

Hermann J. Weimer Vineyard
800-371-7971
www.wiemer.com

Lon J. Rombough
503-678-1410
www.bunchgrapes.com
Grape cuttings

Northeastern Vine Supply
802-287-9311
www.nevinesupply.com

Red Dog Vineyards and Grapevine Nursery
515-577-4192
www.reddogvineyards.com

Winterhaven Vineyard & Nursery
507-234-5469
www.winterhavengrapevines.com

Information on Nuts

Northern Nut Growers Association, Inc.
www.nutgrowing.org

Agricultural Research Service Pecan Breeding Program
http://aggie-horticulture.tamu.edu/CARYA
Pecan cultivars

Nuts Sources

Grimo Nut Nursery
905-934-6887
www.grimonut.com

Nolin River Nut Tree Nursery
270-369-8551
www.nolinnursery.com

Rhora's Nut Farm and Nursery
905-899-3508
www.nuttrees.com
Also some minor fruits

Information on Other Fruits

California Rare Fruit Growers
www.crfg.org

Center for New Crops & Plant Products
Purdue University
www.hort.purdue.edu/newcrop

Elderberries.com
http://elderberries.ning.com

International Wild Huckleberry Association
http://wildhuckleberry.com

KSU Pawpaw Program
Kentucky State University
www.pawpaw.kysu.edu

Other Fruit Sources

Blossom Nursery
www.blossomnursery.com
Pawpaws

McGinnis Berry Crops
250-338-8200
www.berrycrops.net
Gooseberries, currants

Tripple Brook Farm
413-527-4626
www.tripplebrookfarm.com
Less common fruits

Supplies and Equipment

In addition to the sources listed here, many nurseries and some gardening retailers, both local and online, sell products of use to fruit growers.

All Seasons Homestead Helpers, Inc.
800-649-9147
www.homesteadhelpers.com

A. M. Leonard, Inc.
800-543-8955
http://amleo.com

Canning Supply
Division of Kitchen Krafts
888-612-1950
www.canningsupply.com

Fertile Garden
800-373-3880
http://fertilegarden.com
Organic supplies

Gardens Alive!
513-354-1482
www.gardensalive.com

Gemplers
Division of GHC Specialty Brands, LLC
800-382-8473
www.gemplers.com

Homestead Harvest
877-300-3427
www.homesteadharvest.com

Hydro-Gardens
888-693-0578
www.hydro-gardens.com

Midwest Vineyard Supply, Inc.
217-864-9896
www.midwestvineyardsupply.com

Oesco, Inc.
800-634-5557
www.oescoinc.com

Interior Photography Credits *(by page number)*

1. © Ewa Brozek/iStockphoto.com
2. © Elke Borkowski/GAP Photos
5. *almond* © Jill Fromer/iStockphoto.com; *apple* © Dean Turner/iStockphoto.com; *blueberry* © Ewa Brozek/iStock photo.com; *strawberry* © Rosemary Calvert/Getty Images
6. *blackberry* © Frank Lukasseck/Getty Images; *gooseberry* © Valentyn Volkov/iStockphoto.com; *pear* © Nicholas Eveleigh/Getty Images; *raspberry* © Vitaliy Pakhnyushchyy/iStockphoto.com
7. *cherries* © Julia & Vic Pigula/GAP Photos; *peach* © Susan Trigg 2009/Getty Images; *plum* © Ewa Brozek/iStockphoto.com; *walnut* © Kevin Dyer/iStockphoto.com
10. © Angela Wyant/Getty Images; (inset) © Bryan Mullennix/Getty Images
11. © Rosemary Calvert/Getty Images
12. © Jonathan Buckley - East Ruston Old Vicarage, Norfolk
13. © Kevin Dyer/iStockphoto.com
15. © Rosemary Kautzky
16. © Rosemary Kautzky
17. © Jonathan Buckley, design by Isobel Gillan/Alan Titchmarsh
18. © Jonathan Buckley - Chatsworth House, Derbyshire
19. (top) © Jonathan Buckley, (bottom) © Jonathan Buckley, design by Mark Brown - American Impressionists Garden, Giverny
21. © Visuals Unlimited, Inc./Robert & Jean Pollock/Getty Images
22. © Ed Darack/Getty Images
23. (left) © Cosmo Condina/Getty Images; (right) © Heidi & Hans-Juergen Koch/Minden Pictures
24. © Zara Napier/GAP Photos
25. © Uros Petrovic/iStockphoto.com
28. © Joshua McCullough, PhytoPhoto
33. © John Gruen
36. © Jonathan Buckley
37. © Mayya Murenko/iStockphoto.com
38. © Rachel Warne/GAP Photos
40. © Jonathan Buckley
41. © Jonathan Buckley, design by Sarah Raven
42. © Paul Viant/Getty Images
43. © Jonathan Buckley - Great Dixter, East Sussex
44. © Jonathan Buckley
45. © Jonathan Buckley, recipe by Sophie Burnside - Chatsworth House, Derbyshire
46. © Diane MacDonald/Getty Images; (inset) © Dennis Gottlieb/Getty Images
47. © Valentyn Volkov/iStockphoto.com
48. © Jonathan Buckley, design by Sarah Raven
49. © Marilyn Barbone/iStockphoto.com
55. © Jonathan Buckley
57. © Jonathan Buckley, design by Patricia Fox - RHS Chelsea Flower Show
59. (left) © Dave Bevan/GAP Photos; (right) © Mel Watson/GAP Photos
60. © Jonathan Buckley, design by Sarah Raven
61. © Jonathan Buckley
62. © Jonathan Buckley
63. © Vitaliy Pakhnyushchyy/iStockphoto.com
64. (left) © Jonathan Buckley; (right) © Gilles Delacroix/agefotostock.com
65. (left) © Cathleen Albers-Kimball/iStockphoto.com; (right) © Kurt Tysinger
66. © Jonathan Buckley
68. © Jonathan Buckley, demonstrated by Alan Titchmarsh
73. Susan Ellis, Bugwood.org
74. © Jonathan Buckley
76. © Victoria Firmston/GAP Photos
77. © Ermin Guttenberger/iStockphoto.com
78. (left) © AGStock/Alamy; (right) © CuboImages srl/Alamy
80. © John Ewing
84. (left) © Custom Life Sciences Images/Alamy; (right) © Rosemary Kautzky
86. © Bill Johnson
88. © Jonathan Buckley
89. © Valentyn Volkov/iStockphoto.com
90. (top) © Hoekan Jansson/Getty Images; (bottom) © Jonathan Buckley
91. © imagebroker/Alamy
92. © Joshua McCullough, PhytoPhoto
93. (left) © Dave Bevan/GAP Photos; (right) © Paul DeBois/GAP Photos
95. © Keith Burdett/GAP Photos
96. © Jonathan Buckley
98. (left) © Rosemary Kautzky; (right) © Konstantin Mikhailov/NPL/Minden Pictures
99. (left) © Pawel Garski/Alamy; (right) © Rosemary Kautzky
100. © Jonathan Buckley, design by Sarah Raven
101. © Lezh/iStockphoto.com
103. (top left) © Jerry Pavia; (top right) © Vitaly Libo/123RF.com; (bottom left) © Jonathan Buckley; (bottom right) © Joshua McCullough, PhytoPhoto
104. © Rosemary Kautzky
109. © Jonathan Buckley
113. (left) University of Georgia Plant Pathology Archive, University of Georgia, Bugwood.org; (right) Clemson University - USDA Cooperative Extension Slide Series, Bugwood.org
114. Natasha Wright, Florida Department of Agriculture and Consumer Services, Bugwood.org
115. (top left) Mars Vilaubi; (top right) © Nigel Cattlin/Alamy; (bottom left) © Russell Warris/iStockphoto.com; (bottom right) © Emily Norton/iStockphoto.com
116. © Joshua McCullough, PhytoPhoto
117. © Juliette Wade/GAP Photos
120. © D. Hurst/Alamy
121. © Lee Reich
122. © house_red/iStockphoto.com; (inset) © 2009 itsabreeze photography/Getty Images/Flickr RF
123. © Gevorg Gevorgyan/iStockphoto.com
124. © Jonathan Buckley
125. © Melinda Fawver/iStockphoto.com
126. © Jonathan Buckley
128. © Jonathan Buckley
135. (top left) © Joshua McCullough, PhytoPhoto; (top right) © Nigel Cattlin/Alamy; (bottom left) © Dave Bevan/GAP Photos; (bottom right) University of Georgia Plant Pathology Archive, University of Georgia, Bugwood.org

138. © FhF Greenmedia/GAP Photos
139. (top) © Emmeline Watkins/Alamy; (bottom) © Jonathan Buckley, design by Sarah Raven
143. © Pernilla Bergdahl/GAP Photos
144. © Jonathan Buckley
145. © Eddwestmacott/iStockphoto.com
146–147. © Rosemary Kautzky
149. © Jonathan Buckley - West Dean Gardens, Hampshire
151. (top) © FLPA/Nigel Cattlin/Minden Pictures; (bottom) © Antje Schulte-Ant Life/Alamy
152. © Jonathan Buckley, design by Sarah Raven
155. © Jonathan Buckley
156. © Tim Gainey/GAP Photos
157. © Igor Goncharenko/iStockphoto.com
158. (top) © Carolyn De And/iStockphoto.com; (middle) © Natikka/iStockphoto.com; (bottom left) © Juliette Wade/GAP Photos; (bottom right) © Christina Bollen/GAP Photos
160. © Bill Johnson
162. © Friedrich Strauss/GAP Photos
163. (left) © Nigel Cattlin/Alamy; (right) Clemson University - USDA Cooperative Extension Slide Series, Bugwood.org
164. © Jonathan Buckley, design by Sarah Raven
166. © John Glover/GAP Photos
168. © Tim Gainey/GAP Photos
169. © Floortje/iStockphoto.com
170. (left) © Jonathan Buckley/GAP Photos; (right) © Jonathan Buckley, design by Sarah Raven
173. (left) ©Victoria Thurmston/GAP Photos; (right) © Bill Johnson
175. © Jo Whitworth/Garden Picture Library/Getty Images
177. (left) © Frank Lukasseck/Getty Images; (right) © Ed Young/agefotostock.com
179. © Edwin Remsberg
180. © John Glover/GAP Photos
181. © Red Helga/iStockphoto.com
182. (left) © Juliette Wade/GAP Photos; (right) © John Glover/GAP Photos
183. © CuboImages srl/Alamy
185. © Mark Winwood/GAP Photos
186. © Bill Johnson
188. (top) © Flora Press/GAP Photos; (middle) Mars Vilaubi; (bottom) Joseph O'Brien, USDA Forest Service, Bugwood.org
191. (top) © Jonathan Buckley, design by Sarah Raven; (bottom) © Flora Press/GAP Photos
193. © Bill Johnson
194. (left) © Imagewerks/Getty Images; (right) © Skye Hoffmann/Alamy
195. (left) © Jerry Pavia; (right) © Elke Borkowski/GAP Photos
196. (left) © Howard Ric/GAP Photos; (right) © WILDLIFE GmbH/Alamy
197. (left) © Visuals Unlimited, Ltd./Inga Spence/Getty Images; (right) © Maddie Thornhill/GAP Photos
198. © Jonathan Buckley
199. © Andrey Stenkin/iStockphoto.com
201. © Joshua McCullough, PhytoPhoto
202. © Jonathan Buckley
203. © Joshua McCullough, PhytoPhoto
204. (left) © Bill Johnson; (right) © Jonathan Buckley
205. © Joshua McCullough, PhytoPhoto
209. © Rosemary Kautzky
211. © Jonathan Buckley
212. © jasmina/iStockphoto.com; (inset) © Mehmet Hilmi Barcin/iStockphoto.com
213. © Floortje/iStockphoto.com
214. © Jonathan Buckley
215. © Florea Marius Catalin/iStockphoto.com
218. © Joshua McCullough, PhytoPhoto
219. © Michael Howes/GAP Photos
220. © Rosemary Kautzky
222. © Joseph De Sciose
226. © Rosemary Kautzky
229. © Jonathan Buckley
231. © Jerry Pavia
232. © Ron Evans/GAP Photos
233. © Don Nichols/iStockphoto.com
238. © Rosemary Kautzky
239. © Joshua McCullough, PhytoPhoto
240. © Howard Rice/GAP Photos
241. © Floortje/iStockphoto.com
243. © BBC Magazines Ltd./GAP Photos
244. © Dave Bevan/GAP Photos
253. © Jonathan Buckley - Perch Hill, East Sussex
255. © Jonathan Buckley - Great Dixter, East Sussex
256. (left) © Rosemary Kautzky; (top right) © Friedrich Strauss/GAP Photos; (center) © John Glover/GAP Photos; (bottom right) © Michael Howes/GAP Photos
260. © Dave Bevan/GAP Photos
261. © Borut Trdina/iStockphoto.com
263. © Anne Green-Armytage/GAP Photos
264. © Pernilla Bergdahl/GAP Photos
265. Joseph Berger, Bugwood.org
267. (left) William M. Brown Jr., Bugwood.org; (right) © lucielang/iStockphoto.com
269. (top) Charles Drake, Virginia Polytechnic Institute and State University, Bugwood.org; (bottom) © Bill Johnson
270. (top) © Neil Holmes/GAP Photos; (middle) © Geoff Kidd/GAP Photos; (bottom) © FLPA/Nigel Cattlin/Minden Pictures
271. (top) Scott Bauer, USDA Agricultural Research Service, Bugwood.org; (bottom) Clemson University - USDA Cooperative Extension Slide Series, Bugwood.org
272. (top) Brian Perchtel, Bugwood.org; (middle) N.S. Luepschen, Bugwood.org; (bottom) © Dave Bevan/GAP Photos
273. H.J. Larsen, Bugwood.org
276. © Dave Bevan/GAP Photos
277. (all) © Bill Johnson
278. (left) © Paul DeBois/GAP Photos; (right) © Bill Johnson
279. (top) © Bill Johnson; (middle) Clemson University - USDA Cooperative Extension Slide Series, Bugwood.org; (bottom) Eugene E. Nelson, Bugwood.org
280. (top left) © Bill Johnson; (top right) © Geoff du Feu/GAP Photos; (bottom) © Dave Bevan/GAP Photos
281. (top, middle) © Bill Johnson; (bottom) Pennsylvania Department of Conservation and Natural Resources - Forestry Archive, Bugwood.org
284. (left) © Photonic 4/Alamy; (right) Peggy Greb/USDA ARS
285. Mars Vilaubi
292. © Design Pics Rf/Getty Images
293. © Eric Isselée/iStockphoto.com
294. © Geoff Kidd/GAP Photos
295. © Rosemary Kautzky

Index

Page references in *italics* indicate photos or illustrations; page references in **bold** indicate charts.

C

Q

R

S

T

U

V

W

Y

Z

Other Storey Titles You Will Enjoy

The Beginner's Guide to Edible Herbs
BY CHARLES W. G. SMITH
A classic companion planting guide that shows how to use plants' natural partnerships to produce bigger and better harvests. 152 pages. Paper. ISBN 978-1-60342-528-5.

The Gardener's A–Z Guide to Growing Organic Food
BY TANYA L. K. DENCKLA
An invaluable resource for growing, harvesting, and storing 765 varieties of vegetables, fruits, herbs, and nuts. 496 pages. Paper. ISBN 978-1-58017-370-4.

Landscaping with Fruit
BY LEE REICH
A complete, accessible guide to luscious landscaping — from alpine strawberry to lingonberry, mulberry to wintergreen. 192 pages. Paper. ISBN 978-1-60342-091-4. Hardcover with jacket. ISBN 978-1-60342-096-9.

Starter Vegetable Gardens
BY BARBARA PLEASANT
A great resource for beginning vegetable gardeners: 24 no-fail plans for small organic gardens. 180 pages. Paper. ISBN 978-1-60342-529-2.

The Vegetable Gardener's Bible, 2nd edition
BY EDWARD C. SMITH
The 10th Anniversary Edition of the vegetable gardening classic, with expanded coverage and additional vegetables, fruits, and herbs. 352 pages. Paper. ISBN 978-1-60342-475-2. Hardcover. ISBN 978-1-60342-476-9.

The Veggie Gardener's Answer Book
BY BARBARA W. ELLIS
Insider's tips and tricks, practical advice, and organic wisdom for vegetable growers everywhere. 432 pages. Flexibind. ISBN 978-1-60342-024-2.

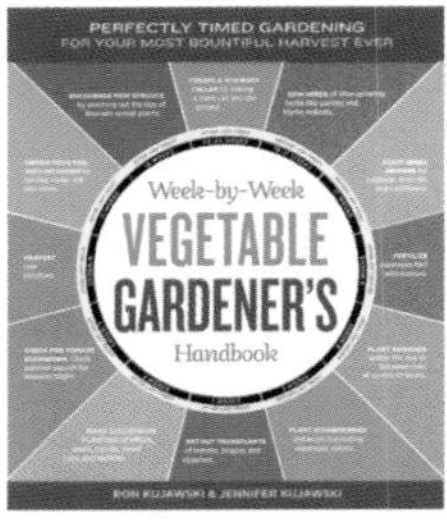

Week-by-Week Vegetable Gardener's Handbook
BY RON KUJAWSKI & JENNIFER KUJAWSKI
Detailed, customizable to-do lists to break down gardening into simple, manageable tasks. 200 pages. Paper with partially concealed wire-o. ISBN 978-1-60342-694-7.

These and other books from Storey Publishing are available wherever quality books are sold or by calling 1-800-441-5700.

Visit us at www.storey.com.